D0768934

ISAAC & ISAIAH

By the same author

Politics and the Novel during the Cold War (2010)

Marechera and the Colonel. A Zimbabwean Writer and the Claims of the State (2009)

The Dancer Defects: the Struggle for Cultural Supremacy during the Cold War (2003)

Joseph Losey: a Revenge on Life (1994)

The Fellow-Travellers. Intellectual Friends of Communism (1988, revised and updated)

Sixty-Eight: the Year of the Barricades (1988)

Under the Skin: the Death of White Rhodesia (1983)

The Great Fear. The Anti-Communist Purge under Truman and Eisenhower (1978)

Collisions. Essays and Reviews (1974)

Cuba, Yes? (1974)

The Fellow-Travellers. A Postscript to the Enlightenment (1973)

The Illusion. Politics, Theatre & the Novel (1971)

Frantz Fanon (1970)

The Left in Europe since 1789 (1966)

Essential Writings of Karl Marx (1966)

Communism and the French Intellectuals (1964)

David Caute
ISAAC & ISAIAH
THE COVERT PUNISHMENT OF
A COLD WAR HERETIC

YALE UNIVERSITY PRESS
NEW HAVEN AND LONDON

For information about this and other Yale University Press publications, please contact:

U.S. Office: sales.press@yale.edu www.yalebooks.com
Europe Office: sales@yaleup.co.uk www.yalebooks.co.uk

Set in Adobe Minion Pro by IDSUK (DataConnection) Ltd
Printed in Great Britain by TJ International Ltd, Padstow, Cornwall

Library of Congress Control Number 2013931820

ISBN 978-0-300-19209-4

A catalogue record for this book is available from the British Library.

10 9 8 7 6 5 4 3 2 1

For Murray Forsyth

Contents

Acknowledgments

I AM INDEBTED to Dr Henry Hardy, Fellow of Wolfson College, for his contributions to this book on behalf of the Isaiah Berlin Literary Trust. He not only supplied the author with copies of letters by Berlin not found, or readily found, in the Bodleian Library's Isaiah Berlin Collection, but he also facilitated access to closed sections of the archive. Dr Hardy also made many helpful suggestions when kindly vetting my quotations from Berlin's writings under copyright. Any remaining errors of transcription or understanding are entirely my own.

I would like to thank Michael J. Hughes, project archivist, The Isaiah Berlin Collection, Bodleian Library, Colin Harris, of the Bodleian Library, as well as the helpful staff of the Bodleian's Special Collections Reading Room. My thanks to the following: the staff of the London Library; the staff of the Royal Institute for International Affairs Library, Chatham House, London; the staff of the Slavonic and East European Studies Library, London.

Regarding the Papers of Isaac and Tamara Deutscher, I am indebted for access and permissions to the director and staff of the International Institute for Social History (IISG), Amsterdam. Mr Bouwe Hijma was invariably helpful. For access to the All Souls College (Codrington) Library, I would like to thank Professor Sir John Vickers FBA, Warden of All Souls, and Dr Norma Aubertin-Potter, Librarian, who has been unfailingly helpful. Perhaps I should add that the main fruits of my research in the Codrington will have to find a place in a future book.

I am indebted to the following for generous help and advice: Lord Briggs (Professor Asa Briggs); Robin Briggs, Emeritus Fellow of All Souls College; Professor Michael Cox, London School of Economics; Professor Jonathan Haslam, Corpus Christi, Cambridge; Dr Cecile Hatier, University of Wolverhampton; Professor Nicola Lacey, All Souls College; Professor Michael Lipton, University of Sussex; Joanna Ryan, for kind permission to quote from two letters by her mother, the late Jenifer Hart; Eva Sadowski, for kindly helping with Polish expressions in correspondence between Isaac and Tamara Deutscher; Professor Sir Keith Thomas, Distinguished Fellow of All Souls College; Professor Bernard Wasserstein, University of Chicago.

I am grateful to Robert Baldock and Candida Brazil at Yale University Press, for their valuable support and good counsel.

As always, my first debt is to the support of my wife Martha Caute, an expert editor of first drafts whose criticisms and suggestions I could not do without.

It goes without saying that had the late Isaiah Berlin and the late Isaac Deutscher not written their enduringly fertile and marvellously erudite works, the world would have been a poorer place and this book would not have been written.

For permissions to quote from works under copyright, I am grateful to the following:

The Isaiah Berlin Literary Trust (Isaiah Berlin); The International Institute for Social History (IISG), Amsterdam (Isaac and Tamara Deutscher); Peter Halban Publishers, for kind permission to quote from *Conversations with Isaiah Berlin* by Ramin Jahanbegloo, first published by Halban Publishers 1992, reissued 1997, copyright Editions du Félin, Paris 1991; the Estate of Jenifer Hart for permission to quote from Isaiah Berlin's Foreword to *Ask Me No More. Autobiography*, by Jenifer Hart, copyright by the Isaiah Berlin Literary Trust 1998. Copyright The Estate of Jenifer Hart 1998; Random House for kind permission to quote from *Isaiah Berlin: A Life*, by Michael Ignatieff, published by Chatto & Windus. Reprinted by permission of The Random House Group Limited, Henry Holt (USA) and Penguin Canada.

Preface

BOTH ISAIAH BERLIN (1909–1997) and Isaac Deutscher (1907–1967) are regarded as major thinkers and politically influential intellectuals of the twentieth century. Both achieved the height of their influence during the Cold War. Their mutual antipathy was intense and in Berlin's case without parallel.

On one occasion Berlin explained to the present writer precisely why Deutscher should not be allowed to hold an academic post – anywhere. This conversation took place in the common room of All Souls College, Oxford, early in 1963. He declined to explain, however, whether he had in mind a specific post at a particular university. That was 'confidential'. Although Berlin's passionate discourse on that occasion made a sharp impression, I never pursued its consequences (if any) – very soon afterwards I became more preoccupied by his stance during the All Souls reform crisis.

Memories from that distant time sprang their lock a few years ago when ongoing research into the cultural Cold War brought me to the Isaiah Berlin archive in the Bodleian Library. There I came across partial evidence of what Berlin had done, or might have done, to Deutscher at the time of my conversation with him. Quite apart from the exceptionally gifted, and indeed charismatic, personalities involved, the story of Berlin's bitter feud with Deutscher held an added attraction: it offered a path into the densely populated controversies between historians and political theorists during the years when American and Soviet systems confronted one other in naked rivalry. Surely that was what the personal antagonism between the devoted liberal and the dedicated Marxist was about?

Yes, to a large extent, but that is far from the whole story. Isaiah Berlin had become one of the presiding voices of Anglo-American liberalism. On virtually every issue he took the anti-Soviet position. Deutscher by contrast remained faithful to his Leninist heritage and resolutely defended Soviet conduct. Although a critic of Stalin, he nevertheless regarded his work as essential to Soviet modernisation. Deutscher relentlessly disparaged Western positions while prophesying a true socialist democracy in post-Stalin Russia.

Berlin and Deutscher clashed bitterly about Marx, Marxism, Lenin and Trotsky. Deutscher ridiculed in print Berlin's warnings about the perils of monism and the determinist doctrine of 'historical inevitability'.

Berlin's famous definitions of liberty were dismissed by Deutscher as little more than an apologia for bourgeois conservatism.

Berlin revered Pasternak, whereas Deutscher disparaged *Doctor Zhivago*. Berlin admired Orwell whereas Deutscher denounced *Nineteen Eighty-Four* for exciting Cold War hysteria.

Almost all of Berlin's close colleagues in the field of Soviet studies regarded Deutscher's writings about East European satellite states with hostility, suspicion, even contempt.

Towards the end of his life Deutscher became a guru and hero to the New Left, which Berlin found intolerable. Deutscher excoriated America's war in Vietnam whereas Berlin, who subscribed to the domino theory, refused to condemn it.

But one must guard against reductionism; in this case, the conclusion that the two scholars can be viewed simply as protagonists for diametrically opposed ideological positions. The further one looks into it, the more apparent become sources of friction rooted in personal history and psychology. In terms of identity, this was a civil war, a fratricidal rivalry. Born two years apart, both of these high-voltage scholars arrived in England as immigrants in flight from totalitarian violence, both acquired exceptional mastery of a language, English, that they had not inherited, both forged intersecting paths into the Anglo-American intellectual establishment, commanding space in the highbrow press and radio while sharing the patronage of (often) the same editors and producers. You can find flattering words about Berlin in *Time* magazine, praise for Deutscher in *Newsweek*, his image on the cover of the *Saturday Evening Post*. Both competed to enlighten English and American audiences about the mysteries of European thought and Russian history, pumping out cosmopolitan oxygen.

Both were non-believing Jews attached to their Jewish identity but with sharply conflicting attitudes towards Israel and Zionism. Deutscher's lauded 'non-Jewish Jews' were not Berlin's. Both lost close relatives during the Holocaust.

Each bequeathed a massive archive: letters to, letters from, diaries, notebooks, press cuttings. From this heavy load of material emerge at least two key facts. First, Berlin was by far the more highly strung and quixotic letter writer, with an inclination to adjust his message and expressed sentiments depending on the recipient.[1] His purchase of a Dictaphone no doubt encouraged his natural loquacity, his ingrained prolixity (what he himself called logorrhoea). Deutscher's letters on the whole are more conventional, more measured and guarded, devoid of Berlin's often impossible syntax and ebullient slapdashery. Deutscher keeps the tighter rein on his emotions – except when orating to mass audiences and thus releasing the Dr Jekyll from Mr Hyde.

The second key fact is that while Berlin's letters convey or betray from the early 1950s an unrelenting animosity towards Deutscher, the fire is not returned and Berlin passes almost unmentioned in Deutscher's correspondence. Deutscher most certainly regarded Berlin as an ideological opponent, a dominant figure in the Anglo-American establishment's intellectual landscape, yet it was enough to leave him for dead in the very occasional book review. Mr Deutscher may not have suspected that these rare burial ceremonies were never forgiven by Professor Berlin.

'May not' – one must speculate for lack of hard evidence. By the time of Deutscher's early death in 1967, he may or may not have known precisely what action Berlin had taken against him regarding the academic appointment he almost desperately sought. I suspect he didn't. In the wake of his death, Berlin entered into a tortuous, self-exonerating correspondence with Deutscher's widow, Tamara. Was he telling her the truth? We shall see. Mrs Deutscher clearly did not believe his version of events but it seems that she – and therefore Deutscher himself, whose working life she fully shared – lacked proof. It would be an exaggeration to suggest that the action taken by Berlin, which he never fully revealed, preferring an elaborate narrative of denial, was to haunt him for the thirty years he outlived Deutscher – but it refused to go away.

It is remarkable how the Deutscher case has passed unmentioned by Berlin's numerous admirers, although Michael Ignatieff alludes to it flectingly. The index of *The Book of Isaiah*, a collection of tributes, some eulogistic, offers a single, passing reference to Deutscher as one of Berlin's 'academic *bêtes noires*' whom Berlin thought 'politically tainted'.[2] But the overwhelming emphasis of Berlin's friends has been on what he thought, believed, wrote and said, or his gift for empathy and instant understanding – not what he did, unless generosity and kindness to interviewers, assistants and students be counted as action. We hear little or nothing about Berlin's behaviour when practical measures were required against an adversary or in the heat of a college crisis.

This book sets out to explore Berlin's actions and allegiances against the background of his professed beliefs. To that extent, it is bound to be a somewhat revisionist enterprise and will no doubt arouse a fierce defence from his admirers. Although my own ideological position is far removed from Isaac Deutscher's, I acknowledge that I am also out of sympathy with Berlin's brilliantly expressed version of liberalism. (He styled me a 'Jacobin', in his lexicon only one step short of 'Bolshevik'.) Actually, I was fond and admiring of him, like almost everyone, and perhaps can do no more in these pages than trim the giant's untended toenails. The affectionate recall, sometimes breathless adulation, he still engenders will rightly survive the narrative set out in these pages – bearing in mind that we were not entirely surprised when we learned that the far side of the moon, the side hitherto unseen, carries the deepest craters.

Introduction

A CONVERSATION IN ALL SOULS

THE CONVERSATION TOOK place in the common room during the first week of March 1963. It was the idle half-hour after lunch when one might drift in from the buttery, with its curved, panelled walls and coffered ceiling shaped as an oval dome, the work of Hawksmoor.

Isaiah greeted me. 'Do you have a moment to spare? I seek your advice.'

He shepherded us into armchairs close to a window overlooking the fellows' garden. It could be no one else's garden since ours was a college uniquely without students.

Then in his early fifties, Isaiah wore thick-framed glasses and a dark suit with waistcoat, his perennial pipe to hand. His thickly moulded features, two deep furrows running down either side of a broad nose, conveyed their characteristic animation – the manifest pleasure of being Isaiah – but on this occasion he seemed faintly ill at ease, the large ears extended, a touch of the troubled elephant.

'I seek your advice,' he repeated, then abruptly asked what, 'in principle', should disbar a man from holding a senior academic post. 'Leaving aside,' he added in his rapid tones, 'lack of acceptable scholarly credentials, drunkenness, wife-swapping – nothing like that.'

I hesitated, as one might. Impatient, he boomed out the answer: 'May I tell you? Dishonesty. Falsifying evidence. Deliberate falsification.'

I asked whether he had anyone in mind.

He nodded. 'Indeed I do. Deutscher. Perhaps you know him?'

'Isaac Deutscher? No.'

'But you know his work. You admire him enormously – most of our young scholars on the Left admire Deutscher.'

I said that I knew Deutscher's *Stalin* and his Trotsky trilogy. I was also familiar with his essays attacking 'renegades'.

Isaiah appraised me. 'Quite sufficient.' Thereupon the dark, sonorous voice boomed and bounded in pursuit of thoughts lodged within long and complex sentences punctuated by elaborate parentheses and diversions. The style of delivery had affinities with that of his old friend Maurice Bowra, warden of my undergraduate college, Wadham, but whereas Bowra sprayed his chosen audience in machine-gun bursts, his features cast in stone, Berlin tended towards a semi-humorous bombardment, softened by pauses, caveats and almost apologetic half-smiles.

He asked whether I had read Deutscher's review of Pasternak's *Doctor Zhivago*. I had. I was aware that Isaiah had known and revered the late Boris Pasternak whereas Deutscher had likened his famous novel to a voice from the grave. I commented that I was out of sympathy with Deutscher's complaint that Pasternak's characters had never heard of Lenin or Trotsky and were allowed to witness few of the major events of the Revolution – most Russians, after all, had not been present at the signing of the Treaty of Brest–Litovsk. It had also struck me that Deutscher, although loudly a Marxist, displayed a marked pre-occupation with Great Men.

Berlin nodded, evidently gratified. 'All very true. Deutscher worships Lenin, you see. He would like us to view Trotsky as Jesus on the Cross – the great modern tragedy.'

I ventured that Deutscher's biographies were impressively researched and extremely well written.

Berlin nodded again but grimly, the pipe between his teeth. 'To read him is to be persuaded unless one knows better. He is not short of followers and devotees, most of them, I have no doubt, sincere people resistant to what Deutscher would call the prevailing "Cold War culture".'

Perhaps presumptuously, I asked whether Deutscher, hitherto a freelance, was now in line for an academic post, but the question was somehow circumvented and got lost in further reflections about the ugly gap between what Deutscher wrote and what he knew.

I had first heard Isaiah's rapid-fire voice (and his name) in the early Fifties, as a teenager listening to his inspirational talks on the BBC's Third Programme. I had known him in the flesh during the three years since I came to All Souls and of course always enjoyed his presence, his wit, his abundant delight in being himself. Genial and affectionate, he took pleasure in maintaining friendly relations with the younger fellows. I was familiar with *The Hedgehog and the Fox, Historical Inevitability* and *Two Concepts of Liberty* – and with his high-profile polemics against the historian E.H. Carr, who often made common cause with Isaac Deutscher. But if he and Deutscher had ever publicly crossed swords I was unaware of it, though they were widely regarded as Titans of opposing camps in the Cold War, at that time raging bright.

'Deutscher's gifts cannot be denied,' Isaiah said. 'But would you not agree that the more a man knows, the less excuse he has for peddling pernicious myths? For dishonesty? For falsifying evidence – deliberate falsification?'

I asked whether his main objection to Deutscher was his attachment to Marxism.

'Not at all. That is covered by academic freedom. We have Marxist academics like Mills and Hobsbawm whom I may even admire, though in complete disagreement with them. But not Deutscher. Evidence must not be suppressed. He ought to know better – and he most probably does. He is not fit to teach.'

I gathered that Deutscher should not be, must not be, received into the academic Ark – anywhere. But where in particular? Berlin again sidestepped my question, citing the demands of confidentiality.

'Think ill of me if you will, but I am really not at liberty to say.'

I mentioned that Deutscher was already a widely invited visiting lecturer in Britain, if still restricted in America.

A nod. 'He mainly lectures to the converted. But serious teaching – a protracted relationship with undergraduates, guiding them in their reading, moulding their outlook, establishing a curriculum – is not the same as the one-off lecture, come and go. How are young undergraduates, much less informed and perceptive than you, to survive his unscrupulous distortions? Believe me, your run-of-the-mill hack who dutifully toes the party line, word for word, chapter and verse, is far less dangerous than Deutscher. He passes for an independent historian, a free spirit. He confesses how, most regrettably, uncontrollable circumstances had by 1920 or 1921 forced Lenin and Trotsky to become Lenin and Trotsky. He explains how the necessary collectivisation and industrialisation of Russia was undertaken by a leader, Stalin, who most regrettably turned into a tyrant. Innocent people believe that Deutscher is an anti-Stalinist. Doesn't he say so, time and again?'

He paused to study me. Isaiah pausing somewhat resembled a car coming in to the garage for more petrol with its engine still ticking over.

'You don't, perhaps, agree? Perhaps you think I am consumed by Cold War hysteria?' He smiled. 'Perhaps not a fair question.'

I asked why none of these strictures against Deutscher applied to his ally in Cold War polemics, E.H. Carr. Presumably Isaiah would have no objection to appointing Carr to a teaching post?

'Quite so. I supported Ted's candidature at Trinity, Cambridge. He and I gave a joint seminar here some years ago, perhaps before your time.' Berlin said that he and Carr had crossed swords on many occasions but he respected Carr and liked him.

'He sends me cricketing riddles which I, a Latvian Jew, don't fully understand. He asks me whether the historian should pay more attention to the batsman who scored a century or the fielder who muffed the catch which would have dismissed him. At worst, his belief in "progress" renders him blind in one eye. In that respect I believe he is mellowing a bit though I dare not say so publicly for fear he would abruptly cease to mellow.'

But surely Carr often wrote in support of Deutscher?

Isaiah chuckled drily. 'True. Not a few of the anonymous reviews of Deutscher's work in the *TLS* have been written by Carr. No, all of them. They say the hammer and sickle flies over Printing House Square.'

'Is the difference in your mind that Carr isn't a Marxist whereas Deutscher remains attached to Marx's utopia?'

'No, no and again no. To be a Marxist is a legitimate stance for an academic. But Deutscher parades as a soothsayer who informs us exactly how the true "socialist man" will emerge in the USSR and put us all, the warped civilisation of the West, to shame and rout. Ted Carr finds such optimism risible, he told me so. He does not believe that you can read the palm of history's hand by way of ephemeral Kremlinology and then collect your shilling. As you say, Deutscher could be held to write exceedingly well if only truth were not a rather vital ingredient of good history. Not that any of us knows the whole truth – but Deutscher does.'

Isaiah had now grown restless, almost as if I had initiated the conversation. Having tested his case on a young historian likely to disagree with him, he was wearying of it. He rose from his chair and pocketed his pipe.

'You must excuse me, I have a boring committee meeting to attend. I must tell you frankly that Deutscher is the only man whose presence in the same academic community as myself I should find morally intolerable. I will not dine at the same table as Deutscher.'

Short of step, with his left arm (disabled by a German doctor's forceps at birth) tucked immobile into his side, he went his way.

PART ONE

ISAAC AND ISAIAH

1

BERLIN: A LIFE

BORN ON 6 JUNE 1909 in Riga, Isaiah Berlin was descended (like the violinist Yehudi Menuhin) from the Chabad Hasidim, now known as Lubavitch. His grandparents, but not his parents, were pious Hasidim. He was born in a fourth-floor apartment in Albertstrasse, in an Art Nouveau block the entrance of which (as he remembered) was guarded by two sphinxes, reclining plaster figures with breasts and a pharaoh's headdress. (Some eighty years later Berlin's biographer, Michael Ignatieff, found the breasted pharaohs still there, 'mossy with the damp and chipped with age'.) The birth was a difficult one. After many hours of labour Dr Hach, a German, used forceps on the infant's left arm and yanked him into the world so violently that the ligaments were permanently damaged.

It was here in Riga that he spent his first six years, brought up speaking Russian and German, though his mother Marie's native language was Latvian (or Lettish). His father, Mendel Berlin, was a prosperous timber merchant and entrepreneur. Riga was then the capital of Livonia, a province of the tsarist empire but one that retained its character as an old Hanseatic trading town, with German the language of culture and commerce. Riga lay outside the Pale of Settlement, to which the majority of Jews were confined by tsarism, and its Jews were exempt from the law forbidding them to own land, to enter certain trades, and the laws banning them from the gymnasium and the universities. Mendel Berlin was a Merchant of the First Guild, a small elite, free to travel and trade throughout the empire. While the sawmills and timber yards of Mendel's business were located in the ghetto and employed ghetto workers, for the young Isaiah the ghetto remained *terra incognita*. Mendel enjoyed extra income as an insurance agent for a London company. He loved not the Talmud and the Psalms but light French comedies and the operettas of Franz Lehár.[1]

Isaiah did not attend school but his intellectual development was clearly precocious. When seven, his companion was Leonard Schapiro, then eight. They would sit on the veranda of their holiday *dacha* or wander through the parks talking earnestly about the art of Alexander Benois, Leon Bakst and other Russian painters of the time – Leonard possessed postcards of their work and even modelled a plaster bust of the dying Marat. These vivid childhood conversations were later to resurface in the precocious cultural reach that awed his English contemporaries at Oxford and no doubt earlier, at St Paul's.[2]

As an industrialist and merchant, Mendel specialised in timber products. He was proud of his descent from a long line of rabbis and scholars. He and his wife were first cousins. They enjoyed a 'grandiose' wedding in Riga in 1906. Mendel Berlin later vividly described the raging Russian anti-Semitism in 1914, when Riga was blockaded. The family moved in 1915 to Andreapol, 340 miles west of Moscow, but a year later they settled in Petrograd, where Mendel worked for the Russian government, supplying timber for the railway system. They lived in a rented flat on Vassilievsky Island in the north of the city. Isaiah still did not attend school.

Petrograd became the eye of the storm. Late in February 1917, Isaiah was at home when crowds began surging through Vassily Ostrov towards the city centre, carrying large plywood banners – 'Land and Liberty!', 'All Power to the Duma!', 'Down with the Tsar!', 'Down with War!'. When the first cordon of troops marched towards them in formation the crowd did not give way; the military line wavered, then broke, crowd and soldiers mingled, tossing caps in the air, singing the 'Marseillaise' in Russian, then setting off across the Neva bridges for Winter Palace Square. Isaiah recalled: 'Looking out of the window I saw masses of people marching, workmen and soldiers intermingled, singing revolutionary songs.' The February Revolution came as a complete surprise to Mendel. He believed that a 'wiser Tsar, not under the evil influence of his wife', could have avoided it.

A traumatic incident occurred when the eight-year-old Isaiah was out in the street with his governess and witnessed a scene that stayed with him all his life: a mob rushed past with a secret policeman in their grasp. A bookseller had laid out his wares on the snowy pavement and the studious Isaiah was bending down to examine a battered Russian translation of Jules Verne when the roadway suddenly filled with a group of men, perhaps fifteen strong, rushing past with a frightened person in their clutches, 'a man with a white face twisting and turning as he was borne away'. The prisoner had evidently been spotted on the roof of a nearby building and dragged down into the street. Berlin recalled: 'The police in the streets were called Pharaohs – oppressors of the people. Some of them sniped at the revolutionaries from rooftops and attics. I remember seeing a policeman being dragged off, pale and struggling, by a mob, obviously to his death – that was a terrible sight that I have never forgotten; it gave me a lifelong horror of physical violence.'[3]

Later commentators have made much of this incident, perhaps rightly. Ignatieff believes that the experience, by 'strengthening his horror of physical violence and his suspicion of political experiment, and deepening his lifelong preference for all the temporising compromises that keep a political order safely this side of terror', prevented Berlin in the 1930s from joining his contemporaries 'intoxicated with revolutionary Marxism'. Christopher Hitchens concluded that the sight of a terrified tsarist cop being dragged away by a mob 'powerfully coloured his view of disorder and insurrection; the more so, perhaps, because his infant imagination furnished the subsequent scene of lynching or drowning that he did not in fact witness. Yet I think it's clear, from his own recurrence to the story, and from other evidence, that it was the disturbance to the natural order that made the young Isaiah tremble and flinch. Other members of his family, including a much-loved uncle and aunt, were quite active supporters of the SR [Socialist Revolutionary] movement. Neither then nor in retrospect did he register any allegiance of that sort.'[4]

By the end of the year the Bolsheviks had seized power. A threatening incident occurred when a group of men with armbands and rifles ordered the tenants to form a house committee with the stoker Koshkin as secretary. Few of the tenants had noticed him because he lived in the basement and kept the boilers filled with coal. Koshkin, dressed in a colonel's striped trousers, began giving the orders. Princess Emeretinsky and Rimsky-Korsakov's daughter were made to stoke the stoves, remove refuse and sweep the yard. But somehow – a judicious bribe perhaps – the Berlins were exempted from such chores. They were also protected by their maid, a peasant woman of strong tsarist convictions who would answer the door and send marauding search parties on their way. The family jewellery, hidden under the snow on the balcony, was never seized.[5]

When the Bolsheviks nationalised the railways, Mendel was hired as a state contractor to provide timber from the Andreapol forests. He was provided with a travel pass, documents exempting him from searches and arrests, food and clothing coupons and a pistol. Nevertheless, during the winter of 1918–19 the Berlins' house committee ordered all the tenants to vacate their extra rooms in order to conserve heat. For the next two and a half years they were reduced to the compass of two rooms. Thanks to his state food coupons, Mendel would obtain the occasional bag of white flour and smuggle it home under his fur coat, past the police checkpoints. The flour was baked into a white loaf exclusively reserved for Isaiah. He was a plump boy. Standing in food queues Isaiah's mother was told, 'With such a fat boy you can scarcely need more food.'[6] On one occasion the house was searched by seamen looking for flour stolen from a naval barracks and bought by the chairman of the house committee, a tsarist general. The Berlins had their sack of flour but got away with the search.

Late in life Isaiah recalled: 'We were never touched: neither my father nor any immediate member of my family was arrested or in any way molested. I remember people standing in queues for bread, or anything they could get: I was left standing to keep a place in such queues for four or five hours on end. We all lived in one room because there was no way to heat more than one. But I was not frightened and felt no sense of oppression – perhaps I was too young to know what was going on, and my parents seldom spoke of it.' The family had to live with police raids, interrogations, illegal thefts, bribes and more bribes.

Isaiah was tutored at home. He read Tolstoy, Turgenev, Pushkin and his tutor Zhukovsky's translations of Heine and Goethe. Above all, the boy treasured the *Jewish Encyclopaedia*, which permanently cemented his love of the Judaic heritage.

Mendel Berlin had succeeded in depositing money in London through trading in plywood. After the October Revolution he evidently burned all papers relating to his trade with England 'in order not to be forced to sign a [sterling] cheque on London and to be taken into custody to prevent me from stopping the encashment of such a cheque'. This was happening to people deemed to have what was known as 'valuta' abroad. His business as supplier to the Moscow-Windava railway continued under a new form after he was appointed a plenipotentiary for the production of timber under the eye of the Bolshevik state security organisation, the Cheka.

The family were summering in a *pension* in Pavlovsk in 1919 when the Cheka ransacked the villa, searching for jewellery. He later recalled the presiding sense of being cut off from the world, habitual spying and capricious arrests, the feeling of being easy prey to 'any hooligan parading as a Bolshevik'. Mendel's ear remained cocked throughout the night, listening for the car that stopped: it meant a search was under way somewhere and somebody was being carried away to prison, torture or death – anything one did was against the law. Even as a child Isaiah regarded the headquarters of the Cheka as 'a torture chamber, a hell from which few emerged alive'.[7]

It was too much. The decision to leave Bolshevik Russia was made but it was not until October 1920 that the formalities were completed. The family had to leave almost everything behind at Angliisky Prospekt, taking only the permitted 3,000 Romanov roubles per person and some jewellery sewn into the lining of Isaiah's overcoat. He was saddest to leave behind his beloved *Jewish Encylopaedia* and the Russian classics.

Due to Lenin's policy of self-determination for nationalities, the Latvian Republic was now recognised by the USSR as an independent state (Livonia having been split between Latvia and Estonia). They reached Riga on 15 October 1920 but the ten-day train journey was fraught. Latvians in their compartment began an anti-Semitic conversation, assuming their neighbours were Russian Jews who would not understand them. After enduring this, Isaiah's Lettish-speaking mother, Marie, observed tartly that though there were many things wrong with the Soviet system, anti-Semitism was not among them. When the Latvian military control came through the train the Latvian passengers accused her of being a communist spy. At Riga station police boarded the train and threatened to lead her away. A Latvian in the compartment informed Mendel that he was a member of the secret service and could secure her release for a consideration. Mendel paid up and Marie was allowed to leave with her husband and son, but throughout the autumn of 1920 the Berlins kept receiving papers warning that she was due to answer charges.

Before leaving for England, Isaiah was tutored by a German, Dr Kupfer, who dinned Latin and German into him and made him read Goethe. 'All his life, Berlin's German remained imperfect, and as for the German professor, he judged his eleven-year-old pupil to be superficial. The judgment lodged in Isaiah's mind for life: "There is a certain truth in it. Dr Kupfer was not wrong".

Fortunately Mendel's London bank, the Midland, cabled that he still had access to the profits from his plywood deals, more than £10,000. Isaiah's mother managed to obtain a visa for them both to travel from Riga to the city of Berlin, while Mendel went ahead to London and got Isaiah accepted at Arundel House prep school. At the end of his first term, Isaiah, who arrived speaking no English and had never been to school, came home with the first prize in English. Meanwhile Mendel set himself up in Bishopsgate as the British and Overseas Trading Company, importing timber from Latvia. The family were now attending a smart West End synagogue. Mendel befriended an eminent QC and sought his advice about schools. Fearing that Westminster might not be the right place for a foreign Jewish boy, he turned to St Paul's, although it didn't have 'the same social mark'. Mendel Berlin and his family lived a year in the sedate safety of Surbiton before the sound of a car drawing up in the street outside no longer brought him to the window and a discreet parting of the lace curtains. When Mendel applied for British citizenship, three of his Gentile friends in the timber trade signed their names to his application.[8]

Isaiah recalled his father as an 'Anglo-maniac'. Civilisation was English: bicycles meant Raleigh, sugar meant Tate and Lyle, steamships Cunard, education the English public school. Decent, incorruptible public authority meant George V.

Established in 1509, St Paul's School on Hammersmith Road was Christian, but it did not exclude Jews or maintain a quota. (When in later life Berlin discovered that the governors of St Paul's had fixed a Jewish quota at 15 per cent he resigned from the Old Paulines.) In 1922, there were about seventy Jewish pupils out of five hundred. Isaiah sat the scholarship exam and was granted a place, but no scholarship. He suffered from an excess of mother-love. Marie felt her husband was dull and dependent, 'so all her love was turned on me'. She nagged and smothered him, couldn't stand him sitting about, demanded activity. Isaiah's parting success at St Paul's was being awarded the Truro Prize for an essay on the theme of freedom. Ignatieff reports that the essay defends the real freedom of inner experience from the determinists, and the real freedom of action in the outer world from the ideal-ists. It also defended 'convention' as a safeguard for liberty and for inner nonconformity. Oxford was to embody these values for Berlin throughout his life. 'From St Paul's onward, he lived inside conventional, rule-ordered institu-tions, rich in lore and custom, absurd perhaps, but absurdly convincing as well.'[9] The main such institution was to be All Souls.

In 1927, he sat the scholarship examination for Balliol but was not granted even a place. As he remembered it, his classics were not up to standard and his viva was hopeless. Weeks later, however, he won a classics scholarship at Corpus Christi. The philosophy tutor, Frank Hardie, would listen each week to the essay and then, in his soft, precise Scots accent, pick it apart, cutting through the purple passages and flights of fancy. Sixty years later Berlin could still recall how Hardie punctuated his comments by smacking the palm of his right hand over the top of his left: 'Obscurity [smack] and pretentiousness [smack] and sentences which doubled over themselves [smack] he wrung right out of me [smack], from then until this moment.' Well, perhaps not entirely.

Ignatieff speculates that perhaps the paramount influence on Berlin's later prose style was Macaulay, whom he first read at the age of fourteen – long sentences that gather momentum, accumulating subordinate clauses as they accelerate. His passion was for the formal grandeur of Victorian prose. This granted, his own prose often more resembles a commentary on the intricate processes of thinking than a firm pathway cleared of undergrowth. Often the piling-up of alternatives or synonyms tends to blunt the impact of each. He appears to be inhabiting a thesaurus.

In 1931 Berlin met Maurice Bowra, the most notorious and celebrated young don of his day, a short, stocky, bulldog-belligerent classicist, then dean of Wadham and later its inspirational warden (extending to my own time). A shared interest in Russian literature drew them together. Berlin recalled that Bowra's words 'came in short, sharp bursts of precisely aimed, concentrated fire as image, pun, metaphor, parody seemed spontaneously to generate one another in a succession of marvellously imaginative patterns, sometimes rising to a high, wildly comical fantasy'. Berlin's biographer comments: 'Here, in other words, was a Paganini of talk, a virtuoso of that apparently wild, yet disciplined free association that was to become Isaiah's own speciality. Berlin's very diction – the rapid-fire gabble – came from Bowra.'[10] But it is worth adding that, whereas Berlin tended to write as he talked, often using dictation, Bowra's prose is severely disciplined. When you read him, you no longer hear him.

Unhappy with a lectureship at New College, in 1932 Berlin became a prize fellow and the first Jew elected to All Souls, and only the third ever to be awarded an Oxford fellowship. His subject was philosophy – he was to recall with awe conversations with the redoubtable Ludwig Wittgenstein. Having stumbled during the ordeal of translating a passage in German before the assembled fellows, he heard the warden, the ex-viceroy of India Lord Chelmsford, say as he left the room, 'At least we don't have to have that one.' He heard later that the bishop of Gloucester had objected to the election of a Jew, which may indicate why Nazi anti-Semitism received so feeble a response from sections of the All Souls establishment. Nonetheless, Berlin was elected and the chief rabbi wrote to congratulate him, while Baron Rothschild invited him for the weekend at Waddesdon, his palatial country house.

In the 1930s, friends called him Shaya, his family nickname. He was set to meet 'everybody'. In November 1933, he encountered Virginia Woolf at a dinner in New College. When Warden Fisher asked her if she enjoyed walking, she said she did because she liked coming upon goats: 'They look so ecclesiastical.' Berlin had a halting conversation with her. She later reported: 'There was the great Isaiah Berlin, a Portuguese Jew by the look of him, Oxford's leading light; a communist, I think, a fire-eater.' On another occasion she wrote: 'argued with Isaiah, who is a very clever, much too clever, like Maynard [Keynes] in his youth, don: a violent Jew.'[11] A residue of anti-Semitism seems to have survived her mutually devoted marriage to the Jew Leonard Woolf. After Berlin dined with them in Tavistock Square in 1936 she grew to like him. He cherished the good opinion of famous intellects – Woolf, Freud, Wittgenstein, Keynes – but he was scarcely exceptional in that regard. With keen interest he attended a course of lectures on the philosophy of history by R.G. Collingwood, who stood virtually alone among Oxford philosophers in his intensely historical approach. Collingwood may have been a significant influence on Berlin's decision a decade later to turn from analytical philosophy (evidently never his forte) to the history of ideas.[12]

Despite his innate preference for neutrality on public issues, Berlin did support the Republican side in Spain, explaining that it was about the only political issue that was clear-cut to him, all propositions on other issues being unjust to someone. The story is told how he cornered the foreign secretary, Sir John Simon, in the All Souls smoking room in the autumn of 1935, demanding that he impose oil sanctions on Mussolini for his invasion of Abyssinia. 'And what then,' Sir John replied coolly. 'Let Italy fall to the communists?'[13] But politics also excited the prankster in Berlin: during the Oxford University by-election of 1938 (the university still elected its own MP), Quintin Hogg (later Lord Hailsham and a fellow of All Souls) ran for Parliament on a straight pro-appeasement, pro-Munich ticket. While university opinion was passionately divided, Berlin found it more funny than serious. Spotting a car parked outside All Souls bearing a sign on its bumper, 'A Vote for Hogg is a Vote for Hitler', and another car nearby exhorting 'Vote for Hogg', Berlin transferred the first sign to the second car, then watched it drive away with the syllogism completed: 'A Vote for Hogg is a Vote for Hitler. Vote for Hogg.'

But Hitler and the outbreak of war was serious business. Now thirty but physically handicapped, active service was obviously out of the question. In June 1940, he received a visit from Guy Burgess, who had joined the intelligence service, and who suggested that Berlin was needed by the British Embassy in Moscow. Restless as a fellow of New College (he had left All Souls in 1938, though he would return in 1950), he longed to be sent to Moscow and wrote (21 June 1940) to Lord Halifax, foreign secretary and a 'distinguished fellow' of All Souls, offering his abilities and services as a press attaché ('no Russian on merely hearing me speak would assume that I was any sort of foreigner').[14] Almost immediately he found himself en route to New York in the company of Burgess (of whose role as a Soviet spy Berlin was innocent), hoping to acquire there a visa to Moscow. This was granted but the whole venture was then vetoed by the Foreign Office. Left adrift in New York, he obtained a post with British Information Services before moving to the British Embassy in Washington, his brief being to keep London informed about the state of American opinion, official and public. During a time of rising Zionist agitation and anti-British feeling in the USA, he was in contact with Chaim Weizmann, David Ben-Gurion, Nahum Goldmann and a host of other important Jewish figures, while attempting to reconcile his own Zionist sentiments with his primary obligations to HMG.

When he returned to New College after the war, following a memorable visit to the Soviet Union in 1945–46, he changed his subject from analytical philosophy (his contemporaries in that field included A.J. Ayer and J.L. Austin) to political thought and what might be called 'Enlightenment Studies', with an emphasis on pre-revolutionary Russian literature. He was now on course to write the succession of essays that made his name. No single factor in his upbringing and early adulthood can explain the essence or orientation of his beliefs, his credo. Yes, he was a Jewish refugee from Bolshevism; yes, his father revered all things English; yes, the war against Hitler cemented his commitment to a free and pluralistic society, likewise the deepening of Stalin's stranglehold on Russian life and lives; and yes, his war years in America deepened his allegiance to the Anglo-American alliance. But his personality, his more private passions? Here we encounter a tension between the reclusive, donnish life required by any scholar set on producing literary work of value, and his inherently outgoing, gregarious and socially ambitious nature. What significance should be attached to his remarkable social life? Obviously weekending with smart, wealthy people did not generate the complex arguments to be found in *Historical Inevitability* or *Two Concepts of Liberty*; on the other hand, the deeper you dig into the core values underpinning Berlin's trademark warnings and exhortations, the more you find, or may find, a passionate defence of the status quo, an extended plea that the things we enjoy and value should not be taken from us. In the course of the present investigation we shall find that red light flashing time and again.

So it is worth mentioning that in the postwar years Berlin increasingly mixed with smart and rich people – a weekend with Guy and Alix de Rothschild at their stud farm in Normandy, friendships with Jimmy Rothschild, Jermaine de Rothschild and Victor Rothschild,[15] as well as Lady d'Avigdor-Goldsmid, wife of Sir Henry (Harry), banker, bullion broker and Conservative politician. Ignatieff mentions Lady Colefax's lunches in Lord North Street, as well as invitations from Lady Cunard and later from Marietta Tree at Ditchley Park in Oxfordshire. Clarissa Churchill – who was to marry Anthony Eden – regarded Berlin's socialising with perplexed disappointment. He might, she thought, have become a genuine sage, yet allowed himself to glitter as a salon conversationalist, 'an intellectual acrobat in the society circus'.[16] The Conservative politician Oliver Lyttelton (Lord Chandos) put him up for membership of the St James's Club in the summer of 1950, only to discover that several members were determined to have no one of Jewish extraction. But then he was proposed and accepted for Brooks's and for the Athenaeum, smarter than which one cannot get.[17]

Even in term time, Oxford retained the atmosphere of an empty place: it accommodated a mere eight thousand students, even when swollen by ex-servicemen, but Berlin still complained about the boredom of teaching too many undergraduates who arrived in their ones and twos to soak up another precious hour that might have been better devoted to writing the book that would establish his reputation as a serious scholar rather than a gilded gadfly. His anxiety on this score was reflected in his decision to reissue his prewar study of Karl Marx, a book that would now be of only minor intellectual interest – beyond its reflections on Marx's refusal to recognise the Jew in himself – were it not the work of the young Isaiah Berlin. Once his teaching duties at New College were behind him, a resumption of his fellowship at All Souls allowed him the freedom to balance his separate existences as scholar and socialite – no doubt an uneasy balance but the early Fifties were productive years and he was by no means 'an intellectual acrobat in the society circus'. He read and he wrote. Berlin's narratives arrived on the page like coracles swept along by rapids and waterfalls, clause upon clause, caveats and parentheses, his disinclination to bring a sentence to a halt indicated by numerous colons or semicolons ousting the much-needed period, the longed-for paragraph break. Words provided not so much a means of communication as a commentary on the process of thinking. The reader or listener found himself clinging to the coracle, buffeted and beguiled. But no *magnum opus* came forth.

Until 1950, his love affairs evidently went unconsummated. Invariably he was attracted to married women like Patricia Douglas who were having other affairs. In that year he began his first sexual relationship, with the former civil servant and academic Jenifer Hart, wife of his friend the legal philosopher Herbert Hart. In 1956, he married the wealthy Aline Halban, née Ginzbourg. Living in a palatial Georgian residence in Headington (while occupying a bachelor 'set' in Albany, off Piccadilly), he could now entertain in the grand style. While in London, he would dine at the Athenaeum.

In 1957, he was elected Chichele professor in social and political theory at Oxford. Nevertheless, his knighthood in 1957 provoked raised eyebrows among friends and colleagues. In 1951, he had commented sardonically on Maurice Bowra's acceptance: 'if people long for knighthoods they shall have them and no one will be the poorer for it.' Berlin's own knighthood, announced in the June 1957 Birthday Honours list, was an offering by Prime Minister Harold Macmillan. It is said that when Berlin told his mother of his intention to refuse it, her eyes filled with tears and he decided that he must accept. He reported to his friend Morton White, the American historian of ideas, the rumour that 'the Prime Minister was dispensing patronage to people who entertain or amuse him in one fashion or another. Which may indeed be true, for the reason for this "elevation" is genuinely obscure to me as to others.'[18] Berlin told T.S. Eliot he felt he was being asked to wear a funny paper hat. His old flame Patricia Douglas sent a feline letter congratulating him on his recognition for services to conversation. On hearing of Berlin's acceptance, Herbert Hart wrote from Harvard to his wife Jenifer (Berlin's former lover): 'How awful about

Isaiah: really horrid. . . . What was it said to be for? Not attacking govt. during Suez? Conversation? Solving problem of Free Will? . . . I feel it really does make him look a bit ridiculous, and the thing about his mother is a very feeble excuse. She's had enough glory out of him already. I long to hear Oxford comments.' A month later, on 19 July 1957, Berlin wrote to Morton White, 'You are quite right, people like the Harts and my predecessor Cole and others do think of me as having "sold out" to some vague establishment.'[19]

The knighthood may have been prompted by the quality that brought the honour to so many stage actors – Sir Laurence, Sir John, Sir Ralph – who penetrated great dramatic parts while appealing to a wide public. Berlin's broadcasting career, beginning in the 1940s and extending to the 1990s, in itself deserved a trip to the Palace. For example, in October–December 1952, he had delivered six weekly lectures on 'Freedom and its Betrayal', his theme being that 'the great eighteenth-century philosophers were ultimately responsible for a lot of intellectual tyranny, ending in the Soviet Union, in the *gulag*; that these good men, who were against superstition, falsification, authority, and were great liberators, had nevertheless preached doctrines which led, albeit in somewhat perverted form, to tragic consequences'.[20] He delivered each of the hour-long lectures extemporaneously from notes, what he called 'a kind of agonised bawling into a machine'. Hundreds of thousands of listeners tuned in. No doubt Berlin's wartime service in Washington and being on the right side of the Cold War did no harm in Prime Minister Macmillan's estimation either – Deutscher also broadcast frequently but 'Sir Isaac Deutscher' was never on the cards, regardless of which party was in office. Sir Isaac's surname was Wolfson, retail magnate and eponymous patron of the graduate college that Berlin himself was to bring to life as its first president.

That Berlin's perspectives and positions sometimes met with sharp-edged scepticism among fellow political theorists is reflected in a letter to him from Jenifer Hart, undated but probably written during the 1963 spring vacation. She had heard Berlin's recent lecture on Machiavelli, evidently delivered to a conference or seminar attended by an elite audience.[21] She mentions sustained argument, 'rather sharp with you': 'It seemed at times almost like a concerted plan to get you down – rather like Communists at a meeting each with his own point and a follow up.' She praises the way he dealt with 'the pedantic scholars': 'I thought you showed yourself to be just as scholarly as them . . . far more important and meaningful than the pale tepid effect produced by the Plamenatz(s). . . . Laslett was horrible I thought and no doubt intended rudeness by doing a Namier on your Christie – going out ostentatiously before the end after he had said his bit.' 'I suppose,' she continues, 'some of them were shocked that you didn't condemn M[achiavelli] more – or indeed at all. You looked unmoved by some of the ruthless and cruel advice he gave. But you didn't give an inch on this – which I thought splendid – thus exemplifying what I take to be your getting-under-the-skin method of doing political theory – which is the only proper way. S. Finer [Professor Samuel E. Finer] on my other side was v. tiresome and talked ostentatiously to [unclear] throughout. At intervals he tried to dissuade me from listening on the ground that it was all rot.'[22]

Although Berlin's social life was global, he was always keen to serve on public bodies, from obscure academic committees to august national institutions like Covent Garden and the Royal Academy. He more than did his bit. An opera addict, Berlin served on the directorial board of the Royal Opera House, chairing the opera subcommittee and suggesting new productions, conductors and singers. Writing (2 March 1956) to the general administrator, David Webster, he expressed concerns about the scheduled opera season for 1957–58, providing an impressive *tour de force* through the operas and composers under consideration.[23] His great love of music reinforced his loathing for political systems that imposed cruel pressures on great composers such as Prokofiev and Shostakovich in the Soviet Union. Soviet propaganda exposing the 'philistine' commercial values governing American cultural life failed to impress him. In November 1966, he was to be found among the guests at Truman Capote's glitzy Black and White Ball at the Plaza, New York, dubbed 'the party of the century'. The American publisher Katharine Graham recalled that when he was asked to speak more slowly if he wanted Americans to understand him, Berlin had replied, 'Yes, I know. I know, I know. But if I did, I should be quite a different person, quite a different person.' His black tie travelled with him; in Oxford he was a stalwart of an elite dons' dining club called, simply, The Club.[24] He belonged to an upper-class generation that habitually employed 'should' instead of 'would', merging the subjunctive imperative with the conditional. Isaac Deutscher, he remarked to the present writer in that memorable conversation in 1963, was 'the only man whose presence in the same academic community as myself I should find morally intolerable'. He did not mean 'I ought to find'.

Fame was his joy and (he liked to feel) his crown of thorns. He both enjoyed and suffered a distinctly perverse relationship with the press. Often in the news, he subscribed to Durrants and kept all press cuttings concerning himself on file. He wrote frequently for newspapers, and even fed them with information off the record, but affected (the right word, I think) to despise journalists and their invariably inaccurate stories, deploring personal publicity and frequently remonstrating with editors – yet clearly fascinated to read about himself. By the end of his life, in 1997, he was covered in official honours and worldwide academic accolades, honorary degrees and prizes. He did not regard himself as one of the innovative thinkers of his time, and noted that his influence was mainly confined to Britain and America.

2

DEUTSCHER: A LIFE

ISAAC DEUTSCHER'S CHILDHOOD and early adult years in Poland present a problem not found in Berlin's – Deutscher himself was the sole surviving witness. Berlin brought his parents to England with him (so to speak) and his father later wrote a revealing, informative memoir. But Deutscher arrived in England alone in 1939. None of the family he grew up with survived the Nazis. He met his future wife, Tamara, in England and she could later relate only what he had told her about his family, upbringing and intellectual formation. We are therefore reliant on Deutscher's word alone for the first twenty years of his life, until he joined the Polish Communist Party.

To be a young Polish Jew before, during and after the First World War (the Pilsudski era) was an inherently dramatic experience. The Deutscher family lived in the Austro-Hungarian Empire at the so-called Three Emperors' Corner. After all three empires (Austro-Hungarian, Russian and German) collapsed, the Deutscher family experienced the landslide of three revolutions. Born in Galicia in 1907, Isaac belonged to the urban middle class – his grand-father and father owned a printing firm which published Jewish religious literature. His uncle was a member of the Polish Upper House, representing the Jewish clerical party, Agudah. Tamara Deutscher relates how, in November 1918, not yet eleven, Isaac experienced a pogrom in his native Chrzanòw, when drunken mobs gave vent to the new patriotism being preached in all churches in the regained motherland. The Deutscher family lived in the centre of town, in the more bourgeois part, having their living quarters on the floor above the printing shop. Isaac's father barricaded the windows and stood behind the bolted door, gripping an iron rod. Through the chinks in the shut-ters the family could see the glow of distant flames as the shrieks and cries for help or pity became louder. The enraged mob passed by, breaking windows in the house next door.[1]

Isaac attended a rabbinical school and until his late teens wore the Hasidic attire, but he eventually rebelled against religious education, left his yeshiva and adopted secular clothes. He was almost thrown out of the Catholic gymnasium he attended part time when he opened a debate on a theme of his own choice: 'Christ was a Jew and a communist.' His father, Jacob, an orthodox Jew in love with German culture, philosophy and poetry, urged him to master German, a world language, unlike Polish. 'You have only to go beyond Auschwitz, and practically nobody will understand you any more, you and your fine Polish language.' (Auschwitz was nearby, on the frontier; during the Second World War his father disappeared into the extermination camp.)

Deutscher sent his journalist colleague, Donald Tyerman, some details about his upbringing in support of his application for membership of the Reform Club in 1954:

> The fact is that I attended regularly a school only during two years of my life, at the age of 8–10 years. I have been to no school since the age of 10. I had a private tutor, a rabbi, who instructed me only in Hebrew, the Talmud, and medieval mystical subjects. In the Jewish orthodox environment in which I grew up it was considered a grave sin to learn or teach any secular subjects, and my Father, who wanted me to be educated in some secular subjects, exposed himself to social ostracism on the part of a fanatical Jewish environment whenever he tried to make me 'sin'. He taught me Latin which he himself knew very well and read with me his favourite authors, Spinoza, Heine, Lassalle, to mention only these.

For three or four semesters Isaac attended courses as an extramural student in history, literature and philosophy at the medieval Yagellon University in Cracow, but he was never officially enrolled there and took no degree. 'Isn't it curious that I should have always been in such an irregular position, unable to claim any formal qualifications or status?' At the age of sixteen his first poems were published in the Cracow Polish-language Jewish journal *Nowy Dziennik*. His early verse carried strong echoes of Jewish mysticism, motifs of Jewish history and mythology, fusing Polish romanticism with Jewish lyrical folklore in an attempt to bridge the gulf between the two cultures. He also translated Hebrew, Latin, German and Yiddish poetry into Polish. At the age of eighteen he left Cracow for Warsaw; he also left poetry for literary criticism, and a more intense study of philosophy, economics – and Marxism.

Deutscher felt himself to be a Polish patriot and regarded Germans as oppressors. In school they had sung the song of Maria Konopnicka, a great poet: 'The German will not spit in our faces, nor will we make Germans of our children.' It was later that Marx and Engels reconciled him to the German language and culture. 'I was an adult before I read them, Lassalle and Bebel, Franz Mehring and Rosa Luxemburg, she who wrote German so wonderfully.' This opened the way to Kant, Hegel and Feuerbach. In 1926–27, he spent many hours in Warsaw with Thomas Mann, translating his work. He also associated with a circle of older people steeped in Russian literature: it was now that he began to read Lenin, Plekhanov, Bukharin and Trotsky.

In 1927, he joined the outlawed Polish Communist Party and very soon became the chief editor of the clandestine and semi-clandestine communist press. His severe critic Leopold Labedz later called him a 'young Talmudist-turned-dialectician'. He became secretary of the editorial board of the Yiddish communist literary monthly *Literarische Tribune*; his own articles appeared under the name 'Krakowski'. He also wrote for the Polish-language monthly *Miesiecznik Literacki*.[2]

In 1931, he travelled widely in the USSR, acquainting himself with the economic conditions of the country under its first Five-Year Plan. This was at the height of the collectivisation famine, involving the expulsion of the kulak families and the deaths of millions. Arthur Koestler embarked on a similar journey at this time.

Then came the rupture that was to colour the rest of Deutscher's life. He was expelled from the Polish Communist Party in the spring of 1932 after publishing 'The Danger of a New Barbarism in Europe', calling for common action between communists and socialists against Nazism and the Pilsudski dictatorship. His expulsion became known as the 'Krakowski affair', after his literary pseudonym. The official reason for it was that he had 'exaggerated the danger of Nazism and was spreading panic in the communist ranks'. Soon after his return from the USSR he had founded, together with three or four comrades, the first anti-Stalinist opposition group in the Polish Communist Party. They protested against the Party line according to which social democracy and Nazism were 'not antipodes but twins'. He recalled that from the day of his expulsion two sleuths shadowed him: one employed by the Polish police, the other a volunteer from the Stalinist Party cell. (Well, perhaps.)

In 1934, Deutscher joined the Polish Socialist Party. He also began working on the Zionist Polish-language daily *Nasz Przeglad* (published in Warsaw), with which he remained associated until he left for England in 1939. In 1938, the entire leadership of the Polish Communist Party, having fled to Moscow from Pilsudski's police, were imprisoned and shot, and the Party itself was dissolved by the Comintern. Although Deutscher had been expelled, he was bonded to the Party by memories: 'I remember the image of [Adolf] Warski at

Theatre Square on 1 May 1928. He was marching at the head of a huge banned demonstration, through the hail of machine-gun fire and rifle shots with which we were greeted by Pilsudski's militia. While tens or hundreds of wounded were falling in our ranks, he held up his white grey beard ... and indomitably addressed the crowd. This was the image of him I had in my mind when some years later he was denounced from Moscow as a traitor, a spy, and a Pilsudksi agent.'[3]

Although classed as Trotskyists, he and his Polish colleagues opposed Trotsky's creation of a Fourth International as futile, if not suicidal. When the founding congress took place in Paris in September 1938, the two Polish delegates arrived with a position paper prepared by Deutscher, objecting to the new International on the ground that 'No significant section of the working class will respond to our Manifesto'. The Poles were heavily outvoted and denounced by the American Marxist Max Shachtman as 'Mensheviks in our midst'.[4]

In April 1939, Deutscher left Warsaw for London as a correspondent of *Nasz Przeglad* – just in time. There he was to meet his future wife, Tamara Lebenhaft, the daughter of a Jewish intellectual family. Schooled in Łódź, then at a college in Belgium, she had worked as a journalist in Poland before escaping from France to Britain in 1940. According to one account, she arrived via Belgium after the fall of France and learned English with the aid of E.H. Carr's leaders in *The Times*. However, she herself was to provide a different version of her escape from the advancing Nazi armies. Interviewed during a holiday visit to Ceylon (Sri Lanka) in 1970, she recalled: 'I smuggled myself to Britain in 1940 as an airman. It was terrifying moving among men and dressed in an airman's uniform but I had to get away from Paris and the advancing Germans'. In pouring rain she passed through the checkpoints from the French to the Spanish border before boarding a ship carrying five hundred soldiers. The convoy was attacked from the air; three ships went down, but hers survived.[5]

Writing to friends after Isaac's death, Tamara recalled:

The whole of Isaac's family perished under German occupation, both his parents, his brother and sister. (One half-sister, from the previous marriage of his father, lives in Israel.) We have no family at all; perhaps some distant cousins scattered in the USA or Australia or Canada. My parents perished in the Warsaw ghetto. My mother did not want to leave it though some friends from the Resistance wanted to smuggle her out – but she was determined to remain with the other victims. My brother tried to cross over to the Russian side. His organisation was discovered by the Germans about two hours before they set out on the journey across the eastern frontier – they were all shot (my sister-in-law expected a baby).[6]

Reaching England, Deutscher zealously applied himself to learning English. E.H. Carr's biographer Jonathan Haslam remarks: 'On arrival his English was extremely weak, but with the aid of an edition of Macaulay, the *Shorter Oxford English Dictionary*, Talmudic self-discipline, a prodigious capacity for memorizing words and a sharp brain, he polished his prose to the point where – except for occasional quaint archaisms – he, like Joseph Conrad half a century earlier, could more than match the fiery eloquence of the best native speaker.'[7]

In 1940, he joined General Sikorski's Polish Army in Scotland (a photo shows him wearing a forage cap perched on one side of his head). According to one account, most of his 'army life' was spent in the punitive camps as a 'dangerous and subversive element' – his reward for his unceasing protests against the anti-Semitism rampant in that army. Released in 1942, he was subsequently employed in the exiled government's Information Department. It was at this time that his English journalism began, with regular contributions to the *Economist* and the *Observer*. 'Considering his linguistic handicaps,' comments Leopold Labedz, 'his technical achievement as a journalist was remarkable.'[8] On joining the staff of the *Economist*, he became the magazine's expert on Soviet affairs, its military commentator and its chief European correspondent. His first piece, 'Underground Europe', appeared on 13 June 1942. In the postwar years he was to produce numerous articles (twenty-one in 1945, twenty-five in 1946, continuing to 1949) on European affairs, reports from Germany and Austria, on mass expulsions in Eastern Europe, the one-party system in the Soviet Occupation Zone, reparations and industrial improvisation, currency reform and elections ('Berlin votes against Russia' was not an early dig at Isaiah).

He also joined the staff of the *Observer* in 1943, writing under the pseudonym 'LIBERATOR' in 1944 and as 'Peregrine' in 1945–46, but equally common was 'By a Special Correspondent'. Polish–Russian relations figured – he showed some sympathy for Moscow's refusal to recognise London's version of the Polish government. With the liberation of Europe, he became a roving correspondent, at one point sharing a room with George Orwell in occupied Germany, with somewhat fateful consequences, as we shall see. He reported from the Soviet zone. 'The Russian Military Government, whatever its failings and faults, does give a sense of purpose and direction to many Germans,' he observed, whereas 'complete industrial standstill' was 'not rare in Western Germany'.[9] Like Orwell himself, he also wrote for Michael Foot's left-Labour weekly *Tribune* in 1943–45, his contributions often unsigned or signed by the editors.

Meanwhile Stalin was taking possession of his native Poland through the leaders he had not executed in 1938. Deutscher could not return, even if tempted to do so. Labedz commented that after 1945 the communist ruling minority in Poland, 'top-heavy with the Jewish remnant (often concealing its ethnic origin), only helped to continue the traditional anti-Semitism in a country from which the Jews had practically disappeared'.[10]

Tamara was his inseparable companion and colleague. As described by the French journalist Daniel Singer, she was a beautiful young woman of great charm and a budding literary critic, admired in the highest circles of the Polish government in exile. She and Isaac travelled together as war and postwar correspondents in Germany. W.L. Webb, literary editor of the *Guardian*, recalled: 'Although they both worked as correspondents following Allied troops across Europe after D-Day, the clever and strikingly handsome Polish journalist, who had saved Corporal Deutscher's sanity when he was having a hard time with anti-Semitic elements in the Polish army in Scotland early in the war, largely abandoned her own writing while he lived.'

With Tamara's encouragement, and boosted by a major commission from Oxford University Press, Deutscher made the major decision to leave salaried journalism in favour of a career as a historian and biographer, influenced by the great English historians Gibbon, Macaulay and Trevelyan. In 1967, he recalled: 'Finally I also found in English my "world language". It gives me great satisfaction when English critics, even those who are politically hostile to me, sometimes compare my prose with that of Churchill or Macaulay, and that the University of Cambridge chose me this year to be its George Macaulay Trevelyan Lecturer.'

He struck up an enduring and significant friendship with the historian E.H. Carr, who had worked for *The Times* during the war. Carr soon became a favourite visitor to the home Isaac shared with Tamara, whom he married in 1947, while she was working as secretary to an expatriate organisation of Polish journalists in London.

In the late 1940s, Deutscher's public image, given his already clear pro-Soviet stance, was remarkably respectable. He worked freelance for most of the principal establishment newspapers and had been taken up by Oxford University Press. Perhaps benefiting from postwar sentiment favouring exiled Poles, not least those whose families had perished in the Holocaust, he was already 'one of us' and eminently courteous in correspondence. He was patronised by BBC producers like Douglas Cleverdon and Laurence Gilliam: in 1947, Deutscher provided notes on the voices of Lenin, Trotsky, Zinoviev, Kamenev, Kerensky and Vyshinsky for a script of his that Gilliam called 'masterly'. In 1948, Cleverdon commissioned a script from him on Karl Marx and the Russian Revolutionaries.[11] Gilliam reported to Deutscher that the conservative historian Hugh Trevor-Roper, of Christ Church soon to be famous for *The Last Days of Hitler*, had passed his name to Giliam for a BBC programme about the anniversary of the Russian Revolution, following which Trevor-Roper sent Deutscher an offprint of his 'The German Opposition 1937–1944' inscribed 'To Isaac Deutscher from Hugh Trevor-Roper'. Hugh Carleton Greene, head of the BBC World Service, wrote to him on 8 December 1949, responding to his enquiry about foreign reactions to broadcasts of extracts from his biography *Stalin* (obviously regarded as good anti-Soviet propaganda). By June 1949, he had been taken up by the Russian-born Anna Kallin, of the Third Programme, who was also Isaiah Berlin's patron. He was acquainted with Adam Watson, head of the Foreign Office's semi-clandestine anti-communist wing, the Information Research Department, responsible for disseminating the works of authors like Orwell and Koestler in Germany and Eastern Europe.[12] In August 1949, R.N. Carew Hunt, a strong anti-communist, solicited him to speak about Stalin to a study group at Worcester College, Oxford, 'under the auspices of the War Office'. On 27 April 1948, he spoke to a general meeting at Chatham House on economic conditions in the USSR, the speech to be published in the house journal, *International Affairs*, and in February 1948 he addressed a course at Chatham House sponsored by the Education Department of the Admiralty and the Air Ministry. In October 1949, Jane Degras, of Chatham House, invited him to discuss current Russian strategy at a meeting to be chaired by Lieutenant-General Sir Ian Jacob (later director-general of the BBC from 1952 to 1960).[13] At the suggestion of Carr, the historian David Thomson, of Sidney Sussex College, Cambridge, invited him to contribute a chapter on the Russian Revolution to volume twelve of the *Cambridge Modern History*. Deutscher accepted. With both Oxford and Cambridge now under his belt, he remarkably found himself professionally incorporated into the British Cold War establishment – despite holding the West entirely responsible for international tensions. The same went for E.H. Carr, of course, but Carr was not a Polish Jewish ex-communist.

Clive James remarked: 'The Jew out of nowhere is in demand everywhere, and he can be excused for loving every minute of it.' He was referring in fact to Isaiah Berlin but the comment applies equally well to Deutscher at this point in his career.[14] Clearly Berlin's animosity did not precede the appearance of Deutscher's biography of Stalin. He obliged when Dan Davin of the Clarendon Press asked him to comment on Deutscher's translation of lines by Aleksandr Blok. Davin reported to Deutscher: 'he comments, truly enough, that your translation contains one or two un-English expressions,' adding: 'Berlin, by the way, seemed a little puzzled that you should have chosen precisely the lines that you did; he thought that there are lines in the same poem which might have been even more relevant.' Deutscher replied: 'Berlin is, of course, right. . . . But I don't think there are any lines there bearing a closer relationship to my subject – foreign policy.' This is the first discovered record of interchange between Berlin and Deutscher, though in this case conducted through an intermediary. The following year, 1949, Berlin recommended Deutscher to Douglas Cater, editor of the New York *Reporter*, as an expert on Soviet society[15] – and, indeed, out of this was to come a full decade of contributions (at 14 cents a word) by Deutscher to that magazine.

A political biography of Stalin, as the Soviet leader approached his seventieth birthday more than ever in the full panoply of power, became for Oxford University Press a major undertaking. Oxford's advance payment to Deutscher was £1,000 (worth about £20,000 in current values), with an extra £200 payable on receipt of the final manuscript.[16] Deutscher found himself at ease with the slightly curious set-up, which had him working with both Dan Davin (his editor) at the Clarendon Press in Oxford and Geoffrey Cumberlege at OUP in London. Meanwhile Henry Z. Walck of OUP, New York, was also fully involved in simultaneous publication in the US.

Davin consulted widely on the manuscript, including Isaiah Berlin (an OUP author) and Sir David Maxwell-Fyfe on a query about the Nuremberg trials. The latter reported back that Marshal Tukhachevsky had come to England for the coronation of George VI, which didn't help him when Stalin decided to do away with him. In fact, the evidence seems to be that Tukhachevsky's visit was cancelled by Stalin shortly before the coronation on 12 May 1937, by which date the marshal was doomed. Given the accusations later levelled against Deutscher regarding his belief that Tukhachevsky really had plotted to overthrow Stalin, this minor point may assume some significance.

Remarkable though Deutscher's rapid mastery of the English language was, his typescripts needed heavy editing. In April 1947, his long-term friend Donald Tyerman, then of *The Times*, sent back chapter one of *Stalin* with comments: '(a) For heaven's sake watch your past tenses and see if you really know the difference, in English, between the perfect, pluperfect and imperfect . . . (b) watch your semi-colons; in 99 cases out of 100 you use a semi-colon where a comma is called for; (c) shun like the plague words like "quite", "rather", "somewhat" and so on; in almost every case where you use them they neither add nor detract from the meaning of the adjective alone.' Tyerman added his admiration for the first two chapters.[17]

The Deutschers' arrival in New York, and with it the launch of *Stalin* in the US, was dependent on an uphill struggle (described below) to obtain an entry visa. Accommodated at the publisher's expense, they immediately found themselves 'rushing from lunch engagements to cocktail parties and from press conferences to dinner engagements'. Deutscher had no objection to that – for the first time in his life he commanded the limelight. In general, the reception of the book on both sides of the Atlantic equalled or exceeded expectations: *Stalin* was generally greeted as a deeply researched and compellingly written objective study, the first definitive portrait of the most powerful man in the world. In the *New York Times Book Review* (2 October 1949), Edward Crankshaw called it the classic biography and work of reference until such time as the Soviet archives became available – 'the daunting nature of his task, so triumphantly, so apparently effortlessly, performed'. The *Saturday Evening Post* (1 October 1949) featured Deutscher on its cover. Two days later *Newsweek*, too, warmly promoted *Stalin*: 'In England, Deutscher's 600-page work, published by the Oxford University Press, has met with the highest praise accorded any book since Winston Churchill's "The Gathering Storm".'[18] The *Chicago Sunday Tribune* (2 October 1949) carried the feature on its cover, although David Dallin complained that the book was marred by unjustified concessions to the Soviet view. Such caveats were the exception rather than the rule, although a critical review by Bertram D. Wolfe appeared in the *New York Herald Tribune Book Review* (31 October 1949), castigating Deutscher's 'complete apologetic' for the partition of Poland between Hitler and Stalin. We are told, continued Wolfe, that we should not have enquired what happened to their officers buried in the Katyn forest. Purges in Eastern Europe and the Balkans are said to be directed against 'the old ruling class', which must include the socialist and peasant parties, democrats and liberals. 'We look in vain for the names of Petkov, Maniu, Nagy, Masaryk.'

OUP issued *Stalin* at 25 shillings in Britain. The book received vast coverage. Figures provided by OUP on 21 March 1958, almost nine years after publication, show nine translated editions, the most successful in terms of sales being in Norway (6,181), followed by Germany (3,544) and France (1,650). Cash received from overseas by the publisher in total amounted to about £1,400 – results perhaps falling short of expectations. Deutscher was advised: 'Neither the Danish nor the French edition has sold sufficiently well to cover the advances received.' Sales figures for the UK and USA have not been found.[19]

Deutscher was naturally hungry for further commissions. Since 1947 at least he had been mentioning a projected history of Soviet Russia or a 'Social History of the Soviet Union', and we find him still with this project on his radar after his visit to the Harvard and Stanford archives in 1950. In May 1952, Dan Davin sent him a cheque for £300 as advance payment but the book never materialised.

In May 1949, the Home Office had accorded him a Certificate of Naturalisation, requiring that he take the oath of allegiance. On 26 September, it took note that Isaac and Tamara Deutscher had been released from Polish nationality by the Warsaw government. OUP was set on bringing Deutscher to the USA for the publication of his *Stalin*. Meanwhile, the Rockefeller Foundation, approached by the Clarendon Press, had provided a grant to enable him to study the Trotsky archives at Harvard. But with the American witch-hunt gathering hysterical pace, would the State Department grant a visa to this former communist?

Applying for a visa, Deutscher explained at the embassy that he had been a member of the Polish Communist Party from 1926 to 1932. Tamara Deutscher later recalled the ensuing period of six months during which letters, cables and fat drafts of affidavits running into thousands of words were written and exchanged, on the basis of which the elusive '9th Proviso Waiver' was (or wasn't) to be granted. While OUP's attorneys in New York negotiated with the Department of Justice, Deutscher refused to express regret at having joined the Communist Party and refused to attest that he had thereafter returned from communism to 'the rabbinical tradition'. He was careful to sign nothing which might conceivably push him over the border separating the 'heretic' from the 'renegade'. What he did agree to was the following (paraphrased): 'It is true . . . that at the age of nineteen I could not have known anything about the uglier features of the Communist Party but I do not regret having joined. I think that my experience in the CP was on the whole a valuable one for my mental development and further work. I have been disgusted by the nature of the recantations from within the ranks of the Communist Party.' This was brave and could have been professionally suicidal.[20]

Eventually he was granted a visa for only three months to work in the Trotsky archives at Harvard and the Hoover Institute, Stanford, but as Tamara Deutscher recalled, he was banned from speaking in public, 'so a whole series of lectures arranged well ahead of time at various colleges and universities had to be called off'. He was, however, allowed to deliver two or three talks to closed meetings and seminars at Harvard's Russian Research Center. The couple liked Harvard: 'to our great relief none of the Harvard professors put any obstacles in Isaac's way: on the contrary, they were helpful, with that mixture of politeness and reserve shown to a political opponent who arouses respect and a sneaking admiration.' Deutscher was virtually the first scholar to work in the Houghton Library's Trotsky archive, so minimal was academic interest ten years after Trotsky's murder in Mexico in 1940.

One important dissenting voice was that of Trotsky's widow, Natalya Sedova. She did not read English and her view of Deutscher's *Stalin* was dependent on her advisers, who regarded the author as an apologist for Stalinism and also a heretical non-orthodox Trotskyist who did not worship at the shrine and was therefore even worse than an infidel. Fortunately her objections were overruled by the Harvard librarian and other members of the faculty. Even Sedova was to change her attitude after she met the Deutschers in Paris in 1956, to which we will return.[21]

After three months at Harvard the couple emerged with 'twelve massive notebooks filled with notes and excerpts from the Trotsky documents'. They now returned to New York with funds running low. 'Mr Walck [of OUP New York] kindly offered me an advance on *Trotsky*, but, because of British currency regulations, I could not avail myself of this,' noted Deutscher. 'The Rockefeller Foundation came up with an additional grant for Tamara, who had actually been doing as much research as myself.' They were then able to proceed to Stanford, travelling by coach and train to San Francisco. Writing to Dan Davin from Stanford (21 April 1950), Deutscher reported: 'The Immigration authorities persisted in their refusal to allow me to speak in public. A score of universities and colleges had invited me to address special meetings, but Mr Walck's office had to cancel all tentative speaking engagements.' The ban on his public appearances had the advantage of allowing him to concentrate on the research, although the banned lectures would have financed the greater part of the couple's stay and travel. At several closed academic gatherings, Deutscher delivered what he called 'a somewhat provocative essay analysing the role of ex-Communists in contemporary literature and politics'.

A proposed visit to Mexico had to be aborted because his one-entry-only visa would not have allowed him to return to America even for a day had he crossed the border. The immigration authorities were adamant about this, saying they took a low view of Mexican communists and the fact that Deutscher wanted to attend a meeting in Mexico made him doubly suspect. In fact, he did not intend to meet Mexican communists.[22] He probably did not know that the treason charges against Julius and Ethel Rosenberg, who were arrested while the Deutschers were in America, hinged on communist courier-contacts with Mexico. (The Rosenbergs, incidentally, were guilty as charged, although their execution three years later was unforgivable.)

Writing to Robert Jackson (16 June 1950) after his return to London, Deutscher reflected on his experiences in the USA, 'the industrial genius of its people, the warm-heartedness and kindness of the average American'. He was proud to have met John Dewey, now ninety-one, who had presided over the 1937 'Counter-Trial' that had found Trotsky innocent of the Soviet charges against him. Dewey had also written a favourable appreciation of Deutscher's *Stalin*. But the downsides of America were immense: 'The vulgarity of the

American press, radio, film and book selling trade is really overwhelming. Yet these are the media by which the mind of the people is shaped and moulded constantly ... this prodigious outpour of stupidity and falsehood.' As for the academic output, most of it is 'so empty, yet pretentious, so far below any European standards, so phoney that we could hardly believe our eyes and ears. And this is in spite, or perhaps because, of fabulous endowments, scholarships, grants, funds of all sorts, the most modern technical facilities for research etc. It takes five minutes at Harvard or Stanford to find a reference, which it sometimes takes a week to in London. Yet, if somebody were to ask for a single important title on Russian topics produced by these happy American "scholars", we would be at a loss to mention one or two.'

By 1949–50, Deutscher's status as an international relations expert was recognised to an astonishing degree by leading establishment newspapers both in Britain and in America. Now in his early forties, newspaper photographs or sketches show Deutscher with spectacles, receding hair cut short and clean-shaven. The aforementioned cover of the *Saturday Evening Post* (1 October 1949) depicted a gentle, smiling Deutscher in the foreground and a looming portrait of Stalin behind him. By the time he attended the funeral of Natalya Sedova at Père Lachaise cemetery in Paris, in January 1962, Deutscher had acquired his trademark moustache and goatee beard.[23]

With the publication of *Stalin*, his journalism flourished.[24] In July 1950, the *New York Times Magazine* carried a huge piece by Deutscher on 'Soviet Strengths and Soviet Weaknesses'. The display copy for the article suggested: 'The current crisis points up the difficulties in gauging Russia's potential for all-out war.' That Deutscher resented this editorial précis is indicated on his cutting of the printed article, where he has crossed it out and substituted another. Like Isaiah Berlin, he also wrote for the State Department's journal, *Foreign Affairs*, in Deutscher's case on the subject of 'Socialist Competition' (March 1952), a study of incentives and competition commissioned by the editor, Hamilton Fish Armstrong. The same year he was delighted to give a talk on Stalin and Trotsky at the invitation of the British Foreign Office. Other speakers included Isaiah Berlin on 'The Transition from Capitalism to Socialism and from Socialism to Communism', Leonard Schapiro, Hugh Seton-Watson, Max Hayward and Brigadier Fitzroy Maclean.[25] Did Berlin and Deutscher meet on this occasion, and if so, was this the first time?

Back in London after six months in the United States, with Tamara expecting a baby, the immediate problem was that their two-room flat would not accommodate 'the three of us', as he explained to Robert Jackson (16 June 1950). By 1951, the family had decided to move from the Haverstock Hill district of north-west London to a more countrified habitat within an easy train ride of the capital in Coulsdon, Surrey (described by Deutscher as 'coun-tryside', with garden and guest room). In the late Fifties they moved again, to Wokingham, Berkshire, before returning to Highgate Hill West, close to Swiss Cottage underground station, in 1963.

But without a regular salary and with a wife and child to support, by 1952 Deutscher was struggling to make ends meet. Discussing Isaac's financial needs as he embarked on his biography of Trotsky (OUP wanted only one volume and refused to offer more money for two), Tamara reflected: 'How to finance the second volume? Apply for a grant? Look for a teaching job? Although quite a few people received grants on the strength of Isaac's recom-mendation, he could receive none, and all efforts of friends who acted on his behalf came to nothing.'[26] The Rockefeller Foundation refused a further grant while the Leverhulme restricted its donations to those who had been of British nationality at birth. The freelance life is perilous and fame is not money – there was doubtless no shortage of intelligent readers who, having read admiring reviews of *Stalin* in the newspapers, felt no need to spend 25 shillings on the details.

Having engaged the literary agent Robert Harben, Deutscher bent his ener-gies to expanding his range as a syndicated journalist: in 1955 he described Harben as 'dealing with my books brought out by Publishers other than O.U.P., and with my journalistic writings. He has represented me in at least fifteen countries to my greatest satisfaction. I have found him a very efficient and reli-able agent.' The resulting income was not princely: Harben's statement for syndicated foreign journalistic earnings in 1963 showed £723 minus £166 commission, but this did not take account of British and US earnings.[27] Working for the bourgeois press, Deutscher may have taken heart from his hero Leon Trotsky. Exiled in Prinkipo, Turkey, Trotsky had supported out of his own literary earnings a burgeoning household resembling a small department of state, with multiple secretaries and visiting devotees, costing US$12,000–15,000 a year. He received $7,000 for the American edition of *My Life* and in 1932 the *Saturday Evening Post* paid $45,000 to serialise his *History of the Russian Revolution*.[28]

Meanwhile for Deutscher both scholarship and journalism had to compen-sate for the underfunding of British libraries, obliging him to subscribe to a wide range of newspapers and periodicals, including the leading Soviet cultural organs, *Voprosy Istorii*, *Voprosy Istorii KPSS*, *Voprosy Filosofii*, *Voprosy Ekonomiki*, *Istoricheskii Arkhov*, *Kommunist* and *Novyi mir*, and the Polish *Z Pola Walki*. He also joined and made extensive use of the august London Library in St James's Square (annual subscription four guineas), with which Isaiah Berlin was closely associated.

Isaac Deutscher's good relationship with the British political and military establishments survived his controversial *Russia after Stalin* (1953). While it is hardly surprising that he accepted them, one assumes that the invitations continued to be issued on the basis of 'we ought to know what the chaps on the other side are thinking'. The speaking engagements he tended to turn down politely were mainly from university societies likely to be small in attendance: if you were Aberystwyth University Labour Group, you might be out of luck. On 2 April 1954, he lectured on 'Russia' at the Royal United Services Institution. He continued to charm the Cold Warriors into the Sixties: in 1961, he addressed the Imperial Defence College and was invited again the following year but declined on health grounds. In July 1963, he spoke to the Conservative Political Centre on 'Contemporary Communism: The Sino-Soviet Argument'. Accepting the invitation, he wrote: 'I feel, however, that I ought to ask whether you are aware that you are inviting a Marxist.' Evidently they were aware. For this engagement he received £2 from the Conservative and Unionist Central Office and was accommodated overnight in Wadham College. All the other speakers were leading Tories like Lord Home and Peter Thorneycroft.[29] Obviously his audiences felt rewarded: on 14 November 1964, he addressed the University Conservative and Unionist Associations on 'China and Communism'.

Equally obviously, he himself felt at ease in such company. On 18 April 1955, the secretary of the Reform Club in Pall Mall thanked him for his 30-guinea entrance fee and subscription for the current year. He had been proposed by Donald Tyerman, who needed his help with the club's question-naire about upbringing and education.[30]

If the publication of *Stalin* had led to the recognition of Deutscher as a leading authority on Soviet affairs and historian of the Russian Revolution, his reputation as a master of English prose was confirmed by his Trotsky trilogy: *The Prophet Armed* (1954), *The Prophet Unarmed* (1959) and *The Prophet Outcast* (1963). Much of the material contained in the third volume is unique, he having in 1956 received special permission from Trotsky's widow, Natalya Sedova, to read through the Closed Section of the Harvard archives which, according to the terms of Trotsky's will, was to remain unopened till the end of the century. Deutscher explained that Trotsky's motive in creating a Closed Section consisting largely of correspondence with family and colleagues was to protect them in an age when Hitler and Stalin were in the ascendant.

While working on Trotsky in the Houghton Library, Harvard, Deutscher filled many notebooks with material on Lenin. He planned to conclude his biographical series with a study of the great man, and expressed the hope that his works would be seen as 'a single essay in a Marxist analysis of the revolution of our age and also as a triptych of some artistic unity'. When again working in the Trotsky archives at Harvard in 1959, he remained banned from speaking in public. It was not until May 1965 that he was able to deliver his first public speech in America, when invited to the National Teach-In in Washington and, the following year, to a mass meeting in Berkeley.

The Deutschers' marriage, as reflected in their correspondence (he was often abroad), was warm and devoted. Tamara was not only his wife and mother to his child but a dedicated and linguistically gifted research assistant who totally embraced Isaac's Marxism and his position on world politics. They wrote to each other in English, with occasional Polish phrases thrown in. ('Marusinka, najukoschańsa ['beloved'],' he addresses her, finishing in Polish: 'I kiss you, my dearest, my beloved, my one and only, wonderful Marusinka.') Tamara's letters from 1959 begin 'Maruś, my darling' or 'Marupuska, my darling', but she also used 'My dear Pa', 'Darling Pa', and 'Darling Maruczek'. In their 1967 letters she addressed him as 'Dearest/Darling Maruczek' and he addressed her as 'Maruczek darling' (a private term between them). 'When you are here you do all the talking,' she wrote, 'and when you are not here I keep on talking to you.' She reported how she had taken their son, Martin, to Amsterdam and how she had cried over Anne Frank's house.[31]

A speaker of spellbinding power and a debater of great argumentative force, in 1965 Deutscher took part in the first Teach-In on Vietnam, in the course of which fifteen thousand students gathered on the Berkeley University campus to hear his indictment of the Cold War. He was in remunerative teaching mode at Harpur College (the State University of New York at Binghamton), and when lecturing at New York University, Princeton, Harvard and Columbia in the spring of 1967. As G.M. Trevelyan Lecturer at Cambridge University for 1966–67, Deutscher at last received his due from British academe, addressing overflow audiences. Published under the title *The Unfinished Revolution*, his Trevelyan Lectures were translated in some fifteen countries. His analyses of major international events continued to appear in Europe, the USA, Canada, Japan, India and Latin America.

He died suddenly of a heart attack in the Mater Dei Clinic, Rome, on 19 August 1967, aged only sixty. The Deutschers were insured with the British United Provident Association, which sent Tamara a cheque for £31.7s.0d to cover the fees of the surgeon and anaesthetist for a minor operation and one day's maintenance. The Royal Automobile Club sent her an account statement for 'the recovery of your car from Milan'. Memorial meetings were held in London and New York, both on 22 September, with 150 persons attending in the US and the UK gathering being chaired by the Marxist academic Ralph Miliband at the Mahatma Gandhi Hall, Fitzroy Square. Carr paid tribute to

Deutscher's personality in his anonymous *Times* obituary (21 August 1967). Deutscher knew his worth but 'There was also a great modesty about him, and a splendid warmth, as well as an unfailing kindness and a touching courtesy – at times, too, hours of sheer boyish glee – in his meetings with friends'. Deutscher's oeuvre was formidable: 'It is a remarkable record for a man working alone, without a university faculty to help him in his research and thinking.' Berlin, who knew why Deutscher's application for a chair was rejected, contrasted his own friendly feelings for Carr – 'unlike Deutscher whom I detest as a nasty human being, quite independently of his views'.[32] This was written a year before Deutscher's death, but the verdict remained unmodified.

The shock of Deutscher's death for Tamara was pulverising, her grief enormous: 'he was my life', she wrote to friends, in November, explaining how the pain did not lessen with the passing days but increased. She was, or felt, financially hard up: 'My financial position is not very good, Isaac had to waste so much of his time and energy on journalism precisely because we could not live on the income from books or from public engagements – they were bringing fame but no money.'[33] She wrote to friends and to the British Museum and BBC Radio Archives in search of part-time work, stressing her linguistic qualifications and her experience as her husband's researcher and editor, and she enquired at the Overseas Students Department of the British Council about taking in a student lodger. Friends like Donald Tyerman were responsive and helpful, yet nothing seemed to turn up. Hugh Seton-Watson (the target of at least one review by Deutscher) wrote sympathetically from the School of Slavonic Studies, recalling his disagreements with Deutscher but fondly remembering earlier days when they saw quite a lot of each other – but he could not suggest a vacancy. She wrote to Arthur Crook, editor of the *TLS*, soliciting reviews: 'I read Russian, Polish, French and Italian.' The future press baron Robert Maxwell wrote from Pergamon Press in Oxford to Tyerman: 'Along with millions of others I was a fan of Isaac Deutscher. . . . It should be possible for us to employ Mrs Deutscher with her great linguistic talents, including research and writing experience.' But evidently nothing came of it. She turned her energies instead to shepherding Isaac's unpublished work through the printers, drumming up contributors to David Horowitz's planned Festschrift and setting up the Isaac Deutscher Memorial Prize.[34]

Deutscher's books and articles had never been published in Russia, where he was labelled an enemy of socialism. Tamara wrote a memo dated 15 July 1969, relating an incident that occurred two years after Isaac's death. A nameless Russian who spoke good English called her on the phone, explaining that he had long wanted to meet Deutscher because 'in our terrible isolation, on our terrible diet, his works were real nourishment to us'. He had managed to read Deutscher's publications because as a sociologist he had lived in Paris for six years, but a number of Deutscher's works had also been smuggled into Russia and passed from hand to hand. The mysterious Russian then visited Tamara at her invitation, telling her that his copy of *Stalin* was falling to pieces and had to be held together with gum paper. Born in 1926, Tamara's visitor remembered the period when people used simply to 'disappear' mysteriously. As a boy of nine or ten he had played with his friends in the courtyard of a block of some twenty flats – there were only three families who had not lost a member in this way. 'One day a boy's father would treat us all to ice-cream and sweets and next day he was gone and nobody asked any questions.' His own parents were both engineers and feared arrest during the trial of the foreign specialists – perhaps a reference to the Metro–Vickers trial in 1933. 'Now I see that my parents never really talked to me, they never took me into their confidence.' The Russian gazed wistfully at the shelves of Deutscher's books and was impressed by the number of foreign editions of *The Unfinished Revolution*. Tamara was glad to offer him a copy but he sadly declined: 'At present it is too dangerous to bring your husband's books in.' So he departed, still nameless but promising to return.[35]

During the years following Isaac's death, Tamara's essays and reviews revealed a lively style, a witty mind and a critical spirit. She produced, *inter alia*, a Lenin anthology (*Not by Politics Alone*) while also dedicating her energies to the publication of Deutscher's essays in book form, among them *Russia, China and the West* (1970), *Marxism in our Time* (1971), and *Marxism, Wars and Revolutions* (1984). She likewise edited and published 'The Young Lenin', the first chapter of a biography of Lenin on which Deutscher was working when he died. Meanwhile, Tamara Deutscher agreed to work for the elderly E.H. 'Ted' Carr as his assistant, researcher, editor and critic. When he came to stay with her at Kidderpore Gardens in NW3, usually for two days every fortnight, Tamara would put him up in her small spare bedroom. It was a rather bohemian household, down to the shots of vodka before dinner. For some years she worked as Carr's valued collaborator in the preparation of the final volumes of his *History of Soviet Russia*. Jonathan Haslam records that in 1973, as a result of his crisis with his current wife, Betty, Carr began to press his attentions on Tamara but she did not want that. 'His track record was, after all, pretty awful; and it is striking how his letters to Tamara sound like the letters to Betty sent in the early sixties.' After Carr's death she wrote a warm appreciation, 'Remembering E.H. Carr'. She died in 1990.[36]

3

THE ISSUES

BERLIN AND DEUTSCHER were of the same generation, both refugees, both British by adoption, both multilingual, opinionated Jews; one Latvian-Russian, the other Polish. Both came to exercise influence not only in academic circles but among the wider British and American public. Both can be viewed as missionary spirits in contention to convince or convert the ideologically naïve English and American natives. To that extent theirs can be viewed as a family quarrel over the legitimate title to a heritage, a domain, entailing the temptation to fratricide. Deutscher's fatal review of Berlin's *Historical Inevitability* may be likened to an episode in the fraught story of Jacob and Esau – but which was the hairy one?

No correspondence between Berlin and Deutscher has been found. As far as one can tell, Berlin never mentioned Deutscher's name in print although his private correspondence reveals an intense hostility. After years of mounting animosity, he took a fateful step to damage Deutscher. The victim may have remained ignorant of the perpetrator's exact role – but that remains uncertain. For his part, Deutscher regarded Berlin as an ideological opponent whom he scarcely knew – they perhaps met twice – not as a figure to be despised and loathed.

Today the name of Isaiah Berlin remains familiar to a wider public than Deutscher's. Even when they have not read his work, educated people recognise him by reputation. By contrast, Deutscher's name is well known to modern historians and students of politics, but not much beyond that circle. The capital city of Germany is easier for us to pronounce (and to spell) than the German word for 'a German', which tends to sit awkwardly on the Anglo-Saxon tongue. Deutscher was of course Polish and, like Isaiah Berlin, avoided writing in German whenever he could. He could talk to Heinrich Brandler in German but wrote to him, with apologies, in English. Both spoke Russian,

Berlin like a native, though he confessed he was not at ease writing more than a postcard. Deutscher pleased Trotsky's widow, Natalya Sedova, when he switched their conversation from French to Russian. Obviously both men possessed a range of linguistic abilities extremely rare among English academics.

Their philosophical differences, their dispute about the nature of history and the proper function of the historian, or what it meant to be a Jew, were lethally transmuted into their view of the contemporary world and the political allegiances it offered. For two decades they stood, heavily armed, on opposite banks of a Rubicon coloured red by deposits of mud and blood.

Berlin's circle of colleagues and friends, some of them Sovietologists and many of them associated, like Berlin himself, with the Congress for Cultural Freedom, stood without exception for the anti-Soviet position. Almost all identified the USA as the indispensable leader of the 'Free World', although individual reactions to McCarthyism varied, with liberals and social democrats tending to regard America's domestic purge as damaging to the image of the West as a bastion of civil liberties. Deutscher intransigently rejected the entire Western system and its international policies, dismissing the 'Free World' as the cosmetics of an expansionist, colonialist monopoly capitalism.

On occasion in what follows I venture into topics where Berlin and Deutscher are not found in overt contention. This applies, for example, to much of Berlin's work on nineteenth-century Russian literature, his playful thoughts about hedgehogs and foxes, and his *Two Concepts of Liberty*. But if their two ships sometimes passed in the night, they tended to arrive back in the same main ports, accompanied by heavy bombardments. Those ports are located in Russia and its history since 1917.

We are looking at the high-water mark of the Cold War, the years between 1945 and 1970, when scarcely any branch of thought and learning, even extending to the natural sciences, remained unaffected by the schism between the 'Free World' and the Soviet sphere of influence. In the USA and Europe, the Cold War consensus comfortably prevailed in politics, the academy and the media from 1945 to 1960; thereafter it came under mounting challenge and suffered a widening fissure as American policies previously contested only by Western communists, or by an 'anti-anti-communist' minority (including Deutscher and E.H. Carr), faced root-and-branch attack from radicals hostile to the ossified Soviet system but committed to the fresh shoots of Third World revolution. The serene self-confidence of the Congress for Cultural Freedom and 'Cold War liberalism' during the 1950s was fraying as critics in the West began to call into question not only the virtue of American foreign and domestic policy but the hierarchical university system. The period of the so-called 'end of ideology' witnessed the birth of a passionate ideological debate, and it was at this juncture that Isaac Deutscher had his day as tribune and prophet, a day unhappily curtailed by his early death. Berlin clearly resented and despised Deutscher's popularity within the New Left, which he took as further proof of the man's unprincipled readiness to prostitute his undoubted learning and abilities.

Deutscher was a valued contributor to Jean-Paul Sartre's periodical, *Les Temps modernes*, but his outlook lacked Sartre's multifaceted flexibility. Whereas the French philosopher had the gift of seeing sideways and backwards through his outwardly lopsided eyes, Deutscher was something of a Cyclops as a judge of global morality. The only ascendant star glimmered in the Russian sky. And yet – to adopt Berlin's own famous metaphor – the nimble, witty and fox-like Berlin ultimately comes across as no less a hedgehog than Deutscher. At first sight Isaac knew One Big Thing whereas Isaiah juggles with many things, but on closer inspection these many things ultimately boil down to One Big Thing: beware those parading a single vision of human destiny, the 'monists'.

Yet this was an intimate family quarrel akin to that of Catholics and Protestants at war over Christ's heritage. Marxists and anti-Marxist liberals alike were children of the European Enlightenment. Both Cold War camps subscribed in the abstract to education, justice, freedom. Unlike the West's current antagonist, Islam, Marxism was a Western product. Marx was not born in Mecca; he worked in the British Museum. In theory if not in practice, Soviet communism regarded itself as the only triumphal outcome of a revolutionary tradition nurtured in England, France and Germany. One notices that throughout the Soviet era Moscow, Washington, Paris and London all attached value and competitive instinct to a common range of cultural activities, from literature and classical music to high-jumping and hurdling; from ballet and opera to chess and aviation; from theatre and cinema to gymnastics and popular entertainment. Both East and West entered their champions for the same Olympic competitions, whether sporting or cultural. Thus Berlin and Deutscher are speaking a common language when they disagree bitterly about Bolsheviks and Mensheviks, about Lenin or Pasternak, about Israel or the Hungarian Revolution, about 'historical inevitability' or whether liberty is inseparable from equality. They are hurling dishes across a family table. Even more do Berlin and Deutscher speak a common language when they disagree about what it means, or should mean, to be a Jew or a Zionist – both having lost close relatives to the Holocaust and both witnesses to the same twentieth-century catastrophes.

How did their theoretical positions as academics relate to their active personal commitments, the actual, here-and-now involvements in the domestic political and social issues of the time – the traffic passing outside the study window? Did they shut the window, close their eyes – or lean out? Berlin tended not to lean out (too far). No recluse – indeed, he was assigned to the British delegation in Washington during the war to exercise his gifts for communication in the national interest – he nevertheless inclined to a donnish withdrawal into Oxford's quadrangles, whence his eloquence would periodically gallop forth. During the years within our frame, he said little publicly about capital punishment, homosexual law reform, the rules governing divorce, immigration to the UK or rising racial tension. Should industries be nationalised, should the welfare state expand? No clear answer. When Victor Gollancz wrote in the hope of enlisting his support for the campaign to abolish capital punishment in the UK, Berlin replied (20 August 1955): 'I wish I knew my mind about capital punishment. I am more against it than for it, and if it were abolished I should, I think, feel relief. Although, at the same time, I do not feel strongly enough to wish to identify myself with the movement of the completely converted.'[1] Likewise it would not be easy to unearth his views about the British military counterinsurgency in Kenya, Malaya, Cyprus and the Canal Zone of Egypt. He did, however, later remark: 'Liberal democracies, unlike tyrannies, by their very natures cannot generate continuous counter-frightfulness for any length of time, at least in dependent territories. So it was in Palestine, in Cyprus, in Kenya, in Batavia, in Algiers.'[2] Was Vietnam omitted from this list because it was technically not a 'dependent territory'? Why did 'liberal democracies' happen to rule so many 'dependent territories' where they lacked any democratic mandate and suppressed rebellion by means of often brutal counterinsurgency? Further afield, he kept his own counsel about black rebellion, ghetto riots and rising animosity between Jews and blacks in the USA. How did he react to apartheid in South Africa or white Rhodesia's unilateral declaration of independence? Only once did he succumb to moral pressure to state publicly, very briefly and clearly reluctantly, his view of the Vietnam War. He liked to describe himself as a man of the Left, or 'left of centre' assailed by both Left and Right – but his right-wing detractors are difficult to locate.

On the majority of front-page issues Berlin neither marched nor denounced in the letters pages of *The Times* those who did. He was no Jean-Paul Sartre, no Bertrand Russell. The major exception to his reticence throughout these years was his support for Israel, for a modified Zionism, and his outspoken views on what it meant, or should mean, to be a Jew. By and large, Berlin remained an impeccably conforming British citizen or 'subject' – fellow of All Souls, knighted in his forties, president of Wolfson College, president of the British Academy, Order of Merit, almost predictably in step (or silent step) with the general line of the British government, the Western consensus. His perceptive essays about the states of mind available to the different types of assimilated Jew living in the West provoked little public controversy; into that minority domain the guilt-ridden majority culture chose not to intrude.

Should our view of Berlin's major works of political theory be affected by what we know of his life as a citizen? A reformist socialist might argue that *Historical Inevitability* and *Two Concepts of Liberty* were perfectly compatible with joining the Labour Party, supporting hunger marchers or embracing liberation movements in the Third World. Berlin would probably not have disagreed in principle, yet he chose not to join. Yet one may surely work for social progress without insisting on its inevitability. One may place one's penny in the vast box of history without declaring history to be a science. One may champion the most obviously urgent needs of the working class and those suffering poverty without embracing some Marxist vision of the proletariat as the class destined to abolish all classes. A missionary doctor in Africa may believe he is following Christ's path, but another doctor may equally pursue his vocation without any supernatural support. Yet Berlin remained virtually immune to the virus of good causes, if only because he regarded action, or active political commitment, as the enemy of clear thinking – although mainly by implication. People no sooner unfurl a banner than they find themselves taken over by those stridently partisan, assertive voices oblivious to reflective doubt and the plurality of values. He admired the New Deal and Attlee's welfare state, but also believed that Lloyd George had saved England from centralised socialism. He was never a joiner. Berlin was not at ease on the back of any camel liable to lumber away on a journey of its own.

Deutscher also remained an essentially private man where domestic British issues were concerned. Though he relished public lectures and broadcasts, he was not a joiner either. For some years, living and writing in or near London, his passions and ambitions were fully realised as a scholar, pundit and prophet. One can surmise that, having experienced acute difficulties with the State Department in acquiring a visa to study the Trotsky archive at Harvard, and wishing to return there, he was prudently avoiding further political entanglements. English bourgeois society remained surprisingly tolerant of dissident views; indeed, in his case patronised them through an impressive range of newspapers, periodicals and public lectures. But he was not inclined to risk overstepping the mark into militant activity or joining picket lines. Prudence, after all, is a revolutionary virtue, like the lack of it.

Deutscher always announced himself as a classical Marxist, which means a revolutionary, a militant of the unfinished revolution. But where was the revolution to be found on this side of the Iron Curtain? Critical of Stalinism, he could not join the Communist Party; contemptuous of parliamentary reformism, he could not join the Labour Party. The Trotskyist factions regarded him as a neo-Stalinist heretic, a betrayer of Leon Trotsky's indispensable teachings. As Deutscher put it, with no army to embrace, he had positioned himself in the 'watchtower'.

He could not visit the Soviet Union, his native Poland or any other People's Democracy. He could lecture (permission was eventually granted) in America but not in the country on which he set his Marxian hopes, Russia. So mount the 'watchtower'. You know the old joke, told in many versions, about the rabbi who is asked whether socialism in one country is possible. He replies: Yes – but take care not to live there. We could adapt this to the question: Is bourgeois-democratic capitalism on its last legs? To which the rabbi would answer: Yes, of course – but go and live there to find out. Deutscher did that and liked it. It may raise a smile to remember that he sought and was granted membership of the Reform Club in Pall Mall, next door but one to Berlin's Athenaeum. He found living in bourgeois England congenial; writing to a friend in 1950, he described 'the calm and the quietness and the political phlegm which still characterize this country. This is a very pleasant atmosphere for literary work.'[3]

However, there is another factor in Deutscher's case which merits more attention than it has generally received. Although a Marxist who constantly reaffirmed that history begins with the actions of the masses, of the working class, his actual publications as a historian were emphatically top-down. It was great men who fascinated him and with whom (there can be no doubt) he empathised and identified. The decision to write history by way of biography – Stalin, Trotsky, Lenin – is in itself a long step in that direction. Experience had taught him that the masses in their millions are more reliable and indeed admirable in theory than in practice. He never said so but the attentive student can tell. The Russian proletariat was not in 1917 numerous or mature enough to assume real leadership of the Revolution through the Soviets; the West European proletariat should by Marx's calculations have been primed for the task but in 1914 the Second International had collapsed into patriotism. Not even four years of decimating imperial war had shaken the grip of reformism on the Western proletariat. Deutscher's subconscious apparently absorbed what his conscious mind would never admit: that when the historian comes to consider the convergence of factors that produce 'revolutionary situations' (mass hunger, war fatigue, peasant revolt), it is nevertheless the actions of outstanding individuals, of great men, of Lenin, Trotsky and Stalin, that make the difference – or are decisive. Once a historian settles into that frame of mind he will most likely opt for a tenancy inside the heads of these major historical players and the archives they left behind. The single human heart and head continues to beckon the single human heart and head. Marxist biography may be a contradiction in terms.

The shadow of Soviet communism, of its intellectual origins as well as its Gulag, fell across almost every page of Isaiah Berlin's *oeuvre* – usually indirectly, by clear implication. The Soviet experience shaped his view of history and his values, rivalled in this respect only by his identity as a Jew. His Foreword to the autobiography of the Oxford don Jenifer Hart, his former lover, contains a striking passage conveying his loathing of the Soviet Union:

> Certainly those who supported the Republic in Spain (myself, for example) had no notion then of the sinister part played in that war by Soviet agents and Spanish communists. If I had not myself spent some years of my childhood in the Soviet Union, I think I too might have drifted in that direction – that was the world I was surrounded by [in the 1930s]. But those few years, even at the age of eight or nine, had completely inoculated me against illusions about Soviet reality – I remained passionately anti-Stalinist, and indeed, anti-Leninist, for the rest of my life; but my words fell on deaf ears; my contemporaries thought that there was something curiously perverse in my failure to understand who were the sheep and who the goats in the political world. There is no doubt that Soviet propaganda remains the most successful hoax ever perpetrated on the human race. . . . My liberal friends – the world in which Jenifer moved – at that time believed that although no doubt mistakes, even crimes, might have been perpetrated in the Soviet Union, yet despite that they were moving in the right direction – they were in some sense on 'our', the decent, social-justice-seeking, side – and much could be forgiven to so backward and impoverished a land . . . in peaceful, civilized England communism must have seemed mainly a strong remedy against illiteracy and injustice, an illusion which persisted in the West for a very long time.[4]

Isaiah Berlin was not, of course, a Whig. To be a true Whig in the tradition of Thomas Babington Macaulay one must be English and Protestant, indebted to Luther or Calvin, and one must look back to the Reformation as the tree from which Liberty sprang, after England had beaten off the Catholic Church, the Stuart claims to absolute monarchy and the constant backsliding of the Tories.[5] Yet Berlin, I think, was a Whig in a reverse sense. His forte was the intellectual and historical origins of disasters. He was as sure that Voltaire and Reason unhappily led to Stalinism as a real Whig was sure that Luther and God happily led to a property-owning constitutional monarchy blessed by the Established Church of England. Deterministic philosophies, Berlin constantly reminds us, are big trees whose overhanging branches blot out the light – the light being our freedom to abide by our subjective values and moral instincts here and now, the only defence in practice against bloodshed and the 'fanatical' despotism of Left or Right. Yet Berlin was strikingly deterministic in his rejection of all determinisms, that is to say, in his often simplified depictions of what he regarded as their fatal consequences. The cry 'All will be well if we follow the sun' sounded to him like a prescription for eternal darkness.

Berlin warns us that history carries no inner meaning, yet the reverse Whig in him tends to hang his essays on the hook of 'where we are now', reading past conflicts as precursors of current ones. We *today* must rebuff all those who insist that the study of history is no less a science than physics or astronomy or medicine. He parades for our admiration the past thinkers who rejected such fallacies; these far-sighted spirits are found crowding supportively around Berlin himself as he confronts the contemporary heirs and disciples of a monist, rationalist or scientific interpretation of historical destiny. He tells us that Herzen's values survive intact, that Montesquieu's 'undogmatic principles are only too relevant to our violent modern conflicts between rival ideologies'. Vico launched a great debate 'of which the end is not in sight'. The moral and political issues raised by Belinsky remain, 'in the West, still open'. At the end of his 'Benjamin Disraeli, Karl Marx and the Search for Identity', he hopes his account of their different solutions to not being Jewish 'may serve as a moral tale, to inspire some and warn others'.[6] And, of course, a direct line runs from his account of the wounds and insults suffered by Turgenev to those endured by liberals like himself under the depredations of the New Left. We hear the clock of his reverse Whiggery ticking loudly.[7]

The paradox is this: the more he strives to view each culture of the past as unique, an *en soi*, the more it becomes irradiated by the contours of the present. He is always commanding the intellectual battlements of a besieged and imminently beleaguered city. Few have propounded the uncertainty principle in more certain tones. Few have advanced the virtues of 'negative' freedom and pluralism in more positive terms. Few have been more dogmatic about the perils of dogmatism. No one has more clearly insisted that historical outcomes are inevitably not inevitable.

Whereas Isaiah Berlin tended to be consistent in his prime values whatever platform he chose – book, essay, lecture, broadcast, newspaper article – there were several Isaac Deutschers. There was the masterly and measured prose of his major works, the fine nuances of judgment, the rapid digestion of archival evidence, the psychological insights and vivid portraits, the willingness to depart from orthodoxy – all of which placed him in the highest rank of historians. But another Deutscher, the polemicist, was something of a street fighter. A phone call from Fleet Street hit him like a nip of vodka. He loved the smell of printer's ink. With success and acclaim, his ego expanded to the frontiers of vanity. Given newspaper commissions, his reservations and doubts evaporated in a volley of prophetic declarations. He sneered at his critics, prisoners of Cold War mythology. He played to his audience: addressing gatherings of students, he tended to strike attitudes, waving his arms, wheeling in his 'classical Marxism', exalting the battle-hardened experience of his own generation, or quixotically affirming his faith in the revolutionary potential of the young American working class (even though he knew better). At the press of a button, this major historian became the Voice of Isaac Deutscher, in possession of its own unique wavelength.

It would be too easy to conclude that, whereas Deutscher was demonstrably wrong about a great deal, because events proved him wrong, Berlin avoided predictions and thus kept his card clean. But it can also be argued that the dice Berlin shook out across British and American lecture theatres were loaded: he provided the answers to the questions he chose to ask. He habitually walked through open doors while impressively demonstrating that they were in danger of being torn from their hinges. Deutscher, by contrast, hurled himself against gates genuinely padlocked by the prevailing Cold War culture. And that may be why, when you climb the main staircase of the London Library (of which both were members), you encounter Berlin's portrait, not Deutscher's.

PART TWO

COLD WAR HISTORY

4

MARX AND MARXISM

Isaac Deutscher was, by his repeated avowal, a 'classical' Marxist. Although Isaiah Berlin often insisted that Marxist scholars were perfectly entitled to occupy university posts, we may begin our investigation of his objections to Deutscher's appointment here. The problem resided not so much in the theory as in its practical application to recent history. That said, one may hesitate: can theory and practice be so cleanly separated? Take, for example, Berlin's sceptical perspective on Karl Marx's commitment to the 'proletariat' (the urban/industrial working class) as the destined vector of humanity's future under socialism.

In his first book, *Karl Marx: His Life and Environment* (1938), Berlin dismisses Marx's visionary attachment to the proletariat as a product of a tormented personal psychology. Never able to become a member of the proletariat, Marx fashioned it into 'an abstract category' embracing 'his own indignant self'. In reality, Marx was really addressing 'persons like himself, alienated members of the world-wide intelligentsia', rather than factory operatives. 'Marx's proletariat is to some extent a class constructed after Marx's own specifications, as a vessel to carry the vials of his justified wrath.'[1] We find here Berlin's aversion to a long line of Jewish Marxists attempting (in his view) to escape from their pariah status as Jews by inventing an alternative, more universal, allegiance. Yet Marx's closest collaborator, the industrialist Friedrich Engels, was almost certainly not a Jew.

Any viable description of the proletariat must be a matter primarily for economists and sociologists. Berlin was neither and was not, as he confessed, inclined to penetrate these sciences. His main argument in his *Karl Marx* was not directed against the predicted demise of capitalism, or the end of private property and the market economy, or against Marx's economic theory in general. He was content to set aside technical arguments about Marx's labour theory of value against the larger truth for the workers – that they alone produce more wealth than they receive, and that the residue is appropriated by the owners of the means of production, machinery, financial credit, etc. Indeed, he granted that *Das Kapital* (1867) 'constitutes the most formidable, sustained and elaborate indictment ever delivered against an entire social order, against its rulers, its supporters, its ideologists, its willing slaves, against all whose lives are bound up with its survival'.[2]

On the other hand, he complained about the almost complete absence from *Das Kapital* of explicit moral argument, of appeals to conscience or to principle. 'The conceptions of natural rights, and of conscience, as belonging to every man irrespective of his position in the class struggle, are rejected as liberal illusions: socialism does not appeal, it demands; it speaks not of rights, but of the new form of life before whose inexorable approach the old social structure has visibly begun to disintegrate.'[3] For Berlin, the great sin of Marx's method was to obliterate the individual, his conscience, his capacity to choose, by reducing his consciousness to a mere mechanical function of his class position. In so doing, Marx subscribed to an intolerably dogmatic, determinist vision of human history.

This was what mattered to Berlin, not the economic arguments. Writing to a friend in 1948, he summarised his objections to Marxism in terms of human consciousness and how in reality ideas and ethical tenets are created. 'We believe, & the Marxists do not, that the value and truth of a man's opinions & activities does not wholly, or even decisively, depend on his place in the economic and social structure ... nor do we believe, as Marxists do, that all ideals are open or disguised material interests; hence we believe that cooperation is possible & the class struggle not inevitable; and that such concepts as truth, goodness, justice, kindness, compromise, etc. are not disguised forms of class interests, but genuinely common to different classes, individuals & societies.'[4]

What he perhaps most deplored in Marx's working method, 'historical materialism', was his systemic certainty, his Hegelian legacy: his determinism. Berlin objected to the obliteration of individual moral choice by the great machine of ongoing History, to the suppression of ethics under the steamroller leviathan of 'historical science'. Marx was found culpable of transferring the meaningful agency of human life from individuals to social classes: the insistence that individuals could not transcend their position in the class structure.

Berlin did, however, grant that Marx's approach to history and individual behaviour was not entirely mechanistic; he recognised the role of human initiative in raising mass consciousness. Nevertheless, 'in his anxiety to avoid any appeal to the idealistic feelings of his audience, [he] systematically removed every trace of the old democratic vocabulary . . . sought to obliterate all references to eternal justice, the equality of man, the rights of individuals or nations, the liberty of conscience, the fight for civilization.'[5] To educate the masses for their socialist destiny was regarded by Marx as the whole duty of the contemporary philosopher. In any case, Hegel and Marx were metaphysicians. The doctrine of movement in dialectical opposites, said Berlin, is not an empirical hypothesis subject to evidence, but a metaphysical belief deriving from a historical intuition.

Here a comment: it can certainly be argued that Marx, as an heir to the rationalist-scientific Enlightenment, managed to achieve a convenient harmonisation of ethics (his own) and history, thus convincing himself that he had transcended by way of historical science (dialectical materialism) the naïve ethical arguments of the utopian socialists, the reformers, the persuaders, the do-gooders. Marx presented his central economic concepts – 'surplus value', 'exploitation', 'pauperisation', etc. – in what looked like objective, value-free language (as with a physical science), whereas in reality the great pundit's human heart beat passionately for the poor and downtrodden, while fervently hating the exploiters and their apologists. But Berlin gave Marx's passion an unpleasant twist: writing to A.D. Lindsay, master of Balliol, he argued that Marx's vision of the future was inspired more by choleric irritation at chaotic social stupidity, at 'knaves imposing on fools', rather than by the kind of moral passion propelling a Proudhon or a Mazzini.[6]

Berlin had set out his stall; it was to be on display in every succeeding denunciation of Marxist determinism. He firmly places Marxism in the tradition of the Enlightenment or, more accurately, 'the Enlightenment Gone Wrong'. Here he characterises the perils of ultra-rationalism: 'Reason is always right. To every question there is only one true answer which with sufficient assiduity can be infallibly discovered, and this applies no less to questions of ethics or politics, or personal and social life, than to the problems of physics or mathematics.' Further: 'Everything occurs as it does as a result of unalterable processes of nature; and no improvement can be effected by the free decisions of individuals, however wise, however benevolent or powerful, since they, no more than any other entity, can alter natural necessity.' Reason had supplanted God. This, Berlin comments, was to become 'the fundamental doctrine of the radical intellectuals of the next [i.e. nineteenth] century' – most notably the Marxists. His hostility to what he regards as the gleaming certainties of the Enlightenment – the science of man – constantly leads him to lament how single-minded foundations and ground plans turned into leaning towers set to topple under the gravitational force of empirical reality, often resulting in mass graves.

However, with Berlin's indirect monologues there is always a fine line between (say) what Voltaire actually said and what Berlin thinks of Voltaire. For example: 'But if Voltaire created the religion of man, Rousseau was the greatest of its prophets.'[7] The word 'religion' (pejorative as employed by Berlin) here belongs to him, not to Voltaire or Rousseau. To cement his argument, he frequently interjects his own dismissive vocabulary: 'faith', 'ruthless', 'fanatical'. For example, Marx is said to figure prominently 'among the great authoritarian founders of new faiths, ruthless subverters and innovators who interpret the world in terms of a single, clear, passionately held principle, denouncing and destroying all that conflicts with it'.[8] But one may ask in what sense Marx was 'authoritarian' and in what sense the founder of a 'faith', a word better linked to (say) religious belief.

Berlin's insistence that the individual is the primary unit of human thought and action, of morality and responsibility, leads him to downplay collective class consciousness while somewhat inconsistently lauding the collective awareness that results in nationalism, not least in its Jewish form. Berlin grants that millions may share the same predicament, may be bonded by similar beliefs, prejudices or fears, but he insists that so belonging cannot fully account for the individual's behaviour. Society and its component subdivisions exist, yes, but only the individual man or woman can choose, decide, act – demonstrate responsibility. Only the individual can be free or unfree. Here one may object that Marx was analysing historical patterns of collective behaviour, but Berlin insists that Marxism obliterates the vital factor of individual choice: 'Yet to seek to explain, or put a moral or political value on the actions of individuals ... is considered by Marxists to be not merely impracticable ... but absurd ... because the "true" (or "deeper") causes of human behaviour lie not ... in the individual's thoughts or volitions (as a psychologist or biographer or novelist might describe them) but in a pervasive interrelationship between a vast variety of such lives with their natural and man-made environment. Men do as they do, and think as they think, largely as a "function of" the inevitable evolution of the "class" as a whole.'[9] This Berlin adamantly rejects. But when the same analysis is transferred to national sentiment – to Zionism, for example – he does not object.

One obvious problem here is that in practice Marxists from the time of Marx to that of Stalin attached singular importance to individual moral capacity and responsibility, hailing heroes, damning renegades, praising courage, excoriating cowardice. History might be the chariot of science but it was up to the individual to leap aboard with clarity of mind, thus overcoming the prevalent 'false consciousness' instilled by bourgeois ideology. Marx's own diatribes against contemporary rivals and deviationists like Proudhon, Lassalle and Bakunin were highly moralistic and riddled with accusations of treachery, venality and other avoidable personal vices. Writing to Engels in 1865, he speaks of Lassalle's 'treachery', glorified in the pages of a 'filthy rag'. Lenin and the Bolsheviks sustained this tradition: every individual was held responsible for his or her own integrity and self-sacrifice. The triumph of socialism might be 'scientifically inevitable' – but in the meantime it required constant agitation, exhortation and appeals to conscience. In the official media, 'heroes' and 'heroines' crowded the front pages, as did derogatory terms like 'renegade', 'traitor', 'philistine', 'lackey', 'hyena', 'snake', 'running dog'. This implicit emphasis on personal responsibility was relentless.

Unlike Berlin, Isaac Deutscher was not a philosopher and, much as he lauded Marxism, he rarely ventured into theoretical justifications of 'dialectical materialism'. He treated it more as the engine room of a self-evidently buoyant vessel to whose mast the historian must rope himself. This attitude became a source of friction for Berlin. On 19 April 1958, he reported to the editor of the *Observer*, David Astor, an encounter with Deutscher that had occurred in Balliol College in October 1954, when Deutscher was the guest speaker at a seminar given by Berlin and E.H. Carr. When Berlin ventured that Marx and Trotsky were 'victims of a false historical theory', Deutscher 'changed colour' and shortly afterwards 'abused me, as he had every right to do, in the *Observer*'. (Here Berlin refers to Deutscher's review of *Historical Inevitability*, 'Determinists All', for which he was never forgiven.) Berlin returned to this fateful Oxford seminar in a further letter to Astor (14 May 1958), castigating Deutscher's cocksure dogmatism. He had met Deutscher only twice, he said, and had been informed on both occasions that Marx was the greatest *philosopher* of the Western world (Berlin emphasised the word 'philosopher' to convey his outrage), greater than Kant, and a greater scientist than Darwin. Challenged about the awful jargon used by Soviet Marxists, Deutscher 'literally rose to his feet' and answered that Einstein and Freud were allowed to use scientific terminology not easily intelligible to the layman. He also asserted that the practical verification of Marxism was to be found in its current global reach 'from Malaya to the Adriatic'. Berlin had retorted that one would surely not defend medieval beliefs by counting the heads that were 'stuffed' with them. From that moment he reckoned that Deutscher had counted him as 'on the wrong side', adding: 'I did not feel that he was very human: I have met his like only among Spanish Jesuits. . . . I think him a wicked man.'[10]

Unfortunately we do not have Deutscher's record of this fraught encounter. Given the violent personal emotions revealed in these last phrases, Berlin's report may be treated with reserve. The claim tossed at Deutscher that Freud's technical terms, unlike Marx's, led to 'predictions verified in practice' was highly disputable, and Deutscher had some justification in pointing to the USSR and the People's Republic of China in response to the challenge.

Paradoxically, Deutscher and Berlin did agree that there was only one Marx. In later years neither was convinced by the advocates of a Marxist humanism recently discovered in the early works. 'I don't think there is an early humanistic Marx, and a later economic Marx, a scientific Marx and a romantic Marx,' Berlin said. 'People seem to me to have tried to think this, because they hate Stalinism and want to rescue Marx from Stalin. But if you read Marx, the continuity in him and from him to Plekhanov, Lenin, Stalin is very clear.'[11] Deutscher had no more time for Herbert Marcuse's Marxism than Berlin did. Tamara Deutscher wrote to friends in similar terms after her husband's death: '[Isaac] did not like and did not use the term Neo-Marxism. He maintained that there was nothing obsolete in Marxism – the method, the theory, the Weltanschauung – all these were, if anything, still so far ahead of the existing societies which were not mature or educated enough to really understand Marxism.'[12]

5

WHAT IS HISTORY?

DEUTSCHER WAS NOT primarily a theorist and his embrace of 'classical Marxism' was not what turned Berlin's stomach and led him to liken this Polish Jew to a Spanish Jesuit, a 'wicked man'. The bile rose with Deutscher's Marxist-Leninist approach to recent history, to Berlin's own early experiences, when the Bolsheviks burned his cradle. The dispute about Marxist revolutionary theory found its flashpoint in Lenin's contribution to the twentieth century, and Trotsky's and Stalin's. Likewise the dispute about the nature of history and the proper duties of the historian was rooted in sharply adversarial interpretations of the living world into which both Berlin and Deutscher had been born, culminating in the Cold War.

Berlin was a historian of ideas, not of 'events', yet his passionate opposition to all 'determinisms' precipitated him into frequent altercations about the duties of historians. Normally Berlin's jousting partner was not Deutscher himself but his ally E.H. Carr, Britain's leading historian of Soviet Russia. Such 'jousting' indicated a degree of amity with Carr – Berlin never stooped to joust with Deutscher. Berlin and Carr exchanged friendly letters, 'Dear Ted', 'Dear Isaiah', and on occasion sent one another advance copies of forthcoming articles, inviting comments that they had no intention of heeding.

Carr was entirely English in personality, a factor that put Berlin at ease, and by no means a Jewish immigrant carrying a lethal cargo of Central European revolutionary metaphysics. When Carr sent Berlin cricketing metaphors to back up his theory of history, Berlin was tickled (though not pink). Indeed, Carr, despite his admiration for Lenin's revolution, was no Marxist. His early work *Karl Marx: A Study in Fanaticism* (1934) had dismissed dialectical materialism as nonsense, the labour theory of value as dogmatic and wrong. This further eased his relationship with Berlin. However, in Berlin's mind Carr and Deutscher enjoyed a sinister alliance. As we shall see, hot on the heels of

Berlin's clash with Deutscher at the Oxford seminar, the publication of Berlin's essay *Historical Inevitability* provoked a public attack by Deutscher sufficiently brutal never to be forgotten or forgiven. Carr's verdict echoed Deutscher's.

That these theoretical exchanges were rooted in sharply opposed positions on the Bolshevik Revolution and the role of Lenin, as well as the anti-Western position adopted by Carr and Deutscher since 1945, is demonstrated by Berlin's review of the first volume of Carr's *The Bolshevik Revolution*, prominently displayed in the *Sunday Times* of 10 December 1950. Carr, he remonstrated, 'is deeply affected by the contempt for liberalism made fashionable in the last century by Hegel; he sees history as a procession of events ruled by inexorable laws . . . and like Hegel (and Marx) the tone of his writing suggests that there is something childish or quixotic in approving or deploring the consequences of these laws'. Carr's version of the Bolshevik Revolution, Berlin complained, proceeded without so much as a backward glance at the casualties of the process. 'If Mr Carr's remaining volumes equal this impressive opening, they will constitute the most monumental challenge of our time to that idea of impartiality and objective truth and even-handed justice in the writing of history which is most deeply embedded in the European liberal tradition.' This was all the more disturbing given the fact that Carr's work amounted to 'much the most important contribution made to its subject for many years in any language'.[1] Deutscher, by contrast, lauded the publication of Carr's *The Bolshevik Revolution* as 'massive and masterly'.

Berlin's closest colleagues were unanimously anti-Carr, who was accused (as Hugh Trevor-Roper put it) of worshipping 'success', of believing that whatever forces prevailed had to. Arthur Schlesinger, Jr. commented to Berlin that Carr 'is the type of intellectual convinced almost in spite of himself by the absolute confidence of totalitarian power'. Berlin agreed.[2]

Deutscher and Carr first met in 1947. The Deutschers were living in Haverstock Hill when Carr came to tea on 23 March. Tamara Deutscher described Carr as 'an unmistakable product of Cambridge . . . schooled in a diplomatic service famous as a bastion of British traditionalism'. Jonathan Haslam writes: 'Thereafter these enjoyable occasions, enlivened by the Deutschers' ample vodka supply, became increasingly frequent, as Ted's attachment to Isaac became increasingly evident. . . . Isaac and Tamara greatly respected him as a scholar, they loved his writings on the romantic exiles, but inevitably held deep reservations about his ruthless realpolitik; they stood much closer to Carr the utopian than Carr the realist.'[3] In July 1948, Carr began reading draft chapters of Deutscher's forthcoming political biography of Stalin, describing them as 'brilliant'. Both men were averagely unscrupulous about deploying influence in the review pages of the *TLS*. For example,

Deutscher wrote to advise Carr how best to review his *Stalin*, given the English aversion to dialectics (and no doubt Carr's as well). 'I shall be anxiously awaiting your verdict.' Carr produced a glowing review in the *TLS* and even titled it 'The Dialectics of Stalinism'.[4]

Although Carr developed a close personal friendship with Deutscher, making common cause with him against 'Cold War' scholarship, and despite Berlin's regular duels with Carr in print (for example, Carr's early attack on Berlin, 'The New Escapism'),[5] Berlin rather liked this idiosyncratic ex-civil servant, his senior by seventeen years, and was able to maintain a more than civil relationship with him despite having been involved in a protracted conflict with Carr at the Royal Institute of International Affairs (Chatham House), where Carr was chairman of a publications sub-committee. This concerned a work in progress by Berlin's boyhood friend Leonard Schapiro, 'Opposition in the Soviet State, 1922–1938'. As related by Haslam, Carr repeatedly thwarted publication of Schapiro's proposal, accusing him of 'embittered prejudice' and distortion of Lenin's policies. When Schapiro eventually wrote a letter of complaint to the chairman and director general of Chatham House, Berlin backed him up by resigning in protest and by enlisting the support of Professor Merle Fainsod at Harvard. Schapiro's *The Origin of the Communist Autocracy* was eventually published in 1955. Schapiro had reviewed volume one of Carr's monumental *The Bolshevik Revolution* (1950) in a spirit of profound disagreement shared by Berlin.[6]

Yet Berlin and Carr agreed to conduct a joint seminar in Oxford. In January 1954, Carr invited Deutscher to address their Modern History Group, but then aborted the invitation, lapsing into Cold War mode when he advised Deutscher against acceptance on learning that St Antony's College, a hotbed of anti-communism, wanted to seize the occasion to invite him to address a college seminar: 'Probably one of several reasons for wanting you is to demonstrate their broad mindedness.' Haslam comments that in this respect Carr's isolation as an academic was self-inflicted. It was at this time that he publicly posed a question about British academic impartiality: 'Would a teacher of international relations in a British university who became known for the skill and effectiveness with which he analysed and demolished the arguments invoked by the Western Powers in the ideological duel with Moscow really improve his chances of promotion?'[7] Carr himself was without a tenured academic post at this time. Berlin provided his implicit answer to Carr's challenge about academic impartiality by supporting his application for a research fellowship at Trinity College, Cambridge: 'His researches are original and scrupulous; he discovers new facts; he is a genuine authority on his subject of a unique kind. . . . I disagree with all his views, I abhor his historical approach, I attack him in print and in lectures, I hold classes with him [in Oxford], but I have a great admiration and indeed affection for him.'[8]

But what British university would employ the freelance scholar Isaac Deutscher? When, eight years later, Deutscher made such an application, Carr served as his referee. We shall duly discover what happened.

Carr and Deutscher were united against Berlin and his associates in regarding the Bolshevik Revolution as necessary and progressive. Carr's rather pragmatic view of the Soviet experiment(s) as a modernising response to the claims of the underprivileged and impoverished masses of one exceptionally retarded country, Russia, was marginally more acceptable, or less unacceptable, than Deutscher's ardently ideological vision of Lenin's revolution as the great leap into a proletarian era which should have been, in 1918–20, universal: workers of all countries should have united, not least in the most advanced capitalist countries like Germany, where the military collapse in 1918 replicated Russia's in 1917. Deutscher understood that after 1920 a Western workers' revolution had been put on hold, that Stalin's 'socialism in one country' was the only viable perspective in the short term, but he was to argue that, after the defeat of Nazi Germany, only Stalin's restraining hand prevented revolution in France, Italy and Greece, escalating elsewhere. Deutscher's essays and polemics conveyed a note of what Berlin called 'fanaticism' not to be found in Carr.

Indeed, Carr and Deutscher increasingly registered their divergent perspectives. Deutscher wrote rather patronisingly about Carr to his German confidant Heinrich Brandler: 'He is, on the whole, inclined to learn and take notice of criticism, but it is very difficult or perhaps impossible for him to get out of his skin, theoretically and ideologically. He is steeped in English empiricism and rationalism.'[9] It was a stricture that Deutscher applied quite widely across the English intellectual spectrum – to George Orwell, for example. In essence, 'rationalism' was a negative word for both Berlin and Deutscher, but when Berlin deployed it he meant Voltaire, Rousseau and Marxists like Deutscher, the mad-dog proponents of inexorable enlightenment and 'progress' – whereas Deutscher meant British-style empiricism, adherence to abstract values, and ignorance of the dialectic of history.

While heaping praise on the ongoing volumes of Carr's history of Soviet Russia as 'massive and masterly', Deutscher regarded his approach to the Russian Revolution as essentially that of the bureaucrat.[10] Was Lenin to be viewed primarily as an ideologically driven revolutionary leader (Deutscher) or as a pragmatic statesman and administrator (Carr)? As Deutscher saw it, Carr displayed 'the peculiar limitations of the bureaucratic mind' in regarding the Russian Revolution as virtually a national phenomenon only, with Lenin acting out the role of 'a Russian super-Bismarck. . . . Mr Carr is a historian primarily of institutions and policies . . . he is preoccupied primarily with the State, not with the nation and society behind it. . . . it might be said that his History of the Soviet Union [sic] is primarily a history of the ruling group.' And further: 'He tends to see society as the object of policies made and decreed from above. He is inclined to view the State as the maker of society rather than society as the maker of the State. . . . His passion is for statecraft, not for "subversive" ideas.' Carr, Deutscher added, saw the revolutionaries giving up their utopian dreams and learning arduously and painfully the ABC of statecraft. Carr himself came back on this at a later date: 'But does not Deutscher lean to the other side? Are not his eyes sometimes so firmly fixed on revolutionary Utopias and revolutionary ideas as to overlook the expediences which so often governed policy – even in the Lenin period?'[11]

Or take Carr's review of Deutscher's *The Prophet Outcast*. Deutscher believed that one day Trotsky's memory would be rehabilitated in the Soviet Union: 'By this act the workers' state will announce that it has at last reached maturity, broken its bureaucratic shackles, and re-embraced the classical Marxism that had been banished with Trotsky.' Carr was not convinced: 'But to assert this is an act of faith.'[12]

While Isaiah Berlin keenly noted these divergences of emphasis, they could not for him subsume the fact that both Carr and Deutscher believed that Lenin and his colleagues had done what had to be done, advancing both Russia and History in a progressive direction. Neither found cause to regret Berlin's burning cradle, the conflagration that drove his family to emigrate.

However, an odd feature of these exchanges is that there was more than one Isaac Deutscher. The actual narratives and analyses to be found in his *Stalin* and his Trotsky trilogy – as distinct from the Marxist theoretical flourishes found in his reviews and essays – were littered with 'expediences' and exigencies of statecraft causing serious deviations from revolutionary ideals. And while Deutscher the theorist insisted that it was 'the nation and society' that made the Russian Revolution, Deutscher the historian frequently focuses on leadership, on 'policies made and decreed from above'. His rhetorical 'society as the maker of the State' is hard to flush out from his narratives: what he calls 'society', when taking Carr to task, emerges from his own pen as a chaotic aggregation of millions dragged along into civil war, into 'war communism', and then deprived of its own voice in 1920–21 by the leadership's decrees.

The ongoing ostracism of Carr and Deutscher by the 'Cold War liberals' was reflected in Berlin's acceptance of the chairmanship of a historians' conference held at the Institut Universitaire de Hautes Etudes Internationales, Geneva, in July 1961. The subject was 'Contemporary History in the Soviet

Mirror'. Attending were many leading historians and political commentators, without exception critical of or hostile to the Soviet system and its policies, most of them well known to Berlin or Oxford colleagues. There was no sign of Carr and Deutscher among them.[13]

Berlin did not deliver a paper at the Geneva conference but his interventions during the discussion periods reflected familiarity with the vicissitudes experienced by Soviet historians from Tarle to the current revisionist-under-a-cloud, Burzhalov. Berlin commented – rather frivolously? – that if one really believed Marxism to be a science, laid down by experts, it would be quite logical to have the chosen experts assume the role of spiritual dictators. The belief that the whole art of government consists in acting as engineers of human souls could, he said, be deduced from the purest Marxist doctrine unadulterated by Leninism or Stalinism. He also asked a separate question about the extent to which Soviet historians applied socialist categories in their work – not artificial categories imposed from above and dictated by the Party line of the moment, but the genuine use of concepts and categories different from those used by bourgeois historians in the West.[14] This question was scarcely less frivolous since Berlin never showed much regard for the work of Western Marxist historians and none was to be found at the Geneva conference. Admittedly, Soviet history and historiography were very rarely the chosen subjects for British socialist historians such as Hill, Hobsbawm, Rudé, Savile and Thompson, who tended to specialise in Western or colonial history. Deutscher and Carr were the conspicuous exceptions, although Carr was no Marxist and something of an oddball. Their absence at Geneva is not hard to explain.

Regularly teaching in the USA, Berlin accumulated distinguished American colleagues and friends, many of them experts on, or interested in, Soviet communism: George Kennan, Merle Fainsod, Arthur Schlesinger, Jr. and Martin Malia were among the most prominent. Berlin's own point of view largely coincided with theirs. Reviewing Carr's fourth volume, *The Interregnum* (1954), Deutscher had taken the opportunity to strike at Berlin's American colleagues. 'Mr Carr is in a sense the first real historian of Soviet Russia, and because of this his work outweighs in substance and importance the output of all the "research centres", institutes and colleges specializing in Russia which have proliferated in recent years, especially on the other side of the Atlantic.'[15] Likewise Carr, despite long and fruitful spells in American library collections, was never slow to express hostility to American Sovietologists like Bertram D. Wolfe (one of the Geneva participants and at that time chief of the ideological advisory staff of the Voice of America). In an anonymous review of Wolfe's *Khrushchev and Stalin's Ghost*, Carr accused the author of preferring 'the role of publicist to that of historian'. 'If not the pope of current anti-Bolshevik orthodoxy in the United States, he is at any rate one of the chiefs of its department of propaganda.'[16] Reviewing a batch of three books in April 1961, Carr observed: 'The cold war ... has never really loosened its grip on American scholarship. The hostility to the United States still persistently manifested in publications from Moscow is matched by a constant flow from the American side of works which, though scholarly in outward appearance and to some extent in content, are none the less dominated by the conception of an all-pervading Soviet aggressiveness and Soviet unscrupulousness, implicitly – or sometimes even explicitly – contrasted with the peaceful policies and blameless intentions of the United States.'[17] Reviewing the proceedings of the Geneva conference when they belatedly appeared under the title *Contemporary History in the Soviet Mirror* (1964), Carr accused some if not all of the participants of adopting 'the demonological view of history'. He did not mention Berlin's role as chairman, or his interventions – or draw attention to his own and Deutscher's absence.[18]

Despite vicissitudes, Carr and Deutscher were to maintain their alliance against the 'Cold Warriors'. Carr's approach to anonymous reviewing could be unscrupulous, as when in an unsigned piece he lauded Deutscher's 'penetrating review of Mr. E.H. Carr's What is History? ... [although] he balances a little uneasily between the objective and subjective, the causal and teleological elements in historiography'.[19] Just as Deutscher had (anonymously) praised Carr's 1961 Trevelyan Lectures at Cambridge, so now Carr (anonymously) returned the compliment when in 1967 Deutscher was accorded the same honour (published as *The Unfinished Revolution: Russia, 1917–1967*). Here Carr spoke for them both when he let fly at the Western capitalist system: 'The fact is that regardless of all Keynesian innovations, our productive process, so magnificently socialized in many respects, is not yet socially controlled. ... Our governments have forestalled slumps and depressions by planning for destruction and death rather than for life and welfare.' Indeed: 'the stupendous progress made by backward Russia ... points the way to what the western nations might achieve by giving effect to "the great principle of a new social organization".' Calling this Deutscher's 'eloquent and well argued appeal', Carr clearly endorsed it himself.[20]

But what of historical theory? What is history? Isaiah Berlin equated Carr's general outlook (and Deutscher's) with the fallacy of 'historical inevitability' – and with the ruthless banishment of moral judgments from the writing of history. Across the years, however, Carr did venture into theoretical questions of great interest: (1) What is 'reason' and what is its role in history? (2) What should we mean by 'progress'? (3) Is history a science and how is it affected by the particular historian's own outlook? (4) Should the historian offer moral judgments on individuals and events? (5) Are the 'masses', as distinct from 'individuals', the proper subject for the modern historian? Carr argued that the contemporary historian must focus on the modern awakening of the masses to their own legitimate claims.[21] Deutscher agreed.

Berlin's more sceptical view of 'progress' is well conveyed in his essay in praise of Montesquieu (1955). Here he associates himself with Montesquieu's preference for slow, organic evolution as against precipitate reform. 'Montesquieu cannot forget that simplicity, energy, speed, are the attributes of despotism, and go ill with individual liberty, which needs a looser social texture, a slower tempo.' According to Montesquieu, 'La nature agit toujours avec lenteur.' (But, one may ask, had not capitalist industrial development operated with 'simplicity, energy, speed', laying waste to 'nature' wherever the profit motive dictated? The quiet pastures of England might rapidly be overrun by a legion of chimney stacks, the smallholders forced off the land by fenced enclosures. One problem here, apparently unacknowledged by Berlin, is that the rationalists he distrusted were by the nineteenth century in large part responding to the depredations inflicted by modern capitalism, constantly crunching individual rights in the iron jaws of innovation.)

Montesquieu – like Sir Lewis Namier, also admired by Berlin – discerned the virtues of hereditary aristocracies and inherited values, against the vices of mechanical equality. Although Montesquieu was later dismissed as 'a frozen Augustan figure in a Roman toga', as Berlin put it, he did not concur: 'On the contrary, I should like to argue that Montesquieu's views have far more relevance to our own situation than those of his nineteenth-century successors' – the apostles of 'progress' who believed that 'Nothing could stand in the path of scientific knowledge, and knowledge alone could make men happy and virtuous, wise and free'. (But here again we notice that Berlin's complaints were invariably directed at the dogmas of the social philosophers who sought remedies – but never at the unflinching scientific positivism of the entrepreneurs who changed the world with the law at their service.)

On the question of 'progress' in history, Carr remarked: 'Certainly, without the hypothesis of progress, there is no history. Men emerge into history when they become aware of themselves as having a past, and consciously use the achievements of the past as a starting point for future achievement. . . . Faith in the future is a condition of meaningful interest in the past.'[22]

For Berlin, by contrast, the notion of inevitable 'progress', both in human development and understanding, is always dangerous, always liable to lead to a dogmatic or monist view of final outcomes. Tractors instead of mules may be progress, but the collectivisation of agriculture the better to utilise tractors could be a disaster in terms of both human welfare and productivity. With unalterable 'progress' goes unalterable 'purpose', a dogma found in both theocracies and secular-humanist societies. According to Berlin, the Ionian fallacy had vitiated much of Western philosophy from Plato to Kant, from Descartes to Marx, the belief that eternal answers can be found to the nature and destiny of man. (But here again one notices that Berlin's objections were invariably directed at the theory and practice of reformers or insurgent revolutionaries. While theory may not provide final answers, the non-theoretical practices of feudalism or capitalism had provided answers in the form of 'facts', of realities, which may seem perfectly final to the multitude who have lost out. The devastated Native Americans and the Russian kulaks brutally ejected by collectivisation could well compare notes.)

Berlin's essay *Historical Inevitability* (originally 'History as an Alibi') was delivered as the Auguste Comte Memorial Lecture, at the London School of Economics on 12 May 1953. E.H. Carr was an interested member of the audience. Berlin's target was historical 'determinism'. Yet who, in 1953, was a 'determinist'? Elsewhere, Berlin approvingly quoted his friend the philosopher John Austin: 'They all *talk* about determinism and they say they believe in it. I've never met a determinist in my life, I mean a man who really did believe in it as you and I believe that men are mortal. Have you?'[23] So which historian, here and now, called himself a determinist? Berlin's *Historical Inevitability* leaves this question unresolved. Various theorists from earlier centuries are brought before the firing squad: Condorcet, for example, had 'no doubt that happiness, scientific knowledge, virtue, and liberty are bound as "by an indissoluble chain", while stupidity, vice, injustice, and unhappiness are forms of a disease which the advance of science will eliminate for ever; for we are made what we are by natural causes; and when we understand them, this alone will suffice to bring us into harmony with "Nature". Praise and blame are functions of ignorance.'[24] But Condorcet belonged to the eighteenth century and Carr suspected that Berlin was flogging a dead horse back to life.

Historical Inevitability is not an easy read; Berlin failed to mediate between what came out of his head and what could intelligibly pass into the reader's. Huge, unbroken paragraphs densely packed with ideas, metaphors, repetitions and alternative phrasings pour forth torrentially, leaving the student gasping for air.

Berlin assailed the apostles of necessary historical violence: for Hegel and Marx, 'the crucial moments of advance ... take the form of violent, cataclysmic leaps, destructive revolutions which, often with fire and sword, establish a new order on the ruins of the old'. (Berlin more frequently expressed aversion to violence that established 'a new order on the ruins of the old' than to the historically more common violence that re-established the old order on the ruins of the new. In Berlin's own time, this would apply to the vast slaughter of the First World War; likewise to the intervention of Western armies on behalf of the Whites during the Russian Civil War, which increased the destruction and famine. What we might term pragmatic, non-theoretical violence in defence of l'ordre établi rarely, if ever, aroused aversion in him.)

Marx must be the central target of complaint if only because the world remained thickly populated by Marxists of various descriptions. They, post-Hitler, were the threat. Marxism is condemned by Berlin as 'deterministic', 'historicist', 'holistic', 'teleological', 'chiliastic'. Like his part-mentor Hegel, Karl Marx is taken to task for adopting an Olympian disregard for the aspirations of ordinary mortals not inducted into the grand design of 'scientific history'. Marx 'conjure[s] up an image of peaceful and foolish human beings, largely unaware of the part they play in history, building their homes, with touching hope and simplicity, upon the green slopes of what seems to them a peaceful mountain side. . . . But the mountain is no ordinary mountain; it is a volcano . . . and their elaborately tended institutions and their ideals and their way of life and values will be blown out of existence in the cataclysm which marks the leap from the "lower" to the "higher" stage.' Marx 'identifies himself exultantly . . . with the great force which in its very destructiveness is creative, and is greeted with bewilderment and horror only by those whose values are hopelessly subjective, who listen to their consciences, their feelings'.[25]

But this is not only a very odd version of Marx ('green slopes of a peaceful mountainside'), it is also a travesty. If revolution is to be likened to a 'volcano', it rarely arrived without preliminary tremors and shocks, strikes, demonstrations, all habitually answered by repression. Marx and Engels point out that for centuries Berlin's 'peaceful and foolish human beings' have lived not on pastoral green slopes but under the rule of force, often terror, inflicted by those who own the property and rule. Berlin's chosen volcanic image seems to carry the nightmare of a cataclysm descending abruptly on the innocent spires of Oxford when all the dons are asleep and dreaming of ancient hieroglyphs. In reality, Marx's view of history is evolutionary as well as revolutionary: the 'values' embodied in the revolution are never brand-new, but derived from ethical tenets cherished more in theory than in reality under the old order.

According to Berlin, determinism eliminates 'the notion of individual responsibility' and of ontological freedom – and therefore destroys the historian's quest for empathy and impartiality. But in practice, says Berlin, we cannot abandon this quest – although it would be tempting to do so, alluring to regard ourselves 'as soldiers in any army' no longer suffering 'the pains and penalties of solitude ... our goals are set for us, not chosen by us; doubts are stilled by authority'. One may shed a tear for the brave but beleaguered defenders of individual responsibility – but who was actually insisting, in 1953, that 'To know all is to understand all, *tout comprendre, c'est tout pardonner'*? Not even Deutscher. As Berlin runs on and on, granting indirect monologues to composite schools of dogmatic determinism, utopianism or *a priori* metaphysics, one increasingly asks who belongs to these schools and whether their members would recognise their own voices as subsumed by their ventriloquist? And even though he mainly confines his strictures to past thinkers, to Zeno, Spinoza, the Gnostics, Leibniz, Hobbes, Hegel, Marx, Lenin and Freud – all held to have preached that knowledge liberates and absolute knowledge liberates absolutely, thus reducing history 'to a kind of physics' – Berlin is clearly culpable of promoting tendencies into absolutes, achieving a *reductio ad absurdum*.[26]

Carr and Deutscher believed that Berlin was tilting at windmills when he confronted purveyors of 'an imaginary science', successor to 'the astrologers and soothsayers', who speak in 'immense, unsubstantiated images and similes, in deeply misleading metaphors and allegories', and make use of 'hypnotic formulae', thereby throwing 'dust in their own eyes as well as ours', confusing an already bewildered public 'about the relations of morality to politics, and about the nature and methods of the natural sciences and historical studies alike'. Again, one may ask who are these successors to the astrologers and soothsayers? Berlin mentions in passing Arnold Toynbee. He also extends his complaint to those experts who attach too much explanatory importance to their own economic, fiscal, sociological, environmental or psychological models, to the 'sociology of knowledge', squeezing the immense variety of individual behaviour into conceptual straitjackets. Fair enough, no doubt, his call for an empirical history subject to Karl Popper's falsification test; but zooming eloquently above the rooftops of actual history writing, Berlin never interrupts himself to examine in detail a case of flawed modern model-building.

Towards the end of *Historical Inevitability* Berlin offers a degree of reassurance – a healthy empiricism was on the rise: 'Our best historians use empirical tests in sifting facts, make microscopic examinations of the evidence, deduce no patterns, and show no false fear in attributing responsibility to individuals.' Yet 'deduce no patterns' was a dubiously large claim. In reality, any analysis, any foray into causation, requires at least a hypothetical general theory of 'patterns'. A work like Crane Brinton's *Anatomy of Revolution*, regarded as a classic in the West, is a determined patterning of the English, American, French and Russian revolutions. The contemporary analyses of totalitarianism produced by Berlin's admired colleagues offered structural parallels between the Nazi and Soviet regimes.

Now Deutscher came at him in a sardonic review of *Historical Inevitability*, covering two columns in the book pages of the *Observer* ('Determinists All', 16 January 1955). Without doubt this was the killer event in Berlin's attitude to Deutscher, and one can see why.

The review begins courteously enough, noting that, with 'Puckish humour', Mr Isaiah Berlin chose the first Auguste Comte Memorial Trust Lecture to launch 'this brilliant, irresistibly eloquent tirade against all those philosophers, historians, political theorists, and writers who, in one form or another, accept the notion of "historical inevitability"'. It was not a new subject of debate but rarely had it been exposed 'to so tempestuous and rapid and roaring a verbal hurricane fire'.

Deutscher agreed that human history and experience should not be pressed 'into all sorts of elaborate and unreal "systems", "categories" and gener-alisations'. Mr Berlin, he wrote, is also on strong ground 'when he protests against the mechanical application to human society of the methods of inquiry and classification which are proper to the study of nature: Auguste Comte's theory offers indeed the textbook illustration of that error. . . . 'And Mr Berlin is fully justified in denouncing those who use the notion of historical inevita-bility as a "moral alibi" enabling them to shift "the weight of responsibility for all human action" on to the "broad backs of these vast impersonal forces – institutions or historic trends. . . ."' Arriving at Berlin's accusations against Marxism, Deutscher gave the point a deft twist likely to infuriate Berlin: historical determinism had been used by, for example, the old German social democrats, the reformists, 'as an excuse for their own moral quietism and political futility' – which, of course, was not at all what Berlin had in mind!

Towards the end of the first column, Deutscher announced: 'But here my agreement with Mr Berlin ends.' And it did. The onslaught began:

> He [Berlin] does not seem to make the necessary distinction between determinism and fatalism. It is patently incorrect to say that determinism is, as a rule, conducive to quietism or moral surrender to things as they are. Is present-day Communism, in its crude way the chief expounder of deter-minism, so quietist and passive? The abuse of determinism as a 'moral alibi' is no argument against the theory of determinism itself, with which Mr Berlin fails to come to grips. The chief weakness of his tirade is that it attempts too much and achieves too little. Mr Berlin protests on almost every page against the generalisations and abstractions of others, but he himself sins in this respect to quite an extraordinary extent. He lumps together scores

of philosophical ideas and systems, determines in a few sentences of sweeping generalisation what is their 'common denominator', and then roundly condemns them all. He throws the heads of nearly all the great philosophers and historians of antiquity and modern times into one vast bag, heaping the same accusation on all of them, and then he hurls them down with one magnificent gesture from the Tarpeian rock. Only two philosophers, I fear, survive the great execution: Mr Karl Popper and Mr Isaiah Berlin.

Deutscher then quotes at length two 'typical statements' of Berlin's (which are indeed 'typical' and require full quotation). First: 'To understand all is to see that nothing could be otherwise than as it is; that all blame, indignation, protest is merely complaint about what seems discordant. . . . This is the sermon preached to us by thinkers of very different outlooks, by Spinoza and Godwin, by Tolstoy and Comte, by mystics and rationalists, theologians and scientific materialists, metaphysicians and dogmatic empiricists, American sociologists, Russian Marxists, and German historicists alike.' And second: 'From Plato to Lucretius, from the Gnostics to Leibniz, from Thomas Aquinas to Lenin and Freud, the battle-cry has been essentially the same; . . . that reality is wholly knowable, and that knowledge and only knowledge liberates, and absolute knowledge liberates absolutely – that is common to all these doctrines which are so large a part of Western civilisation. To explain is to understand and to understand is to justify. The notion of individual responsibility is a delusion.'

Deutscher then surfaces to comment: 'But one would like to interrupt for a moment the torrential flow of Mr Berlin's philosophical monologue and remark that it is hardly correct to condemn Spinoza, the expounder of *Ethics*, or Tolstoy, the moralist, for denial of "individual responsibility", despite the strong streak of fatalism in their thought . . . that Freud, looking into the dark depths of man's subconsciousness, certainly cannot be described as an expounder of absolute knowledge; and that nobody was as emphatic in his insistence on the relativity of knowledge as Lenin.'

(Here one might add: 'Except in regard to Lenin's own.')

Deutscher then proposes that Marx's 'anti-determinism' is proven by his celebrated phrase: 'Hitherto the philosophers have only interpreted the world – the task now is to change it.'

We have reached Deutscher's final paragraph: 'But Mr Berlin does not analyse. He does not even argue his case. He proclaims and declaims it. Like some other great rhetoricians, he is not over-scrupulous or over-precise in his statements. Let us be thankful for his superb, phenomenal rhetoric and submit to the rest as to a . . . historical inevitability.'[27]

All phrases may be equal but some are more equal than others: 'not over-scrupulous' is going to be remembered longer than 'not over-precise'. Blood had been drawn. Writing to Schlesinger (12 January 1955), Berlin complained of 'gibes from the horrible Deutscher in the *Observer*' plus cracks from Carr in the *TLS*: 'I am dead and buried.' Berlin let his hair down to the editor of the *Observer*, David Astor (27 January 1955), indicating that the main target of *Historical Inevitability* was in fact Deutscher: 'the whole gist of my thesis was directly aimed at his own cherished beliefs.' But Deutscher's review was 'nastier than I had conceived possible', ascribing to Berlin a travesty of his opinions and views 'which I certainly do not hold and which, so far as I know, no human being holds'. Berlin had evidently been invited by the *Observer* to write a reply in advance but refused on the grounds that it was wrong in principle for authors to reply to reviewers (a new idea?).[28]

E.H. Carr reviewed *Historical Inevitability* quite briefly by the indulgent standards normally accorded to him by the *TLS*.[29] Berlin, he agreed, was right to identify 'one of the deepest of human desires' as the wish 'to find a unitary pattern in which the whole of experience, past, present, and future, actual, possible and unfulfilled, is symmetrically ordered'. But Berlin was not right to object to this desire. 'In the first place, the events of the past are related to one another by cause and effect, and it is the business of the historian to unravel and establish that relation. The annalist is content to say that one thing followed another; what distinguishes the historian is that one thing led to another.' Carr insisted that the proper task of the historian – as distinct from the theologian or moral philosopher – 'is not to judge but to explain'.

Seeking support, Berlin sent a copy of *Historical Inevitability* to the conservative historian and fellow Zionist Lewis Namier, and was stung by the ironic response (10 February 1955) of a man with little time for theory: 'how intelligent you must be to understand all you write,' Namier wrote.[30]

The argument about historical inevitability was publicly resumed in 1961 when Carr delivered the Trevelyan Lectures at Cambridge, published as *What Is History?*. In an anonymous editorial in the *TLS* the previous year, Carr had come up with a provocative statement: 'But one may reasonably ask of the historian that he should march at the head of the progressive and enlightened movements of his time and not lag behind them.' Of the Bolshevik terror Carr now commented in the lectures: 'Horrible in lands that had known equal justice – not so unnatural in lands that had never known it.' Irritated by charges that he himself subscribed to 'historical inevitability' and 'determinism', Carr was brusquely dismissive, insisting that all events that take place have been determined. He proposed a distinction between 'rational' and 'accidental' causation – most 'rational' of all being the fact that history begins with the masses, with millions of men. The fact that their names are not known does not make them 'impersonal', as T.S. Eliot had implied in his phrase about 'vast, impersonal forces'.[31]

Berlin wrote to Carr (3 July 1961): 'I know of no historians who do not in fact, either by commission or omission, pass moral judgments: after all, you yourself identify some forces or persons as progressive, others as futile or troublesomely reactionary – your evaluation of Lenin – . . . . I was not really trying to urge people to moralise, so much as telling them that they cannot help it in any case.'[32]

Berlin claimed that Carr had a 'Big Battalion view of history', accusing him of equating the 'progressive' forces with those that triumphed – the failures and the minorities belonged, in Trotsky's famous words, to 'the rubbish heap of history'. Carr's image of social life was that of a battleground in which the historian's business was to pick the winners: the good historian will get himself accredited to the winning side.[33] But Carr insisted that the good historian was the one whose vision coincided with the goals towards which history was advancing. Those who tarried over the might-have-beens were engaged in a 'parlour-game'. Confronting Berlin's objections to 'historicism' as a denial of free will and as an encouragement to historians to evade moral judgments, Carr inferred that Berlin was against looking for 'underlying social or economic causes of two world wars' lest this should explain away 'the moral responsibility of Willem II or Hitler or the German people'. He concluded: 'Let us therefore reject the notion of the historian as a hanging judge.' On a later occasion Carr told the writer and Balliol graduate Ved Mehta that 'it is foolish to judge Charlemagne or Napoleon or Genghis Khan or Hitler or Stalin for their massacres'; likewise it was 'absurd' or 'not our business as historians' to praise 'benefactors of humanity'.[34] But why 'absurd'? As a theorist, Carr often gives the impression of the odd-man-out clubman burping heresies over the port.

Deutscher duly weighed in with a review of Carr's *What Is History?* in the *TLS*. This was published anonymously but every paragraph carried Deutscher's intellectual signature and Berlin cannot have missed it. Carr had privately confided to Deutscher (29 March 1960): 'I have been looking for some time for an opportunity to deliver a broadside on history in general and on some of the nonsense talked about it by Popper and others . . . the foolish remarks of Popper, Isaiah Berlin, etc. about history in general and revolution in particular.'[35] Lauding Carr in his review as 'one of the most unorthodox, radical and open-minded British liberals of his generation', yet expressing discomfort with his relativistic side – his tendency to describe 'facts' as dependent on the historian's point of view – Deutscher hailed *What Is History?* as 'in every way a remarkable and masterly book', a contrast with 'the dull and grudging belittlement of [the Russian Revolution's] achievements in many current western accounts.' Deutscher's overview of Soviet history tallied with Carr's: 'It is difficult to see any other course which could so rapidly have raised Russia, and the Russian people, to their present levels of industrial achievement and material welfare. It is indeed difficult to do justice to the magnitude and the astonishing speed of this process – starting in a country devastated by seven years of war and civil war, and interrupted by a further and still more destructive war.'[36]

Deutscher also took this opportunity to renew his attack on Berlin, endorsing Carr's good work in countering 'the fogs of pessimistic conservatism, scepticism, anti-"historicism" and resignation that hang over so much of contemporary history writing'. He approved of Carr's thrust that 'History was full of meaning for British historians so long as it seemed to be going our way; now that it has taken a wrong turning, belief in the meaning of history has become a heresy'. And so to Isaiah Berlin: 'In Professor Popper and Sir Isaiah Berlin the conservative aversion from political philosophy takes the form of extreme subjectivism, of a moralism which expects the historian to act as "hanging judge" (especially vis-à-vis the leaders of the Russian revolution), of a bitter hostility towards the scientific treatment of history and towards every form and variety of determinism. On a more popular level these attitudes produce the naïve view that only "individuals", as opposed to "social forces", are the historian's proper theme.'

Berlin and Popper, Deutscher continued, believed that history is no science and that the methods practised in the natural sciences cannot apply.[37] Deutscher (with Carr) took the opposite view: 'In the chapter on "History, Science and Morality" he [Carr] demonstrates how closely the methods of science and history have in recent decades moved towards each other.' To be applauded was Carr's statement that 'history properly so-called can be written only by those who find and accept a sense of direction in history itself'. Likewise Carr's declaration of faith 'in the future society and the future of history' breaks 'like a strong and refreshing breeze into the stuffy air of intellectual despondency that has so long prevailed in our philosophy of history'. Indeed, historiography could not survive without the sense of progress inherited from the past two centuries.[38]

Clearly Deutscher harboured no misgivings about his assault on Berlin's *Historical Inevitability* six years earlier. At a seminar held this same year, 1961, he (like Carr) presented the case for determinism in terms of the historian's duty to explore cause and effect as he had attempted to do in his own biography of Stalin. As reported sympathetically by Christopher Hill, Deutscher's case was this: 'The historian . . . cannot help being a determinist, or behaving as one if he is not: he has not done his job fully unless he has shown causes and effects so closely and naturally interwoven in the texture of events that no gap is left, unless, that is, he has demonstrated the inevitability of the historic process with which he is concerned . . . what is irreversible has assumed the aspect of the inevitable.'[39] (This is in no sense a valid defence against Berlin's complaint that Deutscher regarded the ultimate victory of socialism as indelibly inscribed on the tablet of historical science. The demonstration of cause and effect, after all, cannot safely apply to the history of the future, one of Deutscher's trademark specialities.)

One should not assume that either Carr or Deutscher was entirely consistent in his theoretical positions. In arguing with each other about the modalities, or with Isaiah Berlin about the core fundamentals, they were also debating with themselves – as when a man moving on from the bar of the King's Head to the Bell and Crown down the road is heard reversing his previous position about the relative merits of football teams. Much depends on who he is talking to. Deutscher, for example, did not hesitate to endorse Trotsky's dismissal of the non-Bolshevik Left (Mensheviks, SRs, anarchists) as the 'rubbish heap of history', but when, after Lenin's death, Trotsky himself fell into a minority position, he adopted a different view. Discussing Carr's impatience with the revolutionary illusions of the early 1920s, including those of the Chinese communists, Deutscher issued a stern warning: 'The historian must not treat unfulfilled possibilities as if these had been, from the outset, nothing but so many stillbirths.' Further: 'There is a lesson here for any writer of contemporary history: he should beware of the temptation to bury the defeated revolutions and "revolutionary illusions" of his time under the mass of his own disdain – the buried may yet stir into life and hit back.'[40]

6

A PORTRAIT OF STALIN

'HOW ARE YOUNG undergraduates,' Isaiah Berlin asked the present writer, though it wasn't really a question, 'much less informed and perceptive than you, to survive his unscrupulous distortions? Believe me, your run-of-the-mill hack who dutifully toes the party line, word for word, chapter and verse, is far less dangerous than Deutscher. He passes for an independent historian, a free spirit. He confesses how, most regrettably, uncontrollable circumstances had by 1920 or 1921 forced Lenin and Trotsky to become Lenin and Trotsky. He explains how the necessary collectivisation and industrialisation of Russia was undertaken by a leader, Stalin, who most regrettably turned into a tyrant. Innocent people believe that Deutscher is an anti-Stalinist. Doesn't he say so, time and again?'

Isaac Deutscher had established his credentials as a historian with a single-volume political biography of Joseph Stalin, written and published while the Generalissimo was still ominously alive. Was this the work of an 'anti-Stalinist Stalinist'?

Among those participating in the 1961 Geneva conference under Berlin's chairmanship was Walter Laqueur, a friend and a kindred spirit. In his *The Fate of the Revolution: Interpretations of Soviet History*, Laqueur provided a summary of Deutscher's alleged distortions in his biography of Stalin. Deutscher, wrote Laqueur, 'has been repeatedly accused of tampering with the facts, of selecting them in accordance with his bias. His account of the purges were [sic] said to be, at best, only half true. His interpretation of the murder of Kirov and of Tukhachevsky's conspiracy against Stalin, to give but one example, while more or less in accordance with the contemporary Stalinist version, is most certainly incorrect.'[1] Berlin undoubtedly shared Walter Laqueur's overview: 'His biography of Stalin, when all is said and done, amounted to an apologia for its hero and to some extent an idealisation.

Deutscher did not conceal the negative features of Stalin's regime, his errors and mistakes, but the word crime was used sparingly if at all.' Laqueur's indictment extends to Deutscher's journalism during the last years of Stalin's life: 'When hard-pressed Deutscher prefers the term "scandal". The purges and the executions of the 1950s, likewise the case of the Kremlin doctors, were "scandals", not crimes.'[2]

One recalls Berlin's damning verdict: 'Falsifier.'

Despite Deutscher's expulsion from the Polish Communist Party in 1932, as an émigré historian working in England he developed an admiration for Stalin's policies after he became virtual sole ruler in 1929. This applies both to his domestic and foreign policies. Deutscher endorsed Stalin's 'second revolution', a social upheaval without precedent, as cruel but necessary. The great reforming tyrants of the past, Ivan the Terrible and Peter the Great, 'seem to be dwarfed by the giant form of the General Secretary'. The long-term benefits are said to have been immense: rapid industrialisation; more than a hundred million peasants were compelled to abandon their small, primitive holdings and set up collective farms; the primeval wooden plough gave way to the modern tractor; tens of millions of illiterates were driven to attend school. In *Russia after Stalin* (1953), Deutscher wrote: 'The core of Stalin's achievement lies in the fact that he found Russia working with the wooden plough and left her equipped with atomic piles.'[3] E.H. Carr held much the same view.

But it *is* a view, a historical perspective, not a 'falsification' – unless Deutscher can be detected suppressing or altering relevant facts. Does he do that?

Collectivisation is justified in terms of the deteriorating supply of food to the towns. 'As things stood, Stalin acted under the overwhelming pressure of events.' But, says Deutscher, such drastic methods of collectivisation as actually occurred were not anticipated or recommended by Stalin. Perhaps he was overwhelmed by the peasant resistance his cadres encountered. Deutscher is nevertheless critical of the all-out tactics pursued: if Stalin had limited the reform to a moderate redistribution of land and wealth to benefit the poorest, 'collectivization would hardly have become the bloody cataclysm which in the event it did become'. Instead of that Stalin despatched his cadres to drive the reluctant 'middle peasants' or small-scale proprietors into collectives while refusing to allow 2 million kulaks (8–10 million with their families) to join the collectives. 'We must smash the *kulaks*,' Stalin declared, 'eliminate them as a class.' As Deutscher puts it, 'Collectivisation degenerated into a military operation, a cruel civil war. Rebellious villages were surrounded by machine guns and forced to surrender.'

(Deutscher travelled at that time in Russia and the Ukraine. In a railway carriage he met a colonel of the GPU, an old Bolshevik, the successor organisation to the Cheka, broken by his experience of ordering his men to fire indiscriminately into the crowds of peasants.)[4]

Deutscher is candid about the statistical outcome of collectivisation (although they are Stalin's own statistics, issued in 1934). Half the nation's 34 million horses had gone. Only 45 per cent of its cattle remained. 'Vast tracts of land were left untilled. Famine stalked the towns and the black soil steppe of the Ukraine.' 'Forced labour, in the strict sense, was imposed on peasants who had resorted to violence in resisting collectivisation. . . . "Re-education" degenerated into slave labour, terribly wasteful of human life, a vast black spot on the picture of the second revolution.' And yet he continued to believe that this 'second revolution' was necessary, dictated by dire circumstances.

Deutscher also highlights its socially progressive dimensions. For many, rapid industrialisation spelt social advance. Press, theatre, film and radio exalted the 'heroes of the production front'. Technical schools proliferated, open to workers from the bench. 'This was, indeed, the generation of Stalin's "frontier men"'. But, he concedes, a vast gulf of stratification and inequality opened up, fostered by Stalin, who denounced 'levellers'.

The Marxist historian draws parallels between building socialism in the USSR and the grim process of the Industrial Revolution described by Marx and Engels in nineteenth-century England, when capital made its claims 'dripping from head to foot, from every pore, with blood and dirt'. He also endorses Stalin's claim that capitalists consider it normal in a time of slump to destroy surpluses and burn excess agricultural production in order to protect prices and profits – whereas Stalin turned force from the midwife of history (to quote Marx and Engels) into the mother of the new society.[5]

Deutscher insists that Stalin 'remained the guardian and the trustee of the revolution. He consolidated its national gains and extended them. He "built socialism"; and even his opponents, while denouncing his autocracy, admitted that most of his economic reforms were indeed essential for socialism.'[6]

Yet Deutscher's overall portrait of Stalin's purges and show trials is almost uniformly hostile, denunciatory: 'The confessions of the defendants were the only basis for the proceedings and the verdicts. Not a single piece of evidence that could be verified by normal legal procedure was presented.' The accusations levelled by Walter Laqueur and others against Deutscher's analysis of the purges seem to boil down to two events: the unsolved murder of the Leningrad Bolshevik leader Sergei Kirov in 1934, and the arrest and execution (without trial) of Marshal Tukhachevsky and senior Red Army commanders in 1937 on charges of treasonous conspiracy with foreign powers. Deutscher is accused of concealing Stalin's role in Kirov's death and of presenting Tukhachevsky's conspiracy as real. In the original 1949 edition of *Stalin*, Deutscher concedes that the facts about the assassination of Kirov had never been proven beyond doubt.[7] On Tukhachevsky one reads: 'The men who tried to put an end to Stalin's rule, Tukhachevsky and his associates, acted behind the back of the people, as a small, strictly secret group of conspirators. Therein lay their fatal weakness.' According to Deutscher, 'The exact circumstances of Tukhachevsky's plot and of its collapse are not known. But all non-Stalinist versions concur in the following: the generals did indeed plan a *coup d'état*. This they did from their own motives, and on their own initiative, not in compact with any foreign power.'[8]

But not often noticed is Deutscher's oddly contradictory comment when discussing the situation at the time of Hitler's invasion in 1941: 'In the face of Hitler's all too real conspiracy, the bogus conspiracies of previous years were as if forgotten. . . . Tukhachevsky's disciples, who had been cashiered and deported, were rushed back to military headquarters.'[9] What is one to make of that?

And how important is it? Deutscher might or might not be wrong, but what motive could he have for deliberately falsifying? Given Deutscher's portrait of Stalin as systematically bent on the physical liquidation of the entire Lenin-era leadership of the Party, no obvious motive emerges. Given the brutal nature of Stalin's regime in the purge era as depicted by Deutscher, is the belief (right or wrong) that Tukhachevsky and the generals plotted to get rid of Stalin any more 'Stalinist' than it is 'Hitlerite' to recognise that in 1944 German officers conspired to assassinate Hitler?[10] In the 1967 edition of *Stalin*, Deutscher did modify, if not entirely abandon, his earlier version of Tukhachevsky's arrest and execution.[11]

A distinctive feature of Deutscher's overview is his insistence that Stalin was a legitimate heir to the work of Lenin. 'In its scope and immediate impact upon the life of some 160 million people the second revolution was even more sweeping and radical than the first.' Here he obviously parted company with Trotsky and his orthodox followers, but Isaiah Berlin, who regarded Leninism as proto-totalitarian, ruthlessly dictatorial, was unlikely to challenge Deutscher's claimed continuity. Berlin's disinclination to recognise that Deutscher frankly set the jewel of continuity in the unpolished stone of the post-1920 or 1921 Lenin–Trotsky dictatorship can be explained by his utter rejection of Deutscher's glowing depiction of the pristine 1917 Revolution: 'The revolutionary party is still marching in step with the majority of the nation. It is acutely conscious of its unity with the people and of a profound harmony between its own objectives and the people's wishes and desires.'

For Berlin, that was hogwash. Deutscher then conceded that by the end of the civil war the dictatorship of the proletariat had become the dictatorship of the Party over the whole people. Misery and famine prevailed. A chasm had opened up between the revolutionary party and the people. 'That', Deutscher wrote, 'is the real tragedy which overtakes the party of the revolution.' For Berlin, the revolution had from the outset been synonymous with naked Bolshevik dictatorship over all other parties and the mass of the population.

Deutscher finds the Lenin–Trotsky dictatorship inevitable and necessary – in the circumstances – though its consequences extended to Stalin's one-man rule. In order to safeguard the achievements of the Revolution, the Party now has to muzzle the people. 'The party of the revolution knows no retreat; it has been driven to its present pass largely through obeying the will of that same people by which it is now deserted. It will go on doing what it considers to be its duty, without paying much heed to the voice of the people. In the end it will muzzle and stifle that voice.' Lenin and Trotsky were driven by circumstances beyond their control to take powers discordant with the main themes of their own lives.[12]

And Stalin's Gulag? Here Deutscher's credibility seriously falters. In the index to *Stalin* one draws a blank under 'camps', 'concentration camps', 'labour camps', 'forced labour', 'Gulag', 'penal system', 'prisons', 'justice', 'penal servitude', 'courts'. There is no entry under 'White Sea Canal'. Even before the Second World War, the Soviet press itself had set a figure of 250,000 prisoners working on the Baltic–White Sea Canal. After the war, calling for an international commission of inspection to visit the USSR, the American Federation of Labor submitted evidence about Soviet labour camps to the UN Economic and Social Council, including a photostat document instructing the MVD (Ministry of Internal Affairs) in the Baltic States as to the categories of people who should be removed to forced labour in Russia: 'Persons who have occupied prominent positions in the civil or communal service. Prominent members of the anti-Communist parties: social democrats, liberals. Small farmers. Active members of Jewish, Bund and Zionist organizations. Mystics, such as Freemasons and Theosophists. Industrialists, wholesale merchants, owners of large houses, shipowners, owners of hotels and restaurants, persons who have been in the diplomatic service, permanent representatives of foreign commercial firms, relatives of persons who have escaped abroad.'[13] But Deutscher is evidently not concerned about mystics, Freemasons and Theosophists – after all, a revolution is not a teddy bears' picnic.

The fullest account of Stalin's purges is found in Deutscher's *The Prophet Outcast* (1963). Here the focus is squarely on Stalin's political victims, the decimation of the Party: 'By this time hardly any of the authentic Trotskyists or Zinovievists were left alive. . . . The terror of the Yezhov period amounted to political genocide: it destroyed the whole species of the anti-Stalinist Bolsheviks.' As for Trotsky: 'He was unaware of the fact that the anti-Stalinist forces had been wiped out; that Trotskyism, Zinovievism, and Bukharinism, all drowned in blood, had, like some Atlantis, vanished from all political horizons; and that he himself was now the sole survivor of Atlantis.'[14] But Isaiah Berlin was unlikely to light candles in memory of Trotskyists, Zinovievites or Bukharinites: the dragon had devoured itself.

Deutscher remained in effect a prisoner of his own fixation with the Old Bolsheviks and their factions, seen as the guardians of Lenin's values. Stalin's victims are named only when prominent. The section on the purges of 1936–38 is confined to the trials and tribulations of the elite men with names, the Party. Testimony from those millions who had suffered from collectivisation or in the labour camps is not heard. Their voices are not quoted but subsumed in generalisations. Deutscher does not carry the story of the purges into the tenement flats and workplaces where informing became a desperate strategy of survival. There is no hint of the Kafkaesque dimension of the purges, the long queues of women waiting on freezing night streets for word of loved ones. Then he seems to correct himself: 'The real mass purges were carried out without the thunder and lightning of publicity, without confessions of the victims, and often without any trial whatsoever. . . . He sent thousands to their death and tens and hundreds of thousands into prisons and concentration camps.' But here again Deutscher seems to be talking only of men and women, Soviet and foreign, who had been active in the communist movement, extending to the bloody purge of the army.[15] So the tally remains 'thousands to their deaths and tens and hundreds of thousands into prisons and concentration camps' – rather than the millions who actually suffered and died in the Gulag.

In this context it is significant that, after Khrushchev's revelatory speech to the 20th Congress in 1956, Deutscher criticised him for mentioning only the loyal Stalinist victims of the purges, breathing not a word about the Old Bolsheviks associated one way or another with opposition. But Deutscher did not complain about Khrushchev's total silence on the terror that struck the population at large.

And the intelligentsia? 'Some of the best writers sought refuge in silence,' we learn, 'others were silenced.' One searches in vain for those great artists who suffered bullying or suppression (Akhmatova, Pasternak, Shostakovich, Eisenstein among them) or death (Mandelstam, Babel, Meyerhold). We learn that Stalin's dull, plodding prose style became the obligatory norm.

According to Deutscher, the birth of the new class was Stalin's great achievement and strength. From 1933 to 1938, about a million administrators, technicians, economists, etc. graduated from high schools. The members of this new intelligentsia, whose ranks filled the purged and empty offices, had been brought up in the Stalinist cult from childhood. In *The Gulag Archipelago* (1974), Aleksandr Solzhenitsyn presents the case of a typical young man of the 1930s (himself). He is of the 'Stalin' generation which grew up full of pride in the new Soviet society, indoctrinated to have absolute faith in the Party. 'Along that same asphalt ribbon on which the Black Marias scurry at night, a tribe of youngsters strides by day with banners, flowers and gay, untroubled songs.' Solzhenitsyn recalls his third year at university in the autumn of 1938. 'We young men of the Komsomol were summoned before the District Komsomol Committee not once but twice' and urged to apply for admission to an NKVD school. 'How could we know anything about these arrests and why should we think about them? . . . we loved forming up, we loved marches.'[16]

Reading this, one is struck by what is missing in Deutscher: mass psychology. He understands the modern political history of Russia but rather less about Russia.

His perspective on Stalin's foreign policy is scarcely less contentious, yet it was far from uniquely his own and probably not to be described as 'falsifying evidence'. He justifies the Nazi–Soviet Pact and even the partition and invasion of his own country, Poland. He justifies the Russo-Finnish War and the seizure of the Baltic States: 'The Baltic working classes probably supported the socialization of industry he [Stalin] decreed; but what was decisive was Russia's armed power.'[17] The Comintern line during the two years of Soviet–German friendship does, admittedly, cause him some qualms, but he underplays the virulence of Moscow's propaganda onslaught against countries now at war with Nazi Germany.

Arriving at the contentious episode of the Warsaw Uprising of August 1944, Deutscher does not accept the allegation that Konstantin Rokossovsky's army sat on its hands while the rising was brutally suppressed; he insists that Rokossovsky had been stopped by the Germans at the Vistula, then thrown back. After some delay Stalin promised help to the Warsaw insurgents: 'But then Stalin did something that sent a shudder of horror through the allied countries. He refused to allow British planes, flying from their bases to drop arms and food to the insurgents, to land on Russian airfields behind the fighting lines.' Deutscher calls this a 'demonstration of callousness' by Stalin: 'He was moved by the unscrupulous rancour and insensible spite of which he had given so much proof during the great purges.'[18] Better might be: 'Stalin was happy to see the Polish nationalists he did not control crushed by the Germans.'

At the war's end Deutscher presents Stalin as enjoying within the USSR 'the full blaze of popular recognition and gratitude. These feelings were spontaneous, genuine, not engineered by official propagandists. . . . The nation was willing to forgive Stalin even his misdeeds and to retain in its memory only his better efforts.' And: 'The truth was that the war could not have been won without the intensive industrialization of Russia, and of her eastern provinces in particular, nor could it have been won without the collectivization of a large number of farms.' Deutscher does not mention the ten or twenty million inhabitants of the Gulag, or the brutal treatment of former POWs. The emphasis remains positive: 'For of Stalinist Russia it is even truer than of any other revolutionary nation that twenty years have done the work of twenty generations'. In Russia the whole nation has been sent to school. The urban population grew by thirty million: 'Its avidity for knowledge, for the sciences and the arts, has been stimulated by Stalin's government to the point where it has become insatiable and embarrassing. . . . Perhaps in no country have the young been imbued with so great a respect and love for the classical literature and art of other nations as in Russia. The works of Pushkin, Gogol, Tolstoy, Chekhov, Belinsky have been issued in millions of copies. No Russian Lessing or Heine has been burned at an *auto-da-fé*.'[19]

Yet there were several contradictory versions of Deutscher. The impression is strong that, as with E.H. Carr, his perspective on Stalin changed after the Soviet military victory over Nazi Germany and the onset of the Cold War. How, otherwise, can one explain Deutscher's vast shift of emphasis from an essay he had written after the Nazi invasion of the USSR but which came to light only some years after his death? This essay displays a degree of anti-Stalin passion missing from his later work. Written in Polish, '22nd of June 1941' condemns the Nazi–Soviet Pact. How many other castles, built not so much in the air as on the wrongs done to nations, Deutscher asks, were to be cemented by the wretched Kremlin architects? On the very day of 22 June, Moscow was still trying to salvage its friendship with the arch-executioner of Europe by recognising his occupation of Yugoslavia, Greece and Norway. Communiqués and denials from the offices of Narkomindel strove to prove that the concentration of German troops presented no danger to the Soviet Union. Deutscher notes the totalitarian regime, with its GPU, concentration camps, cult of the leader and terrible purges. He also condemns the Russo-Finnish War. Yet this angry outburst also insists that the heroic resistance of the Russian workers and peasants is proof of the vitality of the revolutionary society they are defending. An economy without capitalists and landlords is defended not because of, but in spite of, the privileges that the new bureaucracy allocates to itself.[20]

So Deutscher had radically changed his outlook by the time he came to write *Stalin. A Political Biography*. The 'anti-Stalin Stalinist' detested by Berlin was incubated by the course of the war, the Soviet victory and the Cold War. Nevertheless, on page 566 of *Stalin* we find an enumeration of the 'similarities and differences' between Stalin and Hitler: 'Each of them suppressed opposition without mercy or scruple. Each built up the machine of a totalitarian state and subjected his people to its constant, relentless pressure. Each tried to remould the mind of his nation to a single pattern from which any "undesirable" impulse or influence was excluded. Each established himself as an unchallengeable master ruling his country with a rigid *Führerprinzip*.' But Deutscher then enumerates the differences between the great dictators, citing the progressive ideal 'inherent in Stalinism'.[21]

Visiting the Soviet Union in 1988, Isaiah Berlin read in an official journal that Stalin's victims numbered fifty million, not the fifteen to twenty million suggested in the West. He did not find the figure fanciful. 'I think Communism is a total failure, and there are more horrible crimes on its conscience – if it exists – than on that of any other movement in history, not even of the great religious persecutions.'[22] At this late stage of his life Berlin elsewhere reflected: 'What is interesting is to read the enemy . . . brilliant opponents who so to speak put their swords, their rapiers into one and find the weak spot.' But he never ranked Deutscher among these 'brilliant opponents'.

7

IMAGES OF LENIN

YET BERLIN DID not deplore Stalin as deeply as he detested Lenin. Sentiments about Stalin might be complicated by the wartime alliance against the destroyer of the Jews, Hitler, but Berlin was a student of political ideas and Stalin produced few (Berlin and Deutscher agreed on that), despite his pretensions to have the last word on everything, even linguistics. Lenin's published work on the other hand, his theories of imperialism and class struggle, of revolution and the state, still served as holy texts of historical science for thousands of corrupted intellectuals like Deutscher. Lenin was the great contaminator, the self-confident doctor of poisonous medicine, who had in effect chased the Berlins from their family home, their roots.

It was not Marx who was responsible for the Gulag but Lenin. 'Karl Marx did not advocate mass murder – this is a new idea in the West. The true author of this is Lenin. Under Lenin more innocent people were exterminated than in any previous revolution, many more than in 1789 or 1848 or 1870. This was real terror, not on the scale of Stalin, but real terror which hit out right and left, it was on this that Leninism was based.'[1]

As for Deutscher, he was a Leninist fanatic: 'Beneath his appearance of cool judgement and the temperate tone there is, I am sure, an icy fanaticism. He is a complete Bolshevik of Lenin's time.' This was Berlin writing in 1958 to David Astor (who stubbornly continued to commission articles by Deutscher, exasperating Berlin).[2]

Berlin's portrait of Lenin can be found in his essay 'Political Ideas in the Twentieth Century', written in 1949 and commissioned by the US State Department's semi-official journal, *Foreign Affairs*, for its mid-century issue. According to Berlin, Lenin like his successors had little faith in the capacity of the Russian working class to develop a proper class consciousness, and thus he emphasised the necessity of a drastically disciplined elite Party leadership.

Berlin gave Lenin provisional credit for having believed that 'coercion, violence, executions, the total suppression of individual differences, the rule of a small, virtually self-appointed minority, were necessary only in the interim period.' Indeed: 'his practice was strangely like that of those irrationalist reactionaries who believed that man was everywhere wild, bad, stupid and unruly, and must be held in check and provided with objects of uncritical worship.'[3]

Berlin likened Leninism to the tsarism in reverse accurately predicted by Herzen in the mid-nineteenth century. 'Communism is a Russian autocracy turned upside down,' Herzen had written in the Epilogue to his *The Development of Revolutionary Ideas in Russia* (1851). The primary factor for Berlin was Lenin's authoritarian and dogmatic personality. Add to that 'the conception of the Party as a sect ruled ruthlessly by its elders and demanding from its members the total sacrifice upon its altar of all that they most cherished (material goods, moral principles, personal relationships), the more defiant and horrifying to tender-minded morality the better.'[4]

In 1960, Berlin wrote an introductory essay to Franco Venturi's *Roots of Revolution*. Here he deployed the word 'fanatical' repeatedly, applying it to 'the believers in disciplined professional terrorism – Sergei Nechaev (1847–82) and Pyotr Tkachev (1844–86), and their followers who include – for this purpose alone – not only the Social Revolutionaries but also some of the most fanatical Russian Marxists, in particular Lenin and Trotsky'. Alongside 'fanatical', Berlin produced other favoured terms such as 'apocalyptic' and 'utopian'. 'All these thinkers share one vast apocalyptic assumption: that once the reign of evil – autocracy, exploitation, inequality – is consumed in the fire of revolution, there will arise naturally and spontaneously out of its ashes a natural, harmonious, just order, needing only the gentle guidance of the enlightened revolutionaries to attain its perfection. This great Utopian dream, based on simple faith in regenerated human nature, was a vision which the populists shared with Godwin and Bakunin, Marx and Lenin. Its heart is the pattern of sin and death and resurrection. . . . Its roots lie deep in the religious imagination of mankind.' Here Berlin draws a parallel with the faith of the Russian Old Believers, the dissenting sects, for whom, ever since the great religious schism of the seventeenth century, the Russian state and its rulers, particularly Peter the Great, represented the rule of Satan.

But he shifts his ground from terrorism to a quite different heritage, Jacobinism, when he insists that Lenin's strategy in 1917 owed less to Marx and Engels than to the Jacobin tradition passed through Blanqui and Buonarroti to Tkachev and the Russian Jacobins. Lenin succeeded not so much by taking over the bastions of capitalist finance and industry, but by seizing the centres of strictly political power. Growing in confidence, and 'with a tendency to self-perpetuation which no dictatorship seems able to resist', the Bolsheviks created the very hierarchy of centralised power that the populists had warned against.[5]

Lenin's role, personality and motivations sharply divided Berlin from Deutscher and Carr. Most of their theoretical disputes about the nature and study of history – is it a science? – were the pilot fish splashing their tails on the surface above that great, semi-submerged shark, the 1917 Revolution. For Berlin, the spectre haunting the twentieth century was that of Lenin, not Hitler. Deutscher, by contrast, fully embraced the Bolshevik seizure of power in terms intolerably Jesuitical to Berlin. We quote Deutscher: 'In the Soviets the propertied classes were not represented: they were to be disfranchised in the way in which old ruling classes are disfranchised in every revolution. (This did not necessarily imply that they should be deprived of freedom of expression.) ... The existence of opposition and the continued contest of parties within the Soviets were taken for granted. That the ruling party alone should be entitled to form public opinion did not yet enter anybody's mind.'

Really? Nobody's mind?

Deutscher offers two separate accounts of the dissolution of the democratically elected Constituent Assembly in 1917. In his *Stalin* (page 186), we read: 'The Assembly, elected on the basis of a law that had been worked out under Kerensky, probably did not reflect the swing in the mood of the country that took place on the eve of the October revolution. Its dispersal represented no difficulty.' But in fact the elections to the Constituent Assembly took place *after* the October Revolution, giving the Bolsheviks only a minority of seats in the Assembly. This is conceded by Deutscher in *The Prophet Armed* but he remains impatient with democracy: 'Rural Russia, vast, illiterate, boiling over with revolt and revenge, had little grasp of the involved disputes between the urban parties.'[6] But why should Petrograd and Moscow write the libretto for a vast nation? Deutscher admits that in 1917 Lenin had pledged himself to convoke and uphold the Constituent Assembly. He also admits: 'The dispersal was at first justified by the specious argument that the elections had been held under an obsolete law, construed under Kerensky to favour the well-off peasants.' Specious or not, Lenin had 'no qualms' about pulling up by the root what Deutscher grants was 'the first Russian shoot of parliamentary democracy'. Nor did Deutscher.[7]

Where did Isaiah Berlin's retrospective sympathies lie among the *dramatis personae* of 1917? Did he regard the February Revolution as necessary? Did he sympathise with Miliukov, or the Cadets, or Kerensky, or even the Mensheviks? Did he regard the Constituent Assembly as viable? While one might assume that the liberal Cadets would have been his focus of allegiance, his party, in an essay on Turgenev, Berlin places the Mensheviks in the proud tradition of the Girondins, of the defeated liberals of 1848 and of 'the stout-hearted members of the European Left who did not side with the Paris Commune in 1871'. Elsewhere he includes Danton in this stout-hearted tradition, with Robespierre cast as Lenin's fanatical precursor. 'It was not weakness or cowardice that prevented the Mensheviks from joining Lenin in 1917, or the unhappy German socialists from turning communist in 1932.' Such moderates were 'not prepared to break their principles or betray the cause in which they believe[d]'.[8] (On the other hand, the Mensheviks viewed themselves as true Marxists rather than as Fabians or Jean Jaurès-style French socialists.)

Deutscher had little patience with what he regarded as Menshevik equivocations. Writing to Trotsky's former colleague Alfred Rosmer, he described the first major publication by Berlin's friend Leonard Schapiro, *The Communist Party of the Soviet Union*, as 'a piece of apologetic writing from an unavowed right-Menshevik viewpoint.... The Mensheviks and the Right SRs are his heroes – innocent lambs slaughtered by the Bolshevik butchers. One need not at all feel that the Bolsheviks were right in suppressing the Mencheviks to feel that this is a gross misrepresentation of history.'[9] In a Third Programme talk (24 April 1964), Deutscher likened the Menshevik Plekhanov to Erasmus, quoting the historian Johan Huizinga on the latter as 'the man who was not strong enough for his age' when compared with 'the oaken strength of Luther ... the steely edge of Calvin, the white heat of Loyola'. Deutscher attributes 'oaken strength' to Lenin, 'steely edge' to Trotsky.[10]

Deutscher's *Ironies of History* includes a sequence of reflections on the Mensheviks, 'sometimes labelled the Girondins of the Russian revolution.' In joining the short-lived governments of Prince Lvov and Kerensky, 'they were renouncing their own past and their proud convictions'.[11] The Mensheviks were doctrinaires, 'who in the name of an abstract principle or constitutional dogma turned a deaf ear on life's realities: on the peasantry's cry for land and peace, and on the nation's war weariness. They exhorted the nation to go on bleeding itself white; and implored the peasants to have patience with the lords of the manors.' Reviewing a recent book by the veteran Menshevik Raphael Abramovich, Deutscher poured scorn on his claim that Russia had succumbed to the new totalitarian version of the old Oriental despotism – and therefore the USA must use its nuclear supremacy to tame or destroy Bolshevism. 'What an epilogue is this to the story of Martov's party; and how Martov's ghost must be weeping over it.'[12]

On reading this, Boris Sapir sent from New York (23 May 1965) a letter of protest to the editor of the *Listener*, describing himself as a former secretary of the Menshevik Party and its representative in the International of the Socialist

Youth. Sapir also wrote to Isaiah Berlin in Russian on the same day, imploring him to support publication of his letter.[13] There is no archival evidence of Berlin taking any action.

Reviewing Alexander Kerensky's *The Kerensky Memoirs*, Deutscher scathingly dismissed the elderly author's claim that he could have established a parliamentary democracy in Russia if he had not been stabbed in the back by ... (a long list). According to Deutscher, bourgeois democracy 'had no chance of survival in Russia's political and social climate ... having in the middle of a war emerged from centuries of autocracy, with a shattered semi-feudal structure, with a land-hungry peasantry, with an undeveloped bourgeoisie, with the national minorities in uproar, and with a highly dynamic, Marxist-oriented, and ambitious working class'. And the role of Lenin? 'Revolutions are history's unproductive disturbances unless or until their leaders become statesmen. The Russian revolution found its salvation and consummation in Bolshevist statesmanship; and this found its embodiment in Lenin, the builder of the Soviet Republic, the originator of the New Economic Policy, the revolutionary turned into a supreme diplomatist.'[14] (Why did Deutscher complain elsewhere that his friend Carr regarded Lenin as essentially a statesman, a Bismarck? It takes us back to the analogy of the man hurrying from one pub to the next, changing his opinions when he encounters a new debating companion.)

Could the October 1917 Revolution have taken place without Lenin's leadership? On this hypothetical question Deutscher's apparently contradictory stances greatly irritated Berlin and his friend Raymond Aron. They, too, thought that Deutscher's opinion depended on the occasion. The present writer first met Aron at Harvard in 1960 and enjoyed long discussions with him about the nature and roots of French communism, the subject of Aron's celebrated polemic against the Sartreans, *The Opium of the Intellectuals*. We met again when Aron visited All Souls as Isaiah Berlin's guest. After lunch the conversation turned to Isaac Deutscher. Reviewing Deutscher's work in the Congress for Cultural Freedom's Paris journal *Preuves*, Aron had expressed astonishment at Deutscher's off-the-cuff remark that the Bolshevik Revolution could, perhaps, have taken place even without Lenin. Deutscher had duly hit back: 'He [Aron], on the contrary, sees Lenin as the sovereign maker of that revolution, and Lenin's personal role as more important than all the "objective trends".' Deutscher accused Aron of subscribing to the crude belief in the role of historical accidents (Cleopatra's nose) by suggesting that if Lenin's train had been derailed while passing through Germany in April 1917 all might have been different. This, said Deutscher, linked up with Carlyle's idea of the 'hero in history' – an idea perhaps indispensable to fascism, Stalinism and Gaullism. (Aron was a keen Gaullist.) 'Thus half a century of Russian and even world history is seen as springing from Lenin's head, from a single idea in his brain. Should one carry one's contempt for "materialist determinism" as far as that?'[15]

Well, should one? The common room conversation between Berlin and Aron turned to the first volume of Deutscher's Trotsky trilogy, *The Prophet Armed* (1954). Aron could quote it almost verbatim from memory, but I have checked chapter and verse. Here Deutscher wrote: 'Trotsky had more than any single man moulded the mind of the broad mass of workers and soldiers. . . . But the active insurgents had come from the cadres and ranks of the Bolshevik party; and on their minds, Lenin, the founder and unrivalled leader of the party, had even from his hiding place [in the Vyborg suburb] exercised by far the greater influence.'[16] Hearing this, Isaiah Berlin guffawed grimly. Aron commented that if one wrote history as biography, it was an implicit recognition that there are indeed 'heroes in history'. Furthermore, the hesitations and splits within the Bolshevik leadership on the eve of the insurrection made it virtually certain that Lenin's influence was decisive.

Berlin nodded: 'Decisive then, decisive now.'

Had this conversation taken place after Deutscher's *The Prophet Outcast* appeared in 1963, Aron could have derived ironic comfort from the way Deutscher there handled a heresy similar to his own uttered by the great Trotsky himself. In his *History of the Russian Revolution*, Trotsky asks what would have happened if Lenin had not managed to return to Russia in April 1917: 'Is it possible . . . to say confidently that the party without him would have found its road? We would by no means make bold to say that.' Conceivably, 'a disoriented and split party might have let slip the revolutionary opportunity for many years'. In a letter to Preobrazhensky from Alma-Ata (AlMaty), Trotsky had written: 'You know better than I do that had Lenin not managed to come to Petrograd in April 1917, the October Revolution would not have taken place.' But in Deutscher's forgiving lexicon this was an isolated case of 'subjectivism' on Trotsky's part – whereas when voiced by Raymond Aron the same heresy amounted to an unscientific belief in historical accidents and a bourgeois contempt for 'materialist determinism'.[17]

In a later interview Berlin touches on the subject of the irreplaceable leader: 'I believe that there are moments in history when individuals or groups can freely alter the direction of things. . . . The limits exist, but within them, there is space for choice. . . . If Lenin had died or become debilitated in April 1917, there would have been no Bolshevik Revolution; possibly a civil war, Liberals and Socialists versus monarchists, but the Bolshevik regime could not have been constructed by anyone but Lenin.'[18]

To 'If Lenin had died' Berlin might well have added, 'If the Germans had not shrewdly arranged for Lenin and his colleagues to be transported back from exile in Switzerland in a sealed train' (the imperial government knew the shape of Cleopatra's nose, as did the Entente powers, who refused passage by an alternative route). Deutscher was to come under attack when denying, against the evidence, that Germany had in addition supplied the Bolsheviks with financial backing. Whatever 'propagandists of the cold war' might claim, he wrote, the German archives showed no evidence that Lenin and his party had entered into *secret* contact with the Kaiser's government or accepted any money from it.[19] While this debate might appear to focus on Lenin's credibility as a patriot – which was how the Kerensky government presented it when indicting him for treason – it equally brings us back to the historical role of contingency, of the random factor, of our friend the Egyptian queen. Suppose this or that official of the German imperial government had not seen fit to put its money on Lenin? Would he have remained throughout 1917 a powerless spectator in Switzerland?[20]

In short, Deutscher, much as he admired Lenin, wanted to present the October 1917 Revolution as historically determined beyond individual influence. Berlin believed that the event would not have taken place, or in the form it did, without Lenin's German train ticket.

In Berlin's view, Lenin's Bolshevism was proto-totalitarian. Deutscher admits that labour was by 1919–20 militarised, with workers dragooned into 'Labour Armies': 'Thus the party that had promised to abolish the standing army was transforming the working population into an army.'[21] He quotes Trotsky: 'A deserter from labour is as contemptible and despicable as a deserter from the battlefield. Severe punishment to both. Begin and complete your work, wherever possible, to the sound of socialist hymns and songs.' Deutscher describes how at the 10th Congress in March 1921, Trotsky insisted that the Party must exercise its dictatorship even if it 'clashed with the passing moods of the workers' democracy'. He spoke of the 'historical birthright of the party' and 'the indispensable unifying element'. It must not waver because of 'temporary vacillations even in the working class'. Lenin concurred while avoiding Trotsky's inflammatory language. 'The party had to override trade unions, to dismiss their recalcitrant leaders, to break or obviate popular resistance, and to prevent the free formation of opinion inside the Soviets. Only thus, held Lenin, could the revolution be saved.'[22]

Deutscher, as usual, endorses Lenin's position, but here he is quite candid about the facts. No falsification is involved. If we disagree with him it must be in terms of his overriding ideological perspective – Lenin and Trotsky heeded the call of necessity and saved the revolution – rather than because he 'falsified the facts'. He offers us *Lear* not *Macbeth*, tragedy not villainy. However, the same may not apply to his account of the traumatic Kronstadt

rebellion – traumatic because on this occasion it was the vanguard of prole-
tarian rule who mutinied against the Party. The proclamations from Kronstadt
were proletarian, democratic and collectivist. Peter Sedgwick notes that
Deutscher was embarrassed by Trotsky's 'mendacious and evasive apologia',
Hue and Cry over Kronstadt, but Deutscher himself was less than candid.[23]
However, this was not an episode about which Isaiah Berlin was likely to hold
a strong view, the rebels being no more up his street than Trotsky and
Tukhachevsky, who crushed them by force.

In 1921, Lenin banned all organised opposition within the soviets (although
there had been constant harassment of Mensheviks and SRs during the civil
war). Deutscher defends the decision to rule alone on the ground that the
other parties wanted to oust and strangle the Bolsheviks, but he concedes that
the conciliatory faction of the Bolsheviks was correct in its fear that 'a purely
Bolshevik government could be maintained only by means of political terror'.[24]
Deutscher quotes Trotsky to the effect that the proscription of other parties
was not a principle but 'an episodic act of self-defence'. But were the Bolsheviks
not perpetually engaged in self-defence, in 'episodes' and 'emergencies'?
Arguing that the 'party was now at loggerheads with its own nature', Deutscher
asks: 'Should the masses be allowed to jeopardize the whole work of the revolution? Should the Soviets be given back their freedom of action when they
were almost certain to use it for their own undoing?'[25] The implied answer is
no, but one notices that Deutscher has worked himself into the position where
Lenin 'gives' or does not 'give' freedom to the masses and the soviets (rather as
the tsars gave or did not give freedom to indentured serfs). Yet there was no
alternative! No revolutionary government, he insists, can 'abdicate' after a
victorious civil war.

Deutscher's moral justification seems to reside in historical parallelism, a
fatalistic general scheme or pattern of revolutions. The happy relationship
between the party and the masses never lasts; ravaged by war, the country sinks
into a misery that may be deeper than that which originally caused the revolt.
'The rulers acquire the habits of arbitrary government and themselves come
to be governed by their own habits.'[26] The English and French revolutions
were accompanied by protracted civil and foreign warfare no less than the
Russian – one emergency after another, from 1640 to 1660, from 1789 to 1815.
As devoted students of past revolutions, equipped with perspectives unavail-
able to a Cromwell or a Robespierre, Lenin and Trotsky should have known in
advance that a seizure of power would precipitate opposition, create enemies
and bloodshed, invite foreign intervention, civil war, widespread devastation.

Yet Deutscher appears to ignore this when, in a later essay, 'The Moral
Dilemmas of Lenin' (1959), he explains that devastation, chaos and social

disintegration consequent on civil war did not permit a workers' democracy. 'Lenin saw a strong hand was needed to guide [the nation] from above. This conviction gave him what appeared to be an unshakable moral self-confidence in his course of action.' For Lenin, moral action was that which hastened the end of the bourgeois order and the proletarian dictatorship. Deutscher gives this the kind of gloss that earned Berlin's contempt: 'It was, I think, Bukharin who first said that the Leninist philosophy of historic determinism had this in common with the Puritan doctrine of predestination that, far from blunting, it sharpened the sense of personal responsibility.'[27]

So there we have it from Deutscher's own pen: he is, as Berlin alleged, 'a complete Bolshevik of Lenin's time'. Firm, even ruthless, leadership is indispensable, even when the sacred tenets of 'proletarian rule' are ditched. The Party must rule over the masses in a dire emergency (but there is always a dire emergency). Government must be top-down. Stalin merely carries the process a step further by imposing terror on the Party itself – at which Deutscher breaks ranks, though his sympathy (as we have seen) is mainly directed at the Old Bolsheviks, Lenin's ill-fated colleagues, themselves responsible for the total identification of the Party with the state.

In an interesting passage, Deutscher goes on to relate how eventually Lenin's 'self-confidence broke down . . . he was seized by acute doubt, apprehension, and alarm. He realized that he had gone too far, and that the new machine of power was turning into a mockery of his principles.' At a Party congress in April 1922, the last he attended, as he 'watched his colleagues, disciples and followers, he was reminded of the old Tsarist mentalities and methods. He realised that Tsardom was spiritually conquering the Bolsheviks, because the Bolsheviks were less civilized than even the Tsar's bureaucracy had been.' But Deutscher does not, cannot, consider whether the source of Lenin's sudden alienation may have been his own personal loss of power as a result of illness (attacks of sclerotic paralysis). 'He felt alienated from the state of his own making,' comments Deutscher, apparently oblivious to Lenin's despair at no longer making that state, at being sidelined, an honoured spectator.[28] So Lenin wrote his famous will, warning against Stalin and Dzerzhinsky, the head of the Cheka – his own appointees. He spoke of a 'swamp' of oppression, while national minorities were subjected to a revival of Great Russian chauvinism. Deutscher cannot contemplate the fact that Lenin's will was the *cri de coeur* of a man who did not wish to leave the stage – *his* stage – at the age of fifty-four. Indeed, if we glance at the history of virtually every available political system, we may be struck by how rapidly 'conscience' is awakened in men who have recently lost power.

Deutscher's 'The Moral Dilemmas of Lenin' was commissioned as one of a series of Third Programme talks by Anna Kallin, Berlin's own favourite talks producer. Berlin must have complained to her, judging by Kallin's letter to him (3 February 1959): 'What did Deutscher twist about Lenin? If he did, shouldn't you write to The Listener, when his talk is published?'[29] In reply (4 February 1959), Berlin gave way to venom, admitting that he had hated and despised Deutscher ever since his review of *Historical Inevitability*. He added: 'How can I reply to Deutscher? I hate him too much. . . . I cannot be sure that it is only his hateful personality (about which all are agreed), his Communism (which is that mean, dead, talmudical "*parshivy yevrey*" type) and not purely his attitude towards *me* that determines my view of him. I am sure I shall find fault with whatever he does. . . . But to attack him in public looks too like revenge; and that I am not ready for.'[30] The Russian phrase *parsvhivy yevrey* means 'mangy Jew'.[31] One is reminded of Herzen's low opinion of Chernyshevsky, in Berlin's words 'a tedious third-rate, pedestrian figure who didn't understand life or literature or what men lived by'.[32] A letter of Herzen's, intercepted by the tsarist police, provided a pretext for Chernyshevsky's arrest and imprisonment; a letter from Berlin intercepted by no one was to terminate Deutscher's academic prospects. Chernyshevsky never complained to Herzen, just as Deutscher never complained to Berlin.

Isaiah Berlin might well have granted Deutscher's depiction of Lenin's relative cultural tolerance, though uncomprehending and often scornful of the modernist art flowing forth in the wake of the Revolution – constructivism, suprematism, expressionism, futurism, abstraction. Visiting Moscow in November 1945, Berlin sat at the same table as the filmmaker Sergei Eisenstein, who told him that the early post-revolutionary years were far and away the best in his own life as a creative artist, a time when wild and marvellous things could be done with impunity. He spoke nostalgically of surrealists, futurists, formalists and Marxists all quarrelling and stimulating each other. Berlin was impressed: 'The Revolution had stimulated a great wave of creative energy in Russia, in all the arts. . . . Revolutionary art of extraordinary vitality continued to be produced.'[33]

Deutscher lauded Lenin for permitting his cultural commissar, Anatoly Lunacharsky, to lend support to the Proletcult and to the architect Tatlin, for appointing Chagall director of the popular Academy of Art at Vitebsk, for allowing scope to Malevsky the constructivist and Malevich the suprematist, for acting as godfather to Meyerhold's biomechanical theatre and for supporting Eisenstein's epoch-making film projects. Lunacharsky helped to bring to life the famous *Habima*, the first Hebrew theatre in history. Tamara Deutscher agreed: 'What astronomical distance separates spiritually that period not only from the severe barbarity of the Stalin era, but even from the desiccated bureaucratic "liberalism" of the post-Stalin years!'[34]

On the other hand, *The Prophet Armed* says nothing about Maksim Gorky and the suppression by Lenin of his journal *Novaya Zhizn*, even though Gorky had been on personal terms with Lenin since 1905 or earlier. Instead Deutscher takes a swipe at Gorky: 'In Marxist politics, the great novelist was childishly naïve. Yet with the lack of modesty characteristic of a famous self-made man, he assumed the posture of political oracle.'[35] This crude verdict contrasts with E.H. Carr's version: 'After October he [Gorky] accepted the new regime, and for the next three or four years he played an important part in keeping literature alive in the horrors of civil war and famine. He constantly appealed personally to Lenin and received intermittent support.' But one notices that the depredations of the Cheka in Petrograd under the instructions of Zinoviev, about which Gorky bravely complained, are chloroformed by Carr as 'the horrors of civil war and famine.'[36]

Material produced by Tamara Deutscher about Lenin and Gorky strongly suggests her husband's intention to use it in his biography. She cites Lunacharsky's account of a conversation in 1919 in which Gorky again complained about the searches and arrests suffered by some members of the Petrograd intelligentsia:

'But they are the same people,' Gorky added, 'who assisted you personally, hid you in their homes, etc.'

Smiling, Vladimir Ilyich answered: 'Yes, of course they are excellent, good people and that is precisely why their homes have to be searched. Precisely because of this one has sometimes *à contre coeur* to arrest them. Of course ... their sympathy goes always to the oppressed, of course they are always against persecution. And what do they see now around them? The persecutor – our Cheka; the oppressed – the Cadets and S.R.s who flee from it.... And we must catch active counter-revolutionaries and render them harmless. The rest is clear.'

And Vladimir Ilyich laughed, quite without malice.[37]

Gorky's implicit answer is found in his 'Untimely Thoughts', banned in Russia but published abroad, in Berlin: 'Their lordships the Commissars strike with all their might, without distinguishing between who is the opponent of their mad actions only, and who is, through his principles, the enemy of the revolution in general.'[38] In 1921, Gorky left Russia for reasons of health but also due to harassment by Zinoviev, chairman of the Executive Committee of the Petrograd Soviet, the scourge of all 'enemies of the people'. Nothing of this is found worth mentioning by either Isaac or Tamara Deutscher.

Sadly, we do not have Deutscher's intended biography of Lenin but we do have his preliminary study of Lenin's childhood, published three years after his death, a superbly evocative and psychologically sensitive portrait of Vladimir Ilyich Ulyanov's first sixteen years, ending with his admission to university at the moment of the execution by hanging of his elder brother, Aleksandr. The observation of character, not only of the young Lenin, but of his father and his siblings, is acute. The milieu of provincial Russia, of the solid family of a dedicated schoolmaster who believed in the tsar's beneficence while striving to extend education to the poor, is exactly captured. As usual with Deutscher the biographer, the narrative is a masterpiece of composition, compelling to read, utterly convincing. As Vladimir Ilyich enters the stormy seas of adolescence, we encounter the emergence of a short temper, of rudeness, of aggression, of sarcasm extending even to his schoolmasters. His elder sister Anna remarked: 'Volodya's scorn, disrespect, especially towards the mother whom he began to answer back as he would have never dared when father was alive – his impertinence and sarcasm … were absolutely alien to [Aleksandr, the elder brother].'[39] Elsewhere Deutscher notes that Lenin's political writings usually took the form of polemical assaults – there was invariably some fool or knave who had to be cut down. Anatoly Lunacharsky found awesome 'his colossal certainty of the rectitude of his principles. … An argument for him is always a struggle. Lenin always welcomes the transition from a struggle to a fight.'[40]

8

TROTSKY THE PROPHET

DEUTSCHER'S *MAGNUM OPUS* was his three-volume biography of Trotsky, in which he invested years of devoted labour. Only the first volume, *The Prophet Armed*, had appeared when E.H. Carr invited Deutscher to address a seminar he was giving jointly with Berlin in Oxford. Deutscher duly delivered a paper on 'Trotsky at Alma Ata and the Party Opposition'. Jonathan Haslam comments: 'Deutscher clearly underestimated his own unfortunate capacity for inflaming the sentiment of others by getting carried away in wounding and ad hominem polemic.'[1] This probably refers not to the presentation itself but to the altercation about Marxism that followed. Of this we have only Berlin's blood-soaked accounts which emerged in a series of outbursts. For example, Elena Levin asked Berlin to provide an introduction to her translation of Trotsky's *Diary in Exile, 1935* (eventually published in 1958). His reply (30 November 1954), written a month after the fateful seminar, deserves extensive quotation. The main complaint against Deutscher here is not 'falsification' but absurd medieval scholasticism.

He had, he wrote, recently listened to a paper by Deutscher on Trotsky's exile to Alma Ata.[2] Apart from such activities as hunting, 'of which the more sedentary type of Social Democrats seem pathetically and snobbishly proud', Trotsky had engaged in a lot of correspondence with fellow exiles about Stalin's potential manoeuvres and the proper strategic response. If Stalin moved to the left, then 'we' would have to change our opposition to support. 'Deutscher took all this frightfully seriously, and yet the ghastly unreality of it was extraordinary' – what with Trotsky banished to Central Asia, his letters censored, writing to other 'equally feeble and discredited Bolsheviks, still talking the language of 1910', the language of factional intrigue, even though 'all this had become trivial nonsense'. So why did 'people like Deutscher' regard it as so important? 'The whole thing seemed to me a kind of fantastic caricature of the earlier Marxist scholasticism', reminiscent of the fissions within the heresies and subheresies of early Christian theologians. Berlin regarded all this as 'a pathetic and repulsive spectacle, the kind of nemesis which comes on blind and heartless bigots when something goes wrong with the system and their particular carriage slips off the railway lines along which alone they are capable of moving'. Berlin detested 'conscientious, coherent, high-minded doctrinaire torturers of human beings into neat and tidy shapes'. He concluded that one must be 'either a Dantonist or a Robespierrist and I am quite clear that I am the former and cannot really sit at the same table as the latter'.[3]

One is struck by the metaphor 'sit at the same table', which Berlin was again to deploy when explaining to the present writer Deutscher's moral disqualifications from an academic post. Berlin's characterisation of himself as a 'Dantonist' seems to fit his perennial claim to be 'left of centre' – although Georges Danton, it may be recalled, voted for the death of Louis XVI in January 1793: 'The kings of Europe would dare challenge us? We throw them the head of a king!' When all executive power was conferred upon a Committee of Public Safety on 6 April 1793, Danton was elected one of its nine original members. By mid-May of that year, he was calling for the suppression of the Girondins, with whom Berlin on other occasions associated himself.

What can be said about Berlin's letter to Elena Levin? Deutscher's *The Prophet Armed* had recently been extensively lauded. Writing in the *Observer* (21 March 1954), Bertrand Russell had praised 'a most remarkable book worthy of his great theme'. Even political opponents, said Russell, acknowledged Deutscher's attention to detail, his archival research. Merle Fainsod, professor of government at Harvard and author of *How Russia Is Ruled*, described *The Prophet Armed* as 'a magnificent essay in historical restoration. It is written with sympathy, understanding, and a rare detachment.'[4] Indeed, Deutscher's detailed presentation of Trotsky's situation when exiled to Alma Ata was entirely appropriate for a specialist modern history seminar; serious historical scholarship often proceeds by way of arcane, 'scholastic' detail to the broader picture. Berlin, who constantly criticised E.H. Carr for backing only history's winners, seems to be ridiculing Trotsky because he was known to be an ultimate loser. His 'particular carriage' had slipped 'off the railway lines'. Trotsky and his followers 'were living in the imaginary world of heresies and sub-heresies and fissions within the sub-heresies of the earlier Christian theologians – which no longer corresponded to anything that was anything in the "real world"'. Yet Trotsky was real enough to be the alleged cause of every invented plot against Stalin's rule, his followers were imprisoned and executed, and he himself was murdered. Surely they inhabited the 'real world'? Trotsky had, of course, been the second most powerful man in the regime that forced the Berlin family to seek sanctuary in England – and a Jew. Trotsky was no Gandhi; he had proudly sent the Mensheviks and the Socialist Revolutionaries to the 'dustheap of history' – so Berlin doubtless experienced a darkish satisfaction at his eclipse.

Deutscher regarded Trotsky as a 'tragic' figure – this word often comes up – a hero in the Shakespearean mode. A letter to Brandler (19 February 1955) conveys his views on Marxist history writing: 'But I do not think that the dry description of facts is *the* Marxist style in history writing. Dialectical history writing is dramatic writing precisely because it views events in terms of the conflict of opposites.'[5] Peter Sedgwick believed that Deutscher's capacity for historical analysis in his biographies was undermined by his artistic achievement: 'His extraordinary dramaturgical and poetic gifts led him to operate within a group of concepts that have absolutely no place in any analytical work of social history or social theory: particularly those of tragic irony, tragic destiny, tragic hero.' Sedgwick held that 'The concept of tragedy is totally alien to politics . . . there are no tragedies in politics. . . . The biography of a political leader should therefore exclude tragedy, since his failures will reflect the exhaustion of certain social possibilities, not simply his own chances.'[6]

For Berlin, Trotsky was a murderous fanatic, and Deutscher was a dangerous acolyte not only of Trotsky and Lenin, but of Stalin too.

Within the parameters of our pages a worthy account of Deutscher's prodigious, indeed enthralling, exploration of Trotsky's life and achievements would break the bank, likewise his criticisms of Trotsky's stances in exile and his own points of departure from orthodox Trotskyists who joined his 'Fourth International'. A useful summation of Deutscher's version can be found in Marcel Liebman's *The Russian Revolution*, which received Deutscher's endorsement. Liebman signposts the issues about which Deutscher and his followers (like Liebman himself) regarded themselves as uniquely correct against practically everybody else. We may note in particular:

(1) Deutscher's frank recognition that by 1920 'the bulk of the working class, not to speak of the peasantry, unmistakably turned against the Bolsheviks' and 'if the working classes were to be allowed to speak and vote freely they would destroy the dictatorship'. Consequently 'the Bolshevik Party maintained itself in power by usurpation'. Therefore those who believe that 'Stalin destroyed Leninist democracy' deceive themselves.

(2) Devotees of the cult of Trotsky also deceive themselves that Trotsky and the Left Opposition later succumbed to mere gangsterism by Stalin. Trotsky made fatal errors between 1923 and 1926 by failing to align himself with Zinoviev and Kamenev, or with Bukharin, 'an act of suicidal folly'.[7]

(3) From 1923, Trotsky, having spoken for Party dictatorship over the workers, unrealistically advocated the re-establishment of workers' democracy at a time when the working class had been decimated by civil war and weakened by the New Economic Policy. As for permanent revolution, which underpinned Trotsky's programme, in 1923 the last attempt of the German communists to take power failed miserably. Trotsky became 'a fighter against his time'.

(4) Stalin's view of the non-revolutionary potential of the Western working class seemed stronger on the evidence than Trotsky's contrary view. Trotsky blamed Stalin's Comintern for dampening or thwarting the revolutionary impulses of the Western proletariat but Deutscher, while agreeing, objected that the situation in Western Europe was what it was: Deutscher further distanced himself from Trotsky's orthodox followers – and his widow, Natalya Sedova – when he described Trotsky's Fourth International (1937) as misconceived and 'stillborn'.[8]

(5) Stalin stole from the Left its own political platform in 1929 when he launched the second revolution, the authentic successor to Lenin's. Stalinism was therefore not 'Thermidor', as orthodox Trotskyists allege. Trotsky argued that the Stalinist bureaucratic structure strove to abolish public ownership and that its members might soon become the shareholding owners of Soviet industry. Deutscher disagreed. The Stalin bureaucracy represented the socialist sector of the economy, and was bound to defend the nationalised economy, 'the foundation of socialism' by way of a planned economy, industrial expansions and mass education.[9]

However, Deutscher's overall position was largely irrelevant to Isaiah Berlin, along with Bolshevik faction-fighting and theology in general. By the time *The Prophet Outcast* appeared in 1963, Berlin's view of Deutscher as a Stalinist wearing a Trotsky goatee beard while garnering fashionable adulation as a brave dissident was confirmed to his satisfaction. Deutscher's separation from orthodox Western communists could be regarded as more decorative than real.

According to the historian Lord Acton, power corrupts and absolute power corrupts absolutely. This may be extended to the lust for power, just as it is the lust for money, not merely the possession of it, that is the proverbial root of all evil. Berlin believed that the Bolshevik leaders were blown up with power and inevitably corrupted by it.

Was Trotsky, the former commissar for war and number two in the Bolshevik hierarchy, consumed by vanity and in love with power? For Berlin, yes. For Deutscher, such a proposition was blasphemous. Like Marx himself, he refused to weigh power as a disembodied entity. Power must be viewed instrumentally, in class terms, not psychologically, in personal terms – although Stalin's performance did present Deutscher with problems when the dictator developed Louis XIV's celebrated 'l'état c'est moi' into 'la société c'est moi' (as Trotsky put it). However, unknown to Isaiah Berlin, Deutscher did begin to entertain doubts 'off-stage', and it is to these we now briefly turn.

We should begin with Deutscher's vital relationship with Natalya Sedova, Trotsky's devoted widow, who had seen his head smashed by the assassin's axe in 1940 – vital because her goodwill was indispensable if he was to gain access to sections of the Trotsky archive at Harvard where a new, private section had been donated to the Houghton Library's Trotsky archive in 1953 by Sedova. He thus needed to win over this formidable former colleague of Lenin, then in her seventies. An indication that Sedova disagreed with aspects of volume two of his Trotsky trilogy, *The Prophet Unarmed*, is found in a letter she sent him on 5 August 1956, following Khrushchev's attack on Stalin at the 20th Party Congress. She wrote (in French): 'I would now like to pose a question to you: this brutal turn which Russia has just experienced, what do you think about it? I ask myself if it has modified your orientation in the second volume.' Evidently she herself no longer regarded the Soviet Union as a socialist state (an outlook about which Deutscher expressed exasperation in private).

Deutscher clearly engaged in flattery when persuading the elderly widow to open the closed archive at Harvard to him. He wrote to 'Chère camarade Sedova', praising Trotsky's objectivity, his heroic tenacity under adverse conditions, 'the majestic grandeur of the thought and revolutionary character of Trotsky'. Deutscher told her that he often regretted not having tried to enter into personal contact with 'L.D.' in the 1930s. ('L.D.' – for 'Lev or Leon Davidovich' – was virtually a password among those close to Trotsky.) Reporting from Harvard in November 1959 to Trotsky's old colleague Alfred Rosmer, he explained the difficulty of gaining access to the private section of the papers: 'I therefore cabled to Natalya [spelled variously Natalia and Natalya by Deutscher] . . . and asked her authorization.'[10] To his vast relief she soon cabled back her assent. 'For about a month I worked like a beaver, seven days a week from morning to night. . . . Among other things, I have read through with intense interest and fascination the three folders containing the correspondence between both of you [Alfred and Margarita Rosmer] and L.D. and Natalya.'[11] He wrote again to Rosmer in February 1960, soliciting his advice about the papers he had seen at Harvard concerning the most intimate side of Sedova's life with Trotsky. He had found

a few letters so deeply, so incredibly, intimate in content and style that I was greatly surprised to find them there. The letters are written – how shall I put it? – in strong Russian sex-slang; and they record a somewhat bathetic *scène de jalousie* between husband and wife. I was not in the least shocked to see that nothing, absolutely nothing human was alien to L.D . . . I do not think that Trotsky's reputation can suffer from disclosure of these letters. But it would be a great pity if some cheap novelist or sensation-monger (*à la* Bernard [*sic*: Bertram] Wolfe (whose *The Great Prince Died* you may have read) got hold of those documents and exploited them for a vulgar kind of a *vie romance* [unclear] *et scandaleuse de Trotski* . . .) What can be done to prevent it? . . . Handling the matter would, in any case, require discretion and diplomatic cleverness.[12]

No reply from Rosmer is found. Clearly Deutscher wanted to prevent any other historian from seeing the intimate letters, potential rivals being characterised as cheap novelists and 'sensation-mongers' like the renegade Bertram Wolfe. On the other hand, he was evidently fearful of opening a can of worms and therefore was not explicitly asking Rosmer to help him gain Sedova's consent for his own use of the intimate letters in his forthcoming third volume, *The Prophet Outcast*. Shrewdly he preferred to arrange a new meeting with Sedova in person (having previously met her in 1956).

Deutscher wrote an extremely vivid but undated seven-page memo, 'Notes on Talks with Natalia Ivanovna in Paris', in which he describes his meetings with her in 1956 and February 1961. He remarks that all of the 'prejudice' she showed on the first occasion, when they talked in French with the veteran Trotskyist Pierre Frank as a witness, had disappeared on the second, when he talked to her alone in Russian. She expressed happiness about talking in Russian; it was now rare in her life. She was then approaching her eightieth birthday but the conversation lasted more than three hours and did not seem to tire her. She repeatedly brought the conversation round to the situation in the USSR. 'She was far more receptive to my views than five years ago, although she was more inclined to dwell on the negative aspects, especially on the continuing falsification of history where it concerned L.D. But she accepted the positive aspects as well.'

On Trotsky, he told her: 'I was almost alone among his pupils who had reviewed his formulas in the Marxist way. At this point she appreciatively took my hand – the argument obviously appealed to her.'

But what about the main point of their meeting, the sexually charged private archive? 'There was only one point in our conversation which aroused her anxiety: When she realized that, having read the Closed Section of the Archives, I was au courant of the intimate side of their family life, she feared that I misunderstood the relationship between L.D. and Lyova [their son Lev].'

She was not sure whether Deutscher would know how to interpret the conflict between them. But Deutscher's memo makes no reference to what he had confided to Alfred Rosmer about the passages of intimate correspondence between L.D. and Sedova herself. It seems clear that he did not take the dangerous step of raising that topic and risking an indignant refusal. She had died by the time *The Prophet Outcast* appeared, her ashes reunited by her wish with Trotsky's in Mexico.[13]

In *The Prophet Outcast* he went ahead anyway, citing the correspondence between Trotsky and his wife. She had become jealous of someone she referred to as 'F' – almost certainly the artist Frida Kahlo. A crisis ensued. Trotsky wrote to her, imploring her to 'stop competing with a woman who meant so little' to him. He was full of 'shame and self-hatred', vowing eternal love to her. Then his 'vitality surges up and he feels a sexual craving for Natalya . . . he breaks into the slang of sex, and then feels "abashed at putting such words on paper for the first time in my life"'. He rakes up a love affair that Sedova was supposed to have had in 1918, and about which Trotsky had never uttered a word of rebuke. Sedova replies, explaining that the 'affair' was with an assistant 'infatuated' with her, but that she did not allow any intimacy.[14]

Deutscher's description of their final parting at the Paris métro station of Denfert-Rochereau after lunch is both brilliant and affecting. The old lady insisted on going her own way on foot. She, Trotsky and their sons had once lived in that district, it was packed with memories.

I saw her walking along the crowded, animated street in search of the landmarks she retained in her memory. She walked with the octogenarian's small and shaky steps but briskly, a small frail, brittle figure, yet as indestructible, straight, head high up, face marked by endless suffering and intense pride. . . . For a long time I could not turn my eyes away from her – there she was in her dark clothing and black mantilla over her head – the Niobe of our time, in search of the traces of her children and husband – alone with their shadow and her own thoughts in the milling and gay Parisian crowd.[15]

Perhaps as retribution, even in death Sedova decided to haunt him. Reviewing *The Prophet Outcast* in the December 1963 issue of *Encounter*, Alasdair MacIntyre pointed out that in her last political statement in 1961 Sedova stated that Russia and China were as far from socialism as Franco's Spain. And the veteran Trotskyist Alfred Rosmer, added MacIntyre, agreed with her.[16] This claim threw Deutscher. Had all his hard work convincing her of the correct position come to nothing? (Evidently so.) He wrote to Rosmer (22 November 1963) in consternation: 'We must forgive Natalya this imprudence, though the view she expressed is too naïve theoretically for words.' But did Rosmer himself also really believe that capitalism had been restored in the USSR? If not, would it not be useful if he wrote to *Encounter* saying so?[17]

No reply is found. Rosmer died the following year at the age of eighty-seven.

So back to Acton and the corrupting influence of power. Deutscher could not dare to ask Mme Trotsky whether her late husband had enjoyed power, fame, influence for their own sake, but privately he harboured doubts, conceding that in exile 'Trotsky was of necessity exercising a sort of ideal, moral autocracy as sole mouthpiece of the Opposition. He too, in his defeat, loomed as an individual exceptionally, even uniquely, large.' In his *Diary in Exile*, Trotsky had written: 'There is no one except me to carry out the mission of arming a new generation with the revolutionary method.'[18] Oops!

There was further disturbing evidence. Another Old Bolshevik cultivated by Deutscher was the half-Russian, half-Italian Angelica Balabanoff, who had been secretary of the anti-war Zimmerwald movement and had known Lenin well. It was rather like corresponding with one of Christ's still-living apostles: What was He really like? Were you ever present when He performed a miracle or two? Balabanoff wrote in excellent English from Rome in 1954 (no date) in response to a letter of Deutscher's of 28 July enquiring about a passage in her memoirs in which Lenin tells her during the summer of 1917 that what keeps him and Trotsky apart is 'ambition, ambition, ambition' – he meant Trotsky's, not his own. (Deutscher found this shocking, almost unbelievable.) She had also written that her view of Trotsky as ambitious and vain was reinforced by her correspondence with him in the late 1930s. In her reply to Deutscher, Balabanoff confirmed this, remarking that the effect of power on many revolutionaries and Marxists was to make them prey to the lure of popularity, by contrast with Lenin, who was immune to such weakness.[19]

Balabanoff's damaging comments about Trotsky are found in the Deutscher archive but not in any of the volumes of his Trotsky trilogy. Why so? Had Isaiah Berlin known about this, it would doubtless have confirmed his view of Deutscher as a 'falsifier'.

In 1984 the New Left historian Perry Anderson paid tribute to Deutscher's abilities as a biographer: 'In the life of an individual, he could join the discourses of morality and necessity that Marxism has often found it hard to hold together. . . . Deutscher's exceptional psychological grasp was the medium in which the two – causality and responsibility – achieved synthesis in his writing.'[20]

9

BERLIN, CHRISTOPHER HILL – AND DEUTSCHER

SOME YEARS BEFORE Deutscher's death, he had acquired a perhaps unlikely admirer in the shape of the Oxford historian Christopher Hill, renowned for his marvellous explorations of religion and politics in the age of the English Revolution. Hill's once-friendly relationship with Isaiah Berlin had been pitched into a deep freeze as a result of Hill's membership of the British Communist Party and his admiration for Lenin. Berlin always insisted that he had nothing against Marxist academics but this did not apply if their Marxism was converted into Leninism.

Hill was to describe Deutscher's Trotsky trilogy as 'splendid'.

Berlin had first got to know Hill in the 1930s when both were prize fellows of All Souls – two very different personalities in background, temperament and fields of study. While Berlin was voluble, extrovert and socially gilded, Hill was from a middle-class Methodist background, a quiet man intently focused on the English and Russian revolutions. As a Balliol undergraduate, he had embraced Marxism, joined the Communist Party and, according to Jenifer Hart, even suggested that she should recruit Berlin into its ranks. By an odd conjuncture Berlin undertook his study of Marx at the same time that Hill accepted a commission to write a short book on Lenin and the Russian Revolution, a project that took him to the Soviet Union in 1935.

While there, he generously supplied Berlin with Russian editions of Marx's texts not readily available in England. On 14 December 1935, he wrote to 'Dear Berlin' from a Moscow hospital where he was to undergo an ear operation after venturing out into the Moscow winter after having the flu: 'Buying books by catalogue is a touching act of faith. I expect about half of them will be in stock.' The letter was signed 'Yours Christopher Hill' – not a sign of close intimacy.[1] On 1 February 1936, he reported having sent Berlin four Plekhanovs and seven Lassalles, 'miserable paperbacks'. Should he pick up more Plekhanovs and send them? He reported with dry humour about standing in queues for books at the Lenin Library and for everything everywhere. It was now 30 degrees below zero and his diet of bread and sausage left him hungry. The historian Keith Thomas recalls an anecdote told by Hill: on one occasion he was among a group of foreign visitors who were informed that they were going to visit the first hospital in the world to ensure painless childbirth. They set off but the chauffeur got lost – they located the maternity hospital only when they eventually heard the screams.[2]

Berlin later recalled that he knew Hill 'extremely well, but I never knew that he was a member of the Communist Party. Everybody else did.' He came to believe that Norman O. Brown, who had met Hill while they were both under-graduates at Balliol, and whom Berlin tutored, had converted Hill. Clearly Hill was putting himself to considerable trouble in Moscow on Berlin's behalf; how well appreciated the archive gives no clue. Fifty years later Berlin was to recall using Moscow editions of Marx's works, but without mentioning Hill's assist-ance. Hill wrote again to Berlin: 'I don't think I want to come back to Oxford: do any provincial universities yearn for a historian? Or should I join the Daily Worker which has become an excellent paper?'[3] He did in fact take up a temporary teaching post in Cardiff before rejoining his undergraduate college, Balliol, as a fellow in 1938. Two years later he published 'The English Revolution 1640', a tercentenary essay, asserting the socially and ideologically revolutionary nature of the crisis.

In 1940, Hill was commissioned as a lieutenant in the Oxfordshire and Buckinghamshire Light Infantry, before becoming a major in the Intelligence Corps. Later, after the Nazi invasion of Russia, he served as liaison officer with Soviet military engineers who were in Britain to inspect tanks. He was then assigned to a small unit that was preparing to be parachuted into the Baltic States to foment rebellion, but the mission was shelved and he was seconded to the Northern Department of the Foreign Office from 1943 until the end of the war.

Clearly Hill was a communist – but what species of communist? When he died in March 2005, aged ninety-one, reports accused him of having concealed his membership of the Communist Party, first when in Military Intelligence, then at the Foreign Office. In *The Soviets and Ourselves: Two Commonwealths*, published by Harrap in 1945 under the pseudonym K.E. Holme, Hill provided a picturebook guide to the Soviet Union, illustrated with isotype statistical charts, urging solid English patriots to understand Soviet achievements and how Soviet expectations and values could not be the same as ours, though often superior for the worker and peasant. The English multiparty democracy with its separation of powers was fine for the well off, but had no place in a socialist society joined in the knowledge that the Party and the government were 'ours' and where every factory, power station and collective farm belonged to the people. Strong measures during collectivisation had been necessary and the trials of 1936–38 had dealt with the 'fifth column'. The editor of the series, Professor John Macmurray, explained that the author 'is obliged to conceal his identity'. *The Soviets and Ourselves* clearly fits into the same ideological box as E.H. Carr's equally manipulative propaganda exercise, *The Soviet Impact on the Western World*.[4]

On 29 May 1945, Berlin wrote from the British Embassy in Washington to Hill at Northern Dept., Foreign Office, SW1. He would be calling on him 'officially' to talk about 'this sudden visit to the USSR which Sir A. Clarke Kerr appears to have arranged behind my back with my post facto warm approval'. Hill replied, handwritten (16 June) from the FO, now addressing Berlin as 'Dear Shaya' but mentioning practically nothing about Berlin's trip to Russia, preferring gossip about Stuart Hampshire's ('Hants') chances of being elected to Balliol. Hill reported that when visiting All Souls for the first time in years, taking two friends as guests, they drank from a whisky decanter they found in the common room, not knowing that one should sign for it, and received an offensive letter of rebuke from Dr Ernest Jacob.[5]

Had it taken place, Berlin's conversation with Hill before setting out on his memorable visit to Russia in 1945 would have certainly been interesting, so divergent were their points of view, but no record of such a meeting has been found.

Then, on the evidence of the Berlin Papers, came a great silence between them. It seems that Hill's decision in 1947 to issue an updated edition of his 1937 *Lenin and the Russian Revolution* caused the breach. 'First and foremost,' wrote Hill, 'Lenin symbolizes the Russian Revolution as a movement of the poor and oppressed of the earth who have successfully risen against the great and the powerful. That was and is the most important single fact about the revolution, both in its internal and international effects.' The book's factual errors all gravitated in one direction. For example: 'Gorky, who on many occasions of the hard times of civil war intervened with Lenin on behalf of suspected intellectuals ... never met with a refusal.' In reality, 'the hard times of civil war' was the Cheka's terror in Petrograd; Gorky's *Novaya Zhizn* was closed down on Lenin's orders. Hill (like Isaac and Tamara Deutscher) was not short of touching anecdotes about Lenin, who loved children. Coming across a father who said it did no harm to get a healthy child tired, Lenin got off his bicycle to help the child up a steep hill, saying: 'People like you should not be allowed to have children at all.' 'In the hectic days immediately after the October Revolution Lenin found time to see a totally unknown armless man who came to him with a proposal for a producers' co-operative; and Lenin remembered to ask the official to whom he referred the armless man what action had been taken.' According to Hill, Lenin's purposefulness, realism, common sense, willpower and pugnacity had been conspicuously lacking in the Russian intelligentsia satirised by Chekhov. Unlike Cromwell and Napoleon, Lenin was also a thinker. 'No one since Calvin has combined the two roles.'[6]

Berlin was incensed by Hill's justification of Lenin's dissolution of the Constituent Assembly because the peasants had no confidence in it, and by his claim that the SRs elected by the peasants did not truly speak for their interests. Hill got word of Berlin's reaction, but a meeting failed to restore their relationship. When in 1950 Carr commented that F.I. Dan, the Menshevik leader, had the merit of recognising that 'socialism could not be realised in a free democratic form' in Russia, he received an enthusiastic letter of support in the TLS from Hill: one should not assume that democracy 'must take the forms appropriate to a capitalist society'.[7]

Hill regarded his postwar membership of the new Communist Party Historians Group as a decisive influence on his subsequent work. He was involved with the journal Past and Present, which generated ground-breaking historiography for the next quarter of a century. But in 1956 Hill became sharply critical of the official Party position on events in Hungary. Although elected to the Commission on Inner-Party Democracy in 1957, he and two others wrote a minority report that was not accepted and thus led to Hill leaving the Party.

Hill and his work had been iconic to the present writer when I regularly carted to my public school loads of Soviet pamphlets picked up from Collett's bookshop in the Charing Cross Road, all published by the Moscow Foreign Languages Publishing House, dirt cheap, all proving the superior social system prevailing in the USSR. At that time I already knew Hill's *The English Revolution, 1640* and his *Lenin and the Russian Revolution*, and I knew that he was a member of the Communist Party. Emboldened by a letter from Sir Maurice Bowra offering me a history scholarship at Wadham, I wrote to Hill explaining my political beliefs, hoping that I might attend his lectures when I 'came up' after my national service, and requesting what I rather fatuously called 'a private conversation' before I was conscripted. I remember that I planned to ask him whether I should actually join the Party, but the meeting never took place and when I emerged from service in the Gold Coast and Nigeria all such temptations were blown away during my first term at Wadham by the winds of the Hungarian Revolution and its suppression by Soviet tanks.

Choosing the English Commonwealth and Protectorate as my special subject, I did finally attend tutorials with Hill. He struck me as a reticent, somewhat distracted man whom one could assume was weighed down by the schism within the Communist Party (about which he did not speak), and only out of duty focusing on why Charles I's head had to come off. Later he kindly read a draft of my novel about Winstanley and the Surrey Diggers of 1649.[8] Isaiah Berlin was aware of my admiration of Hill – he was an encyclopaedia of personal connections – and on one occasion alluded to it guardedly when talking about early English versions of utopia. He remarked that Hill's work benefited from the fact that the visions of Winstanley et al. had never taken earthly form, whereas Lenin's had, leading Hill 'up a very rocky garden path, with inexcusable innocence'.

So back to Hill's estrangement from Berlin and his embrace of Isaac Deutscher. Berlin wrote to Hugh Trevor-Roper (15 March 1957), mentioning Hill as among the Balliol worthies 'who find me instinctively distasteful'.[9] Confirmation of the causes of their long-standing rupture is found when their correspondence resumes in a 'Dear Shaya' letter from Hill (4 July 1962), thanking Berlin for proposing a lunch – but regretting that he would be away for most of the summer vacation. Could they try again next term? Referring to an (undiscovered) letter from Berlin, Hill adds: 'But there are a lot of other subjects we shall have to avoid too: what about Carr's excellent book?' (Presumably *What Is History?* – a red rag to Berlin.) And hardly less provocative: 'I very nearly made overtures myself by sending you a revised copy of my Lenin but thought you would be more annoyed by what remained than gratified by what was changed.'

Berlin replied (9 July 1962): he would be in Harvard next term until the following January: 'So we must wait till the spring. I shall leave the initiative to you.' He added: 'About Lenin I genuinely do not propose to talk to you: on that subject we both made up our minds many years ago.' He had thought of sending Hill his revised book on Marx, which now contained 'an exposition on the subject of alienation, to which I paid as little attention in the 30s as you did in the 40s to Trotsky'. (The spiked mention of Trotsky may have reflected awareness of Hill's admiration for Deutscher's biography.) The next found letter is from Hill (30 January 1965), by now elected master of Balliol, thanking Berlin for a kind letter. But: 'Because of the [ridiculousness?] that has built up between us, [it] does make it difficult for me to rush at reconciliations. . . . Perhaps we could meet in AS [All Souls] "so we could take it gradually".'[10]

By this time Hill was a declared admirer of Deutscher and the awkward stand-off with Berlin persisted.

The text of Hill's Third Programme talk 'Marx's Virtues' appeared in the *Listener* (10 August 1967), days before Deutscher's death and read in parts like a direct challenge to Berlin. For example: 'Everyone who has never read him knows that Marx was an economic determinist, who saw men as the puppets of blind economic forces ... [but] he was a historian of genius whose insights into intellectual and religious history were no less brilliant than his economic history.' The challenge was extended by carrying this claim into Berlin's own field of study: 'Some of the best Marxist-influenced historical writing in English has been in the history of ideas: George Thomson, Benjamin Farrington, Joseph Needham, Eric Hobsbawm, Isaac Deutscher, Edward Thompson, C.B. Macpherson.' Implicitly turning his fire on Berlin's well-known affirmation of the need for moral judgments, Hill commented that most modern historians of the English or French revolutions would now analyse them in terms of social classes, rather than 'in terms of [their] goodness or badness'.

No, Marx was not a determinist: his 'profound view of the history of civilisation as a whole is far removed from the vulgar optimism of the 19th-century bourgeois. History is a tragedy, but it need not be a meaningless tragedy.... The organisation of society depends on you, me, and millions of others.' Marx hoped that the lost rights of man would be regained in a classless society, based on the higher technique developed during centuries of inequality and suffering.[11]

Hill was by now convinced by Deutscher's broad historical perspective on repeated revolutionary cycles since the time of the English Revolution. He embraced Deutscher's theory that a bourgeois revolution – unlike a proletarian revolution – does not necessarily mean one made or consciously willed by the bourgeoisie acting as a coherent entity. His endorsement of Deutscher's overview is clear from his supportive account of two seminars (not attended by Hill) given by Deutscher at Harvard in 1950 and at Harvard's Russian Research Center in 1959. He extended his praise to Deutscher's work in general: 'No historian before Deutscher has written so sensitively, so sympathetically and yet so critically, in showing how analogies, illusions and shibboleths from the past drastically affected political action in Soviet history. Le mort saisit le vif.' He added: 'Deutscher's life and writings demonstrate that one can be a heretic without becoming a renegade, indeed that in his time heresy was necessary in order *not* to become in some sense a renegade.'[12]

In short, Hill was at one with Deutscher in refusing to carry criticism of Stalinism to the point of repudiating either Marxism or the Soviet Union. However, it seems likely that Deutscher and Hill never met, though one cannot be sure, and no correspondence between them is found in the Deutscher archive. A letter from Hill in the year following Deutscher's death (23 April

1968) begins 'Dear Mrs Deutscher': it would be nice to meet her. He refers to 'your husband', not 'Isaac'. Hill was concerned about obtaining the Harvard Russian Research Center's permission to use transcripts of Deutscher's Harvard seminars for a planned Festschrift. Tamara's reply begins 'Dear Professor Hill' (Hill actually did not hold a chair at Oxford) and concludes: 'It would give me great pleasure if I could have the opportunity of meeting you personally.'[13]

Isaac and Tamara Deutscher (International Institute of Social History, Amsterdam)

PART THREE

WHAT IS LIBERTY?

10

TWO CONCEPTS OF LIBERTY

WHY IS THE Marxist or Leninist vision of true freedom, a vision shared by Isaac Deutscher, a travesty? Berlin painstakingly set out his answer in the work that perhaps more than any other encapsulated his credo, *Two Concepts of Liberty* (1958). At first sight this is a further case of his ship and Deutscher's passing in the night – no public comment by Deutscher is found. Despite the obvious influence of the nineteenth-century Russian enlightenment (Herzen, Turgenev), Berlin's thesis belongs to an essentially English and empirical tradition of political philosophy – Mill, Green, Bentham, and back to Hume, Locke, Harrington, Hobbes – a lineage peripheral to Deutscher's concerns and in his view finally transcended by Marxism. For Deutscher, discussions of liberty under capitalism were as antiquated as a renewed debate about the earth orbiting the sun.

Neither *Historical Inevitability* nor *Two Concepts of Liberty* is presented as primarily directed at Marxism; on both occasions, Berlin's artillery strikes at a wider spectrum of targets. But there is no disguising that for Berlin the most dangerously ascendant enemy of pluralist liberty was the geographically expanding Soviet system and its Marxist-Leninist underpinning, endorsed in the West by dedicated communists and fellow travellers, and by innocent do-gooders and milky utopians (like Berlin's predecessor in the Chichele chair, G.D.H. Cole) – all of them joined together by the belief that true liberty is inseparable from equality. In *Two Concepts of Liberty*, Berlin sets out to demonstrate the contrary. In his earlier essay 'Equality', he argues that the demand for equality is not self-evidently either reasonable or unreasonable, not necessarily compatible with other values – for example, the conductor's necessarily authoritative role in shepherding his orchestra to musical excellence. He also suggests that extreme equality may be achievable only by authoritarian rule, i.e. by extreme inequality.[1]

For the Left – the socialist tradition since the seventeenth century – a key issue in political theory is always property: who owns what and how unequal possession is acquired and defended in the name of liberty and individual rights (as distinct from the utopian tradition's emphasis on collective rights). Berlin is an unrepentant liberal; for him, liberty starts and stops with the singular individual. Yes, you can come together as a subjugated nation or class to demand equality or social justice collectively ('positive' liberty), but you are free only to the extent that nobody else deliberately impedes your desired actions ('negative' liberty).

Building on the approaching centenary of John Stuart Mill's *On Liberty* (1859), Berlin sets out the stall of contemporary liberalism. Mill's subject was 'the nature and limits of the power which can legitimately be exercised by society over the individual' (to quote Mill himself). Berlin is more concerned with defining what liberty or freedom means than with prescribing how much of it we should enjoy. However, this distinction becomes hazy at the edges.[2]

In February and March 1952, Berlin had delivered the Mary Flexner Lectures at Bryn Mawr College, Pennsylvania, assembling for the first time his vision of the passage from Enlightenment to Romantic ideas of freedom. By his interpretation, Enlightenment rationalism supposed that conflicts between values were a heritage of ignorance or injustice and could be swept away by education, by rational reforms, by demonstrating that individual interests could be fully realised by working exclusively for the common good. Both Rousseau and Robespierre envisaged a state in which freedom was experienced as submission to rational necessity. The stand taken by Berlin – it became his trademark – was against the claims of philosophers, social engineers and revolutionaries who professed to understand men's objective needs and aspirations better than they did themselves.

Late in life Berlin told an interviewer:

Hegel and Marx saw history as a play with a dénouement, but like Herzen I do not believe in a libretto, nor history as a theme created by God or Nature, not a carpet with a recognizable pattern. . . . I see no reason to see history as an autobahn from which major deviations cannot occur. I am interested in Vico's and Herder's beliefs in the plurality of culture, each with its own centre of gravity – in a variety of cultures with different, novel, unpredicted outlooks and conflicting attitudes . . . Voltaire thought of history as a kind of continuous progress of reason and knowledge . . . broken by terrible interruptions – collapses into barbarism – e.g. the superstitious Christian Middle Ages. I see no incremental progression. . . . Can anybody in the twentieth century – certainly one of the worst centuries of human history – really believe in uninterrupted human progress?[3]

How does this relate to liberty? Berlin means that I am free when I am able to do what I want to do, not what someone tells me I ought to want to do, or what is in my best interests. My ontology is singular, so is my liberty. I am not a member of a choir singing to a libretto created by God, by Nature or by History.

'Two Concepts of Liberty', his inaugural lecture as Oxford's Chichele professor, was an event – the present writer expectantly attended as an undergraduate before withdrawing to a cell meeting of grumbling *enragés* and egalitarians in the Cadena café. Delivered in Oxford's Examination Schools Building on 31 October 1958, it attracted a record audience and was relayed to an overspill in the North School. Striving to slow his machine-gun delivery, Berlin spoke for an hour and ten minutes. His thesis was in its essence not original and had been broadly anticipated six years earlier by J.L. Talmon, of the Hebrew University, Jerusalem, in his *Origins of Totalitarian Democracy*, which describes two antithetical types of democracy, 'liberal and totalitarian'. According to Talmon, an admirer of Alexis de Tocqueville, the liberal approach assumes politics to be a matter of trial and error, while regarding political systems not as super-solutions but at best as pragmatic contrivances of human ingenuity and spontaneity. The totalitarian democratic school, by contrast, is based upon the assumption of a sole and exclusive truth in politics, which Talmon termed 'political Messianism' in the sense that 'it postulates a preordained, harmonious and perfect scheme of things. It widens the scope of politics to embrace the whole of human existence.' The liberal school, Talmon argued, defines liberty as the absence of coercion – whereas the totalitarian-democratic trend 'believes it is to be realized only in the pursuit and attainment of an absolute collective purpose'.[4]

As Berlin defines 'negative' liberty, 'You lack political liberty or freedom only if you are prevented from attaining a goal by human beings. Mere incapacity to attain a goal is not lack of political freedom.' Here he quotes Helvetius: 'it is not lack of freedom not to fly like an eagle or swim like a whale.' In other words, human underprivilege does not of itself amount to a lack of freedom. A realistic approach to life always involves a choice between competing values, between the claims of justice and mercy, between liberty and equality: 'To avoid glaring inequality or widespread misery I am ready to sacrifice some, or all, of my freedom . . . but it is freedom that I am giving up. Everything is what it is: liberty is liberty, not equality or fairness or justice or human happiness or a quiet conscience.' It may in certain circumstances be desirable for society to reduce freedom in the interests of equality or social justice – but this does not entail substituting one freedom for another. Berlin does not argue that freedom is necessarily what all people in all circumstances most urgently desire: 'The Egyptian peasant needs clothes or medicine before, and more than, personal liberty, but the minimum freedom that he needs today, and the greater degree of freedom that he may need tomorrow, is not some species of freedom peculiar to him, but identical with that of professors, artists and millionaires.'[5]

Here one may pause to consider the case of a law forbidding the employment of children as chimney-sweeps. Can one say that the benefiting child gains in social justice but not in freedom? More generally, does not the human impact of economic exploitation incur a reduction of freedom? Berlin agrees that the freedom of some must at times be curtailed to secure the freedom of others, the abolition of slave-ownership being an obvious example. Where's the difference? Perhaps the child chimney-sweep can be distinguished from the indentured slave in so far as the child is notionally 'free' to say no, to refuse the work, yet if the child were *really* 'free' to refuse, he would. For him, economic necessity is every bit as dominant a taskmaster as the slave-owner's shackles.

But Berlin is right that if the slaves (or chimney-sweeps) rebel, break free and establish their own republic, this will not guarantee 'negative' freedom. Using the word 'democratic' in its original Greek sense, the rule of the 'demos', Berlin points out: 'But there is no necessary connexion between individual liberty and democratic rule.'[6] John Stuart Mill, he adds, had spoken of the tyranny of the majority. To ensure true democracy we need to incorporate the liberal notion of minority rights and individual liberty through the rule of law – civil or human rights being essential 'negative' liberties codified.

'Positive freedom', by contrast to 'negative liberty', is to do with our desire to be part of the community that makes decisions, but Berlin immediately injects into the tradition of positive freedom the Platonist-Hegelian notion of the 'true' or 'higher' self which is schoolmaster to our childlike desires. Berlin calls this a 'monstrous impersonation, which . . . is at the heart of all political theories of self-realization'. He quotes Kant: 'Nobody may compel me to be happy in his own way. Paternalism is the greatest despotism imaginable.'[7] Berlin is here challenging 'the metaphysical heart of rationalism', by which social and historical 'laws' are first 'discovered', then held to be immutable, like the laws of physics. Anyone who opposes or ignores these 'laws' is contemptuously dismissed as no more 'free' than the lemming who believes he will sprout wings when he reaches the edge of the cliff. 'This is the positive doctrine of liberation by reason . . . at the heart of many of the nationalist, communist, authoritarian, and totalitarian creeds of our day', leading to 'an authoritarian state obedient to the directives of an élite of Platonic guardians'.[8] He quotes the Bolshevik leader Nikolai Bukharin: 'Proletarian coercion, in all its forms, from executions to forced labour, is, paradoxical as it may sound, the method of moulding communist humanity out of the human material of the capitalist period.'

Soviet Russia is the most conspicuous contemporary example of the imposition of 'positive freedom'. Never a 'Sovietologist', Berlin tended to attack Soviet totalitarianism at its philosophical roots rather than by detailing its actual behaviour. He regarded the absolute optimism that Marx inherited from the Enlightenment as not only flawed but potentially murderous – this went for all monist doctrines insisting that 'knowledge' led to a single, unitary truth that subsumed all conflicting moral values. Berlin admired Hume, who knew how to call a thing what it was – whereas metaphysicians like Marx had collapsed the categories, then rolled them up into a single, overriding concept of 'liberty', utterly contemptuous of the individual and totally determined to dictate what was best for everybody: in Rousseau's phrase, men must be forced to be free.

Berlin, however, recognises that freedom cannot be discussed purely in terms of individuals. Man experiences himself within society and in terms of the categories he belongs to (sex, class, race, occupation, language, religion); therefore his or her desire for more freedom may in the first instance take the form of a demand for greater recognition, respect or status for the categories to which he belongs. 'It is this desire for reciprocal recognition that leads the most authoritarian democracies to be, at times, consciously preferred by its members to the most enlightened oligarchies.'[9] But, he warns, this yearning for social status should not be confused with freedom. This confusion is a powerful weapon for dictators.

Berlin's heritage, as he explains, lies with Benjamin Constant, Jefferson, Burke, Paine and Mill. Each compiled a different catalogue of individual liberties 'but the argument for keeping authority at bay is always substantially the same'. This, in Mill's terms, is the only way to sustain progress, originality, moral courage, spontaneity – the only way to prevent men being crushed by 'collective mediocrity'.[10]

Authentic liberty is therefore that which allows each autonomous human being to decide what is best for him and what he shall do. When Marxists or socialists insist that the poor man is not 'free' to dine at the Ritz, Berlin replies, 'Yes, he is, if he can find the money. And if he cannot find the money, it is not his freedom which is curtailed but the economic means to translate his freedom into the desired action.' By contrast, if a man finds revolutionary guards posted outside the Ritz, turning back anyone who wishes to dine there, then his freedom is curtailed. Loss of 'freedom' occurs only when one is thwarted by the deliberate actions of other humans. Somebody must be intentionally stopping you doing what you want to do. The legless man may lack the capacity to walk, but not the 'freedom' to do so. Berlin quotes Rousseau: 'The nature of things does not madden us – only ill will does.'[11]

So one may ask in passing whether the (obviously deliberate) refusal of members of the St James's Club to admit Berlin to membership (which he obviously wanted) in 1950 diminished his negative liberty. If not, how did their veto differ in category terms from that of the Red Guards posted outside the Ritz and physically barring entry? Or have we stumbled across a new factor: can it be that when by definition not every candidate can be granted member-ship of a football team or club or a first-class degree, then the applicant's liberty is not involved? His desires or ambitions, although deliberately thwarted by other human beings, are nevertheless not to be confused with his liberty?

Berlin does, however, acknowledge that the man who lacks the means to buy a loaf of bread is as little able to have the loaf as if it were forbidden him by law. This brings us back to slaves and child chimney-sweeps. Here Berlin wobbles nervously: 'unable' to buy bread means 'unfree' to do so only if the man is, or believes himself to be, deliberately deprived by others, by the social system, of the money to buy the bread. Berlin's general argument is now in deep trouble: the notion of a *deliberate* victimisation of the man without bread yields to a deprivation for which society may be held morally responsible. On this question Berlin was to waver.[12]

Who is to define 'deliberately'? What is meant by the 'deliberate' thwarting of one man's wishes by another? Have not the ruling classes invariably, every-where, deceived themselves about what the lower orders in their employment want, or can reasonably want? In C.B. Macpherson's essay 'Berlin's Division of Liberty', Berlin is held to understate the role of impediments to liberty, i.e. 'lack of access to the means of life and the means of labour'. Berlin wavers by arguing that a causal relation between a man's unfreedom and wider economic arrange-ments lies within the mind and is a matter of disputable doctrinal interpreta-tion, e.g. the socialist view. Macpherson asks what thinker of repute would deny the link between poverty and social arrangements – certainly not Adam Smith, Bentham, Mill or Green (with the possible exception of Malthus).[13] Berlin's negative liberty, or the loss of it, is confined to 'deliberately' intended coercion by the state or other individuals, and does not embrace dominance and subser-vience that may not be 'intended' or 'deliberate' but is a result of the prevailing system of property (laws of property and contract).

In Macpherson's view – and he is right – lack of access to the means of life and labour is by definition an impediment to freedom. It reduces negative liberty since dependence on others for a living 'diminishes the area in which they cannot be pushed around'. In his introduction to his *Four Essays* (where he seems to merge 'negative liberty' with 'pluralism'), Berlin implicitly replied to such criticisms by arguing that the condition of the nineteenth-century working class made their legal freedoms 'an odious mockery' – yet he still insisted that these conditions did not deprive them of liberty but only of some of the conditions of liberty. Conflicts of values are inevitable: likely to conflict with negative liberty are such laudable aims as equality, justice, status, prosperity, power, fraternity, public order, democracy and efficiency. Thus Berlin still refuses to bracket lack of access to liberty alongside coercive impediments to liberty. No, lack of access is a question of justice or equality. Indeed, Berlin adds waspishly, reformers and revolutionaries have been so preoccupied by creating the conditions for freedom that they have forgotten freedom itself.[14]

In *The Political Theory of Possessive Individualism: Hobbes to Locke* (1962), Macpherson pinpointed what he called 'the dilemma of modern liberal-democratic theory . . . it must continue to use the assumptions of possessive individualism, at a time when the structure of market society no longer provides the necessary conditions for deducing a valid theory of political obligation from those assumptions'.[15] The monist, totalitarian version of positive liberty – Stalinism, for example – comes into being 'only after long-continued and intensive refusal of the beneficiaries of unequal institutions, on a world-wide scale, to permit any moves to alter the institutions in the direction of more nearly equal powers'.[16] (Where reformism fails, revolution follows.) Macpherson also argues that of the three senses of positive liberty provided by Berlin, the third, 'conscious self-direction, the right to be my own master, even if only collectively', cannot logically be distinguished from his 'negative liberty'.

Berlin also came under criticism from two younger colleagues at All Souls, Charles Taylor and G.A. Cohen (the latter succeeded to Berlin's Chichele chair with Berlin's support). Cohen commented that not uncommon in liberal circles was the idea that Roosevelt's New Deal (much admired by Berlin) reduced liberty for the sake of economic security. 'I contend that no coherent concept of individual liberty justifies these descriptions. When a man's economic security is enhanced, there typically are, *as a result*, fewer "obstacles to possible choices and activities" for him. . . . My criticism of Isaiah Berlin respects his distinction between liberty and the conditions for it . . . of which economic security is one. I do not say that economic security *is* liberty, but that typically, and certainly in the context of Berlin's comment, it causes liberty to increase, just as equality in education (also not a form of liberty) does, to take Berlin's own example.'[17]

In 'What's Wrong with Negative Liberty', Charles Taylor argued that Berlin's thesis not only separated external impediments to freedom from freedom itself, but also internal impediments such as ignorance, false consciousness and psychological repression. (We are thinking here of hat-doffing servants and serfs.) According to Taylor, we can't say that someone is free if, for instance, he is totally unaware of his potential or he is paralysed by the fear of breaking with some norm that he has internalised but that does not authentically reflect him.[18]

According to the more abrasive critic Perry Anderson, *Two Concepts of Liberty* was 'the most influential text of its genre'. With Berlin, said Anderson, political theory becomes a timeless elucidation of concepts, separated from any historical or sociological context. Berlin's 'two eponymous concepts' produced two opposing lineages which functioned somewhat like genealogies in the Bible. Anderson dismissed the genealogies as 'capricious'.[19] Berlin, he said, was peddling 'a manichean morality tale, whose teleological outcome is the present struggle of the free world against totalitarian communism'. Clearly influenced by Macpherson's work, Anderson noted that Berlin mentioned the word property just twice in *Two Concepts of Liberty* – and it played no role in his conceptual analysis.

As Berlin's critics, including friendly ones, have pointed out, damaging ambiguities attend his central notion of an autonomous individual will permitted or not permitted by others to do what it wants to do. Should we apply this 'I want' to the expressed desires of children or lunatics in danger of harming themselves? Do we deprive a drunk of his freedom if we physically impede his intended passage across a street despite fast-moving traffic? Mill himself argues that liberty should be accorded only to a man 'in the maturity of his faculties' – not to those lacking the proper stage of moral and intellectual development. One may add that every adult knows that a law banning smacking is a curtailment of liberty, while every child knows that the same ban is an extension of liberty. The legal age at which a child becomes an adult and is granted autonomy is always arbitrary. We used to conscript young men and send them to their deaths, while denying them a vote on grounds of immaturity. Or take the case of the perfectly sane adult pedestrian who insists on crossing a footbridge in defiance of a policeman's warning that it is too damaged and dangerous to cross safely. Does the policeman infringe the pedestrian's 'negative liberty' if he forcibly restrains him? George Crowder points out that if Berlin were to admit that internal constraints – ignorance, illusion, fear – vitiate a person's negative liberty, this would open the door to the notion of the 'divided self' and the insistence of the monists who claim to understand how people authentically *ought* to be. However, it turns out that the dichotomy between 'negative' liberty (I want to be free to do whatever I want at a given moment) and 'positive' liberty (you insist that I am drunk, drugged, in shock, under age or suffering from dementia) is rarely neatly perforated. Entirely non-Stalinist societies have equated suicide (perhaps the ultimate exercise of an autonomous free will) with 'unsound mind'. As the joke goes, it used to be punished by death.

It is reliably said that during Isaiah Berlin's youth his pampering mother used to rouse him from sleep with the question, 'What are we going to do today?' To which the answer was: 'Nothing.' Perhaps Marie Berlin became the nicest kind of Stalin in his subconscious.

We may also note that the kind of representative democracy on the Western model implicitly approved of by Berlin contains more than a hint of Platonic guardianship. The individual citizen is granted the right to elect a member of the legislature – but, once elected, the MP is under no legal obligation to heed the views of his constituents. Popular referendums on major issues of principle were unknown in Britain in 1958, when Berlin delivered his lecture. Underpinning this non-mandatory parliamentary system is not only the belief that regular, decision-making gatherings of the whole people on the Greek model or Rousseau's are impracticable – but also the conviction that the elect are better placed than the electors to understand the issues and to interpret the interests of the community. The individual citizen must delegate, and thus derogate, his liberty to say yes or no to legislation, including measures designed to restrict civil liberties and the 'negative' freedoms. Further delegation to the executive occurs within Parliament under the Royal Prerogative but Berlin is not found registering a complaint.

Two Concepts of Liberty was a full-frontal attempt to copyright the precious notions of freedom and liberty in the name of Liberalism. The significance of this in terms of Cold War ideology was clear to all parties, from the Congress for Cultural Freedom to Isaac Deutscher. For Marxists like Deutscher, freedom, equality and economic emancipation were inseparable. Bourgeois 'freedom' was a sham: as Anatole France had observed, the destitute are free to sleep under the bridges of the Seine. The relevant question was who owned what. But Berlin (and to some degree Deutscher, too) recognised that under the Soviet system 'who owns what' had transmuted into 'who governs whom'.

The question arises: have socialists correctly diagnosed Berlin's doctrine as an apology for economic *laissez-faire* and a market economy? George Crowder believes not because Berlin, as a value-pluralist, granted that the relief of poverty might take precedence over complete liberty. Crowder quotes Berlin as saying that unrestrained capitalist competition has led historically to 'brutal violations . . . of basic human rights', while referring to 'the bloodstained story of economic individualism'.[20] In later years Berlin (privately) deplored Thatcherism and hoped for a return to the values and economic strategies of Roosevelt's New Deal, which he had always admired.

This granted, the fact remains that *Two Concepts of Liberty* appeared at the time to involve a condemnation of state-managed economies as recipes for despotism. Berlin vividly related a Moscow reception in 1945, when he was dressed down by Mme Afinogenova, 'a handsome lady who had been one of Lenin's secretaries and was married to a famous Soviet writer'. She told him: 'We are a scientifically governed society, and if there is no room for free thinking in physics – a man who questions the laws of motion is obviously ignorant or mad – why should we, Marxists, who have discovered the laws of history and society, permit free thinking in the social sphere? Freedom to be wrong is not freedom; you seem to think that we lack freedom of political discussion; I simply do not understand what you mean. Truth liberates: we are freer than you in the West.'[21] Berlin had since returned to the USSR one more time, and found such attitudes still in place when he wrote *Two Concepts of Liberty*. For Berlin, only pluralism, enshrined civil liberties and a separation of powers could prevent dictatorship and Orwellian uniformity. This may have been why Jenifer Hart heard the word 'rot' from Berlin's 1963 lecture audience when – as we can assume from his 'The Question of Machiavelli' (1971) – he audaciously described the Florentine author of *The Prince* and *The Discourses* as 'one of the makers of pluralism and … acceptance of toleration', claiming that Machiavelli had exploded the myth of 'the ultimate compatibility of all genuine values' – the cardinal sin assigned by Berlin to the Enlightenment. Hart's companions doubtless objected that *The Prince* offered the Medici a prescription for violent autocracy. For Deutscher, on another wavelength, the Western call for pluralism in the Soviet Union entailed the restoration of private property and the loss of collective liberty.

John Gray has remarked that, for Berlin, mankind has no common destiny. He rejects the Enlightenment idea that cultural diversity is transitory; on the contrary, it is the propensity to cultural difference that is most essentially human. This is the radical anthropological form of his value-pluralism. He does not reject the Enlightenment's moral commitment to human emancipation, he rejects the delusive anthropology. Does Berlin therefore deny the existence of 'natural justice' and 'fundamental rights' as universal values? Within the terms of his philosophy, logically it must be so: 'justice' and 'rights' are subjective desires falsely fortified by the claim that they are inherently inscribed on the human condition. But if in practice Berlin does grant the reality of moral progress (the abolition of slavery, of serfdom, the acceptance of a universal franchise), as he indeed does, on what principle is that 'progress' to be recognised as such if not as a movement, a trajectory, in the direction of universal values? If Berlin finds himself accepting such values, he is himself an advanced product of the post-seventeenth-century rationalist Enlightenment that he refuses to embrace.[22]

Berlin wants the diversity of communities and cultures to prevail over a homogeneous, monist and universal prescription. Empathy and understanding must replace rationalist bullying. For this reason he finds more acceptable the illiberal cultures practised by self-enclosed communities – for example, Hindus, Shintoists, Orthodox Jews – than the universalist claims of illiberal Marxist, utilitarian, Platonist, Christian or Muslim theologies. One must therefore ask him this: to what human units should the demand for negative liberty properly apply? Suppose a broadly pluralistic European society harbours ethnic or religious minorities who exercise extreme patriarchal power, who do not educate female children, who practise female circumcision, who impose forced marriages or who in some extreme cases torture children to rid them by voodoo of evil spirits? Is the young Muslim or Hindu girl, who is destined for a marriage she does not want, first and foremost a member of an inviolable, semi-sovereign 'community' – or an individual entitled to equal rights with the nation's other girls?

In summary: the exaggerated emphasis on the role of articulated ideas, of philosophy, in human history is incarnated in Berlin's view that the Enlightenment has given us scientism, technocracy and ultimately Soviet totalitarianism. Here the role of the Word is deified. Marx reads the Enlightenment philosophers and Hegel, Lenin reads Marx, Stalin reads Lenin. Books become as potent as the rays of the sun. But history is not made in libraries and philosophy is only one minor component of the ideology that promotes or justifies actual behaviour. To claim that Stalin's five-year plans were ultimately the product of the Enlightenment's monist-utopian faith in science or 'scientism' requires a parallel explanation for Henry Ford and Krupp. To view Soviet collectivisation as the product of philosophical monism requires a parallel explanation for the ruthless colonisation of North America and Australia, not forgetting the slave trade.

And how should we explain the horrors of the First World War? Was the war fever that possessed Berlin, Vienna, St Petersburg, Paris, London, Istanbul and Rome really a product of Isaiah Berlin's counter-Enlightenment, the romantic affirmation of instinct, force, nationalism, unreason? The British cabinet in 1914 had not been reading Maistre or Nietzsche before pressing its young men into a slaughter more extensive than the one generated by the 'monist-utopian' mind of Lenin. The general flaw in recent theoretical studies of Berlin is that they replicate his own abstract vocabulary and categories, pursuing him into orbit above actual history without ever touching down.

11

THE HEDGEHOG AND THE FOX

BERLIN SEEMED DRAWN magnetically to dualities and dichotomies, to starkly opposing outlooks arrayed like medieval armies. Here we meet the hedgehog (who knows one big thing) and the fox (who knows many things). The odd thing is that he always insisted on the sheer complexity, the irreducible variousness and multiplicity of human life – yet apparently found irresistible the impulse to boil it down to starkly opposing schools of thought. However, as he ventured deeper into the tunnel of a dichotomy – or suffered informed criticism – he tended to retreat. In *The Hedgehog and the Fox* (1953), he begins by drawing his dichotomy with impressive assurance – but not for long.

'There is a line among the fragments of the Greek poet Archilochus which says: "The fox knows many things, but the hedgehog knows one big thing."' Berlin comments that, taken figuratively, these words may indicate

one of the deepest differences which divide writers and thinkers, and, it may be, human beings in general. For there exists a great chasm between those, on one side, who relate everything to a single central vision, one system less or more coherent or articulate, in terms of which they understand, think and feel – a single organising, universal principle in terms of which alone all that they are and say has significance – and, on the other side, those who pursue many ends, often unrelated and even contradictory, connected, if at all, only in some *de facto* way, for some psychological or physiological cause, related by no moral or aesthetic principle; these last lead lives, perform acts, and entertain ideas that are centrifugal rather than centripetal, their thought is scattered or defused, moving on many levels, seizing upon the essence of a vast variety of experiences and objects for what they are in themselves, without, consciously or unconsciously, seeking to fit them into, or exclude them from, any one unchanging, all-embracing, sometimes self-contradictory and incomplete, at times fanatical, unitary inner vision.

Coming up for air, the reader would be hard-pressed to pass an exam on what has actually been said. To hack deep into this thicket is to risk never coming out. But we notice straight away that Berlin has signalled 'one of the deepest differences which divide writers and thinkers, and, it may be, human beings'. It is not unlike being warned that humans can be divided into extroverts and introverts – worrying for all of us. But while we are still anxiously feeling our backsides for a fox-like tail, or the top of our heads for the stiff defensive bristles of Mr Hedgehog, we find that Berlin is close to abandoning his dichotomy. 'Of course,' he writes, 'like all over-simple classifications of this type, the dichotomy becomes, if pressed, artificial, scholastic and ultimately absurd. But if it is not an aid to serious criticism, neither should it be rejected as being merely superficial or frivolous.'[1] (Well, you could equally argue that all mankind can be divided by temperament and belief into Cavaliers and Roundheads, an entertaining party game until you confess engagingly that you did not really mean it.)

Berlin was aware that many would have regarded him as the quintessential nimble, quick-witted fox, but at a deeper level he was in quest of the one big truth essential to hedgehogs. He did not take full possession of it until the Cold War imposed a choice and the intellectual elaboration of that choice. A nice example of the nimble fox at work is Berlin's letter to Alan Pryce-Jones, editor of the *TLS*, on behalf of this particular 'little book': 'Don't send my Büchlein to some grim literary strigil – but to someone imaginative and humane: yourself! Yourself! Yourself! Why not?' Pryce-Jones responded by handing it over to E.H. Carr, a strigil who duly scraped away at Berlin's listed literary hedgehogs and foxes. Berlin reported to Noel Annan that Carr had tried to be polite about his book – but 'is too philistine & cheaply political to understand much anyhow: I like him but he is a hopelessly mediocre vulgarian all the same.'[2]

Berlin once told the present writer that he would rather be a great novelist (he named Tolstoy) than a great philosopher (more oddly he named Hegel). When he frowns on Tolstoy the hedgehog in *War and Peace* he is really censuring Tolstoy's panoramic musings on history, 'a coherent, sometimes elegantly contrived, but always fictitious construction'. By contrast, Tolstoy excites and convinces when he depicts 'real life – the actual, everyday, "live" experience of individuals'. It is hard to visualise what would have emerged had Berlin chosen to be a novelist, and who would have been his Pyotr, his Andrei, his Natasha, his count, his prince, his young countess. As a political theorist he found in himself the Paradoxical Hedgehog – time and again he comes back to one big thing: namely, that big things are recipes for travail and tyranny.

In *The Hedgehog and the Fox*, Berlin then passes on to what he admires and dislikes in modern novelists. He touches on Virginia Woolf (whom he met in the 1930s and admired):

> Utterly unlike her as he is in almost every other respect, Tolstoy is, per- haps, the first to propound the celebrated accusation which Virginia Woolf levelled against the public prophets of her own generation – Shaw and Wells and Arnold Bennett – blind materialists who did not begin to understand what it is that life truly consists of, who mistook its outer accidents, the unimportant aspects which lie outside the individual soul – the so-called social, economic, political realities – for that which alone is genuine, the individual experience, the specific relations of individuals to one another, the colours, smells, tastes, sounds, and movements, the jealousies, loves, hatreds, passions, the rare flashes of insight, the transforming moments, the ordinary day-to-day succession of private data which constitute all there is – which are reality.[3]

We can scarcely doubt that Berlin is associating his own sensibility with the one he attributes to Virginia Woolf, yet she did not, for example, regard the historic condition of women in general as more 'unreal' than the patter of a butterfly's wings on a hot windowpane. But when she wanted to let her hair down about the plight of women in general, she deliberately chose to discard fiction in favour of polemic: e.g. *A Room of One's Own* (1929). She did not, as Berlin asserts, accuse what we may call the social writers, Shaw, Wells and Bennett, those 'blind materialists', of writing about mere 'outer accidents which lie outside the individual soul'; indeed, the wife of Leonard Woolf increasingly read widely about social and political issues, and was not reluctant to deliver lectures or speeches from time to time. Her complaint against Shaw, Wells and Bennett was aesthetic and modernist: what is the proper domain of 'imagina- tive' writing? When she sat with her pen poised over the head of Mrs Dalloway, her character's direct experience of walking along Piccadilly must not in the next breath be 'explained' in terms of some overarching theory about wealth and privilege. Here Berlin was at one with her. But in Woolf's fiction the neces- sary servants (without whom many of the delicate reveries would have to give way to the washing of floors) exist only as trees stand in the garden. And the maids' 'souls' might well be permeated by such 'outer accidents' as their low wages and hours of work. One imagines that Isaiah Berlin never in his life cooked his own dinner, never washed his own underwear, not as a bachelor, not as a married man. (But I may be inexcusably wrong; he may have been in the high-street laundromat every other day while reading Hume.)

When we consider Berlin's embrace of the 'individual experience' in fiction, 'the specific relations of individuals to one another', as found in the novels of Tolstoy and Woolf, one is bound to notice that their upfront individual characters belonged to that small minority of the population who did not have to launder their own clothes, light fires on cold mornings, clean their own boots, harness and groom the horses, or slave in the kitchen to provide meal after meal. Likewise Proust. While visiting Russia in 1945, Berlin shocked his hosts by confessing that he had never read James Aldridge or Walter Greenwood. In Greenwood's memorable *Love on the Dole* (1933), the individual 'souls' are almost totally invaded by such 'outer accidents' as poverty, the declining level of the dole and the fear of being laid off. And this, surely, is what the 'social' novelists and playwrights, Shaw, Wells, Bennett, Zola and Gorky, were at pains to illustrate. Berlin did not share these pains: what he heard was the threatening voices of the apostles of progress and reason, that long, straight avenue that leads to the guillotine. When Sheila Grant Duff told him that the sight of the hunger marchers tramping through Oxford made her ashamed to be living in the ivory tower, he reprimanded her for 'Tolstoyan sentimentalism'.

Berlin recalled the strained exchange in Moscow: 'What could I say about them? I realised that these [Aldridge and Greenwood] were names of contemporary writers, but confessed that I had never heard of them . . . – what had they written? This was clearly not believed.' He later discovered that their works had been translated and published in large editions in Russia. 'It was my impression that my hosts thought that I was less than honest when I said I knew nothing of these two authors whom they mentioned, because I was an agent of a capitalist power, and therefore obliged to ignore the merits of left-wing writers, much as they themselves were committed to pretended ignorance of most émigré Russian writers and composers.'[4] This was a somewhat self-serving defence; he was not so much 'an agent of a capitalist power' as a coddled bourgeois.

Nowhere in Berlin's extensive corpus of critical writing about works of fiction do we find a study of a novelist or playwright who chose a proletarian or 'lowlife' setting. Where is Maksim Gorky's *Mother* or *The Lower Depths*? Of course, Berlin is wide awake to the social and political dilemmas, the agonising choices, conveyed, for example, by Turgenev. Yet these choices all belong, in Turgenev, to characters who can expect to find their hot breakfast waiting for them in the morning, the horses saddled for their day's journey to the trembling frontier of a notional rebellion. The 'nihilist' character Bazarov may display his rationalist modernity by collecting insects for microscopic examination, and by discounting God, but he would not dream of cleaning his own boots: ' "Come, hurry up, bushy beard!" said Bazarov, addressing the driver.' Reaching Arkady Kirsanov's home, Bazarov speaks abruptly to the father: ' "Only give orders for my little box to be taken there [to his room], and this garment, too," he added, taking off his frieze overcoat.'[5]

Love on the Dole should have been known to any young British intellectual with an interest in contemporary literature – not least one embarking on a study of Karl Marx. Admittedly, it was a first novel by an unknown writer, self-educated and raised in that unknowable region (except to Orwell), industrial Lancashire. But on publication *Love on the Dole* was widely praised and hailed as authentic and powerful by the *Manchester Guardian*. A stage version earned the plaudits of *The Times*. A bestseller, taken up in the USA, translated into Russian, the novel describes grinding, merciless poverty in Hanky Park (Salford) at the height of the Depression, with three million unemployed, the apprentices of Marley's thrown out of work as soon as they qualified, the National Government reducing the dole from 17s.5d. to 15 shillings while imposing family means tests to deprive individuals even of that. Compared to the novels of Virginia Woolf, *Love on the Dole* falls short on psychological subtlety, offering stock characters who serve as ciphers for an essentially documentary report on a desperate world where every two-up, two-down, or one-up, one-down, is a scene of grim overcrowding, penny-counting, family relationships ground down into acrimony. Yet Walter Greenwood's novel enjoyed sufficient popular impact to inspire debates in the press and questions in Parliament about the benefit system. These evidently escaped Isaiah Berlin's attention.

One can see why the Russians eagerly translated this unequivocal indictment of British capitalism, and of the feeble capitulation of the Labour Party to form a National Government, although the revolutionary perspectives of the Communist Party are missing from the novel and the conclusion is one of hopeless despair. No doubt the Soviet edition omitted Greenwood's prefatory quotation from Rosa Luxemburg's prison letters, she being under Stalin another 'Trotskyite', but perhaps the accompanying quotation from D.H. Lawrence was retained: 'Oh, it's time the whole thing was changed, absolutely. And the men will have to do it – you've got to smash money and this beastly possessive spirit. I get more revolutionary every minute, but for *life's* sake.'

Since Berlin was writing his study of Marx in the 1930s, *Love on the Dole* might have usefully drawn his attention to how little British industrial relations had changed since Friedrich Engels published his *The Condition of the Working Class in England* in 1844. Yes, the working class now enjoyed the vote but what use was it to them when the press spoke of 'economic cycles' and 'downturns' as if they were cyclones or floods beyond human control? (Which brings us back to Berlin's *Two Concepts of Liberty*.) Greenwood's leading character, Harry Hardcastle, can bring home £1 a week if he is lucky, receiving back from his mother 2s.6d. pocket money. This was the normal amount wagered on bets in the All Souls common room – A.L. Rowse tells us that the common room betting book went back to 1815. In 1934, Isaiah Berlin bet Rowse 2s.6d. that, in the event of a war between Japan and Russia, if Japan won, Trotsky if alive would return to power (evidently forgotten twenty years later when Berlin derided Deutscher's exposition of Trotsky's position in 1928). On 11 May 1935, Douglas Jay bet Berlin the huge sum of £1.2s.6d., at three to one, that Dr Kurt Schuschnigg would no longer be chancellor of Austria on Encaenia Day 1936. Meanwhile, in Hanky Park, Harry Hardcastle ventures into betting shops only in the desperate hope of picking up a fag end not yet burnt out.[6]

(So would Dr Kurt Schuschnigg still be chancellor on Encaenia Day? Every summer, at the close of the university year, a degree-giving ceremony in Christopher Wren's Sheldonian Theatre is followed by a vast luncheon in All Souls, the new 'doctors' splendid in scarlet, the tables laden with silver and flowers extending the length of the vast Codrington Library. The present writer recalls such an occasion in the early 1960s as Harold Macmillan, prime minister and chancellor of the university, led the exodus after lunch on to the smooth turf of the Hawksmoor quadrangle, attended by Warden Sparrow and Sir Isaiah Berlin, the great and the good. I gawped at the regal spectacle while nursing a thought: that All Souls' vast wealth was about to come under public scrutiny. Berlin and I sat on the same policy committee – which way would he lean? But that is another story.)

If Isaiah Berlin would rather be Tolstoy than Hegel, he certainly did not endorse Tolstoy's polemics in *What Is Art?*. Tolstoy denounced the upper-class fallacy that art is the quest for beauty, resulting in an elitist art celebrating hedonism and sensuality, yet unintelligible to the majority of mankind. He had no time for the powerful modernist current that runs from his *bêtes noires*, Baudelaire, Verlaine and Mallarmé, the Symbolists and Decadents, to the French Impressionists. The old man rejected modernism as a godless repudiation of a world previously held together by coherent meaning. The subject of true art must be the experiences of the majority of men, including the whole world of work: 'The life of a labouring man, with its endlessly varied forms of labour on sea and underground: his migrations, his intercourse with his employers, overseers and companions ... his struggles with nature and wild beasts, his association with domestic animals, his work in the forest, or on the steppe, in the field, in the garden, the orchard.' By contrast, 'almost all the feelings of people of our class amount to three very insignificant and simple feelings – the feeling of pride, the feeling of sexual desire, and the feeling of weariness of life'. These 'form almost the sole subject-matter of the art of the rich classes'. Among such contemporary writers he included Turgenev and Goncharev (who once told Tolstoy that after Turgenev's *Sportsman's Notebook* there was nothing left in peasant life to write about).[7]

This was not for Isaiah Berlin. Turgenev was his idol. He depicted Tolstoy as struggling to resolve irresolvable contradictions between innocence and education, the claims of spontaneity and those of obligation, as condemning upper-class values while being unable to escape from them.[8] Berlin admired Turgenev for his 'enlightened scepticism', for his condemnation of his hero Bazarov's arid 'nihilism' and philistine contempt for the arts, women and romantic love. Turgenev has Bazarov scornfully dismiss art, poetry and music: 'That's all romantic, nonsensical, aesthetic rot.' When he hears Arkady's father playing Schubert's *Expectation* with much feeling on the cello, Bazarov scoffs. After he catches the father reading Pushkin, he tells Arkady: ' "He's not a boy, you know; it's time to throw up that rubbish." ' Bazarov prefers German scientific books. In short, he is the ideologue, the 'fanatic', deeply distrusted by Turgenev and Berlin.[9]

Berlin's equation of materialism with philistinism is again apparent when he quotes Chernyshevsky: 'A pair of boots is something more important than all the plays of Shakespeare.' But Chernyshevsky was talking about the values of poor peasants; his essays on aesthetics offer an interesting – and at the time novel – materialist explanation for varying ideals of beauty. Marx himself was far from being a 'Bazarov'; indeed, he was a passionate admirer of the imaginative capability not only of the classical dramatists and Shakespeare, but also of the major historical novelists who created fictive personal relationships embodying the underlying reality of society. Soviet criticism certainly deplored any departure from Classical-Renaissance models of 'realism', closing the door to modernism, but no observer of the Soviet scene could deny the passionate devotion to art and literature by which, after all, singular individuals are depicted wrestling with conscience and morality. Berlin's version of materialism as blind or hostile to art carries something of the banality of statements frequently heard in his day from American politicians – that communists acknowledge no moral values because they are 'godless materialists'.

Berlin praises Turgenev's 'clear, finely discriminating, slightly ironical vision', 'his detachment, his inveterate habit of doing justice to the full complexity and diversity of goals, attitudes, beliefs'. Turgenev was a 'well-meaning, troubled, self-questioning liberal, witness to the complex truth'. The author of *Fathers and Children* and *Virgin Soil* was (like himself) repelled by all that was general, abstract, absolute: 'his vision remained delicate, sharp, concrete, and incurably realistic.' Berlin carried the implicit parallel further: 'Hegelianism, right-wing or left-wing, which he had imbibed as a student in Berlin, materialism, socialism, positivism, about which his friends ceaselessly argued, populism, collectivism, the Russian village commune . . . these came to seem mere abstractions to him, substitutes for reality . . . which life, with its uneven surface and irregular shapes of real human character and activity, would surely resist and shatter if ever a serious effort were made to translate them into practice.'[10]

But Turgenev's Russia was more dangerous for a writer than Virginia Woolf's England. He was living in the West when, in January 1863, he heard that he was the subject of a Senate enquiry. The summons to St Petersburg arrived in February. He wrote to the Tsar-Emperor himself expressing surprise and, because of his poor health, begging His Majesty to order that questions be sent to him in writing. Nine questions duly arrived through the Paris Embassy. The Senate was interested in his relationship with Bakunin, and with a leading St Petersburg radical, N.A. Serno-Solovievich, but mainly with the London exiles and Herzen's journal *The Bell*. Turgenev's replies are models of servile cringing. He appended letters from Herzen and Bakunin to demonstrate how far apart he was from them. He accused his friend Herzen of having learned to preach 'with the noisy exaggeration which characterizes sceptics when they become fanatics. I saw him ever more rarely, and felt more estranged from him every time.' (Berlin inherited Turgenev's appetite for the word 'fanatic'.) Moreover, Herzen, Turgenev continued, having become a republican and a socialist under the influence of Ogarev, no longer had anything in common 'with any right-thinking Russian, who did not separate the tsar from the people, or honest love of sensible freedom from the conviction of the necessity for the monarchical principle'.

Returning to St Petersburg in January 1864, Turgenev was duly interviewed by the Senate. A few days later he felt completely reassured when the chief of police spoke to him amicably at a grand party given by the Italian ambassador. He was free to return to Baden. Herzen, who thought his erstwhile friend had sold his soul, published a sardonic note in *The Bell* (15 January 1864): 'Our correspondent tells us about a certain grey-haired Magdalen (of the male sex) who wrote to the Emperor that she had lost sleep and appetite, her rest, her white hairs and her teeth, tortured by the thought that the Emperor does not yet know of the repentance which has overtaken her, on the strength of which "she has broken all connections with friends of her youth".'[11]

Herzen had supported the Polish rebellion of 1863, whereas Turgenev considered the uprising futile from the start: 'A revolt in the Kingdom can only do harm to Poland and to Russia, like every revolt and every conspiracy.' He consistently opposed violent means as ineffective as well as immoral. This went for his attitude to the 1848 revolution in Paris, the Polish rising of 1863, and the Paris Commune of 1871. Attempts on the life of Alexander II filled him with indignation. One of his biographers writes: 'Turgenev throughout his life remained a Hamlet who wished he had been born a Don Quixote.'[12] But these are rather noble analogies: perhaps he was a Malvolio who did not regret it. Perhaps he would have approved of Isaiah Berlin writing to Lady Eden in 1956, when Eden launched his military operation against Nasser, congratulating 'Anthony, if I may so call him', for having 'saved England'.

Herzen may have thought ill of Turgenev's panicky conduct, his kowtowing to the tsar, but Berlin deeply admired them both. He described Herzen as a 'revolutionary' but, on the whole, Herzen parted company with Russia's genuine revolutionaries and Berlin found himself captivated by Herzen's 'deep distrust (something that most of his allies did not share) of all general formulae as such, of the programmes and battle cries of all the political parties, of the great, official, historical goals – progress, liberty, equality, national unity, historic rights, human solidarity – principles and slogans in the name of which men had been, and doubtless would soon again be, violated and slaughtered, and their forms of life condemned and destroyed'. Herzen contrasted these abstract ideals 'with the concrete, short-term, immediate goals of identifiable living individuals'.[13]

After petitioning the new tsar to free the serfs and initiate bold reforms, Herzen issued a paean of praise to Alexander II: 'Thou hast Conquered, O Galilean.' The young Chernyshevsky, writing under the name 'A Russian', warned Herzen that 'Russia had been ruined for a hundred years past by believing in the good intentions of the Tsars'. Berlin empathised with his cruel predicament: 'Herzen realised that the criticism and abuse showered upon him as an obsolete aristocratic dilettante by these "nihilists" (as they came to be called after Turgenev's novel *Fathers and Children*, in which this conflict is vividly presented for the first time), was not altogether different from the disdain that he himself had felt in his own youth for the elegant and ineffective reformers of Alexander I's reign; but this did not make his position easier to bear.' Berlin shared Herzen's fear that the new barbarians would 'raze to the ground the edifices of their oppressors, and with them all that is most sublime and beautiful in Western civilization'.[14] He often cited Herzen's phrase, 'history has no libretto'.

E.H. Carr's study of Herzen (1933) makes clear the contempt in which he came to be held by Russian radicals. In an issue of *The Bell*, he attempted to pay tribute to Chernyshevsky, who suffered imprisonment, penal servitude, then exile for the rest of his life. Herzen claimed that there had never been antagonism between them. 'We served as the mutual complement of one another.' This olive branch provoked indignation among Geneva's Russian exiles. An open letter by Serno-Solovievich, privately printed at Vevey, mocked the claim: 'So you were the complement of Chernyshevsky! You marched shoulder to shoulder with Chernyshevsky! . . . Look more closely at what is going on around you, and you will then perhaps understand that dry leaves and paper snakes interest nobody . . . that you, Mr Herzen, are a dead man.'[15] Carr disputed Berlin's quasi-eulogy for Herzen, who 'ended in opposition to all causes he had once seemed to espouse. . . . Herzen was too well off and liked order and comfort too much. In his last years he reached the ultimate point of scepticism which rejects every remedy as potentially worse than the disease.' He remained an armchair critic 'while Bakunin, the fantastic visionary, became a prophet'. A letter from Berlin to Morton White (8 May 1956) describes Carr's review of his 'Herzen and Bakunin on Individual Liberty' as a 'hideously unfair attack upon me'.[16]

Tolstoy did not admire Turgenev. When mocking bogus revolutionaries, even reformers, Turgenev has a tendency to resort in his fiction to grotesque lampoon not infrequently laced with snobbery. At the end of part one of the late novel *Virgin Soil* this treatment is accorded to the dinner given for the young populist missionaries by the drunken and boastful merchant Golushkin, who orders up champagne: 'In frozen flakes and lumps it dropped from the neck of the bottle into the glasses. "To our . . . our enterprise!" cried Golushkin.' The lame Palkin 'soon saw what was required of him and began abusing everything . . . and everybody; conservatives, liberals, officials, barristers, judges, landowners, district councils, local assemblies, Moscow and Petersburg!' Golushkin then bawls, 'Everything is rotten with us, go where you will. . . .' No half-measures, the drunken diners agree, tear it all up by the roots! 'Vasya, drink, you dirty dog, drink!' Even our idealistic hero Nezhdanov gets drunk, declaring it time to 'act', enough of words, but then he contradicts himself by complaining that he finds no sympathy or understanding in the people themselves, the peasantry he has come to liberate. Meanwhile the dour revolutionary Markelov keeps up a monotonous, insistent drone, 'as if he were chopping cabbage'. Turgenev reduces their serious social concerns to incoherence: 'Like the first flakes of snow . . . words began flying, tumbling, jostling . . . progress, government, literature; the taxation question, the church question, the woman question, the law-court question; classicism,

realism, nihilism, communism; international, clerical, liberal, capital. . . .'
And more.[17]

Berlin loved it, lauding Turgenev's 'negative capability', the wide angles of
his vision: 'He faithfully described them all – the talkers, the idealists, the
fighters, the cowards, the reactionaries, and the radicals, sometimes, as in
Smoke, with biting political irony, but, as a rule, so scrupulously, with so much
understanding of all the overlapping tides of every question, so much unruf-
fled patience . . . that he angered almost everyone at some time.'[18] For Berlin
'angering almost everyone' was a self-awarded badge of honour. As he put it
when talking to the Iranian philosopher Ramin Jahanbegloo, 'But then everything I have written has usually been attacked from both sides, from the Right
and the Left, with equal vehemence.'[19]

Isaac Deutscher also liked to remark how he was attacked from all sides, by
Cold Warriors, by Stalinists, by True Trotskyists. But in his case it was true.

PART FOUR

RUSSIA BY DAY AND BY NIGHT

12

ANNA AKHMATOVA

THE BERLIN FAMILY had emigrated in 1920, when Isaiah was eleven. In the autumn of 1945 he returned to Russia for the first time, accredited to the British Embassy on a diplomatic passport. His mission was to assess the prevailing state of Soviet opinion, the lie of the land. Foreign Minister Molotov initially opposed his diplomatic accreditation with the comment, 'We don't want any of the old ones.' He therefore had to wait from June to September 1945 for official consent, and was duly accommodated in the embassy. This was to be his first close-up encounter with Stalin's domain – the experience was to fill him with fear and loathing, not least on behalf of members of the extended Berlin family who had remained in Soviet Russia. Dare he impose the risks of a visit on them?

Berlin's father, Mendel, businessman and timber merchant, had returned for the first time in October 1935, visiting his brother in Moscow. But subsequently tragedy had descended: Isaiah's grandfathers, an uncle, an aunt and three cousins were to be murdered by the Nazis in Riga in 1941. The last message the London family had received was from Isaiah's maternal grandfather, Solomon Volschonok, by way of a postcard dated January 1940, before the Red Army marched into Latvia and severed all communication with the outside world. In fluent English, Grandfather Solomon wrote, 'Let God help you with all the Good!', going on to enquire about 'Shaja' and informing them that in Riga there was nothing new to report. On the bottom left-hand corner of the postcard was affixed the swastika stamp of the German postal service. It was the last communication from the family in Riga. In July 1941, the German army drove out the retreating Russians; by November–December, the Jews had been rounded up by Latvian fascists and German police, then taken to pits on the outskirts of the city, shot and thrown into a mass grave. The Volschonoks and Schneersons perished, including both of Isaiah's grandfathers. He did not learn their fate until the end of the war.

His uncle Leo had settled in Moscow after the Revolution and was a professor of dietetics at the university. On two occasions in 1945 Isaiah slipped out of a ballet performance at half-time to visit Leo and his family in their 'cosy, cramped, book-lined refuge, full of Jewish cheer and Riga memories'. On his second visit he found the extended family assembled, including his uncles Samuel and Solomon, one in Red Army uniform, and his aunt Evgenia. But no one mentioned the loss of the entire family who had remained in Riga. This doleful subject was suppressed. Nor did the mild and charming Leo venture into political discussion. When Isaiah suggested that life as a university professor might not be so bad after all, Leo asked him pointedly whether he had ever visited Florence or Venice. Isaiah nodded. 'We would like to go there too,' Leo said.[1] But worse was to befall Uncle Leo.

At that time the fate of many Soviet writers taken in the purges remained unknown, or unclear, in the West. The Oxford classicist Maurice Bowra wrote to Berlin in the summer of 1945: 'Mandelstam is, I am pretty certain, dead, starved by being put bottom on the list for food tickets because of his disloyal verses. What about Akhmatova? Said to be alive in Leningrad.' (Mandelstam had in reality been executed seven years earlier; Bowra had translated some of Akhmatova's early poems and included them in his wartime collection of Russian verse.)[2] Berlin made and merited his own luck when he met Boris Pasternak and then Anna Akhmatova during his visit to the USSR: 'Even Pasternak and his friends were firmly convinced that there was a golden West where writers and critics of genius had created, and were creating, master-pieces concealed from them . . . by the rigid Soviet censors.' Broadly sharing this belief were other liberal writers to whom Berlin was introduced, Chukovsky, Marshak, Zoshchenko, musicians like Prokofiev, directors like Eisenstein and Tairov, painters, critics whom he met at receptions given by the Society for Promoting Cultural Relations with Foreigners (VOKS). Berlin interpreted this rosy view of the West as partly a reaction to the crude vilification of Western culture in the Soviet press and radio. 'I tried to indicate that our cultural development' was less irresistibly triumphant than they generously supposed.'

In November 1945, he sat at the same table as Sergei Eisenstein, whom he described as in 'a terrible state of depression' because of Stalin's condemnation of his new film, *Ivan the Terrible*.[3]

Returning to Moscow by train after visiting Pasternak at Peredelkino, Berlin encountered two young Russians on the station platform. It began to rain. They were standing in complete darkness and could barely make out each other's faces. A conversation began. '"Why," I said, I admit not altogether innocently, "can people not speak their minds now on social issues?" "If anyone tries," said the young man, "he is swept away as with a broom, and we do not know what happens to him; no one ever sees or hears from him again." The train arrived and we entered different carriages – the conversation could not have continued before others."[4]

Berlin came away from his visit to the USSR with a dim view of current Soviet literature, music and architecture. The young and hugely popular Konstantin Simonov 'has poured out a flood of work of inferior quality but impeccably orthodox sentiment, acclaiming the right type of Soviet hero, brave, puritanical, simple, noble, altruistic, entirely devoted to the service of his country'. Berlin likened the USSR to a vast school: visitors were treated 'much as strangers found loitering round a school and found talking to the boys', 'the severe type of English public school – say Wellington' whose inmates 'feel hideously confined but not exactly imprisoned'.[5]

Travelling to Leningrad, which had only recently emerged from its terrible siege, he found the city less xenophobic and more Western-orientated than Moscow. Arriving in the company of Brenda Tripp, an organic chemist representing the British Council, the pair checked into the Astoria Hotel, then walked through the snow to seek out the old Berlin family apartment on Angliisky Prospekt. He found the inner courtyard still as dank and dilapidated as thirty years before, the railings of the little basement shop, where an old tinker had repaired samovars and household goods, still broken. He followed the Neva embankment to Nevsky Prospekt, where the tramcars overflowed, crawling along, as he recalled, like 'gigantic disabled wasps, covered with human barnacles'.[6]

Meeting the critic Vladimir Orlov in a bookshop, he enquired after Akhmatova and was told, 'Why yes, of course, she lives not far from here on the Fontanka in Fontanny Dom. Would you like to meet her?' Orlov made a phone call and Berlin was informed she would receive them that same afternoon at three o'clock. At thirty-six, he was twenty years Akhmatova's junior and knew her only by reputation, having apparently never read a word she had written – but Berlin did not tell her that. They talked through the night in her sparsely furnished apartment and shared a dish of boiled potatoes. Tears filled her eyes when Berlin asked after the fate of her friend Osip Mandelstam.

When she asked him how London had survived the war, he was unaware of her poem 'To the Londoners', written in 1940, calling the bombing of London, of which she reads in the press, 'the twenty-fourth drama of Shakespeare', something 'we don't have the strength to read'.[7] He told her stories of his childhood in Riga, his early years in Petrograd and how, when she was already a poet so famous that her admirers could recite the whole of her latest collection verbatim, he was still a child, alone in his father's study, reading Mayne Reid's cowboy stories. She in turn spoke of loneliness and desolation, recalling her past loves: her first husband, Nikolai Gumilev (shot in 1921, father of her son), her second husband, Vladimir Shileiko, and her third, Nikolai Punin. She read her *Requiem* to him from a manuscript, broke off and spoke of the years 1937–38 when both Punin and her son, Lev Gumilev, had been arrested and sent to camps.[8]

At some juncture Berlin confessed he was in love with someone (clearly Patricia Douglas). Michael Ignatieff comments that Akhmatova seems to have conveyed a 'wildly garbled' version of his love life to Korney Chukovsky, whose later memoirs depicted Berlin as a Don Juan engaged in adding Akhmatova to his conquests. Ignatieff holds that no Russian reading *Cinque*, the poems she devoted to their evening together, could believe that they did not become lovers.[9] But on the evidence Berlin had never slept with anyone.

On 3 January 1946, he returned to her, taking the Red Arrow from Moscow overnight. He was due to leave for Helsinki from the Finland Station. She was alone, waiting for him, as regal as ever. He gave her a copy of Kafka's *The Castle* in English and a collection of the Sitwells' verse. She presented him with volumes of her poetry, inscribed. On one volume she wrote out a quotation from *Poem without a Hero*, as if the lines had foretold their meeting:

No one knocks at my door. Only the mirror dreams of a mirror,
And quietness stands guard over quietness – A. 4 January 1946.

On another volume she inscribed lines composed after his first visit. He was to discover that they formed part of *Cinque*, a cycle of love poems charting the course of her own enchantment, her battle against hope, her exhilaration and her sorrow at his departure. He was deeply moved by what he saw as the unrelieved tragedy of her life. The young Isaiah had evidently made a lasting impression on the beleaguered Akhmatova – she had never met such a brilliant young conversationalist in Russian, educated in England and with 'Oxford' stamped on his brow, a philosopher by vocation, an intense and sympathetic listener. She could not have guessed from his fluent, idiomatic spoken Russian that he had some difficulty in writing it to the same high standard. He later wrote to Elena Levin (30 November 1954): 'Akh, esli b[y] ya tol'ko mog pisat' po russki – vse bylo by luchshe i bolee authentic' ('Oh, if only I could write in Russian – everything would have been better and more authentic').[10]

In a stanza of *Poem without a Hero*, written rapidly after he departed, Akhmatova chose Berlin as her unnamed 'Guest from the Future' – indeed, she confided as much to Pasternak. After his return to England he received a letter from Pasternak dated 26 June 1946: 'When Akhmatova was here, her every third word was – you. And so dramatically and mysteriously! At night, for example, in a taxi on the way back from some evening or reception, inspired and weary, and slightly in the clouds, in French: Notre ami (that's you) a dit. . . .' Pasternak added how everyone was asking him what Berlin was like: 'Everyone loves you and recalls you with great warmth.' Returning to Oxford, Berlin proposed an honorary degree for Pasternak, but the vice-chancellor, Richard Livingstone, expressed misgivings (1 June 1946): 'nor do I feel this is the moment for a "gesture" to Russia.'[11]

Later, in May 1947, Berlin was to write privately to Boris Nicolaevsky about Akhmatova and her son, Lev Gumilev. As far as he knew, she still received a pension of 600 roubles a month. He had met Lev when he turned up at her apartment ('but please do not publish this or talk about it, otherwise the poor young man may suffer'), recently back from Berlin where he had been an anti-aircraft gunner. A very competent Central Asiatic historian, a pupil of Yevgeny Tarle, Gumilev had impressed Berlin as 'exceptionally well educated, imaginative, charming, and devoted to his mother'.[12]

As he later recalled, his meetings with Akhmatova and Pasternak brought home to him 'the conditions, scarcely describable, under which they lived and worked, and . . . the treatment to which they were subjected . . . permanently changed my outlook.'[13] His report on the Soviet Union (23 March 1946), sent from the British Embassy in Washington, was clearly influenced by what he had been told about the era of purges and trials during his encounters with Akhmatova, Pasternak and Chukovsky: 'Then came the great debacle which to every Soviet writer and artist is a kind of St Bartholomew's Eve . . . and which is scarcely ever today spoken of other than in a nervous whisper. The government . . . struck at all supposedly "doubtful" elements, and innumerable innocent and harmless[,] with a thoroughness to which the Spanish Inquisition and the Counter-Reformation alone offer remote parallels. The great purges and trials of 1937 and 1938 altered the literary and artistic scene beyond all recognition.' Berlin's list of victims included Mandelstam, Meyerhold, Babel, Pilnyak. 'Not a trace of any of these writers and artists has been sighted by the outside world.' He was convinced that the authentic voice of Russian culture remained the 'ageing but articulate intellectuals, deeply civilised, sensitive, fastidious and not to be deceived, who have preserved unimpaired the high critical standards . . . of the pre-Revolutionary Russian intelligentsia.'[14] Ignatieff adds: 'For the rest of his life they remained the gold standard, the touchstone of moral integrity.'

Shortly after these lines were written, the notorious Party resolution on literature of 14 August 1946 reflected the emboldened stiffening of official policy since the turn of the military tide against Germany in 1943. A.A. Zhdanov, Party boss of Leningrad, produced a report on the journals *Leningrad* and *Zvezda*, which had imprudently published *The Adventures of a Monkey* by the popular satirist Mikhail Zoshchenko, portraying (Zhdanov claimed) Soviet people as lazy, stupid and crude – 'the venom of bestial enmity towards the Soviet order'. In fact, Stalin had been angered by what was in essence a tale for children describing the escape of a female ape from the zoo of a city under bombardment. Finding nothing to eat and the citizens standing in absurd lines for food, the ape acquires her bunch of carrots by apelike means. Stalin's ire against the long-term offender Zoshchenko led to a Central Committee resolution accusing the satirist of 'slanderously presenting Soviet people as primitive, uncultured and stupid'. Only 'the scum of the literary world' could write such works, declared Zhdanov, while blasting the literary group known as the Serapion Brothers, to which Zoshchenko belonged, for 'philistinism, superficiality and lack of political belief'. The Leningrad literary journals were also accused of encouraging Akhmatova to poison the minds of the young. 'What has this poetry in common with the interests of our state and people? Nothing whatever.' The journal *Leningrad* was held guilty of 'kowtowing to the contemporary bourgeois culture of the West' and was closed down by decree of the Central Committee.[15]

As news of this purge reached the West, Berlin was to show little sympathy for Zoshchenko, whom he regarded as a time-server and opportunist. What acutely alarmed him was Zhdanov's accompanying attack on Akhmatova, 'with her petty, narrow personal life, her paltry experiences, and her religiously mystical eroticism'. There was no doubt that Berlin's visit to Fontanny Dom had been reported and held against her. At one juncture during their conversation a bellowing Randolph Churchill had turned up, worsening the guilt by association. Nadezhda Mandelstam visited her in the summer of 1946 and remembers the shadowy figures 'with ugly mugs' who followed them whenever they went out walking. While visiting the Writers' Union in August, Akhmatova noticed that people were avoiding her. On the way home she bought some fish and had it wrapped in a newspaper. She met Mikhail Zoshchenko by chance; he asked her in distress what they were to do. Only when she unwrapped the fish did she read that a Party resolution had censored two Leningrad magazines for publishing their work. Zhdanov's report described her as 'a frantic little fine lady flitting between the boudoir and the chapel', a 'harlot-nun, whose sin is mixed with prayer'. On 4 September, she was expelled from the Writers' Union and her book of poems, the one she had promised to send Berlin, was pulped. In April 1948, friends in the British Embassy in Moscow advised Berlin that anti-foreign xenophobia was running so high that any attempt by him to contact her again would endanger her further. With the arrest of Lev in 1949 for the crime of being her son, her desolation was complete. For the next six years Berlin had no further contact or news.

Ignatieff reports that the St Petersburg headquarters of the security organs holds three files totalling nine hundred pages of denunciations of Akhmatova, reports of phone taps, confessions of those close to her. The files, which date back to 1939, are titled 'Hidden Trotskyism and Anti-Soviet Attitudes'. In 1993, the former KGB operative Oleg Kalugin gave a lecture on the files to a conference organised by the Heinrich Böll Foundation. He disclosed that the KGB forced a Polish woman, who was translating Akhmatova's work, to inform on her. The Polish woman said the English spy Berlin had visited on two (or several) occasions and declared his love for her.[16] One should add that in 2009 the Anna Akhmatova Museum, St Petersburg, published a version throwing doubt on aspects of Berlin's own account of his visits to Akhmatova.[17] The authors conclude that he disguised the fact that in reality he visited the poet five times (or maybe three), not just on two occasions in November 1945 and January 1946, as he claimed. A further allegation is that Berlin's first visit to Akhmatova had been arranged in advance through intermediaries, from Moscow, and was not merely the happy result of a chance meeting with Vladimir Orlov in a Leningrad bookshop. An additional insinuation that Berlin's retrospective account was designed to mask his mission as a spy seems an odd one, since the Soviet authorities knew that his entire itinerary in the postwar USSR served to inform the British and American governments about Soviet ideology, culture and the personal fates of those affected by the purges of the 1930s whether they survived or not. Berlin was to look back on his visit to Akhmatova in Fontanny Dom as the most important event in his life. He came away from Russia with a loathing for Soviet tyranny, which was to inform nearly everything he wrote in defence of Western liberalism and political liberty thereafter. He let it be known that he had lived in fear during his entire visit, the fear that they would come and lay hands on him: 'You are Latvian by birth, come with us and work with us – or worse.'[18]

He returned to Russia in 1956 for a month-long visit as the guest of the British ambassador, Sir William Hayter. This was the occasion when Pasternak thrust the typescript of *Doctor Zhivago* into his hand. But should he revisit Anna Akhmatova? Berlin had evidently allowed his tongue to run away with him when in 1953 he talked to Michael Straight, American editor of the left-leaning *New Republic*.[19] Following the conversation, Berlin was acutely upset by a report in the magazine (24 August), clearly based on what he had told Straight, describing the walls of Akhmatova's Leningrad apartment as dingy and the furnishings as ancient. Berlin had also said that a painting of Mme A. by Modigliani hung on her wall. She had confided that the painter was handsome, with curly black hair, and had only one old sweater to wear; the artist had given her the portrait for a loaf of bread and a bottle of wine. She struggled to remember his name and said, 'I always wondered what happened to that poor boy.' She did not seem to know that the painter had become famous since she had met him in Paris before 1914. Berlin's indignant letter to Straight (27 August) claimed that what he had said was not told as a true story for which he had solid evidence but as a current anecdote. Straight also described how Akhmatova had been temporarily rehabilitated after the war because Stalin's daughter had found some of her poems and liked them, and asked her father what had become of her. In his letter Berlin remonstrated with Straight that this was based solely on what he again called unsubstantiated 'anecdote' – his own. Berlin feared that people would think of him as 'a liar and a vulgarian, and an unspeakably nasty cad, and rightly so'.

On the same day he wrote to Arthur Schlesinger, Jr., likening Straight to David Astor, editor of the *Observer*: 'He and David Astor both represent a kind of neurotic, twisted, poor-little-rich-boy character of whom pre-Nazi Germany was full, and who at present flourish most richly in New York.'[20] Clearly, Berlin had enjoyed reminiscing to Straight about the legendary Russian poet whom he alone knew, and the violence of his subsequent attack on Straight was a not untypical reaction when his penchant for gossip got him into trouble. He always enjoyed talking to the press but was quick to distance himself from the results. There is no indication that Akhmatova ever heard about Straight's report in the *New Republic*.

When Berlin visited Russia during the summer of 1956, her son, Lev Gumilev, whom Berlin had liked and admired in 1945, had only recently been released from a camp (again). Pasternak advised Berlin that she felt acutely nervous about seeing foreigners, 'but that she wished me to telephone her; this was far safer, for all her telephone conversations were monitored' (and so not subject to conjecture by the authorities). When they did speak, Akhmatova revealed a pained sensitivity about Berlin's recent marriage and the fact that his wife, Aline, was with him in Russia. 'Is she English or perhaps American?' 'No, she is half French, half Russian.' 'I see.' There followed a long silence. 'I am sorry you cannot see me,' Akhmatova said. 'Pasternak says your wife is charming.'[21] Still beleaguered by official disapproval, her distress can be imagined: the brilliant young man 'from the Future' who had dropped out of the Leningrad sky in 1945 and who had ever since belonged to her imagination had now moved on.

Berlin's month-long sojourn in Moscow was his first visit to the country in ten years. He discovered the extent to which members of the Berlin family still living in Russia had suffered during the anti-Semitic campaign of Stalin's last years, with the added factor of Stalin's personal anger about Berlin's visits to Akhmatova in 1945–46. Uncle Leo had been arrested in 1952, at the time of the 'Jewish doctors' plot'. He was accused of belonging to a British spy ring which included his brother Mendel and his nephew Isaiah. The accusers linked the 1935 and 1945 visits of father and son, alleging that British intelligence had placed Leo in the university dietetics clinic to gather information on the health of Stalin and other Soviet leaders. Leo was beaten, then confessed. Held in prison for over a year, he was released in February 1954. Walking in the streets of Moscow, weak and undernourished, he suddenly caught sight of one of his torturers crossing the road in front of him. He suffered a heart attack and died alone in the snowy streets.[22]

The Moscow Berlins evidently judged it wiser not to receive Isaiah. He reported to his mother: 'I know nothing about Zhen or Lyom, only that their brother M. does *not* wish to see me.'[23] By 'Zhen' he meant Evgenia Landoberg, his aunt, who had in fact died in 1954. 'Lyom' was Solomon Berlin, an engineer, one of his two surviving uncles, who died in 1978. 'M' was Samuel Berlin, twin brother of Solomon, also an engineer, who died in 1988.

He continued to detest the Soviet Union. His low view of Soviet philosophy was only confirmed when he visited the Academy of Sciences, which he was invited to address on the initiative of Lazar Kaganovich, 'just before his fall from grace and power'.[24] In fact, this low view extended back to the pre-Soviet era. Russia had produced profound 'thinkers' in the realm of general ideas, but not philosophers, he said. Philosophers since the time of Aristotle had addressed the topics and methods that constitute philosophy: 'the disciplines of logic, epistemology, ethics and metaphysical speculation, carried on systematically, *i.e.*, in accordance with recognized and teachable rules.' The Russians had not done so. He dismissed Soviet histories of philosophy as 'crude travesties executed by official hacks and sycophants', largely confined to materialists or political radicals, of whom 'only four have achieved official apostolic status': Belinsky, Herzen, Chernyshevsky and Dobrolyubov. 'Lenin and Stalin soar above the categories: above even Marx and Engels, omniscient and infallible, their genius is universal and defies classification.'[25]

Berlin's experiences with Anna Akhmatova clearly heightened his sensitivity to the ambiguous fate of Soviet Russia's leading composer, Dmitri Shostakovich, now lauded, now damned and cast out, now resurrected. Both the poet and the musician had once been members of the brilliant circle of artists that had briefly been allowed to burn brightly in Petrograd after the Revolution. Akhmatova rarely missed a Shostakovich première. In 1958 she dedicated an edition of her 'Poems' to him 'in whose epoch I loved on earth'. It is said that they did not actually meet until 1961. 'We sat in silence for twenty minutes,' she wrote. 'It was wonderful.' Shostakovich visited the Berlins' home in Headington in 1958, seven years before she did, when he received the honorary degree of Doctor of Music. Berlin described the tensions of the visit in a letter to a friend. The previous day the Soviet Embassy had apparently refused to allow the composer to attend a musical reception given by the British Council, which therefore had to be held without the guest of honour – 'much bad blood, general indignation, telegrams, anger, tears'. Shostakovich materialised at the Berlins' Headington mansion on the Tuesday. Berlin described him as 'small, shy, like a chemist from Canada (Western States), terribly nervous, with a twitch playing in his face almost perpetually – I have never seen anyone so frightened and crushed in all my life'. When Shostakovich's cello sonata was played at a musical evening at the Trevor-Ropers', the composer complained to the two cellists that they had rendered two passages incorrectly. The score supported the cellists. Realising that it had been edited by Gregor Piatigorsky, he took out a pencil and substituted his own version. '[Shostakovich's] face will always haunt me somewhat,' Berlin recalled, 'it is terrible to see a man of genius victimised by a regime, crushed by it into accepting his fate as something normal, terrified almost of being plunged into some other life, with all powers of indignation, resistance, protest removed like a sting from a bee, thinking that unhappiness is happiness and torture is normal life.'[26] But maybe Shostakovich distrusted the company he was obliged to keep on this occasion. Cruelly persecuted under Stalin, he was nonetheless the USSR's hugely lauded lion-composer, frequently travelled abroad and was capable of defying the orthodoxies.

During Berlin's visit to Russia in 1956, Boris Pasternak had related how the actor Livanov was to have performed in and produced Pasternak's adaptation of *Hamlet*. At a Kremlin reception the actor asked Stalin, 'Iosif Vissarionovich, how should one play *Hamlet*?' Stalin at first replied that he was no expert on theatrical matters, then added: '*Hamlet* is a decadent play and should not be performed at all.' Rehearsals were at once broken off and there were no further performances of the play until after Stalin's death. Shostakovich's *Testimony* confirms this anecdote: Livanov's production had evidently been scheduled for the Moscow Art Theatre. Shostakovich adds sardonically that Stalin also hated *Macbeth*: 'And he was so naïve, Shakespeare. Pangs of conscience and guilt and all that. . . . And what about the fate of our best translator of Shakespeare – Pasternak?'[27]

But no such anecdotes were likely to pass from the composer's tight mouth while in the Berlins' Headington drawing room. Pasternak had recounted the *Hamlet* story at Peredelkino when he entrusted a copy of *Doctor Zhivago* to a reluctant Berlin. By the time of Shostakovich's visit to Oxford two years later, the storm of retribution was breaking over Pasternak's head, a matter of deep concern to Berlin. But Shostakovich never uttered a public word in defence of the poet.

Akhmatova and Berlin were to meet again, for the last time, when at his instigation she visited Oxford in 1965 to receive an honorary degree (and was able to view the mansion Lady Berlin had brought him, Headington House). She confided that Stalin had been personally enraged by Berlin's visit to her apartment in Fontanny Dom in 1945. 'So now our nun receives visits from foreign spies', he had shouted, followed by 'obscenities which she could not at first bring herself to repeat to me'. She told Berlin that she was convinced that Stalin's fury about her meetings with him had unleashed the Cold War – that she and he had changed the history of mankind. Berlin asked her whether she would ever annotate *Poem without a Hero*: the allusions might be unintelligible to those who did not know the life it was concerned with. She answered that the poem would and should die with those who understood it.

Akhmatova died the following year. In March 1988, Berlin revisited Leningrad and Moscow, where his friend Alfred Brendel gave two recitals, and walked for the last time past Fontanny Dom.

13

BORIS PASTERNAK

'As a poet he is curiously antiquated, compared with Mayakovsky and Yessenin, his contemporaries. . . . A voice from the grave . . . the survivor of a lost tribe.' This was Isaac Deutscher's burial of Boris Pasternak. We come, then, to *Doctor Zhivago*.

Berlin described his first visit to Pasternak's dacha at Peredelkino, outside Moscow, on a warm day in September 1945. 'He [Pasternak] was once described by his friend, the poet Marina Tsvetaeva, as looking like an Arab and his horse. . . . He spoke slowly in a low tenor monotone, with a continuous even sound, something between a humming and a drone . . . each vowel was elongated as if in some plaintive aria in an opera by Tchaikovsky, but with far more concentrated force and tension. . . . He talked marvellously, he was a little unhinged at times . . . in my experience only Virginia Woolf talked somewhat like that. She, too, of course, was a trifle crazy.'[1]

When Pasternak told him that the *Soviet Encylopaedia* made no mention of his work after 1928, a visiting neighbour, Lydia Seifullina, said her fate was the same. The last lines of her entry stated that 'Seifullina is at present in a state of psychological and artistic crisis'. '"For twenty years," she said sardonically, "I have remained in the same state of crisis."' She added: 'We are like people in Pompeii, you and I, Boris Leonidovich, buried by ashes in mid-sentence.' (But they both continued to enjoy accommodation belonging to the Writers' Union, the site at Peredelkino having been granted to the union by Stalin.)

Berlin concluded that Pasternak wanted to forget his Jewish origins and be regarded as a true Russian writer, even as a Slavophile – he gave the impression of wishing to have been born a flaxen-haired, blue-eyed peasant's son. Pasternak believed that Jews should assimilate and considered himself a believing, if idiosyncratic, Christian. Perhaps a negative reaction to Pasternak's repudiation of his Jewishness may explain why Berlin did not actually read the chapters Pasternak gave him to take to his sisters in Oxford. The book was then called 'Boys and Girls, the Story of a Russian Faust: From the Unpublished Papers of the Zhivago Family'. Berlin duly delivered them unread.[2]

'After Pasternak returned to Moscow I visited him almost weekly, and came to know him well.' He spoke of the 'incomparable genius' of Tolstoy. His father, the painter, had taken him to see Tolstoy on his deathbed. Pasternak recounted how Stalin had telephoned him on a terrifying occasion in 1934 to enquire about the poet Osip Mandelstam; when Pasternak seemed to equivocate, Stalin snapped, 'If I were Mandel'shtam's friend, I should have known better how to defend him' – and put down the receiver.[3] Pasternak had suffered another painful trial of nerve in 1936 when the Writers' Union demanded the execution of Kamenev and Zinoviev in *Pravda*. The article was entitled 'Wipe Them from the Face of the Earth'. Pasternak was one of sixteen writers who signed it. In conversation with Berlin, he was obsessed that his continuing survival and publications could be construed as accommodating to the Party and state.

This fear immediately resurfaced in 1956 when Berlin again visited Peredelkino.

'Boris Leonidovich, I am happy to see you looking so well. But the main thing is that you have survived. This seemed almost miraculous to some of us.'

His face darkened and he looked at me with real anger: 'I know what you are thinking,' he said . . . in a breaking voice. . . . 'Do not prevaricate . . . . You think – I know what you think – that I have done something for *them*.'[4]

Berlin by now (August 1956) viewed the great poet with adulation: 'his views, his sense of life, his politics, his faith in Russia, in the Revolution, in the new world to come, which is very deep, have the clarity and concreteness of a poetical vision. . . . It is difficult to think of any figure comparable to him in gifts, vitality, impregnable integrity and moral courage and solidity anywhere in the world.'[5]

Once Pasternak had become certain that *Novyi mir* – and therefore any other Soviet literary magazine – would not allow publication of *Doctor Zhivago* in the USSR, he had entrusted the typescript to Agnelli, an agent of the Italian publisher Giangiacomo Feltrinelli, for publication abroad. Now, soon afterwards, he thrust another finished typescript into Berlin's hand – with the result that his wife, Zinaida Nikolaevna, begged Berlin to dissuade her husband from going ahead with a reckless act that could only destroy his family and children. (She was also convinced that Pasternak was being propelled into recklessness by his ambitious mistress, Olga Ivinskaya.) When Berlin carried Zinaida's case to Pasternak, he reacted angrily. 'He had spoken to his sons. They were prepared to suffer. . . . I was not to mention the matter again. . . . I was shamed into silence.'[6]

Timorous (or cautious) by nature, Berlin would have liked to bury copies of *Doctor Zhivago* in all the world's continents while persuading the author not to go ahead with publication. The uproar following its appearance in the West turned out to be even more virulent than anticipated. Inhibited about adding fuel to the fire, Berlin nevertheless published an appreciation in his 'Books of the Year' selection for the *Sunday Times* (21 December 1958): '*Doctor Zhivago* . . . seems to me a work of genius, and its appearance a literary and moral event without parallel in our day. . . . a magnificent poetical masterpiece. . . . the life, decline and death of a man [Yuri Zhivago] who, like the heroes of Turgenev, Tolstoy and Chekhov, stands at the edge of his society . . . and preserves his human shape, his inner life and his sense of truth under the impact of violent events which pulverise his society, and brutalise or destroy vast numbers of other human beings.' Berlin did concede some short-comings: 'It is an uneven book: its beginning is confused, the symbolism at times obscure, the end mystifying. . . . But all in all it is one of the greatest works of our time.'[7]

In fact, he muted in print the criticisms of the novel that he conveyed to friends. To Gladwyn Jebb he had commented (1 September 1958) that Pasternak's attempts to introduce his characters and involve them in a plot were 'too clumsy and confused'. It was difficult to follow who was who, the incidents came across as 'jerky and inconsequent'. The book only really got going when it became obviously autobiographical, with the advent of the 1914 war. The marvellous pages were the Siberian ones, the civil war, the heroine Lara. And 'the quality of Russia 1917–21, as felt by a civilised and Westernised figure, has never been described anywhere at all. And the "metaphysical" excursions – Christianity and all – seem to me wonderful.' But the first hundred pages were *so* bad. After the Nobel Prize was awarded to Pasternak, Berlin wrote to David Astor of the *Observer* (27 October 1958), emphasising his reluctance to bring on Pasternak's martyrdom though Pasternak himself seemed to seek it. Berlin regarded it as 'wicked irresponsibility' when the BBC's Russian Service broadcast extracts from the novel. 'Every little thing may help to destroy him.' Nevertheless, he saw no objection to a profile of Pasternak in the *Observer*, 'provided it suppresses some of the truth and omits his obviously anti-Soviet attitude'.[8]

Isaac Deutscher's overview of *Doctor Zhivago* ('Pasternak and the Calendar of the Revolution') merely inflamed Berlin's hostility, as he told me. The piece first appeared in Sartre's *Les Temps modernes* in January 1959 as 'Boris Pasternak et le calendrier de la Révolution', then in the spring issue of the New York journal *Partisan Review*. Deutscher had offered the American rights to the more radical of *Partisan*'s two coeditors, Philip Rahv. After an ominous silence, Rahv had eventually written back on 7 March 1959 to say it would appear with a contrary opinion of Pasternak's novel by Irving Howe. 'Personally I go along with you in your view of *Dr Zhivago*, but I am sure that the majority of our readers will be deeply affronted. The cold-war indoctrination has gone so far among us that even the intellectual elite has been reduced to a pulp. Consider the ecstatic review of the novel that Edmund Wilson wrote in *The New Yorker*. He swallowed everything Pasternak dished out, including the warmed-over Christianity.' In reply, Deutscher noted that in England the ascendancy of intellectual conservatism was beginning to give way to 'a refreshing rise of radicalism'. He thought this likely to happen in the United States, too, among young people reacting against 'the indoctrination, especially as the facts of international life clash ever more strongly with the main tenets of cold war propaganda'. Meanwhile Deutscher responded to a letter of 11 March from the other coeditor, William Phillips (unfound): 'Disagreement with my assumptions and conclusions is not surprising.'[9] The twinned editorship of Rahv and Phillips, increasingly positioned on opposite sides of the political fence, was a distinctive feature of *Partisan Review* in these years.

The spring issue of 1959 advertises on its cover: ' "The Politics of Boris Pasternak: An Exchange", Isaac Deutscher, Irving Howe.' Deutscher's central complaint against Pasternak was one of historical content rather than literary form. Accusing Pasternak of failing to distinguish between the early years of the Revolution and the Stalin period, Deutscher complained that only the most attentive reader would grasp that the main story of *Zhivago* ends in 1922. Pasternak was accused of projecting 'the horrors of the Stalin era' back into 'the early and earliest phases of Bolshevik rule'. During the civil war Zhivago and Lara are described by Pasternak as already revolted by the tyranny of the monolithic regime, which, according to Deutscher, 'in fact was not formed until a decade later'.[10]

Deutscher cites, for example, a passage in which Lara is clearly describing in specific detail the time of the civil war. This kind of regime, she comments, 'goes through certain regular stages. In the first stage, it's the triumph of reason, of the spirit of criticism, of the fight against prejudice and so on. Then comes the second stage. The accent is all on the dark forces, the false sympathisers, the hangers-on. There is more and more suspicion – informers, intrigues, hatreds.' Lara tells Zhivago (and he wholeheartedly agrees): 'I can still remember a time when we all accepted the peaceful outlook of the last century. It was taken for granted that you listened to reason. . . . And then there was the jump from this calm, innocent, measured way of living to blood and tears, to mass insanity.'[11]

Deutscher complained that what Lara (i.e. Pasternak) is describing fits only the later Stalinist regime. But here we are back again with the two Deutschers, the historian and the polemicist. The historian speaks in *The Prophet Armed*: 'The grotesque sequel to the October insurrection . . . was a prodigious, truly elemental orgy of mass drunkenness with which the freed underdog celebrated his victory. The orgy lasted many weeks and at one time threatened to bring the revolution to a standstill and to paralyze it.' The army largely disintegrated. Crowds of ruffians, mostly soldiers, broke into wine cellars and pillaged wine shops.[12]

For Deutscher, the other most striking negative characteristic of the novel was its 'archaism, the archaism of the idea and of the artistic style alike'. It was 'a parable about a vanished generation'. A broad, pantheistic Christianity remains the hope and refuge, quasi-fatalistic and rejecting the attempt to remould human society. Pasternak 'speaks the language of the dead and not of the living': 'Yet as a poet too he is curiously antiquated, compared with Mayakovsky and Yessenin, his contemporaries.'[13] He also belittled Pasternak's character, claiming that he had never been interfered with until now, putting up only 'passive resistance' in Stalin's time: 'In his poems he escapes from the tyranny, he does not defy it' – which was why he had survived while others had either committed suicide or been arrested and annihilated. Stalin 'watched over his security and welfare' because he knew 'that he had little to fear from his poetry'. Leopold Labedz commented: 'Even the letter of rejection by the editors of *Novyi mir* was not so disparaging as Deutscher's review of *Doctor Zhivago*.'[14]

Deutscher compared Pasternak unfavourably to Tolstoy, because 'Tolstoy takes the characters of *War and Peace* straight into the centre of the great events of their time. He throws them right into the stream of history.' By damaging contrast, 'Pasternak places his characters in the backwoods and backwaters. They do not participate in any single important event; nor do they even witness any such event. . . . He runs away from history, just as all the time his chief characters flee from the scourge of revolution.'[15] Deutscher lists the events, the 'stream of history' ignored by Pasternak: the Treaty of Brest-Litovsk, the move of Lenin's government to Moscow, the uprising of the Socialist Revolutionaries, etc., etc. It is indeed the case that Pasternak's novel mentions Lenin only once, Trotsky, Stalin and other leading Bolsheviks not at all. His characters know them not. This may have been caution on Pasternak's part, but he also grasped what life meant for ordinary Russians spread across the chaotic vastness of Siberia. Was it food and firewood or a faraway figure called Lenin? Was it the hellish conditions on trains caught in snowdrifts and beset by bandits or the terms of the Treaty of Brest-Litovsk? What did Deutscher mean by 'backwoods and backwaters'? Was this not most of Russia?

We may decide that Pasternak does no damage to real history if his fictional hero takes no part in the storming of the Winter Palace, is never elected to a soviet, never meets Lenin, is never privileged to hear an oration from Trotsky – and may never have heard of either. What Pasternak's novel records is local history, the lottery of rape and murder, hunger, destitution – and incomprehension: what is going on? Why is all this chaos and killing happening? Pasternak illuminates how Russia's vast terrain, wrapped in snow-drifts, turns 'history book history' into local chaos and dark rumour. There are endless queues for uncertain trains. Passengers have to board the train half a mile down the line because the platforms are filthy, and the tracks in front of the platforms unusable because of dirt and ice.

It is a paradox that Deutscher, despite his Marxism, saw History with a capital 'H' much as conservative historians had always done: great men, great battles, great events. He wrote biographies of Trotsky and Stalin much as traditional historians had written about Caesar, Wellington, Napoleon, Washington – the top-down view that normally indicates a degree of psycho-logical association between the historian and his subject. For Deutscher, Pasternak's lack of correct political perspective was inexcusable; like his hero Trotsky, Deutscher wanted what he called an *histoire politique*. He bristled at the fact that the fictional Zhivago, when captured and enlisted as a field doctor by Red partisans, bitterly resents this captivity whereas he had accepted conscription into the tsar's army.

By contrast, Berlin saw only merit in the fact that Yuri Zhivago, 'like the heroes of Turgenev, Tolstoy and Chekhov, stands at the edges of his society'. Berlin totally agreed with Pasternak, not Deutscher, about terror in Lenin's time. As he later recalled, his own parents were not persecuted: 'But I did have memories of the Soviet regime, which were not happy: one or two people we had known were shot quite early in 1918, not for political reasons. There was no explanation of this from any source. There were a great many executions – there was a terror, nothing like what it grew to be in Stalin's reign, but still, a good many people were shot [for reasons] that were never revealed to the public except in general terms – "enemies of the Soviet Union", "speculators", "counter-revolutionaries", "supporters of the bourgeoisie", and the like.'[16] (The 'Soviet Union' actually dates from December 1922.)

We may add that one of Pasternak's major achievements was to illuminate the feminine condition, the sex war within both imperial war and revolutionary war. When Lara falls on her knees before her husband, Antipov, begging him not to volunteer and desert his family, she echoes the prayer of almost every woman. The killing fields and the great causes that foster them have always been first and foremost the remote, uncontrollable province of men, male egos, male honour, male claims on history. Despairing of being allowed to visit her husband Antipov/Strelnikov in his military headquarters, Lara cries out: 'What do wives matter to them at a time like this? The workers of the world, the remaking of the universe, that's something! But what's a wife?'[17]

Deutscher, however, was careful to distance himself from the banning of the novel and its author:

When all this has been said, one cannot react otherwise than with indignation and disgust to the suppression of *Doctor Zhivago* in the Soviet Union, and to the spectacle of Pasternak's condemnation. There exists no justification and no excuse for the ban on this book and the outcry against it, or for the pressure exercised on Pasternak, to make him resign the Nobel award, or the threat of his expulsion from the country, and the continuing witch-hunt. The Writers' Union of Moscow and its official instigators or accomplices have achieved nothing except that they have given proof of their obtuseness and stupidity. What are Pasternak's censors afraid of? His Christianity? But the Soviet State Publishers print in millions of copies the works of Tolstoy and Dostoyevsky, every page of which breathes a Christianity far more authentic than Pasternak's. His nostalgia for the *ancien régime*? ... The work of the revolution can no longer be undone or reversed: the huge, formidable, and ever growing structure of the new Soviet society will hardly stop growing.... Zhivago still represents a powerful force, frequently felt and heard, in Poland, Hungary, Eastern Germany, and elsewhere in Eastern Europe; but in the Soviet Union he is the survivor of a lost tribe. Pasternak's censors ... distrust their own, modern and educated, society which is growing mightily above their heads as well as Pasternak's ... the mass of its people is seizing anew the sense of socialism.[18]

Irving Howe's reply was scathing. Deutscher, not Pasternak, 'speaks the language of the dead', he wrote. In reality, young Russia revered Pasternak – the students of Moscow had hailed him a few years ago, chanting a request that he read his translation of Shakespeare's sixty-sixth sonnet ('And art made tongue-tied by authority'). What Howe saw in Russia was a party state still in opposition to the values of democracy and socialism, and systematically silencing those who spoke of freedom. Pasternak's hero, Zhivago, represented the permanent revolution of man against the total state – and not, as Deutscher claimed, representing the middle class of 1912–14, after they had turned their back on their own radicalism of 1905. Howe quoted a passage from Pasternak: 'Microscopic forms of cardiac haemorrhages have become very frequent in recent years. . . . It's a typical modern disease. I think its causes are of a moral order. The great majority of us are required to live a life of constant, systematic duplicity. . . . I found it painful to listen to you, Innokentii, when you told us how you were reeducated and became mature in jail. It was like listening to a horse describing how it broke itself in.' And this passage: 'Dudorov's pious platitudes were in the spirit of the times. But it was precisely their conformism, their transparent sanctimoniousness, that exasperated Zhivago. Men who are not free, he thought, always idealize their bondage. So it was in the Middle Ages, and later the Jesuits exploited the same human trait. Zhivago could not bear the political mysticism of the Soviet intelligentsia.' And this: 'To conceal the failure [of forced collectivisation] people had to be cured, by every means of terrorism, of the habit of thinking and judging for themselves, and forced to see what did not exist.'

Howe – one of Deutscher's despised ex-communist renegades and co-author of a study of the American Communist Party – also disparaged his token attack on the censors for their obtuseness in not recognising that the book presented no threat within Russia, while admitting that it did so throughout Eastern Europe. In that case perhaps the Soviet censors were not so obtuse? He associated Deutscher with a wider outlook, 'left authoritarianism', usually associated with the belief that a nationalised economy is the ultimate guarantor of progress, even when acting beyond or against the desires of living men. Howe approvingly quoted Marx when he spoke of 'the categorical imperative that all conditions must be revolutionized in which man is a debased, an abandoned, a contemptible being' – he meant the Soviet Union. Death spared him the difficulty of explaining the volte-face from '22nd of June 1941' to the book that made his name. Reviewing *The Prophet Outcast* five years later, Howe reiterated that for Deutscher and the 'left authoritarians' nationalised property was the guarantor of progress, with the expectation of a moderate democratisation within the limits of the ruling party's ethos and power. But events showed otherwise.[19]

Berlin's virulent reaction to Deutscher's 'Pasternak and the Calendar of the Revolution' is found in a letter to William Phillips (8 October 1959): 'I suffer from profound, perhaps exaggerated antipathy to all his writings – I think him specious, dishonest, and in any case possessed of some quality which causes some kind of nausea within me.'[20]

In fact, some of Deutscher's criticisms of *Doctor Zhivago* were widely shared. He complained: 'Not only the author sings his hero's praises – nearly all the characters do the same. Nearly all adore Yury, approve his ideas, echo his deep reflections, and nod their heads at whatever he says.'[21] In truth, even Pasternak's devoted friends tended to agree privately. Anna Akhmatova complained that the characters 'lack vitality, they are contrived'. In her view Zhivago himself was neither a 'Zhivago' (a play on the adjective *zhivoy*, meaning 'alive') nor a genuine doctor of medicine. Immediately after Pasternak's expulsion from the Soviet Writers' Union on 27 October 1958, she told Lydia Chukovskaya: 'Boris lost himself in it. That's why the novel is so bad, except for the landscapes. Speaking frankly this is a Gogolian failure – the second volume of *Dead Souls* [where Gogol begins to preach]. . . . Because of this he has put the people very close to him, as well as his friends, in such a horribly difficult position.' In addition, Akhmatova revealed a degree of personal asperity, detesting Pasternak's attachment to Olga Ivinskaya, whom she refused to receive: 'I do not wish to meet with this bandit.' She brooded about the international uproar: 'where was he when they evicted me from the Sheremetev Palace? He didn't say a single word! And really, in comparison with what they did with me and Zoshchenko, the story of Boris is – a battle of butterflies.' Dismayed by such a comparison, Chukovskaya, loyal both to Akhmatova and Pasternak, had to agree about the weaknesses of *Doctor Zhivago*: 'The main figures aren't alive; they're made of cardboard, and the most cardboardy of the lot is Doctor Zhivago himself.' Nadezhda Mandelstam's verdict was scathing. Aleksandr Gladkov, an unstinting admirer of Pasternak's poetry, felt he would have done better to write a memoir of his times. His fictional characters were mere mouthpieces of the author.[22]

As we have seen, Berlin shared some of these reservations, but he never thought fit to expose them in print. Instead, fearful for Pasternak's safety, he engaged in a futile effort to persuade the Western media to play down the anti-Marxist passages in the novel. His initial belief that the Soviet literary establishment ('Surkov and other old Stalinists in the Writers' Union') were more or less on the defensive 'and there was no question of penalising Pasternak himself' soon evaporated. Again, he blamed the Western press, requesting

Raimund von Hofmannstahl, who worked for *Time* in London, to forward to New York his warnings about the proposed cover of the magazine featuring Pasternak. But *Time* went ahead (15 December 1958) with 'The Passion of Yurii Zhivago'.[23] '*Time* and *Life*', Berlin complained, 'are regarded as the spearhead of the Cold-War party in the West. For them to play up Pasternak's heroism and martyrdom ... is to align him with the enemies of the Soviet Union so openly' as to put Pasternak at grave risk. He saw a parallel in the support by the English and French press for the Polish rising in 1863, which 'turned the majority of Russian liberals and even revolutionaries into supporters of Tsar and Church against the West'. That was why 'Lord Russell, T.S. Eliot, Rebecca West and the others who sent an open letter to Khrushchev were so careful to insist on *Zhivago* as a personal testimony and not a political piece'.[24]

Doctor Zhivago sold 46,000 copies in Italy within a year. By January 1959, 300,000 copies had reportedly been sold in France. Publication in the USA took place in September 1958; 50,000 copies were sold within weeks. Pasternak's novel was an alternative selection of the Book of the Month Club.[25] But not until the award of the Nobel Prize, announced on 23 October 1958, was the full fury of the Soviet Party unleashed. The author sent a telegram of acceptance to Stockholm: 'Immensely thankful, touched, proud, astonished, abashed. Pasternak.'

In 'A Provocative Sally of International Reaction', *Literaturnaya gazeta* (25 October 1958) described the Nobel award as 'an intensification of the cold war against the Soviet Union ... and against the idea of all-conquering socialism'. Pasternak's novel provided only 'the life story of a malicious philistine, an enemy of the Revolution'. The following day *Pravda* published 'Reactionary Uproar over a Literary Weed' by the veteran hatchet-man David Zaslavsky: 'The snake is wriggling at our feet. It is irresistibly drawn downward to its native swamps where it enjoys the odours of rot and decay ... warm and comfortable in the poetical dungwaters of lyrical manure.' On 27 October, the presidium of the Writers' Union expelled Pasternak, alleging (perhaps correctly) that he wanted the world to believe that the Revolution had been neither inevitable nor necessary. On 31 October, some eight hundred Moscow writers requested the government to 'deprive the traitor B. Pasternak of Soviet citizenship' and proposed that this 'cosmopolitan' (the anti-Semitic term was deliberately revived) be deported. Greatly alarmed, Pasternak sent a telegram of retraction to Stockholm: 'Considering the meaning this [Nobel] award has been given in the society to which I belong, I must reject this undeserved prize presented to me.'

Given this Soviet onslaught, one may be surprised to find Berlin writing to Patrick Corbett in 1963, describing Deutscher's 'Pasternak and the Calendar of the Revolution' as 'an attack on *Dr. Zhivago* considerably more violent than any delivered in the Soviet Union; it ended by costing him the favour of *Dissent*, the *New Left Review* and other non-Communist left-socialist publications, which decided to break off relations with him at the time, although the *New Left Review* have repented of this decision.[26]

An interesting dimension of Deutscher's aversion to Pasternak nowhere surfaces in 'Pasternak and the Calendar of the Revolution'. We know that Isaiah Berlin was disturbed by Pasternak's renunciation of his Jewish heritage, his desire to appear a 'Slav', but Berlin evidently held in check the pain of a renunciation he usually condemned (notably in the case of Karl Marx). Deutscher's attitude comes to light when we examine a correspondence begun by William Zukerman, editor of the *Jewish Newsletter* in New York, who sent him an article, 'Pasternak's Message to the Jews', described as containing a 'Christological' doctrine, and inviting Deutscher to comment for publication.

Zukerman's article quotes one of the heroes (unnamed) of *Doctor Zhivago* blaming Jewish leaders for the futile perpetuation of the Jewish problem, 'petty second-raters who are only too happy when some nation, preferably a small and wretched one, is constantly discussed'. Pasternak's hero contrasts this with the Kingdom of Heaven, where there are no nations, only individuals. 'For what purpose are these innocent old men and women and children, all these subtle, kind, humane people, mocked and beaten up throughout the centuries? . . . Why didn't the intellectual leaders of the Jewish people ever go beyond facile *Weltschmerz* and ironical wisdom? . . . Why didn't they say to them, "Come to your senses, stop. Don't hold on to your identity. Don't stick together, disperse. Be with all the rest. You are the first and best Christians in the world." '

Deutscher's response to Zukerman (15 November 1958) assumed that the views expressed by the positive, admired characters in *Doctor Zhivago* represented Pasternak's own: 'Their national idea [that] has forced them to be a nation and nothing but a nation' was wrong, wrote Deutscher; Jewish nationalism had resulted from 'their peculiar role in non-Jewish society and the persecution culminating in the extermination of the bulk of European Jewry'. Pasternak's character then asks, 'What use is it to anyone, this *voluntary* martyrdom?' and goes on to describe the 'literary friends' and intellectual leaders of the Jewish people as 'untalented'. Deutscher commented bitterly: 'I would not exchange a single one of Shalom Ash's earlier novels or a single story by Shalom Alejchem for *Dr. Zhivago*!' No one was entitled to tell the Jews not to hold on to their identity. 'It is curious to see that on this point Pasternak, allegedly the heroic non-conformist, lends, perhaps unwittingly, support to an official [Soviet] policy which found its expression in the liquidation of Jewish writers.' Agreeing with Zukerman that Pasternak displays a 'Christological form and tone', Deutscher added that his own 'intellectual opposition to Judaism is only part of an opposition to all forms of theological thinking'.[27]

Sir Isaiah Berlin 1974 (Clive Barda/Arena PAL)

PART FIVE

COLD WAR ALLEGIANCES

14

THE COLD WAR AND THE PEOPLE'S DEMOCRACIES

HIGHLY PROVOCATIVE TO mainstream Western opinion were Deutscher's theses on the origins and ongoing causes of the Cold War, extending to the People's Democracies established by the Soviet Union after 1945. Although his insistence on the socially progressive nature of communist regimes in Eastern Europe was tempered by a more or less frank acknowledgment that they had been installed by external force, by Stalin, his equivocal reactions to the East Berlin rising of June 1953, then to the rebellions in Poland and Hungary in 1956, only cemented his reputation as a crypto-Stalinist.

When it came to his native Poland, his involvement carried, I think, a tragic dimension. Having broken with the Communist Party at an early age, having renounced his citizenship and rendered himself unable to set foot in Poland, he still yearned to be recognised as an influential voice by Gomulka and the leaders of the ruling Polish Workers' Party. At the same time there was an element of the fatuous in his published interventions, not least when in 1956 he struck the pose of the veteran Leninist advising the young dissidents who led the resistance to Stalinism not to overreach themselves.

Deutscher's basic perspective on the Cold War was that an exhausted and depleted Russia had no intention of expanding or attacking anyone. America, by contrast, emerged from the war unscathed, buoyant and spoiling for global dominance. Only after Churchill's 'iron curtain' speech in 1946, the proclamation of the Truman Doctrine in 1947, the creation of NATO and the decision to rearm Western Germany, did Stalin feel compelled to increase his armed forces to five million. 'But never before had responsible statesmen raised a scare so gigantic and unreal as was the alarm about Russia's design for world conquest and world domination, the alarm amid which the North Atlantic Alliance came into being.'[1]

In his articles for the *Economist* and the *Observer* during the years 1942–47, Deutscher repeatedly prophesied Soviet democratisation. This was well received by a war-weary British public. In his first despatch from occupied Germany for the *Observer*, Deutscher reported that German soldiers serving on the eastern front had been 'very favourably impressed by the collective farms in which, they said, they saw efficiency as well as social justice'. On 3 March 1946, he reported: 'Here in the Russian zone, German culture has unexpected life and liberty. . . . The Russian Military Government, whatever its failings and faults, does give a sense of purpose and direction to many Germans.'

For Russian exiles in Western Europe he expressed hostility, denigrating *Possev* [Seed, or Sowing], the Russian émigré magazine based in West Germany. He had visited émigré camps during his postwar journeys in Germany: 'I found them, or most of them, to be worthless Stalinists in reverse.' Many émigré organisations during the interwar years were 'simply tools of the GPU'.[2]

As for the purported threat from Russia's so-called fifth column in the West, it was paradoxically Stalin's moderation that had rescued Western Europe from revolution. On Stalin's instructions the French communists meekly served in General de Gaulle's government as junior members, disarming the Resistance and urging moderation on the workers. The Italian Stalinists obediently followed a similar course of accommodation. According to Deutscher, it was doubtful whether the bourgeois order would have survived in Western Europe if the Communist parties had not willingly assisted. Stalin cynically abandoned the Greek communists to military suppression by Churchill, while adhering to their secret agreement of October 1944 on future spheres of influence. Under that agreement, Russia was to exercise 90 per cent of influence in Eastern Europe and the Balkans. 'To this grotesque gentleman's agreement Stalin adhered to the letter.'[3]

Deutscher turned a blind eye to Western fears that if Stalin could order the French and Italian parties to collaborate, he could enlist the same absolute obedience in the contrary direction. This was precisely what happened after the Cominform, founded in 1947, replaced its predecessor, the Comintern, defunct since 1943. The zigzags of Comintern strategy were alive in the memory: the left 'social-fascist' phase of 1928–34, the abrupt switch to the united and popular fronts, the reversal after the Nazi-Soviet Pact, the reversion to patriotic collaboration after Hitler invaded the Soviet Union. Following the Comintern line after 1947, the French Communist Party instigated strikes, organised dockers to blockade arms shipments to Indo-China, and waged a propaganda campaign likening American economic and cultural penetration to fascism.

Deutscher's claim that it was only after the communists had been ejected from the French and Italian governments that Stalin began to eject the anti-communists from the governments of Eastern Europe and to establish the single-party system was challenged by the historian and Sovietologist Robert Conquest, who listed a series of Soviet-forced expulsions of non-communists from governments, and destructions of social-democratic parties through shotgun weddings, in Romania, Bulgaria, Poland, Hungary and East Germany – all of them prior to the dismissal of the French and Italian communist ministers in May 1947.[4]

Deutscher's interpretation of Stalin's secret 'gentleman's agreement' with Churchill in 1944 ran into a contradiction: on the one hand, such archaic Great Power diplomacy was 'grotesque'; on the other hand, Stalin honourably abided by the agreement. 'Yet this treacherous tyrant was also in his way strangely strict and almost scrupulous in his dealings with bourgeois diplomatic partners. . . . Even in Stalinizing Eastern Europe he still acted within the letter of his war-time agreements with Churchill and Roosevelt as he interpreted them.' This was to overlook that the 'Declaration on Liberated Europe' agreed at Yalta bound the Three Powers to help the nations of Eastern Europe 'to form interim governmental authorities broadly representative of all democratic elements in the population and pledged to the earliest possible establishment through free elections of governments responsive to the will of the people.'[5]

Clearly Stalin violated this commitment, but according to Deutscher he did so only after the Western governments 'tried to wrest from Russia the zone of influence that Churchill and Roosevelt had yielded to her at Teheran and Yalta'. And why? Because under their class interest and class psychology they mistook Soviet power for revolutionary power, a threat to the capitalist system. 'They sought to contain Stalin's power at the frontiers of the USSR. . . . It speeded up the disaster it was designed to prevent. It provoked Soviet power to erupt all the more violently, to cover hermetically the whole of the Soviet zone of influence.' Unlike orthodox Western communists, Deutscher had to concede that 'Stalinism had pressed all its subjects into a single totalitarian mould and had imposed an absolute dogmatic, though unprincipled, uniformity upon the entire Communist movement. . . . It goes without saying that [Stalin's] actions and the ruthlessness and brutality with which he clamped down a regime of terror on the whole of Eastern Europe provided in Western eyes a justification, one might say a *post factum* justification, for the Truman Doctrine and for the other measures of cold war.'[6] Deutscher dismissed the democratic aspirations of Truman's containment policy as mere rhetoric. It not only failed but was a moral sham.

Yet Western opinion could scarcely accept the *coup d'état* in Czechoslovakia, traditionally a democratic state and one in which the communists had been losing ground in recent elections. The virtues of ballot-box democracy never weighed with Deutscher; he described the Cold War as a conflict between capitalism and communism, 'which some prefer to describe as a conflict between democracy and communism'. He said little or nothing about the Berlin blockade of 1948–49, or the North Korean invasion of the South in June 1950 sponsored by Stalin and Mao. In 1966, speaking at Berkeley, he declared that the Korean War 'gave one a sense of solidarity with a small nation so ruthlessly attacked, so ruthlessly crushed by the most powerful, the greatest, the richest nation in the world'. He never modified his analysis of the Cold War, repeating the same phrases and arguments across twenty years. In his overview, 'the class struggle, suppressed at the level on which it had been traditionally waged, would be fought … as rivalry between power blocs and as cold war'.[7] Implicit in this was a closure on revolutionary perspectives in the West. As the Trotskyist Tony Cliff acidly commented, the workers had no H-bombs or sputniks.

Deutscher described Stalin's postwar takeover of Eastern Europe clinically, but always sympathetic to Soviet determination to remove the old ruling classes. 'Intermediate groupings, which might have stood for parliamentary government, lacked any substantial tradition and were extremely weak or ineffectual' – yet when they became so 'ineffectual' that their ranks swelled, they were subjected to the purge, allowing the Communist parties to achieve a monopoly of power. Deutscher did not conceal that these 'revolutions' were top-down and masterminded by the police. He admitted that communist stratagems included falsification of the popular vote: 'sooner or later 99 per cent of the voters must vote for the powers in being.' As a result, 'even their friends were irritated by the crude hypocrisy of their pretensions'. Yet always he insisted that Stalinism rescued the subjugated peoples of Eastern Europe from feudalism, 'savage poverty and darkness'. In Poland and Hungary, 'the Communist-inspired land reform fulfilled, perhaps imperfectly, a dream of many generations of peasants and intellectuals'. All this was ideologically consistent with Deutscher's support for Stalin's forced collectivisation and militarised industrial programmes after 1929.[8]

That Deustcher took a strategic view of the truth comes out clearly in his private correspondence with Heinrich Brandler, a witness to the entire history of the communist movement and personally acquainted with Rosa Luxemburg, Lenin, Trotsky, Bukharin and Stalin. Deutscher's first five-hour conversation with Brandler took place in London on 15 February 1948, the second three weeks later. Briefly vice-president of the Comintern, Brandler had served as assistant to the ruthless Cheka boss Dzerzhinsky. He told Deutscher that his phone conversation with Lenin was tapped. Deutscher noted: 'Everybody tapped everybody's telephones! Even Dzerzhinsky's phone was tapped.'[9]

Persona non grata in the Soviet zone, Brandler chose to return to West Germany where he became president of a new radical opposition organization called the Gruppe Arbeiterpolitik (Labour Policy Group) and editor of its journal, *Arpo*. Deutscher always wrote to him in English; Brandler replied in German. (Deutscher told Rudolf Hanke: 'my German has got so rusty that I hardly dare use it in writing.') To Brandler he confided (24 August 1949) what he would never have declared publicly – that he was impressed by the high turnout in the West German elections. We may need, he added, 'to view the Bonn experiment somewhat more cautiously'; this he would admit only privately, among trusted comrades. In this respect he was not unlike communist writers (Louis Aragon, for example) who knew many things they did not choose to disclose, or admit when challenged, because disclosure would not serve 'peace' or 'socialism'. Deutscher was of the same breed: strategic calculations constantly moulded what he said and did not say. On 16 February 1953, he told Brandler that he understood his 'reluctance to *appear* to say the same things which are shouted now from every anti-Soviet housetop; and with this motive I am in wholehearted sympathy'.[10]

The Berlin uprising of June 1953 came as a major blow. Deutscher responded in a letter to Brandler (15 July): 'It goes without saying that the workers of Berlin had their very good grievances and that the Russians and their marionettes have done everything to provoke the storm. Nevertheless it seems to me that the effect of the Berlin revolt has been objectively counter-revolutionary ... a local just cause was exploited for purposes which had nothing in common with it.' He now rebuked Brandler for associating himself 'with the anti-Russian movement'.

Brandler disagreed (1 August 1953): 'The workers rose against the mismanagement of the SED [Socialist Unity Party of Germany] bureaucrats, the transfer of Russian methods to Germany, and the spoliation of the country through reparations. . . . The occupation policies of the Soviet Union have driven millions into the camp of the United States and German imperialism. In East and West Germany there are millions of workers who say today: if what is happening in the Eastern Zone and in the Soviet Union is socialism, then let us rather have American capitalism.' On 16 September, Deutscher returned to the Berlin workers' revolt, which 'soon acquired the character of a political revolt against the Pieck-Ulbricht government. Because of this they inevitably strengthened the position of the Adenauer government and of its American protectors. Eisenhower, Dulles, even McCarthy greeted the Berlin demonstrators as their allies in the struggle for "freedom". What a paradox. Or is it a paradox?' Brandler might be right in claiming that in both East and West Germany there were millions of workers who preferred American capitalism to conditions in the Eastern zone, but Deutscher insisted that the practical alternative lay between the capitalist regime of Adenauer and 'the bureaucratic, quasi- (or if you like pseudo-) socialism of Pieck and Ulbricht'. He conceded that the Pieck–Ulbricht regime was hated but insisted that it was preferable to a restoration of capitalism.[11]

Although himself Polish, he passed over Roosevelt's opposition to Stalin's behaviour in taking control of the deeply divided country immediately prior to FDR's death. He did, however, write a revealing parable about an apocryphal state called 'Polrugaria', heavily modelled on Poland. In 'The Tragic Life of a Polrugarian Minister' (written in 1950, published in 1955), his fictitious hero, Vincent Adriano, a former inmate of Stalin's labour camps, has been released and rehabilitated in 1941. After the Liberation, the Stalinist Committee of Liberation becomes the provisional government, and then the actual government of Polrugaria. Adriano recognises that the people show little enthusiasm for the revolution, even though the large semi-feudal estates have been divided among land-hungry peasants – and despite public ownership of large-scale industry, progressive social legislation and ambitious educational reform. Adriano's priorities are Deutscher's: 'The most active and energetic allies of the West in Polrugaria are those who have had a stake in the old social order, the privileged men of the pre-war dictatorship, the old *soldateska*, the expropriated landlords and their like.' Given the opportunity, they would 'let loose a White terror the like of which had never been seen'; the real choice, as Adriano sees it, 'is not between tyranny and freedom, but between Stalinist tyranny, which is in part redeemed by economic and social progress, and a reactionary tyranny which would not be redeemed by anything'.[12]

This reflected Deutscher's line on the People's Democracies in general. Under the impact of the Polish and Hungarian revolts in 1956, he did acknowledge that communist rule was still associated with 'Russian conquest and domination', and outraged national dignity and the longing for independence turn automatically against communism as well as Russia'. Yet Poland had witnessed something like a proletarian revolution from below which adopted the communist regime in order to free it from the Stalinist stigma while keeping the 'Thermidorian forces at bay'.[13]

According to Leopold Labedz, writing about the 1956 upheaval: 'At the time of the Party counter-offensive against the press in Poland, when the "springboard of October", the celebrated magazine *Po Prostu*, and other periodicals were being suppressed, he [Deutscher] gave an interview to the weekly *Swiat* in which he approved of "limitations on democratic freedoms at certain periods" provided they were not presented "as a virtue, still less an eternal virtue". *Swiat* published a translation of Deutscher's 'The Ex-Communist's

Conscience', which distinguishes fertile Marxist heretics from reactionary renegades. On 3 March 1957, *Nowa Kultura* published a riposte by a young communist writer, A. Braun: 'Deutscher recommends abstention from activity as the only attitude worthy of an intellectual. . . . One has to remember that in our country people were destroyed and liquidated not for any activity but for that very attitude.' Following this, Deutscher then sent a letter to the journal (7 April 1957) in which he warned young 'revisionists' that they might be wrong in their attitude to the Russian Revolution 'because they are too near to it'. He again reminded them of the distinction between a heretic and a rene-gade, and was duly applauded in the official journal *Polityka*. K.T. Toeplitz responded in the *Nowa Kultura* of 21 April with the remark that Deutscher lived in England and probably understood the anecdote of the rabbi who advised: 'You can build socialism in one country, but you have to live in another.'[14]

And the Hungarian revolution? Initially he admitted that the Hungarians 'rejected Russian bayonets together with the revolution which was originally brought to that country on those bayonets. This was not a counter-revolution carried out by a hated and isolated possessing class defending its dominant position against the masses. It was, on the contrary, the ardent work of a whole insurgent people.' The description sounds unexceptional until Deutscher's historicism intervenes with the notion of a historical 'clock': 'It may be said that in October–November, the people of Hungary in a heroic frenzy tried unwit-tingly to put the clock back, while Moscow sought once again to wind up with the bayonet, or rather with the tank, the broken clock of the Hungarian Communist revolution. It is difficult to say who it was who acted the more tragic, and the more futile or hopeless role.' In 1957 he claimed that 'Nagy and his faction played the role which Trotsky at one time assumed Bukharin and Rykov would play in Russia', i.e. that of counter-revolution. In 1963, he remarked that in Hungary 'what was revolution and what was counter-revolution was determined by the balance of international power, not the balance of social forces in the country'. He later let fly a bad-tempered footnote in *The Prophet Unarmed*: 'Eastern Europe (Hungary, Poland and Eastern Germany), however, found itself almost on the brink of bourgeois restoration at the end of the Stalin era; and only Soviet armed power (or its threat) stopped it there.'[15]

For his part, Isaiah Berlin reported to Arthur Schlesinger, Jr.: 'I have just signed a violent document about Hungary, which will deprive me of a Soviet visa for ever and put an end to my scholarly career.' Elsewhere he reflected: 'As for the relative value and importance of the desire for national independence, it is perhaps enough to point to recent events in Hungary, in Poland and else-where for evidence that the orthodox Marxist interpretation of national feeling and its lack of influence upon the working classes of a nation conspicuously no longer capitalist, contains fallacies that have proved tragic enough to many of those involved in them.'[16]

The year before his death Deutscher had to admit that de-Stalinisation had juddered to a halt in Poland. On 28 April 1966, he released 'An Open Letter to Wladyslaw Gomulka and the Central Committee of the Polish Workers Party', protesting the secret trial and imprisonment of Ludwik Hass, Karol Modzelewski, Jacek Kuron and others charged with circulating leaflets and a pamphlet containing 'false information detrimental to the State and its supreme authorities'. After rehearsing the tragic history of the Polish party, Deutscher reminded Gomulka that he had protested when Gomulka was imprisoned and slandered during the last years of the Stalin era. He invoked his own essay 'The Tragedy of Polish Communism between the World Wars' (1957), and how Polish censors, Stalinists of the so-called Natolin group, had confiscated the essay when *Polityka* tried to publish it – but Gomulka had ordered it to be widely distributed among party members. 'Do you wish these trials to mark the tenth anniversary of your own rehabilitation?' he asked the Polish leader.[17] Here again Deutscher was claiming 'I belong'. The degree of self-deception – the desire to be recognised by Gomulka as a good comrade – was tragic.

Deutscher died the year before the anti-Zionist campaign led by Interior Minister Mieczyslaw Moczar, which coincided with the invasion of Czechoslovakia by Polish and other troops of the Warsaw Pact, following which some 13,000 Jews, including Holocaust survivors, were forced to leave Poland, and were stripped of their citizenship.

Possibly the most vehemently relentless assault on anyone in the annals of Cold War historical scholarship occurred when Leopold Labedz published 'Deutscher as Historian and Prophet' in April 1962. In fact, the polemic, which appeared in *Survey: A Journal of Soviet and East European Studies*, more or less confined itself to Deutscher's role as 'prophet'; a second article on the 'historian' was long delayed due, at least in part, to Deutscher's resort to legal action. Labedz was also a Polish immigrant to Britain but of a different stripe – a snapping terrier of the Cold War.[18] 'An assessment of Deutscher's views', Labedz begins, 'is impossible without taking into account his youthful traumas. His attachment to some illusions of his youth and his ambiguities are rooted in the earlier, little-known part of his biography. His pro-Soviet sympathies, his Trotskyist hagiography, his work for "bourgeois" newspapers while remaining on the side of History and the Proletariat – all these characteristic elements are already present in the earlier experience.' Derisive if somewhat manic terms like 'his "Olympian affidavits"' and 'lofty intellectual parentage' swarm in as Labedz embarks on a survey of Deutscher's writings on contemporary history, beginning with an article in the weekly *Wiadomosci Polskie*, written in 1942 under a Polish version of his name, Ignacy Niemieczycki. Labedz reports that here Deutscher explained the Soviet annexations of the Baltic States in 1940 as being motivated by 'none of the typical factors which determine the behaviour of any genuine imperialism. There was no search for markets, for sources of raw materials, or for profitable investment opportunities. Soviet annexations were ... only moves in the defensive politico-strategic game.'

Later, during the Stalinist terrorist heyday, 1948–53, Deutscher 'withdrew into a defensive position, disapproving of the persecutions but also of those who voiced their outrage without realising the dialectic of terror and progress. ... Deutscher deprecated Stalinist malevolence, but even more the aggrieved outcries on behalf of its victims by the "cold warriors" and the "anti-communist crusaders".'[19] Labedz quotes from Deutscher's *Heretics and Renegades*: 'Up to the time of the scandal with the Kremlin doctors, that is up to 1953, there was no unearthing of sinister conspiracies in Moscow, no hectic search for traitors and enemies of the people, no witches' Sabbath comparable to that of 1936–8'. Yet Eastern Europe had witnessed one show trial after another. Unknown to Labedz, a letter from Deutscher to Brandler (19 January 1952) regarding the actions taken against Clementis, Slansky and Gomulka is revealing of what he was keeping to himself. (The Czechs Vladimir Clementis and Rudolf Slansky were later tried and hanged in December of that year.) 'I can understand why you are careful not to join the general chorus of hypocritical defenders of those men (especially in Germany),' wrote Deutscher, 'but it seems to me that it is equally wrong to lend the slightest support to their persecutors.' On 29 November he wrote again: 'I find the Slansky trial a horrible affair, which we ought not and should not swallow or excuse ... while the motives and logic of the great Moscow trials of 1936–8 were quite clear to me, or so at least I think, I do not pretend to understand the motives behind the Slansky, Rajk, Kostov trials at all. Do you?'[20]

Yet Deutscher remained resolutely silent in public. Labedz accused him of 'moral ambivalence ... matched by political equivocation', adding: 'After a careful analysis of Deutscher's saying and writings, precious little remains of critical independence and historical impartiality; and this explains the suspicion that all his protestations of liberalism and objectivity, justified by occasional reservations and reluctant strictures, are nothing but a mask necessitated by "bourgeois" journalism and academic convention. Deutscher appears to be at bottom unable to shed his dogmatic style of thinking and cannot understand free thought unbound by a body of scriptures.'

He continued: 'The picture that emerges is of a man who takes himself much too seriously as an analyst, who is careless about evidence, always ready to shift the argument to prove his oracular presence, reluctant to admit an error, more concerned with the recovery of faith than with the discovery of truth.' As a *homo politicus* he was 'less than candid; as a prophet he was, and still is, in demand because . . . his own private unpuzzled vision of the communist wave of the future coincides with a universal longing for peace which induces many people to look at Soviet affairs through rose-coloured spectacles, thus assuaging their anxieties'.[21]

Almost immediately after this onslaught, punitive even by Cold War standards, Deutscher contacted (10 April 1962) the solicitor Sydney Silverman, also Jewish and a radical MP more than once expelled by the Parliamentary Labour Party for defying the whip. Silverman was in practice at the Middle Temple. Deutscher's case, as conveyed to him, may appear naïve because Labedz's attack was largely political, thus covered by 'fair comment', and well documented – yet elements of it could be construed as libellous. Deutscher complained: 'He also imputes to me journalistic dishonesty by saying that I present usually my "conjectural suppositions" as facts, which is untrue.' More generally: 'The purpose of the *Survey* article is, in my view, to discredit me morally and politically and to make impossible my continued work for the many newspapers and periodicals with which I have been associated in this country and abroad.' He informed Silverman that he had been 'under persistent and malignant attack from writers associated with the Congress for Cultural Freedom for many years'. His first letter concluded: 'It is perhaps time that I should react to this smear campaign; and I shall be much obliged for your opinion on the legal aspect.'

Even so, he was worried by the financial hazards: 'I cannot afford to take the risks which Harold Laski or Barbara Castle took – no one will pay costs for me, even if the sum were much less than £10,000 or £5,000.' He came up with a quotation from the Moscow journal *Voprosy Istorii (Questions of History)*, where he was described as a renegade Trotskyist in open alliance with anti-Soviet reaction, etc., etc. One may blink when he adds: 'The method by which *Survey* and the Soviet periodical arrive at their opposite conclusions is the same: wilful falsification.' Less than a year later the word 'falsification' was to dominate Isaiah Berlin's indictment of Deutscher in the All Souls common room.

Silverman suggested a consultation with the barrister Gerald Gardner, QC, recently famous for his successful defence of Penguin Books in the case of D.H. Lawrence's *Lady Chatterley's Lover*. On 17 July, Silverman despatched Gardner's opinion, which Deutscher found 'rather Delphic': on page 3, Gardner says 'I should have thought that any sensible jury would find the article to be defamatory of him', but on page 4 he warns that a sensible jury might not find it defamatory! Deutscher asked Silverman to drop the case. Silverman suggested a letter to *Survey*'s solicitors, 'using suitable extracts from Mr Gardner's opinion for this purpose' – page 3, not page 4. Deutscher agreed that 'suitable extracts' might be in order.[22]

Silverman duly wrote to Messrs Oswald Hickson Collier, representing *Survey*, on 31 July, listing fourteen allegations against Deutscher found in Labedz's article, none of which needs detain us, culminating in a ritual summation: 'In so far as these statements are statements of fact they are untrue, and in so far as they purport to be comment they are not fair comment.' He wanted to know 'what your Clients are prepared to do to vindicate my Client's character and repair the damage done to his international reputation.'[23] The matter evidently drifted into limbo. Deutscher must have known that if had gone to the Royal Courts of Justice, the witnesses against him would have been queuing up along the Strand as far as Fleet Street. (Berlin had surely had wind of Deutscher's failure to press an action when he discussed his 'falsifications' with the present writer.) On 10 May 1963, Deutscher informed Silverman that he had decided not to go to court, but he would avail himself of the right of reply if granted complete freedom of expression. Some time later, perhaps in August, this was granted in principle. There is no discovered record of legal accounts rendered or fees paid.

A postscript: on 26 August 1964, Labedz wrote to the strikingly named Hirsch Mendel Shtuckfish, of Tel Aviv: 'I am trying to find out biographical details on Isaac Deutscher. . . . Pierre Naville told me that you were one of the two delegates from Poland at the foundation of the Fourth International in 1938 and Deutscher claims in the book on Trotsky that he was the actual author of the political platform presented by the two delegates. I wonder if it was so? Neither Max Shachtman nor Pierre Naville can recollect any role played by Deutscher.' Labedz also asked Shtuckfish whether he knew of any inaccuracies in the third volume of Deutscher's biography of Trotsky, recently published. What remains unclear is how this letter, on its original airletter form, found its way into Deutscher's possession. One must assume that Hirsch Mendel Shtuckfish sent it to him.[24]

15

ORWELL AND THE RENEGADES

On several occasions Deutscher addressed closed meetings at Harvard during his first research visit in 1950. At one such gathering he delivered a highly provocative analysis of the 'Ex-Communist's Conscience' – later the opening essay in *Heretics and Renegades* (1955). The article first appeared in the *Reporter* (25 April 1950) under the headline: 'What Can Ex-Communists Do? Isaac Deutscher suggests: Observe, but keep out of, Politics.'

Every day during his first visit to Harvard and Stanford the newspapers brought sensationalist accounts of the escalating Congressional investigations of communist subversion, lining up witnesses and victims, many of whom took refuge in the Fifth Amendment – 'Are you now or have you ever been ... ?' The leaders of the American Communist Party went to jail while Senator Joseph McCarthy denounced 'twenty years of treason' in the wake of the Alger Hiss perjury trials. It was in this climate that Deutscher's disgust took shape. Following his return to London, he reported to Robert Jackson (16 June 1950): 'It so happened that our visit coincided with an enormous intensification in the notorious witch-hunt. Two or three days after our arrival Hiss was convicted and this had its immediate effect. Then came the [Owen] Lattimore case with all its ramifications. During the last days of our stay in California, [J. Robert] Oppenheimer (the atomic physicist, not his brother) was charged with having been a Communist before a Committee of the Californian State Senate ... the heresy hunting took the form of a chain reaction the end of which was unpredictable.'[1] It produced 'a spate of loyalty statements and recantations, the like of which could be seen only in Moscow in the early thirties'.

European émigrés figured prominently among the ex-communist witnesses. The former German communist Ruth Fischer had testified before the House Un-American Activities Committee against her brother, the gifted musician Hanns Eisler, friend of Brecht and composer of the 'Comintern March', resulting in his blacklisting and deportation back to Germany in 1948. She also testified that her other brother, Gerhart Eisler, was a major communist agent (a fervent Stalinist, he settled in East Germany). Deutscher wrote to Heinrich Brandler: 'I shudder to think what fantastic recantations Ruth Fischer and her like must have signed in order to become such welcome guests in the States.' He had in fact been invited by Geoffrey Cumberlege of OUP to give his opinion of Ruth Fischer's *Stalin and German Communism*, which he found to be a 'contribution to scholarship' with 'a high documentary value', she having led the German Communist Party in the early 1920s, although potentially of less appeal to the general reader than to specialist students interested in the intricate struggles and rivalries between largely forgotten 'coteries and cliques in the German Communist Party and the Comintern'. (This was disingenuous in so far as he grilled Brandler for his recall of the same coteries and cliques.) He wrote to A. Ciliga, reporting that he had met Ruth Fischer in London: 'Her mind is so much warped and distorted by her anti-Stalinism and so much involved in the most vulgar type of anti-Stalinist campaigning.'[2]

Another 'renegade' enjoying a high-profile welcome in the United States was Arthur Koestler, author of *Darkness at Noon*, who had later played a key role in the publication of *The God That Failed* in London. A Jew from Budapest, and likewise a former communist who had escaped to England soon after Deutscher, Koestler became Deutscher's principal target. In 'The Ex-Communist's Conscience', Deutscher says of the contributors to *The God That Failed*, including André Gide, Richard Wright and Stephen Spender: 'All have left an army and a camp – some as conscientious objectors, some as deserters, and others as marauders. A few stick quietly to their conscientious objections, while others vociferously claim commissions in an army which they had bitterly opposed. All wear threadbare bits and pieces of the old uniform, supplemented by the quaintest new rags.'[3] Ignazio Silone was the only contributor to this book who commanded his respect, because the Italian writer conveyed the intellectual excitement and moral enthusiasm of communism in the early days. The main attack was directed against Koestler: 'as a rule the intellectual ex-communist ceases to oppose capitalism. Often he rallies to its defence, and he brings to this job the lack of scruple, the narrow-mindedness, the disregard for the truth, and the intense hatred with which Stalinism has imbued him. He remains a sectarian. He is an inverted Stalinist.'[4]

However, here again the public position diverged from the private view. In a letter to Brandler, Deutscher admitted that 'in arguing against the nonsensical "theories" of Koestler it is only too easy to give the impression of unwittingly whitewashing some of the least attractive sides of Stalinism'.[5] But this he

did not declare publicly. Indeed, later, in *The Prophet Outcast*, Deutscher drew
a direct lineage from his hero Trotsky to the renegades: 'Not only did
[Trotsky's] *The Revolution Betrayed* (1937) become the Bible of latter-day
Trotskyist sects and chapels, whose members piously mumbled its verses long
after Trotsky's death. The effect of the book was felt more widely, in the literature of disillusionment produced by western ex-communists in the nineteen-
forties and nineteen-fifties.' He mentioned James Burnham, Silone, Koestler,
Orwell. But much of *The Revolution Betrayed* remained true and powerful, he
admitted, particularly on Stalinist thought control and rigid uniformity in the
arts and sciences.[6]

In *Heretics and Renegades*, Deutscher pressed a parallel between the new
breed of ex-communists and the embittered ex-Jacobins of the Napoleonic era.
Wordsworth and Coleridge were fatally obsessed with the 'Jacobin danger;
their fear dimmed even their poetic genius'. Deutscher elevates Shelley to a
contrasting position of moral integrity, quoting his sonnet on Wordsworth:

> In honoured poverty thy voice did weave
> Songs consecrate to truth and liberty –
> Deserting these, thou leavest me to grieve,
> Thus having been, that thou shouldst cease to be.

Shelley remained true to the Jacobin-Republican ideal: it was as a Republican,
and not as a patriot of the England of George III, that he greeted the fall of
Napoleon, that 'most unambitious slave' who did 'dance and revel on the grave
of Liberty'. Deutscher extends his praise to those, like Jefferson and Goethe,
who refused to identify themselves with either Napoleon's military despotism
or the Holy Alliance, Europe's 'hypocritical deliverers'. Deutscher clearly saw
himself in this light, refusing to choose between Stalinism and the North
Atlantic Alliance, stationed in his 'watchtower'. 'What a pity and what a shame
it is that most ex-communist intellectuals are inclined to follow the tradition
of Wordsworth and Coleridge rather than that of Goethe and Shelley.'[7]

Unlike the admirable 'heretic' (himself), the 'renegade' does not break with
the Party bureaucracy in the name of true communism, he goes on to break
with communism itself. 'He no longer throws out the dirty water of the Russian
revolution to protect the baby; he discovers that the baby is a monster which
must be strangled. The heretic becomes a renegade.' The ex-communist renegade advances bravely in the front rank of every witch-hunt, his blind hatred
leaven to the forces of reaction. 'He insists that the world should recognise his
uneasy conscience as the clearest conscience of all', camouflaging his guilt by
a show of extraordinary certitude and frantic aggressiveness. Indeed, he may

be heard denouncing the mildest brand of the welfare state as 'legislative Bolshevism'. (None of the contributors to *The God That Failed* did so.)

Deutscher claims that the genuine 'heretic' like himself 'cannot join the Stalinist camp or the anti-Stalinist Holy Alliance without doing violence to his better self'. Some years after Deutscher produced this essay, Leopold Labedz commented sardonically that the 'heretic' 'will refrain from breaking with communism, notwithstanding the Leningrad affair, the hanging of Kostov and Rajk, the Crimean case, the Slansky trial, and the doctors' plot'. Yet, added Labedz, was it not noteworthy that this particular 'heretic', while suffering from an inverted apostasy complex, contrived to defend Stalin's Russia 'in the most influential press organs of the wicked Holy Alliance'?[8]

Isaiah Berlin wrote to David Astor (14 May 1958), linking Deutscher with 'other perverters of truth who squeeze the facts into iron frameworks of doctrine, against all that their hearts or consciences tell them'. It was no surprise that Deutscher regarded Koestler, Borkenau and other 'renegades' as behaving '*indecently*' in attacking their old gods'. Deutscher might have a quarrel within the Communist Party, but he totally rejected the Western world. Not a single idea could be found in his articles since Stalin's death that 'a Russian Communist could radically dissent from'.[9]

Deutscher's scathing attack on George Orwell in *Heretics and Renegades* appeared at a time when Orwell enjoyed a semi-iconic status in England and America that could be likened (though inexactly) to that of Pushkin in Russia. Orwell did not fit Deutscher's 'renegade' category because he was never remotely a communist, but the popular influence of *Animal Farm* and *Nineteen Eighty-Four* far outstripped that of *The God That Failed*. Deutscher noted that such Orwellian terms as 'Thought Police', 'Crimethink' and 'Hateweek' now regularly occurred in newspaper articles and political speeches. Big Brother had appeared on cinema and television screens on both sides of the Atlantic.[10]

In Orwell's novel, or dystopia, *Nineteen Eighty-Four* (1949) we witness the systematic, totalitarian cleansing of the mind by brainwashing and unashamed leader-worship (Big Brother), while only a few exceptional individuals possess the values, the resilience, to say no. The cowed masses meekly watch the hysterical exhortations emanating from television screens and obediently report suspected deviants to the Thought Police. Deutscher assailed this novel as a huge threat to sanity; Berlin found it impressive.

Deutscher had known Orwell when they shared a room as correspondents of the *Observer* reporting from occupied Germany. The presiding tone of his demolition of *Nineteen Eighty-Four* was intellectually patronising – only the *deus ex machina* of classical Marxism, understood on the Continent of Europe, could rescue Orwell's English audience from their myopic and antiquated provincialism. Ignoring Orwell's earlier novella, *Animal Farm* (1945), and the tradition of Swiftean satire still alive in Gulliver's native island, Deutscher insisted that Orwell had failed to understand Stalin's purges because, as a provincial English rationalist lacking Marxist education, he was incapable of analysing the real motivation behind the seemingly irrational. (This line of argument closely echoes that of Maurice Merleau-Ponty's *Humanisme et terreur*, a Marxist critique of Koestler's *Darkness at Noon*.) Deutscher was unforgiving: '*1984* has taught millions to look at the conflict between East and West in terms of black and white, and it has shown them a monster bogey and a monster scapegoat for all the ills that plague mankind.'[11]

Arguing that Orwell's dystopian vision was far from original, Deutscher made much of his acknowledged debt to Yevgeny Zamyatin's futuristic novel *We*. Applying the debt both to the plot of *Nineteen Eighty-Four* and to its underlying idea, Deutscher cites Orwell's tribute to Zamyatin's intuitive grasp of the irrational side of totalitarianism, the indulgence in human sacrifice and cruelty as ends in themselves, the worship of the leader credited with semi-divine attributes. Deutscher here attempts to darken this heritage by depicting Zamyatin as a counter-revolutionary from the outset: 'In 1917 Zamyatin viewed the new revolution with cold and disillusioned eyes, convinced that nothing good would come out of it. After a brief imprisonment he was allowed by the Bolshevik Government to go abroad; and it was as an émigré in Paris that he wrote *We* in the early 1920s.' But this was not the case: in reality Zamyatin had been a Bolshevik sympathiser who initially greeted the revolution with enthusiasm. He was never imprisoned. He wrote *We* in Russia, not in Paris. He did not go to Paris until 1931, after a dignified request to Stalin to be allowed to emigrate was granted on the advice of Gorky.[12]

Deutscher's central purpose was to depict Orwell, like the ex-communist 'renegades', as a convert to black reaction: '*1984* is a document of dark disillusionment not only with Stalinism but with every form and shade of socialism. It is a cry from the abyss of despair.' A mere rationalist with no grasp of Marxism, unfamiliar with the dialectic of history, Orwell remained 'at heart a simple-minded anarchist' for whom 'any political movement forfeited its raison d'être the moment it acquired a raison d'état'.[13] So: Orwell simpleminded rationalist; Orwell simple-minded anarchist; Orwell enemy of socialism.

Deutscher then inducts the reader into the proper method of analysis of Soviet reality which Orwell (and other anti-totalitarians) had failed to understand: 'To analyse a complicated social background, to try and unravel tangles of political motives, calculations, fears and suspicions, and to discern the compulsion of circumstances behind *their* action was beyond him. Generalizations about social forces, social trends and historic inevitabilities made him bristle with suspicion. . . . His gaze was fixed on the trees, or rather on a single tree, in front of him, and he was almost blind to the wood.'

Here again there was more than one Deutscher. The polemicist had a tendency to overlook what he had written as a historian – or to count on his readers overlooking it. Consider his own description of Stalin's behaviour and motivation during the era of the purge trials and liquidations. In his *Stalin*, Deutscher introduces Dostoyevsky's *Brothers Karamazov*, where the Grand Inquisitor enters into passionate controversy with Christ. In an entirely fictive scene, Deutscher visualises the increasingly remote autocrat Stalin imagining himself representing the Church in revolt against the Gospel. 'We have corrected Thy deed and based it on Miracle, Mystery and Authority. . . . And men were delighted that they were led once again, as a herd, and that there had been lifted from their hearts, at last, so terrible a gift, the gift [of freedom] that had brought them to such torment. . . . Why then hast Thou now come to hinder us?'[14] Not much about the 'compulsion of circumstances' here, and not much properly 'dialectical' analysis; indeed, had Orwell himself been able to read this when writing *Nineteen Eighty-Four*, he might well have served it up for Big Brother's breakfast.

Venturing further into Deutscher's *Stalin*, we learn that during the trials of the Old Bolsheviks Stalin never appeared in court although he was 'the invisible author, manager and producer as well. . . . Not a single piece of evidence that could be verified by normal legal procedure was presented.' Indeed, Deutscher was treading the same ground as the hated Koestler in *Darkness at Noon* when he wrote in *Stalin*: 'Ever since the middle twenties recantation had been something like a ritual habit, an accepted routine, with the broken men of the opposition. They had begun with the admission of ordinary offences against discipline and they ended by confessing apocalyptic sins. . . . Each time they made a recantation, they agreed to confess some sin only slightly graver than the one confessed before. Each time they hoped, of course, that this would be the last sacrifice demanded of them for the sake of the party and for their own redemption.'[15]

So what is the 'dialectical' explanation for this? We are not told. Something to do with power-lust, perhaps? But no: according to Deutscher, Orwell's distrust of historical generalisations led him to adopt and to cling to 'the oldest, the most banal, the most abstract, the most metaphysical, and the most barren of all generalizations: all *their* conspiracies and plots and purges and diplomatic deals had one source and one source only – "sadistic power-hunger". Thus he made his jump from workaday, rationalistic common sense to the mysticism of cruelty which inspires *1984.* Deutscher presses this point: 'It is the collective cruelty of the party . . . that torments Oceania. Totalitarian society is ruled by a disembodied sadism. . . . The party is not a social body actuated by any interest or purpose. It is a phantom-like emanation of all that is foul in human nature. It is the metaphysical, mad and triumphant, Ghost of Evil.' Orwell's diabolical Party apparatchik O'Brien confides to his prisoner, the good Winston Smith: 'If you want a picture of the future, imagine a boot stamping on a human face – forever.' Deutscher insists that Orwell's mistake was to project 'the spectacle of the Great Purges on to the future' and to fix it there forever, 'because he was not capable of grasping the events realistically, in their complex historical context'.

How should one treat Stalin's purges 'realistically'? Deutscher agrees that they were highly irrational but he who treats them irrationally is very much like the psychiatrist whose mind becomes unhinged by dwelling too closely with insanity.[16]

In fact, Orwell saw 'cruelty' and 'power-for-power's sake' as the end product of totalitarianism, the nauseous gas it released, not as its source or origin. It is an odd feature of his essay that Deutscher nowhere refers back to Orwell's *Animal Farm*, the brilliant fable or 'fairy story' (as Orwell called it) in which the step-by-step progression of the Pig Party from rebellion on behalf of all the farm animals against man's cruel domination finally culminates in Pig Rule and the triumph of the human vices, not excluding power for the sake of power, cruelty for cruelty's sake.

Deutscher held that Orwell was a paranoid personality addicted to conspiracy theories. He recalled conversations when both worked as *Observer* correspondents in post-war Germany. While interested by Deutscher's commentaries on Russia in the *Economist*, the *Observer* and *Tribune*, Orwell struck Deutscher as embodying a Freudian sublimation of persecution mania (a doubtful reading of Freud).[17] In Orwell's distorted perspective, Stalin, Churchill and Roosevelt were consciously plotting to divide the world and subjugate it in common. Here, Deutscher adds, one finds the origins of Oceania, Eurasia and Eastasia in *Nineteen Eighty-Four*. Yet Deutscher himself made much of the secret 'gentleman's' agreement reached by Churchill and Stalin in October 1944, dividing Europe into spheres of influence. When Deutscher pointed to the underlying conflict among the Big Three, he said, Orwell disagreed – yet elsewhere Deutscher always stressed that there need have been no underlying conflict if the Western powers had not panicked. 'What struck me in Orwell was his lack of historical sense and of psychological insight into the political life coupled with an acute, though narrow, penetration into some aspects of politics and with an incorruptible firmness of conviction.'[18]

A year earlier Deutscher had written to Heinrich Brandler (16 February 1953): 'The only credit which one must and ought to give Stalinism is that it has been creating in Russia and in the countries of the Soviet orbit the *material and organizational preconditions* of socialism. In *social psychology* and *culture* it has fostered on the contrary, bureaucratic rigidity and stupidity on the one hand and an almost zoological individualism on the other.'[19] But Orwell's version of the zoo somehow lacked 'historical sense and psychological insight'.

Reviewing (anonymously) Deutscher's attack on Orwell in *Heretics and Renegades*, E.H. Carr pointed out that the degradation of the 'Proles' in *Nineteen Eighty-Four* is reflected in their addiction to 'rubbishy newspapers containing almost nothing except sport, crime and astrology, sensational five-cent novelettes, films oozing with sex' – characteristic evils, commented Carr, not of the Soviet but of the British and American scene. This was true. In Orwell's imagined totalitarian England, the Proles are depicted as degraded by two distinct factors: the rule of the Party and the debasement of popular taste by the old capitalist press. Orwell fails to signal where the seams between these two factors are being sewn, yet one suspects that he expected a British totalitarian party to exploit the local habits and debased tastes of a specifically British working class, turning them into 'the Proles', a class now deprived of any voice of its own.[20]

Deutscher was not without his admirers. Another who, like Carr, greeted warmly the first edition of *Heretics and Renegades* was Bertrand Russell, who described its author as 'to my mind the most intellectually satisfying of the many writers on Soviet Russia'. His massive works on Stalin and Trotsky 'presented these men as nearly as possible with historic impartiality'. Regarding the essay on ex-communists, Russell found the parallel with the English ex-Jacobins of Napoleon's time, Wordsworth and Coleridge, accurate and fruitful (Coleridge even denigrated a bill for the prevention of cruelty to animals as 'the strongest instance of legislative Jacobinism'). The ex-communists of our day, Russell continued, 'will support any abomination provided the Communists are opposed to it'. But Russell (like Carr) was more sceptical about Russia's future transition from 'the violence and cruelty of Bolshevism' to democracy. Industrialisation did not, as Deutscher thought, guarantee it: take the examples of Japan and Germany.

We do not have much to go on regarding Isaiah Berlin's view of Orwell's two satires on Stalinism, beyond the clear implication that he knew them. He mentioned the 'hair-raising satires of George Orwell and Aldous Huxley' when charging the communist states with refusing to foster 'the critical, or solution-finding, powers of their citizens'. Communist policy was dedicated to 'the training of individuals incapable of being troubled by questions which, when raised and discussed, endanger the stability of the system'. Towards the end of his life Berlin praised Orwell for discerning how the idea of positive liberty, 'which is of course essential to a decent existence, has been more often abused or perverted than that of negative liberty. . . . George Orwell is excellent on this.'[21]

Although the dying Orwell was at pains to issue a statement rectifying any impression that *Nineteen Eighty-Four* amounted to a renunciation of socialism in all its forms, Deutscher and Carr were far from alone in claiming the opposite. Deutscher's polemic to some extent anticipates E.P. Thompson's critique of Orwell's earlier essay 'Inside the Whale', in which he famously called progress 'a swindle' – more accurately: 'Progress and reaction have both turned out to be swindles.' Clearly both Deutscher and Thompson suffered exasperation that Orwell had implicitly dismissed as blind folly their own years of dedicated commitment to the communist cause.

Orwell's 'Inside the Whale' contains a punishing description of the totalitarian temptation in its communist version: 'For it was simply something to believe in. Here was a Church, an Army, an orthodoxy, a discipline. . . . All the loyalties and superstitions that the intellect had seemingly banished could come rushing back under the thinnest of disguises. Patriotism, religion, empire, military glory – all in one word, Russia. Father, king, leader, hero, saviour – all in one word, Stalin. God – Stalin. The devil – Hitler. Heaven – Moscow. Hell – Berlin. All the gaps were filled up.' And more: 'To people of that kind such things as purges, secret police, summary executions, imprisonment without trial, etc. etc. are too remote to be terrifying. They can swallow totalitarianism *because* they have no experience of anything except liberalism.' Once inside the whale's belly you need never know whether the whale was 'leaping up through the waves or a mile down'.[22]

Thompson laments ('hard to forgive') another virulent passage about the leftist English intelligentsia in Orwell's 1941 essay 'England Your England': 'They take their cookery from Paris and their opinions from Moscow.' They are ashamed of their own nationality. In left-wing circles one must snigger at every institution from horse racing to suet puddings. They would 'feel more ashamed of standing to attention during "God Save the King" than of stealing from a poor box'. The British fellow travellers are sometimes 'squashily pacifist, sometimes violently pro-Russian, but always anti-British'. The intellectual sabotage from the Left (claimed Orwell) was partly responsible for fascist nations judging England to be sufficiently decadent to risk war against.[23]

Thompson complains that Orwell's *Selected Essays* 'must appear like an endless football game, in which one side (Fascism, Reaction) is invisible, while the other side (Anti-Fascism, Communism, Progress) spend their whole time fouling each other or driving the ball into their own goal. Orwell is like a man who is raw all down one side and numb on the other.' He equates the Right with 'decent people', the 'average thinking person', the Left with 'bearded fruit-juice drinkers who come flocking towards the smell of "progress" like bluebottles to a dead cat'. Thompson's rejoinder to Orwell, delivered twenty years after Deutscher's, is superior in tone and understanding but in the end it, too, founders before the simple truth that to embrace Stalinism was a ghastly mistake. Thompson comes close to Deutscher when he complains that *Nineteen Eighty-Four* 'helped to blind a later generation to the forces within Communism making for its transformation. . . . Its political *raison d'être* is the containment of communism, not in order that they may build the good society but so that we may preserve a philosophical tradition which teaches that no society can ever be good.'[24] (Having left the Party, Thompson waited in vain for the 'transformation' of communism but did live to witness its collapse.)

Worth noting is Deutscher's public silence about the dramas staged by ex-communist 'renegades' in Paris. In terms of the evidence and witnesses assembled, and of the public impact, London's *The God That Failed* was a mere sideshow compared to Paris's extended Kravchenko libel trial, staged in 1949, with the Soviet state flying in its own witnesses to refute the indictment of Stalinism by the defector Victor Kravchenko (whose book *I Chose Freedom* was alleged by the communist defendants in the trial, the editors of *Les Lettres françaises*, to have been ghostwritten by the CIA). It was in the course of this court case and a subsequent libel action brought by David Rousset that the full horror of Stalinism was most irrefutably exposed. Witnesses like Margarete Buber-Neumann and Alex Weissberg had entirely validated stories to tell that carried the camera into the heartland of Stalinist power during the years before the events of 1941 changed the libretto. Reading Buber-Neumann's scrupulous first-hand account of the purge era in Moscow, of her arrest and incarceration, of being handed back to the Gestapo by the NKVD, of her subsequent years in a Nazi concentration camp, it would be hard for Deutscher or anyone to denigrate her testimony as that of a 'renegade'. Finally, as the German army scattered before the Soviet advance into Germany, she and her fleeing companion came upon the Americans. 'They stood there silently spread out in open order. . . . We came up to the nearest man. He had a round, red, friendly face and he looked at us curiously.' In broken English she explained the coloured patches on her miserable camp clothes and her fear of the Russians. ' "OK, sister," he said. "Go through." ' He made a gesture of invitation with his hand. 'I never heard such a beautiful arrangement of words before in my life.'[25]

These two Paris libel trials persuaded Jean-Paul Sartre and Simone de Beauvoir to abandon their doubts about Soviet concentration camps, although never allowing themselves to follow Koestler into the Western orbit. The reality of Soviet forced labour and concentration camps was now beyond dispute (although not for the French Communist Party), but Sartre's outlook, like Deutscher's, was intensely strategic: what counted was who deployed these indubitable facts against whom. In polemical exchanges with Rousset and Albert Camus, Sartre argued that such 'facts', even if correct, did not serve the cause of 'peace', of 'socialism', of France's independence from American hegemony. Ironically, the communist press employed the same logic when responding angrily to the open acknowledgment by Sartre and Merleau-Ponty, in *Les Temps modernes*, that forced labour was operated on a massive scale in the USSR. Utterly ignoring their evidence, the communist writer Pierre Daix posed the familiar question: 'With whom are you? With the people of the Soviet Union, who are building a new society, or with their enemies?' (Later Daix was to disown the party line on everything.)[26]

Deutscher remained a valued contributor to Sartre's *Les Temps modernes*. His real, private knowledge of the Gulag Archipelago can be extracted from his response (11 October 1950) to the typescript of a brochure he received from Heinrich Brandler: 'this passage about the forced labour camps goes too far in explaining and justifying. It is true that planned economy requires planned husbandry of manpower. But you know very well that the human factor is the cheapest in Stalin's eyes.'[27]

16

POST-STALIN RUSSIA:
THE PROPHECIES

EVEN IN THE late Stalin era, Deutscher had insisted that the Soviet totalitarian system was not immutable. During his US visit in 1950 a small gathering of Harvard scholars hotly debated his prognosis that Stalin's end would inevitably be the end of Stalinism and that Russian society was not at a standstill. Deutscher immediately responded to Stalin's death (about which he had been speculating since 1949 in syndicated articles) with an article in *The Times*, 'The New Structure of Soviet Leadership. Mr Malenkov and Stalin's "Old Guard"'.[1] His book *Russia after Stalin* (1953) appeared soon after the dictator's death and received an immediate attack in *Encounter*, which accorded Deutscher the right of a lengthy reply.[2] He was to continue speculating about the inevitable process of Soviet democratisation for many years, while engaging in the despised bourgeois practice of 'Kremlinology'. His predictions were relentlessly wrong and for that reason can be treated with brevity – but not forgetting that it was by no means clear at the time, with cosmonauts orbiting the Earth, what course Soviet communism would take.

His 'Post-Stalinist Ferment of Ideas' appeared in *The Times* (16–18 November 1954), and gave rise to controversy in the correspondence columns. For Deutscher, it was all happening as predicted:

Economists have vented their resentment at an orthodoxy under which they were reduced to the role of Stalin's gramophone records. Biologists have reacted against the humiliation they have suffered at Lysenko's hands. Physicists have declared that they have had enough of the chauvinistic Great Russian swank. . . . Painters and sculptors have revolted against that 'socialist realism' which has compelled them to dress, in shoddy style, Stalin and his entourage as demi-gods. Novelists and poets have expressed disgust . . . at the compulsion to produce dramas without real conflict, novels without living people. . . . The youth of Russia, the students of the Universities of Moscow, Leningrad, and Kiev, have rebelled against the hypocrisy and rigid formalism of the Stalin cult. . . . Even in the concentration camps in the Polar regions, if recent ex-inmates are to be believed, the deportees have formed themselves into distinct groups, produced their political programmes and blueprints for the future.

However, he conceded, the attitude of the Soviet power elite, Stalin's direct successors, remained equivocal. 'Two souls seem to dwell in the breast of the Malenkov government. . . . Stalin's closest associates and successors were indeed the first to break the ice. But soon they began to wonder in perplexity where the drifting floes might not carry them.'[3]

A letter from Isaiah Berlin to Hamilton Fish Armstrong (23 December 1954) refers to Deutscher's 'Ferment of Ideas in Russia' as 'clever rubbish'. Writing to David Astor (27 January 1955), Berlin extended his diatribe, expressing 'the greatest contempt for Deutscher', whom he regarded as dishonest even in terms of his own Marxist framework. Berlin distrusted him 'as a person and as a writer' and regarded his *Stalin* as 'a deception'. His perspective on Russia rather resembled that of one of those Germans who admired Hitler until, say, 1938, but condemned his later blunders. Deutscher was no defender of liberal values, and also 'cunning, dishonest and cheap by comparison with E.H. Carr . . . a sweet human being and a decent public personality'. The truth did not interest Deutscher; his articles on the contemporary Soviet Union had been falsified by events more frequently than those of any other Soviet expert. 'About that he is marvellously unblushing.'[4]

In a letter to Frank Wisner of the CIA (4 May 1955), Berlin continued his attack: '[Deutscher] is a full-sized charlatan and not a word he says, it seems to me, is to be believed.' No one had made more false predictions during the past three years and his pose as an expert was 'shocking'. Berlin allowed himself his own prophetic view, denying any possibility of genuine reform while the Party remained in power. He advised Wisner that disagreements within the Politburo were never genuinely ideological, or even primarily personal, 'but always and explicitly strategical and tactical'.[5]

Deutscher hit back at his detractors (although not aware of Berlin's private correspondence). In 'A Reply to Critics' (March 1954), first published in *L'Esprit*, he defended his *Russia after Stalin* of the previous year. 'I have also drawn the wrath of the professional propagandists of the cold war, and quite especially of the anti-communist crusaders fighting under the lofty banners of the "Congress for Cultural Freedom". On the other hand, many serious and able writers have defended my views with much conviction and effect.' He continued: 'The cold war propagandist bases all his arguments and slogans on the assumption of an unchangeable and irredeemable evil in Stalinism or communism at large. . . . He therefore stubbornly refuses to see that the "evil" has been historically determined.' The USSR was an expanding society on the basis of a planned economy, 'making it immune from that extreme economic and moral instability which in a bourgeois society tends to produce fascist mass neuroses'. Continuous expansion was inherent in a planned economy of the Soviet type, just as the ups and downs of the trade cycle prevailed under capitalism. 'This is the hard core of truth in all communist propaganda' – even when wrapped in layers of crude fiction.[6]

By the mid-Fifties Deutscher's commentaries on world communism were in rising demand among France's left-wing papers, mainly the new arrival *L'Express*, with whose editor, Jean-Jacques Servan-Schreiber, he corresponded in flattering terms: 'May I use this opportunity to congratulate you on that feat of high-class journalism that Express has already become.' Founded in 1953, *L'Express* drew contributions from Sartre, Camus, François Mauriac. Deutscher also established a relationship with J.M. Domenach, of *L'Esprit* and Editions du Seuil, which published *Russia after Stalin*, Domenach checking the translation. Sartre's *Les Temps modernes* paid 100,000 francs (only £100 at that time) for serialisation of *The Prophet Armed*, with the same terms for *The Prophet Unarmed* when completed. Deutscher's Italian contacts were good, particularly *L'Epoca*; likewise in Scandinavia. He was admired in the Indian subcontinent, published by the *Statesman* of Calcutta and by the *Ceylon Daily News*. He wrote regularly for the New York *Reporter* from 1950 to 1961, producing ten syndicated articles a year, earning about $400 for each contribution, until he fell out with Max Ascoli over a piece on Chinese-Russian relations.[7]

When Deutscher announced in *The Times* that the Soviet regime was mellowing, Berlin used the same term as before, 'clever rubbish', while writing to his mother (19 April 1955). Berlin had recently been in Rome, where he had met the first Soviet historians allowed out since Stalin's death. They were full of hearty bonhomie, but it all seemed like an orchestrated performance. Berlin's article 'Generalissimo Stalin and the Art of Government' had outlined the zigzag pattern of Soviet behaviour, now loosening, now tightening the reins: the latest thaw was a zig but a zag was sure to follow.[8]

Answering questions posed by the *Partisan Review* (autumn 1956), Deutscher spoke with his usual confidence: 'The break with Stalinism is now felt in every aspect of Soviet activity and thought: in domestic and foreign policies, in education, in philosophical writing, in historical research, and indeed, in the whole atmosphere of Soviet life.' He ventured further: 'The autocratic system of government, bequeathed by Stalin, is shattered. The backbone of the

M.V.D., the political police, is broken. The *universe concentrationnaire* is dissolving.' Already post-Stalin Russia had achieved greater economic equality, an end to piece-work payment and Stakhanovism, the abolition of all fees for education. This advance of egalitarianism 'outweighs in importance volumes of abstract political theorising about the "impossibility of reform in a totalitarian system"'. He discerned 'a striving for government by consent'.

Here we may consider what was meant by the term 'totalitarian'. As the Cold War hardened it had become common currency in the West. 'There isn't any difference in totalitarian states,' remarked President Harry S. Truman. 'I don't care what you call them, Nazi, Communist or Fascist.' In America, 'Red Fascism' also gained wide currency as a more headline-friendly, populist synonym for totalitarianism. In February 1947, FBI director J. Edgar Hoover published another of his dire warnings (in *American Magazine*), 'Red Fascism in the United States Today'. For the American Federation of Labor's George Meany, Stalin was 'the Russian Hitler'. In other words, the enemy we now face is no less of a menace than the one we have just defeated on the battlefield.

In the first sentence of *The Open Society and its Enemies* (1945), Karl Popper speaks of 'historicism and its connection with totalitarianism'. Isaiah Berlin declared his debt to Popper, who argued that the relation of the individual to the hierarchy of rulers in Plato had many similarities to modern totalitarian regimes. Bertram D. Wolfe described totalitarianism as the 'master key' to the Soviet system. Berlin applied the term 'totalitarian' to what he regarded as the twin nightmares, horribly coupled, of the twentieth century, nightmares that could probably be dispelled only by external force, as had happened with Hitler. In Berlin's work we find no definition, or structural analysis, of either Nazi or communist totalitarianism. When he employed the term it was usually tossed in to a wider historical indictment of the consequences of 'monism', 'utopianism', Enlightenment rationalism, scientism or the belief in predetermined progress leading inexorably to a single, unitary vision of man's destiny. But Berlin left it to colleagues and friends to produce detailed definitions of the totalitarian systems, which by and large they located as specific to the twentieth century and distinguishable from such ancient antecedents as authoritarianism, dictatorship and despotism.

If one takes the liberty of amalgamating the various definitions – although there was no shortage of disputes – the agreed common factors emerge. Totalitarianism is inseparable from modern 'mass society', from the mobilisation of a 'whole people' in the Cause. There is a doctrine, a programme, incarnated in a single ruling Party, guided by a single infallible Leader, supported by a police force beholden to him and enjoying unchallengeable powers including monopoly control of communications. Political opposition is banned, likewise ideas that might foment opposition. Censorship is systemic. The message, the compulsion to subscribe and conform, is conveyed by every available modern mass medium: the press, the radio, agitpropaganda, cinema and newsreels. All this requires, paradoxically, a modern 'democratic' society because the Party rules in the name of, in the interests of, the whole regenerated people or nation: mass literacy and education, not excluding females, distinguishes totalitarian systems from their feudal and authoritarian predecessors. Also modern is the induction of new classes, previously underprivileged or ignored, into the institutions of the ruling system. Science rather than religion prevails but it may be pseudo-science deployed against the utterly rejected enemies of the people, be they Jews, be they bourgeois. Permanent enemies are a vital necessity for totalitarian regimes.

In *The Origins of Totalitarianism* (1951), Hannah Arendt diagnosed the phenomenon as an evil unleashed by the social havoc of the industrial revolution and exacerbated by the domineering, racially elitist ethos of nineteenth-century European imperialism. In her view, the real dynamic was not the declared goals of the Third Reich or Stalin's Russia but the perpetual motion of hamsters on a wheel. 'The practical goal of the movement', she wrote, 'is to organize as many people as possible within its framework and to set and keep them in motion; a political goal that would constitute the end of the movement simply does not exist.' What she found distinctive in totalitarianism – compared to traditional despotisms – was the development of terror beyond the function of eliminating opposition, and its application to constantly growing lists of 'objective enemies' such as Jews or kulaks. In Arendt's perspective, a basic totalitarian tenet is that 'the world is divided into two gigantic hostile camps, one of which is the movement, and that the movement can and must fight the whole world.' Ideology ensured that there was never any shortage of 'objective enemies' of the regime; no genuine police detection was necessary: this applied to the Jews under Nazism and the former ruling classes in the Soviet Union. The 'objective enemy' is not defined by his actions or even intentions; he is a 'carrier of tendencies', like the carrier of a disease. The term 'police state' therefore was a misnomer: 'Like the army in a nontotalitarian state, the police in totalitarian countries merely execute political policy and have lost all the prerogatives which they held under despotic bureaucracies. . . . The secret services no longer know anything that the Leader does not know better; in terms of power, they have sunk to the level of executioner.'[9]

According to Berlin's friend and ally the historian Arthur Schlesinger, Jr., totalitarianism offered the illusion of meaning and purpose, of security and comradeship against the 'loneliness and rootlessness of man in free society'. Schlesinger unearthed a new, composite 'totalitarian man', ruthless, determined, extroverted, free from doubts or humility, and, in the higher echelons of the Party, infallible: 'The totalitarian man denies the testimony of his private nerves and conscience until they wither away before the authority of the Party and of history. . . . We know well the visages of these new men in the Gestapo or the MVD, in the Politburo or in the Assembly of the United Nations – the tight-lipped, cold-eyed, unfeeling, uncommunicative men, as if badly carved from wood, without humour, without tenderness, without spontaneity, without nerves.'[10]

In *The True Believer* (1951), Eric Hoffer also engaged in the prevalent psychological impressionism: 'When people are ripe for a mass movement, they are usually ripe for any effective movement. . . . In pre-Hitlerian Germany, it was often a tossup whether a restless youth would join the Communists or the Nazis. . . . The religious character of the Bolshevik and Nazi revolutions is generally recognized. The hammer and sickle and the swastika are in a class with the cross. . . . They have articles of faith, saints, martyrs and holy sepulchres. . . . And it is easier for a fanatic Communist to be converted to fascism, chauvinism or Catholicism than to become a sober liberal.'[11] Hoffer embraced the fashionable antithesis of the 'moderate' (democratic) personality and the 'extremist's' embrace of totalitarianism.

One obvious problem here is that the Hitler movement in Germany (as Hannah Arendt observed) drew considerable support from large numbers of 'respectable', non-deviant Germans, good sober family men, who had hitherto supported 'moderate' conservative parties under the Weimar Republic, eschewing mass rallies, political uniforms and any form of 'fanaticism'. Another difficulty is that the term 'totalitarian' is not only descriptive and analytical but also polemical and pejorative. No party ran for election in the West under the banner 'Totalitarians for Terror'. Virtually no one admitted to being a 'totalitarian' – fascist, yes, communist, yes – but they regarded each other as deadly enemies, as scum. Reading French communist literature you may come across the name of Stalin eulogised a hundred times, and you may draw your conclusions about leader-worship, the cult of personality and Big Brother, but no communist writer is ever found associating Stalin with 'totalitarianism'.

Isaac Deutscher distrusted this term from the Western lexicon but occasionally lapsed, as when he applied it to Stalinist deformations. Trotsky himself, in his despairing exile, had hurled the term 'totalitarian' against Stalin's regime. Louis XIV had declared *l'état, c'est moi*. 'The totalitarian state goes far beyond Caesaro-Papism. . . . Stalin can justly say, unlike *le Roi Soleil, la société c'est moi*.'[12] On occasion, Deutscher used the word as applicable both to Stalin's

Russia and Hitler's Germany. 'In the second decade of the revolution the totalitarian monolith took shape. Finally, the rule of the single faction turned into the personal rule of its chief.' But – he objected – anti-communists lump together fascists, Nazis, Stalinists, Leninists and just Marxists as totalitarians 'and then assure us that totalitarianism, being a completely new phenomenon, rules out the possibility of any change and evolution, let alone quasi-liberal reform'. By this deterministic approach, he added, politics was determined by politics alone.[13]

The totalitarianism of the Third Reich, Deutscher argued, was designed to impose the most draconic discipline on the working masses and on the German bourgeoisie itself in preparation for the final struggle for German domination of the world. Stalinist totalitarianism, by contrast, is a product of the combined difficulties of building socialism in a backward peasant country and of the struggle of the new bureaucratic structure for a privileged position in postrevolutionary society. 'In spite of all the crimes committed by the USSR against European socialism, in spite of concentration camps, mass deportations and violations of human dignity in the USSR', the Cold War was in essence '*a war between socialism and capitalism*'.[14]

A 'Thermidor' in the USSR was out of the question. By this term Deutscher meant a return to capitalism, to private enterprise. 'Not only the old possessing classes have vanished. The political parties of the old Russia are also dead and beyond resurrection. ... They have since been uprooted from the nation's memory.' Any new political movements 'are bound to seek to achieve their aims within the framework of the institutions created by the October Revolution and falsified by Stalinism'.[15]

Conditions within the USSR improved rapidly after Stalin's death in March 1953. Physical liquidations and 'legal murder' ceased. Legality became the watchword. Many prisoners were released from the Gulag and officially 'rehabilitated' (Aleksandr Solzhenitsyn among them). Liberalisation and freedom of expression progressed by zigzag to the point where dissidents began to emerge into the open (though not with impunity). The powerful KGB now tended to follow guidelines set down by the Party rather than engage indiscriminately in the mayhem, the Kafkaesque nightmare of the Stalin-Yezhov-Beria era.

These ameliorations had only just begun to emerge when Isaiah Berlin made his second visit to Russia in 1956, described in his 'Four Weeks in the Soviet Union'. He found continuing anti-Semitism, though not so fierce as during the last years of Stalin. The basic divide in Soviet society remained that between the governors and the governed. 'The governed are a peaceful,

courteous, gentle, resigned, infinitely curious, imaginative, unspoilt population
... who look upon the outside world with wonder and a little hostility, even
fear.' He encountered an amiable cynicism about all governments and all
publicity. As for the governors, he described them as 'a tough, ruthless, mili-
tantly nationalistic group of proletarian roughnecks, whose resentment of what
can broadly be described as "Western values", or indeed of their own intellectuals, springs as much from their social origins and feelings as from any
ideology which they have imbibed'. He knew of 'no society in which one body
of men is more firmly, systematically and openly "exploited" by another than
the workers of the Soviet Union by their overseers. . . . These controllers . . . act
far more like the capitalists of Marxist mythology than any living capitalists in
the West today.'[16] Michael Ignatieff reports: 'The Politburo, whom he met at an
embassy reception, made him think of a thuggish group of Oxford college
porters, "at once smooth and brutal, class conscious and corrupt, hideously
jovial and with an easy gangsterish flow of sentimental reminiscence".'[17]

Repeatedly Berlin likened Soviet citizens to adolescents. 'Taste remains
simple, fresh and uncontaminated.' He did not attend a recent exhibition of
French art at the Hermitage but spoke to one foreigner who reported that
Russian visitors to the show 'admired few pictures after the 1850s, found the
Impressionists, particularly Monet and Renoir, difficult to like, and quite
openly detested the paintings of Gauguin, Cézanne and Picasso, of which there
were many magnificent examples. There are, of course, Soviet citizens with
more sophisticated tastes, but few and far between, and they do not advertise
their tastes too widely.'[18] In fact, when the first Picasso exhibition was staged
at the Pushkin Museum later that year, after his visit, the queues stretched as
far as the eye could see. Nor was mainstream Western taste as 'sophisticated'
as he implied: an exhibition of Soviet art held at the Royal Academy in 1959
drew far more visitors than a contemporaneous show of American Abstract
Expressionism at the Tate. Sir Alfred Munnings, a president of the Academy,
lauded Soviet pictorial realism, and the British public evidently went along
with this illustrious horse-painter. To understand why Muscovites flocked to
Picasso, one may cite the admiration Berlin himself had expressed for Soviet
audiences in 1945: 'The principal hope of a new flowering of the liberated
Russian genius lies in the still unexhausted vitality, the omnivorous curiosity,
the astonishingly undiminished moral and intellectual appetite of this most
imaginative and least narrow of peoples.'[19]

Isaac Deutscher's ongoing analyses of faction-fighting among the post-Stalin
Soviet leadership make for unhappy reading. In April 1953, before Beria's fall,
he reported that Beria was a leading liberaliser, along with Kaganovich and

Voroshilov. After the execution of Beria, Deutscher characterised Khrushchev as the most diehard Stalinist, surpassing even Molotov. Khrushchev thereupon denounced Stalin to the 20th Congress of the CPSU. By 1957, the 'Stalinist diehards' (Molotov and co.) were cast by Deutscher as enemies of Mao, who stood for the 'inevitability of gradualness', Khrushchev as Mao's ally. According to Deutscher, Mao had repudiated Stalinism and in effect proclaimed China's NEP – unfortunately three weeks earlier the *People's Daily* had launched an attack on the 'rightists' and made clear the liberal interlude was over. In 1960, Deutscher announced that while Indians were growing hungrier, the Chinese were 'greatly increasing their food output', indeed, distributing an abundance of rice to their workers free of charge.[20] Unfortunately, again, Mao embarked on the 'Great Leap Forward', the People's Communes, massive famine – and defence of the late Stalin against the new Soviet 'revisionism', causing Mao's incensed 'friend' Khrushchev to withdraw Soviet technicians from China. As Mao's Cultural Revolution and its Red Guards swung into action in 1966, Deutscher was advising a Berkeley audience: 'However, I think that the violence in China already is much smaller than it was in Russia. The irrationality of the Chinese Revolution, though goodness knows there is a lot of irrationality, so far is much less.'[21]

As he put it, after the Russian Revolution the old cleavage between the propertied classes and the masses had given way to the division between the rulers and ruled. The bureaucracy emerged as the manager of the totality of the nation's resources, the result being 'an almost permanent orgy of bureaucratic violence over all classes of society'. Far from withering away, the state gathers into its hands such power as it has never had before. Could the entrenched bureaucracy legitimately be termed 'the new class' (as the Yugoslav dissident Milovan Djilas and numerous Western observers now called it)? No. It was not a class. Soviet bureaucrats could not pass their prosperity and wealth to their children. (In fact, they could and did.) 'The privileged minority in the USSR has no absolute interest – it may still have a relative and temporary one – in perpetuating the economic discrepancies and social antagonisms that were inevitable at a lower level of economic development. Nor need they cling to a political regime designed to suppress and conceal these antagonisms behind a "monolithic" façade.'[22] (But they did.) Was the USSR nevertheless still a 'workers' state', still authentically 'socialist'? Yes.

But had not Trotsky correctly predicted that the establishment of a genuinely socialist society must and would be achieved without 'the whip of a bureaucracy'? Said Trotsky: 'It will have to be broken in pieces and burned at a public bonfire before you can speak of Socialism without a blush of shame.' Said Deutscher (and this is 1957): 'The whip is being broken into pieces.' Then followed a characteristic stab at the bourgeois outlook. How many in the West viewed this bureaucracy for what Trotsky called it and for what it was, 'the most disgusting inheritance from the old world' – rather than as the 'inevitable' result of socialism or communism? Trotsky wrong or Trotsky right? Deutscher told the *New Statesman* (24 August 1957): 'Even his erroneous hypotheses and predictions contain important elements of truth and most often follow from premises which retain full validity. He is in this respect not unlike Marx: his thought is "algebraically" correct even when his "arithmetical" conclusions are wrong.' (Observing the current faction fights between Khrushchev, Malenkov, Molotov, Bulganin, Kaganovich and Zhukov, not forgetting the bureaucratic cliques clustered round these bosses, readers of the *New Statesman* should presumably brush up on their algebra.)

Deutscher elaborated his historical perspective during a high-level seminar he gave at Harvard's Russian Research Center on 26 October 1959. His subject was 'The Historian and the Russian Revolution'. Merle Fainsod, professor of government, was in the chair. Richard Pipes, Richard Lowenthal, Adam Ulam, B. Schwartz, James H. Billington and Lazar Volin entered the subsequent discussion, which was sometimes sharp, though always polite (everyone referred to everyone else, including close colleagues, as 'Mister'). The main topics for debate and dispute were economic planning and the prospects of Soviet liberalisation, subjects about which Deutscher was very much on his own. Asked whether he dissented from the general theory of Professor Crane Brinton's *Anatomy of Revolution*, widely regarded by American historians as a classic, he told his audience that he had never read it. Brinton describes common patterns or 'uniformities' between the English Revolution of the 1640s and the American, French and Russian revolutions: each is said to have followed a similar life-cycle from the Old Order to a moderate regime, then to a radical regime, finally to Thermidorian reaction. Deutscher, too, insisted on a definite pattern in revolutions, on a cycle of phases in which the inner logic of the revolutionary process manifests itself – but, unlike Brinton, he did not equate Stalinism with a Thermidorian reaction, and indeed ruled out any such scenario in the future.

During the ensuing discussion he was accused by Harvard faculty members of excessive optimism in using the analogies of 1688 and 1832 in order to predict the progressive liberalisation of the Soviet Union. Deutscher insisted that Western students of Soviet affairs, including his own critics, had tended to overrate the totalitarian aspect of the Soviet system and its capacity to resist popular pressures.[23] In 1960, he published a general evaluation of post-Stalin international politics, *The Great Contest: Russia and the West*. Here he lauded Leninism, 'the pre-Stalinist Bolshevik tradition', as the democratic centralism which was currently challenging the bureaucratic centralism of the Stalin era. What was this 'democratic centralism'? According to Deutscher, it implied 'free and open debate, at least within the party and the trade unions, over major issues of policy and organization; and the freedom of the rank and file to choose between conflicting viewpoints and to elect their leaders'. But Khrushchev's Russia, Deutscher somewhat lamely admitted, was nowhere in sight of such ideals. Nor, he might have added, was Lenin's Russia.

In *The Great Contest* is to be found a gem of Deutscherite intellectualism, no doubt discovered through the garden window of his home in Wokingham: 'Marxism has entered the very core of the [Soviet] national consciousness; and as that consciousness grows more educated, complex, and subtle, it rejects the Marxism of the *pays légal*, the orthodoxy and the ritual; and it rediscovers in Marxism the *Weltanschauung* and the critical school of thought which had absorbed and blended the best traditions of Western philosophy and radical political thought. . . . What is going to emerge is probably . . . [a Marxism] as free from dogmatism as the pristine Marxism was – or even freer – but immensely enriched by new experience and able to comprehend and interpret it.' Perhaps his gaze then wandered from the shrubs to his desk, for he had the decency to add: 'But here I am perhaps running too far ahead and indulging in what may still only be a fond intellectual hope.'[24]

Too fond or not, he was happy once again to have nailed 'our cold war propagandists and our Congresses for Cultural Freedom [who] assumed that the Stalinist monolith was immutable and that it was going to survive Stalin for a long, long time to come'.[25]

Isaiah Berlin was only one of many who noted that Deutscher's essays on post-Stalin Russia never contemplate, as a condition for 'socialist democracy', a pluralist, multiparty state. The anticipated erosion of the 'monolithic party' does not entail an end to the Party's monopoly of power, only to its control by a single faction suppressing 'diverse currents of opinion'. Even in his despairing exile, Trotsky had called for the revival of other parties that followed 'the path of October', but Deutscher envisaged no such revival: 'All politically minded and active elements of the nation are, anyhow, in the ranks of the Communist Party, if only because there has been no other party to turn to.'[26]

Deutscher frequently wrote for the *Manchester Guardian* and its successor, the *Guardian*, although, as with the *Observer*, there were resident Sovietologists who looked askance at his opinions.[27] In 1961, the *Guardian*'s resident Kremlinologist, Victor Zorza, weighed in to a widely reported controversy following Deutscher's long article in the London *Sunday Times* (2 July 1961), 'New Russia–China Clash Revealed', which carried the subheading 'Khrushchev

Accuses Mao: "Inciting World War"'. Deutscher claimed to have based his scoop on a 'secret document' from the Kremlin about Sino-Soviet relations that had reached him through an unnameable source. But it soon turned out that this 'secret document' read like a free English translation of a text already published in *Voie communiste*, a monthly organ of the Trotskyist opposition in Paris, for which Deutscher himself wrote. The *Voie communiste* text was in turn based on a widely circulated Kremlin pamphlet, 'For Ideological Unity in the World Communist Movement', accusing the Chinese leadership of denouncing peaceful coexistence as treason.[28] On 23 July, Deutscher was forced to issue an explanation in the *Sunday Times*, denying that the *Voie communiste* version had been his principal source (though he had read it); his original source remained, as he had claimed, a secret Kremlin document obtained from an unnameable 'important Communist'. It was at this point that Zorza took up the issue in tones of undisguised scepticism in the *Guardian* (24 July 1961), as subsequently did Leopold Labedz.[29]

Deutscher's prominence in the bourgeois press was always fraught with dangers. David Astor's *Observer* blew hot, cold, hot again. Following Deutscher's 'scoop' in the *Sunday Times*, but prior to the assault on its credentials, Astor offered Deutscher payment for the UK rights in ten to fifteen syndicated pieces a year, 'and your services on Saturday afternoons and evenings to provide explanatory comment on Soviet or other Communist news breaking that day'. The retainer was 'a comprehensive £2,000 per annum' but for one year only. Astor assured him that 'the question of ideological viewpoint, which led to our earlier disagreement', would be no problem. Easy to say but, as soon became apparent, unrealistic.

On 4 November, the paper's deputy editor, J.M. Douglas Pringle, wrote to Deutscher explaining that a news story of his had been spiked because it had 'too many contradictions in it with other stories we were receiving from correspondents in Moscow and Berlin', putting the paper's news editor, Mark Arnold-Foster, 'in an impossible position'.

> I also think I should tell you that your style of writing does provide certain difficulties for a news story, which are not apparent in a column. That is to say, you make definite statements which are generally quite correct and are proved correct later but which appear at the time to be pure supposition. . . . I know you cannot reveal your sources and I am not asking you to do so, but, without any supporting evidence, these stories ask both the News Editor and the reader to take a good deal on trust. . . . I feel that news stories which come from Wokingham place the News Editor in a rather difficult position!

Deutscher replied argumentatively (8 November) about the spiked story. As for Pringle's jibe about news stories from Wokingham, 'if you care to come down here and have a glance at the files of my enormous correspondence, you might find out that more information on these matters probably comes to Wokingham than to the whole of Fleet Street'. Pringle did not take up this dramatic offer, merely reiterating (11 November) that he preferred Deutscher to 'stick to informative columns'. But things evidently got no better; for both ideological and temperamental reasons, the *Observer* staff resented the sage of Wokingham's flamboyant presence on the paper. A letter from Deutscher to Astor (27 March 1962) conveys hurt surprise that the editor did not intend to renew the annual retainer: 'you will realize that the eagerness with which you appealed to me last summer ... [made me] reject a financially far more tempting offer from *The Sunday Times* for the sake of the moral advantages of working for *The Observer*'. He commented bitterly that 'from the moment when I submitted my first article I have been made to feel the hostility of certain members of staff ... I met with persistent obstruction.' On 10 May, Astor confirmed termination, pleading lack of space.[30] Isaiah Berlin had in effect long been urging Astor to dispense with Deutscher. Writing to Frank Roberts, British ambassador to Moscow, Berlin described as 'absurd' an *Observer* article by Deutscher predicting that the Russians were planning to move out of East Germany. Two years later he wrote to Andrzej Walicki (7 September 1964): 'Deutscher is the least objective and factually least reliable writer among serious writers of politics to be found today: under the cover of dispassionate objectivity he hurls poisoned darts into the left and the right, all except his own tiny faction of Trotskyists and semi-Trotskyists.'[31]

Coming after the *Sunday Times* furore, this must have been one of the most serious financial and professional setbacks that Deutscher suffered, occurring as it did almost simultaneously with Labedz's 'libellous' attack on 'Deutscher as Historian and Prophet' in the Congress for Cultural Freedom's journal *Survey*. Here we may return to Labedz's indictment: 'Deutscher conveniently forgets ... all the *specific* predictions he made which were disproved by events. Whenever possible, he follows in the footsteps of the Delphic oracle and makes his predictions vague, conditional, and qualified enough to leave himself a way out whatever happens.' Deutscher's references to Soviet agriculture were constantly misleading because of his commitment to the collective farm system. In his 1959 Canadian lectures, he had declared himself confident that within ten years Soviet standards of living 'are certain to have risen above Western European standards.'[32] Deutscher, said Labedz, lacked the basic integrity required by both historians and journalists: 'His stylistic devices include such practices as reporting conversations between Soviet leaders in inverted commas, as if

Deutscher himself had heard them, as when he reports the exact words of an altercation between Khrushchev, Molotov and Kaganovich, "Your hands are stained with the blood of our party leaders and of innumerable innocent Bolsheviks!" "So are yours!" etc.' The cocksure Deutscher always knows: he 'knows' that Khrushchev will abandon East Germany, a unilateral withdrawal if necessary, regardless of the consequences.[33]

Within months of reading Labedz's attack and being let go by David Astor, Deutscher was to make his first ever application for an academic post, a senior lectureship at the University of Sussex.

By 1963, he was expressing doubts about his own predictions of an imminent liberalisation in Russia. Interviewed by the *Review* (Brussels), he confessed himself taken aback by the 'slow pace in intellectual, literary, cultural affairs, in the moral-political atmosphere. I would have expected by now an open political debate to be possible in Russia. In this respect I was mistaken.' In 'The Failure of Khrushchevism' (1965), he wrote: 'Under Stalin the bureaucracy was only a praetorian guard, devoid of a political identity of its own. Now the praetorian guard has become a ruling stratum ... careful not to extend democratic rights to workers and peasants, to the lower ranks of the bureaucracy, and to the intelligentsia.'[34] So goodbye to the goodbye to the 'whip of bureaucracy'?

One feature of Deutscher's writing on post-Stalin Russia is a disinclination to consider the influence of Western economic and cultural life – just as he awarded little attention to the impact of the Marshall Plan on Western Europe. He was not inclined to discuss the communications war, the East Berliners who watched West German television, the role of Western short-wave radio stations, jazz from the Voice of America, reports from the BBC, Deutsche Welle and Radio Liberty – the penetration of the People's Democracies by Radio Free Europe – and the furious Soviet jamming of these Thermidorian wavelengths. He did not ask why the Soviet government clamped down on the importation of Western books, even during book fairs arranged at international level. He did not face up to the increasing ascendancy of the West in the cultural Cold War and the cybernetics war. Reading Deutscher, you might have concluded that the Soviet population, eager for the coming of 'a Marxism cleansed of barbarous accretions', was tuning in to a clandestine radio transmitter called 'The Voice of Lenin'.

At the sadly premature end of his life, he was invited by Hamburg television to give his vision of the world in 2000: 'I imagine that by about the turn of the century something like a United States of Socialist Europe will exist ... probably closely linked with the Soviet Union, which will by then have overcome the heritage of Stalinism, producing a free socialism, a working day of

3–4 hours and higher education for all.' In that case 'certain theoreticians, let us say in Harvard, will have to construct a theory of "capitalism in one country"'.[35]

Seventeen years after Deutscher's death, in 1984, Perry Anderson paid tribute to his 'serene political fortitude ... the product of his absolute independence of thought – the entire freedom of his person and outlook from those fashions and phobias which have swayed the intelligentsia of the Left ... successively Stalinist or Maoist, structuralist or post-structuralist ... Eurocommunism or Eurosocialism'.[36]

Looking back from a fine old age in 1992, Isaiah Berlin remained scathing about all the variants of actually existing socialism: 'If Russia has betrayed the ideal, then Yugoslavia is better. If no longer Yugoslavia, then China. Later Cuba, Nicaragua. But basically the phenomenon of Communism in power has been discredited ... the first purpose of Socialism, apart from social justice, is to give food to the hungry and clothe the naked. No Socialist government has yet succeeded in doing that; Socialist economics have not delivered.' He added: 'They believe that if blood must be shed to create the ideal society, let it be shed, no matter whose or how much. You have to break eggs to make this supreme omelette. But once people get into the habit of breaking eggs, they don't stop – the eggs are broken but the omelette is not made.'[37]

PART SIX

THE *PAX AMERICANA*

17

AN ANGLO-AMERICAN

Soon after Berlin was elected to All Souls in 1932, he received a visit from the historian Lewis Namier, his senior in years and achievement, and like himself a Jewish immigrant. The young Berlin was clearly deeply impressed by Namier's anglophilia. 'He went to England, which to him as to many Central and East European Jews appeared the most civilised and humane society in the world, as well as one respectful of traditions including his own.' Indifferent to ideology, suspicious of abstract principles, Namier's prototypical Englishmen recognised the real ends of life, 'pleasure, justice, power, freedom, glory, the sense of human solidarity which underlay both patriotism and adherence to tradition'. He took pleasure in visiting the houses of the aristocracy to examine their muniments and family papers. 'He has, at times, been accused of being a snob. There is something in this; but Namier's snobbery was of the Proustian kind – peers, members of the aristocracy, rich, proud, self-possessed, independent, freedom-loving to the point of eccentricity – such Englishmen were for him works of art.'[1]

Written decades later, in 1966, was this tribute close to a self-portrait?

Berlin's heartbeat belonged to the Anglo-American alliance. In 1940, he worked for the Ministry of Information in New York as a propagandist, diligently making contact with trade unionists and Jewish groups. He lived in mid-Manhattan hotels and went to work at British Information Services on the forty-fourth floor of a building in the Rockefeller Center, sifting through piles of press clippings arranged in shoeboxes, compiling a weekly report on the state of American opinion (80 per cent of the public opposed American involvement in the war and the isolationists were in the ascendant). He was moved to the embassy in Washington. The prestige of his despatches gave him a reputation in Whitehall that percolated through to the upper reaches of London society. The songwriter Irving Berlin found himself mistakenly invited to dinner by Churchill, who had expected Isaiah. Society hostesses invited him to dinner, the BBC invited him to broadcast, Beaverbrook invited him to write a column for Express newspapers. A.J. 'Freddie' Ayer told him that he had been introduced at a party in London as 'the cleverest man in England' and someone had immediately exclaimed, 'Oh, so you must be Isaiah Berlin.'[2]

While living in the USA, he began to establish the personal connections that were to play a large role in his later life and commitment: the journalist Joe Alsop, bright young New Dealers, Arthur Schlesinger, Jr., Katharine and Philip Graham, publishers of the *Washington Post*, Eugene Mayer, Charles E. Bohlen, George Kennan, Edward Prichard and others. Supreme Court Justice Felix Frankfurter and his wife were friends from the Thirties. His time in Washington sealed his attachment not only to his many American friends but to the underlying continuity of US policy from Roosevelt to Kennedy. Henry Luce, publisher of *Time* magazine, was among his admirers. On 13 August 1945, the magazine wished him well: 'After three years in the Washington bivouac, rumpled, tubby, articulate Isaiah Berlin has left the British Embassy staff . . . contributed more than any other one person to official British knowledge of the current US . . . accumulated in part in an interminable round of dinners and cocktail parties.' In fact, Berlin had hopes of attending the Potsdam Conference as the foreign secretary's interpreter but this was vetoed by Eden: 'I can't have Isaiah chattering around the place.'[3]

No doubt Luce had not seen Berlin's summary of anti-British attitudes written for the Foreign Office in September 1942. This is a brilliant document – or would be if Berlin could have boiled down his twenty-three factors to, say, a dozen. While *Time* magazine held that his 'Oxford-accented observations' charmed Americans, Berlin's own report mentioned 'Irritation caused by over-civilised English accent . . . which conveys artificiality, insincerity, etc', as opposed to the advantage 'without qualification' of having a Scots, Welsh, Yorkshire or cockney accent. In general his pinpointing of American anti-British sentiment at that time is penetrating.[4]

He viewed the history of the British Empire with oblique affection. Having visited Moscow and Leningrad in 1945, he reported that Russians were obsessed by the mid-nineteenth-century expansion of imperial Britain, which as Marxists they viewed as part of a long-term, Machiavellian scheme dictated by the laws of a capitalism hurrying to its doom – whereas in Berlin's view 'ours is a hand-to-mouth policy, operating by fits and starts, and often an absentminded one at that'.[5] (Yet the mouth of the queen–empress had been a large one and the hand persistently fed it.)

Berlin was one of eight people whom Churchill consulted on the general structure and historical detail of his memoir of the 1930s, *The Gathering Storm*. Berlin wrote to Churchill (14 February 1948), welcoming the last batch of proofs and endorsing the changes in the text, some clearly made on his own recommendation: 'and I now more than ever think it is a literary and political masterpiece.' But he did draw attention to a passing remark of Churchill's in 1933: that Hitler's hostility to the Jews was unjustified, although 'if the Jews were acting against their country, they must be put in their place.' Such an aside was liable to be misconstrued, Berlin warned, and should be deleted.[6] He reviewed Churchill's second volume, *Their Finest Hour*, in the *Atlantic Monthly* (September 1949), praising the archaic and baroque style forged to align the author with the grand sweep of English history, heroically enhancing the nation's virtues. He met the great man in December 1949 at a dinner given by Oliver Lyttelton and could not like him. The old lion roared that he was looking forward to returning to power and pitching into the fight with Stalin, contemplating the possibility of renewed war in Europe with obvious pleasure. Berlin was both enthralled and repelled. 'He was too coarse, too brutal, and I didn't want him back in.' Ignatieff reports that Berlin regarded the Attlee government as the 'miserable grey on grey', but he did not vote for Churchill in 1950: he voted Liberal. One would be interested to know how he voted in the years ahead.[7] Bryan Magee recalls: 'I have it from his own lips that he voted Conservative on one occasion. But I also have it from his own lips, and near the end of his life, that he had "always" voted Labour.'[8] This may parallel his reiterated conviction that he was 'left of centre'.

In the summer of 1947, Oliver Franks had asked for his services at the Paris conference on the establishment of the Marshall Plan for Europe. Berlin went to Paris and observed that the Europeans acted like 'lofty and demanding beggars' approaching an 'apprehensive millionaire'. But drafting the tortuous language of international compromise did not appeal and after two weeks he returned to Oxford.[9]

In 1949, he waived his normal reticence about adopting public positions on current events when in a radio talk, 'The Anglo-American Predicament', he defended the Marshall Plan as no threat to the UK. 'British fortunes', he declared, 'are today indissolubly tied to those of the United States.' The 'stereotypical mythological image of Britain used to be that of a great unredeemed imperialist oppressor, and it is that image that has become altered in America. . . . The latter day British sins . . . India, Palestine, even Ireland, despite the agitation carried on by the Government of Eire – are today virtually dead or dying issues so far as the majority of Americans are concerned.' The Marshall Plan could only benefit Britain and Europe and posed absolutely no threat to their independence. A critical response came in from the communist historian Rodney Hilton, pointing out that America was far from the democracy Berlin claimed her to be: eleven of thirteen members of the American Communist Party's National Committee had been sentenced to prison 'simply for being Marxists, but their defence attorneys are also imprisoned for defending them'. Hilton was a member of the British Communist Party's Historians Group, along with Christopher Hill, whose book on Lenin caused Berlin to break off relations.[10] *Foreign Affairs*, the journal of the American foreign policy establishment, invited Berlin to contribute; the two articles he wrote made his reputation in America as an expert on Russian affairs. Chatham House invited him to lecture, then the Labour, Conservative and Liberal summer schools followed suit – paradoxically Isaac Deutscher, as we have seen, received similar invitations. In 'Political Ideas in the Twentieth Century' (1950), Berlin argued that both Soviet Marxism and postwar Western social democracy were prey to the same rationalist illusion: that with sufficient social engineering human evils could be abolished and individuals happily assimilated into a seamless social consensus. He ventured into Deutscher territory with 'Generalissimo Stalin and the Art of Government', published in *Foreign Affairs* in 1952 under the pseudonym O. Utis. He explained to the editor, Hamilton Fish Armstrong (16 August 1951): 'as I have (I hope still) relations in the USSR and as I visited innocent litterateurs there, I have always followed the policy of publishing nothing about the Sov. Union directly under my own name, because that might easily lead to something frightful being done to people I talked to there.'[11]

So what of Rodney Hilton's rebuke to Berlin for whitewashing American democracy in 'The Anglo-American Predicament'? Under Truman and Eisenhower, the Communist Party and all organisations listed as subversive by the attorney general remained 'legal' under the constitution (freedom of association) – but anyone who joined them ran a gamut of risks and penalties, from arrest under the Smith Act to deportation or loss of job and reputation. Federal judge Charles E. Wyzanski pointed out that if a citizen's passport was withdrawn because of activities protected by the First Amendment, then that protection was threatened or curtailed. This happened to Arthur Miller, Paul Robeson, Owen Lattimore, Corliss Lamont, the artist Rockwell Kent, Supreme Court Justice William O. Douglas, and leading Hollywood directors and writers. Not a word about these depredations was heard in public from Isaiah Berlin although he was frequently in America during these years.

On occasion he privately regretted the plight of persecuted fellow academics. He himself ran into difficulties when, in May 1949, he arrived at Harvard for a lecturing engagement and a good citizen took it upon himself to report his doubts about this suspicious foreigner to the FBI. Lecturing at Mount Holyoke College, Massachusetts, on 'Democracy, Communism and the Individual', Berlin explained that the roots of communism were to be found in the eighteenth-century Enlightenment belief that there was one right way for human beings to live. The day after his lecture the *New York Times* ran a small story reporting that he had urged American universities to take up Marxist studies. The heading of John H. Fenton's report (29 June 1949) was 'Study of Marxism Backed at Parley: UN Institute at Holyoke Told Russian Revolution Was Paramount Event'. Hastily Berlin sent a nervous letter (30 June) to the editor, emphasising that his principal purpose had been to stress the importance of studying Marxism, and specifically of not placing a ban on such studies. If Marxism were to be refuted it must be first understood: 'my actual lecture stressed the incompatibility between any form of democratic belief and Marxist doctrine.'[12] The letter was published on 8 July. Simultaneously he wrote to the provost of Harvard to assure him he was not a fellow traveller. He even asked George Kennan to compose a reassuring note on his behalf to the FBI liaison officer at the State Department. A week later Berlin wrote a shame-faced letter to a friend: when heretics are being burnt it was perhaps 'not the bravest thing in the world to declare one's loyalty to the burners'. Berlin also wrote to Joseph Alsop (1 July), speculating that the rest of his life might be spent denying to people like the provost of Harvard 'that I am an ambiguous snake of some sort'.[13] He reported to E.H. Carr that he had turned down a $10,000 offer of a permanent chair at Harvard.

Although he was hostile to McCarthy and John Foster Dulles, expression of his thoughts remained confined to private correspondence. He regarded McCarthy as 'really a kind of radical of the Rasputin type'. He told Anna Kallin (15 October 1953) how he disliked ex-communists like Goram Davis who testified to McCarthy's Senate committee against former colleagues. Writing to Schlesinger, he described Rebecca West, a public apologist for the witch-hunt, as a dreadful woman who had come to see him and had talked absolute drivel about McCarthy's aides Shine and Cohn. 'I think she sincerely believes that there are communists under every bed and every chair.' He speculated that this must have something to do with H.G. Wells having long ago left her for the left-wing baroness Moura Budberg.[14]

America remained attractive. In the same letter to Schlesinger he added: 'meanwhile I had a fantastic time with a body of men organised by the Ford Foundation which sat in Grosvenor House for the purpose of discussing how their millions might be spent on the betterment of man.' He established friendships with leading historians such as Morton White, Martin Malia, Adam Ulam, Richard Pipes, Marc Raeff and James Billington, and with the literary critics Edmund Wilson and Lionel Trilling. He got to know the Harvard Soviet expert Merle Fainsod, the Italian scholar and anti-fascist hero Gaetano Salvemini, Irving Singer, a young philosophy graduate, Elliot Perkins, master of Lowell House, and Perry Miller, author of *The New England Mind*. He had first met Schlesinger, now achieving fame for his *Age of Jackson*, in Washington during the war. Both were gregarious liberals, avid for gossip and intrigue, fascinated by power and influence, but whereas Schlesinger relished public controversy, Berlin didn't. The grandest Boston hostesses, Mrs Warren and Mrs Chandler, invited him to their afternoon teas – he found Boston high society talk to be a parody of Henry James, unlike the racy and amusing conversation at London dinner tables.

When Schlesinger joined Kennedy's White House, the door was open to Berlin. At the invitation of his friend the columnist Joe Alsop, a close confidant of the president, he attended a private dinner with John F. Kennedy in October 1962, the heyday of Camelot. As he later recalled to Schlesinger, after dinner Kennedy took Berlin aside and his manner became intense and businesslike. Why were the Russians not making more trouble in Berlin? What did Russians typically do when backed into a political corner? Berlin replied as best he could while Kennedy listened 'with terrifying attention'. The president seemed obsessed with greatness: whenever he mentioned Stalin, Lenin or Churchill, 'his eyes shone with a particular glitter'. The next morning Kennedy announced that American overflights had discovered Soviet missiles on Cuban soil. Once the ensuing crisis was over Berlin was invited to a small celebratory dinner at the White House. In a letter to Noel Annan he reflected that he was 'really no good at a round table discussion of ICBMs, of middle-range weapons, the strategic importance of Assam or even the secrets of British Minister of Defence' (no doubt a reference to the sexual scandal afflicting John Profumo, caught wind of by journalists in December 1962 but not yet known to the public). When Berlin relaxed sufficiently to tell the president 'a rather frivolous story' about Lenin's private life, Kennedy cut him off abruptly. Berlin did tend to fall into this anecdotal trap – it had happened with Pablo Picasso after a dinner in the south of France.

As a result of a further invitation to an informal seminar at Bobby Kennedy's home, Berlin found himself lecturing to the president and a glittering company about the nineteenth-century Russian intelligentsia. At the end of the talk the president asked him what had been the fate of the intelligentsia after the Revolution; who had collaborated, who resisted and what difference it had made. The president, he sensed, was engaged in meas-uring men up, calculating who would remain firm under pressure, who would break – including, perhaps, himself.[15]

Berlin was back in England when Kennedy was assassinated. An interesting anecdote is told by Tim Bayliss Smith, of St John's College, Cambridge. On the evening of Friday, 22 November 1963, Berlin gave a public lecture to the Workers' Educational Association in Brighton on the subject of Machiavelli. The lecture took place in the Drill Hall, Lewes Road, and as the audience assembled beforehand the news circulated that President Kennedy had just been shot dead in Dallas. 'Berlin was under no obligation to stick to his title, and most of us expected and hoped that he would digress onto the subject of political assassination in the modern world, and its relevance to Machiavelli's ideas about statecraft. To our surprise, the lecturer made no mention of President Kennedy, and in fact did not stray beyond the sixteenth century.'[16]

The Congress for Cultural Freedom (CCF) was born in 1950, much under the inspiration of Arthur Koestler, and its London-based magazine, *Encounter*, was launched in 1952. From the outset an American (initially Irving Kristol) was placed in the driver's seat, but Berlin's friend Stephen Spender, a contributor to *The God That Failed*, was given charge of the literary and cultural pages, and from the moment of its launch this monthly gained the esteem of British writers and readers. Like the weekly *New Statesman*, it presented a blend of political and literary contributions, but *Encounter* had space for longer essays, reviews and fiction than the *New Statesman*. In political terms, when you opened *Encounter* you knew which side of the Cold War presided; with the *New Statesman*, particularly under the editorship of Kingsley Martin, you were not so sure. *Encounter* relentlessly charted the suppression of democracy throughout the Soviet sphere of influence; show trials in Eastern Europe, purges, Stalinist anti-Semitism, Zhdanovism in the arts; an ever-ascendant cult of personality; an utterly mendacious Soviet 'peace' campaign. Here also were to be found the distinguished voices of anti-totalitarian political theory: Berlin, Popper, Mannheim, Arendt, Talmon, Aron, Lipset, Friedrich, Polanyi and others.

Isaiah Berlin himself certainly knew all the main figures directing the CCF's publications: *Encounter* (Spender, Kristol, Lasky), *Preuves* in Paris, *Tempo presente* in Italy (edited by Nicolo Chiaromonte) and *Der Monat*, an early product of American cultural policy in postwar Germany edited by Melvin Lasky. Berlin was a close friend of Nicolas Nabokov, secretary of the CCF in Paris. He also knew the CIA's presiding cultural agent in Europe, Michael Josselson. In the late 1940s, there had been a further deepening of what Schlesinger called the 'quiet revolution' in the State Department. Under the influence of such intellectuals as Kennan, Bohlen and Berlin himself, 'State' came to understand and support the ideas of the formerly isolated non-communist Left (NCL) in Europe. As Peter Coleman puts it, a convergence was established between NCL intellectuals and 'that combination of Ivy League, anglophile, liberal can-do gentlemen, academics and idealists who constituted the new CIA'.[17]

Berlin was from the outset a prominent contributor to *Encounter*'s cultural pages alongside the 'politicals' like J.K. Galbraith, Irving Kristol, Nathan Glazer, Arthur Koestler and Dwight Macdonald, and alongside leading liberal professors and intellectuals like Raymond Aron, Max Beloff, Stuart Hampshire, H. Stuart Hughes, James Joll, Denis Brogan and George Steiner. Meanwhile Stephen Spender as coeditor brought into its pages such distinguished writers as the late Virginia Woolf, Albert Camus, Hugh Trevor-Roper, W.H. Auden, Herbert Read, Christopher Isherwood, Robert Graves, Nigel Dennis, Iris Murdoch, Edith Sitwell, Cecil Day Lewis, Kenneth Tynan and John Osborne.[18]

The masked funding of the CCF by the CIA's International Organizations Division, through such 'fronts' as the Farfield Foundation, remained unknown to the majority of contributors. Berlin was on friendly terms with Frank Wisner, who worked for the CIA from 1947 until 1962 as head of the Directorate of Plans, responsible for covert anti-communist operations worldwide from 1952 to 1958. Wisner was one of the Georgetown set in Washington, close to many of Berlin's friends. Writing to him on 4 May 1955, Berlin ruminated about the current Soviet scene and its leading personae, Malenkov, Khrushchev et al. One must nevertheless accept – though some have not – Michael Ignatieff's verdict that Berlin had had no official or unofficial link with British Intelligence or the CIA, and had been unaware that the CIA was covertly funding magazines to which he himself contributed, 'though he may have heard rumours and may have had his suspicions'.[19]

We come to the crisis of the mid-Sixties, when things dramatically turned sour. In 1966, Conor Cruise O'Brien, recently appointed Schweitzer professor of the humanities at New York University (NYU), launched an attack in the *New Statesman* on the occasion of an anthology of contributions to *Encounter* during its first ten years. Cruise O'Brien subsequently returned to the subject in the *Washington Post's Book Week* and in an expanded version delivered as a lecture at NYU. The success of *Encounter*, as he put it, 'lay in inducing distinguished writers of high principle to lend unwitting support to the "more purposeful activities" of lesser writers'. These writers of high achievement and complete integrity were led unconsciously to validate *Encounter*'s intellectual credentials by coexistence with those who 'were engaged in a sustained and consistent political activity in the interests – and as it now appears at the expense – of the power structure in Washington'. (By 'at the expense of' he meant 'funded by'.) Cruise O'Brien also alleged that *Encounter* had been subsidised by the CIA.[20]

Although the magazine's principal editor since 1958, Melvin Lasky, knew the truth of the matter, he printed a polemical rejoinder by a member of the editorial staff, Goronwy Rees, vehement cold warrior, denying the facts and denigrating Cruise O'Brien in sarcastic terms. 'O'Brien' (so rendered), said Rees, had once described his role as the United Nations envoy in Katanga (during the Congolese civil war, a major episode in the Cold War) as that of 'a Machiavelli of Peace'. But, said Rees, 'his blunders in Katanga showed little of the fine Italian touch urged by Machiavelli on the Prince'. His use of the phrase must mean 'that, in the cause of peace, O'Brien was theoretically prepared to indulge in any of those subterfuges, stratagems, mendacities, betrayals, duplicities, which Machiavelli regarded as essential weapons in the Prince's armoury'. Rees went on: 'Yet the air of bad faith combined with moral elevation which was implicit in his claim continues to impregnate his writings.'

Rees took up Cruise O'Brien's claim that the mendacity of the West was more subtle and insidious than that of the communist world. According to Cruise O'Brien, 'The distortions and misleading facades which he [the English-speaking critic and analyst] will most often encounter – I use the verb advisedly – are pro-American and anti-communist distortions and facades.' This, retorted Rees, was reminiscent 'of the kind of smears that used to be laid before the Un-American Activities Committee in the days when the junior Senator from Wisconsin was king'. (In fact, Joseph McCarthy was never a member of HUAC – a common mistake.)

Rees thought fit to mention that, while the dissident writers Yuli Daniel and Andrei Sinyavsky were now in a Soviet prison, 'Mr O'Brien's martyrdom' takes the form of 'his richly endowed professorial chair in New York'. And what evidence had he for his claim that the CIA stood behind *Encounter*? He apparently based the allegation on two articles in the *New York Times* about the history of the CIA, which mentioned *Encounter* in a passing sentence. But when the London *Times* reprinted these articles, it noticeably omitted any mention of *Encounter*. Further, when the *New York Times* was challenged to produce evidence, it did not do so, refused to name its source and duly published *Encounter*'s letter of correction and denial – indeed, the editor of the *New York Times* went on to affirm that the magazine was 'a distinguished international journal of independent opinion'. Several European newspapers and periodicals had likewise hurried to publish retractions and apologies. Not content with tossing Goebbels into the pot, Goronwy Rees offered himself a second stab at the McCarthy parallel: 'Yet there are also elements of high comedy in the transformation of the Machiavelli of Peace into the Joe McCarthy of politico-cultural criticism.'[21]

Conor Cruise O'Brien took the step from which Deutscher had shrunk when lambasted by Leopold Labedz: shrewdly he sued for libel in his native Dublin. This coincided with the present writer's arrival at NYU, at Cruise O'Brien's invitation, as visiting professor in his new department. Simultaneously Isaiah Berlin arrived in New York for his annual semester at City University, where Arthur Schlesinger, Jr. held the parallel Albert Schweitzer $30,000 p.a. chair to Conor Cruise O'Brien's at NYU. As a White House insider, Schlesinger had long been sitting on the truth about CIA funding of the CCF, and if he did not take the opportunity of disclosure to Berlin one could be surprised. Indeed, earlier in the year (1966) Berlin had deepened his relationship with another and more recent White House insider, McGeorge Bundy, special assistant to Presidents Kennedy and Johnson. One of Bundy's first actions as the incoming president of the Ford Foundation was to authorise the generous endowment that launched the new Wolfson College at Oxford, of which Berlin was to be the first president. Bundy knew the facts about the CIA's funding strategies as well as anyone.

On arrival in New York, Berlin was still supporting *Encounter*'s innocence of CIA involvement. On 5 October, he wrote to Melvin Lasky: 'I was sure that you would agree with the letter in *Time* magazine and am very glad that you wrote your own. . . . It sets the record straight.'[22] Lasky sent Berlin a cutting from the *Sunday Telegraph* (9 October) in which the paper apologised for suggesting, 'entirely without foundation', that *Encounter* had engaged in under-cover propaganda activities as a beneficiary of, and in complicity with, the CIA. Lasky attached a handwritten note in the margin: 'Dear Isaiah, We issued a writ. They also agreed to apologise in court, and to pay costs. Will this end it all? Devoutly to be wished. (Do you see – hear – anything of your Irish Schweitzer colleague?)'

The tide was apparently flowing in favour of *Encounter* but Cruise O'Brien's libel action could not be disregarded. If he was proven wrong about CIA funding, did this justify Goronwy Rees likening him to McCarthy or Goebbels? Worse, Lasky knew the truth, even if he kept it from Stephen Spender and other editorial colleagues. On 11 November, Spender wrote to Berlin, urging him to talk Cruise O'Brien out of his libel action, and to assure him that rumours were false that *Encounter* held a personal dossier that might be used against him in court. These rumours had inflamed Cruise O'Brien's fighting spirit, never short of kerosene.

Should he agree to talk to Isaiah Berlin? Should he regard Isaiah as an intermediary in good faith or as 'one of them'? The atmosphere within NYU's

Schweitzer Department on the fifth floor of 1 Fifth Avenue was not without its tensions in view of the boss's inflammatory politics – he was currently engaged in proving that the Warren Report on Kennedy's assassination was a cover-up, and he would not accept that the plane crash at Ndola in which his former chief at the United Nations, Dag Hammarskjold, lost his life could be down to pilot error. The rumour about CIA funding of *Encounter* was grist to his mill but could it be substantiated? He insisted that what was being unveiled was the long-term hypocrisy of America's 'Free World' propaganda.

The fratricidal conflict among the intellectuals was now bitter. The sharp edge of the acrimony was no longer between Cold War liberals and real communists (an almost extinct species in the wake of the purges) but rather those same liberals and what Schlesinger called the anti-anti-communists in good standing, most prominently Cruise O'Brien, whose voices were heard in the press and the literary supplements. The New Left was on the rise; the postwar consensus was fractured; American democracy had forfeited its virtuous image. Cruise O'Brien was an anti-anti-communist not because he harboured any illusions about the Soviet system but because his current emphasis – and it was all about emphasis – was directed against the hypocrisy and wrongdoing of the USA (France and Britain granted walk-on parts). He held Kennedy responsible for the downfall and murder of the Congo's first prime minister, Patrice Lumumba. It was now all about the war in Vietnam and the detested LBJ.

He did agree to talk to Isaiah Berlin. On 17 November, Berlin reported to *Encounter* that he had spoken to Cruise O'Brien and passed on the message about there being no 'dossier'. Regarding Goronwy Rees's polemic, he added: 'I must say that I am surprised that your libel lawyers should have passed these references to Goebbels and McCarthy.'[23]

There matters stuck until *Ramparts* magazine confirmed the CIA's subsidy to *Encounter* by means of an interview with an unrepentant veteran of the Agency's covert cultural operations, Thomas Braden. Nothing to be ashamed of, said Braden. The *New York Times* took courage and further denial was impossible. Early in 1967, both the CIA's Michael Josselson and *Encounter*'s Melvin Lasky wrote to Berlin, appealing to him to contain Stephen Spender, who was visiting the USA and in a spin of indignation, shared by a former editor of the magazine, Dwight Macdonald, about years of deception. Now distancing himself from Lasky, Berlin replied to Josselson on 16 April, recommending publication of a statement claiming that the editors of *Encounter* had not been aware of the sources of funds – which, he added, 'will be true at any rate for most of them – how much Lasky did or didn't know I have, of course, no means of telling'. Two days later Berlin wrote to Lasky, advising that the magazine settle with Cruise O'Brien out of court, while attaching a statement that Rees's allegations against him had been made in ignorance of the new revelations about the CIA etc. This letter opens a large window onto Berlin's mind: 'You could perfectly well say that like other organisations in need of financial assistance you went to the Congress for Cultural Freedom; they went to other Foundations of a prima facie respectable kind; that recipient bodies are not in the habit of examining the sources of income of the prima facie respectable bodies which support them.' The proper role of *Encounter* was simply to say that it acted as it did in ignorance of CIA funding, like a great many other organisations. Men of sense and goodwill would understand this; while others would 'continue to snipe anyway'.[24]

Berlin changed his position when it could no longer be concealed that Lasky and Josselson had been privy to the CIA subsidy and had 'compromised decent people'. He, like his friend Spender and all the other innocents, had been betrayed. He kept silent in public. During the late spring of 1967, it was Spender and Dwight Macdonald who publicly rocked the boat, expressing indignation in interviews and TV appearances, one of which brought a fraught ingathering of the intellectuals to a studio in New York. Cruise O'Brien and Schlesinger both spoke. Spender, who resigned from *Encounter*, offered a distraught personal testimony. But there was no sign of Berlin.

Berlin later explained his ultimate position to Michael Ignatieff: 'I did not in the slightest object to American sources supplying the money – I was (and am) pro-American and anti-Soviet, and if the source had been declared I would not have minded in the least. . . . What I and others like me minded very much was that a periodical which claimed to be independent, over and over again, turned out to be in the pay of American secret Intelligence.'[25] (But surely the actual editorial independence of the magazine was a separate question from whether the funding was covert or overt?)

Can one plausibly argue that *Encounter* was a Greek gift horse concealing CIA Cold Warriors pursuing a sinister agenda while morally raping innocent Trojan highbrows? You only had to read the magazine to understand its politics. Nor was the early CIA altogether the ugly customer it later notoriously became. Working to associate the American image abroad with the higher culture, its bright young men had to proceed clandestinely to forestall uproar among the Congressional backwoodsmen who claimed that every 'ism' in the arts originated in Moscow. This was the time of the noisy conservative backlash against every kind of modernism launched by Dondero, McCarthy, McCarran, the American Legion, the Catholic War Veterans, the China lobby, the Daughters of the American Revolution and a plethora of vigilante pressure groups claiming that modernist artists were really pinks and cryptos.

Meanwhile Moscow was sedulously encouraging West Europeans to believe that the Soviet Union represented the classical European cultural heritage against the cheap commercial ephemerality of American jitterbug, Coke, silk stockings and pop comics. To meet the challenge of the Bolshoi and the Kirov, of Shostakovich, Sholokhov and Brecht, the more enlightened end of Washington – the CIA, the US Information Agency and the New York Museum of Modern Art – invested in de Kooning, Pollock, Copland, Bernstein, Menuhin, Cliburn . . . and *Encounter*. The Congress for Cultural Freedom was the cultural Marshall Plan.

18

THE NEW LEFT AND VIETNAM

TOWARDS THE END of his life Isaac Deutscher became the prophet or attendant priest to something he had not predicted. The 1960s witnessed an unforeseen eruption of the young middle-class intelligentsia in the West, students with an agenda of their own and disturbing anarchist leanings. Suddenly universities became the Bastille, the Champ de Mars, the cruiser *Aurora*, the Winter Palace. The revolting campuses were now places where history began today.

Isaiah Berlin's letters to Anna Kallin confirmed his view of Deutscher as a Marxist demagogue pandering to the mindless radicalism of the young, the 'Bazarovs' of the insensate Sixties whom Berlin was to denounce passionately in a major lecture on Turgenev (1970). Yet Deutscher was of the same generation as Berlin and showed no greater enthusiasm than he for students demanding reform of the universities – whether the hierarchical structure of authority, the multiple links to the 'military-industrial complex' and the 'power elite', or the curriculums they offered, their grading and examination practices. Visiting Professor Deutscher did not believe the young should teach their seniors how to teach them. The Old Left in general was shocked by such iconoclasm. Deutscher was not only a 'professor' by immense scholarly achievement, he saw his own life, not least his direct knowledge of the European revolutionary movement, as a source of indispensable knowledge for the ignorant young. In this respect he differed little from Professor Berlin.

This attitude shone with brutal clarity during a New Left Forum debate in the spring of 1967 at Harpur College, New York State, where Deutscher spent six weeks as distinguished visiting professor of political science. From the outset of the debate Deutscher was chiding other members of the panel for believing there was anything 'new' under the sun. 'But in what sense are you

the "new people"? You are young?' He could endorse their emotional alienation from this 'self-satisfied, complacent, well-fed and yet stupid bourgeois
society' – but he could not accept the wholesale rejection of the older generation. He dismissed 'humanism' as an ethical value 'too vague and much too
broad to have any meaning at all', reminding them that the radical groups of
the Thirties – his own generation – correctly aspired to oppose and overthrow
the social order. From this vantage point he challenged the New Left of the
Sixties: 'Do you see in social control and social ownership of the means of
production a vital principle? In a word, are you socialists?' He chided them:
'You are shying away from these questions, and this only weakens you.' When
told that the New Left stood for the racially and economically oppressed
minorities, he retorted: 'Do you consider the majority of the white workers
in this country are not being oppressed?' Then he began to quote Marx all
over again.

He was politely told that the New Left, under the influence of the late
C. Wright Mills, had now abandoned the belief that the working class was the
decisive force for change. Deutscher insisted that the Left's analysis in the 1930s
remained valid: 'Today I have much sympathy for students of your age group,
but I am worried about the confusion in your mind and about your conceit, and
about your shirking the really great issues, and also about your isolation from
your society. You sow your wild oats within the campus, but you have no
missionary zeal to carry your message to people outside the campus.'[1] He
continued: 'What in fact is the campus? It is only a bus in which you spend
three, four or five years; then you take your final exams, you get off, and look
round for a job.' The role of students, he pointed out, is transient. 'They are not
a stable element in society; they are . . . ideologically unstable.' He himself was
ideologically stable (very). Ninety-nine per cent of the New Left, he complained,
'takes on a supercilious attitude and echoes that Marxism is obsolete. Never
have so many talked about a thing they knew so little.'

So the New Left was enthusiastically involved in the civil-rights movement? Deutscher described Negroes as 'a minority on the margin of the
process of production. Their possibilities are also marginal and verbal; and I
am not sure that they don't talk often in racial terms instead of class terms.'
Black power was deviationary. Just as Lenin instructed Klara Zetkin that
the German women comrades should stop discussing their female identity,
should focus on the class struggle, so Deutscher sent a parallel message to
America's blacks.

And radical reform of the universities? 'But do not delude yourselves that
your aim – "participatory democracy", or, as you yourselves put it, "that each
individual should have a say in the decision-making process", is anything more

than a vague and meaningless slogan. It implies that you want to participate in the management of society as it is, but the society as it is excludes you from participation by definition.'[2] It's amazing his auditors didn't drown him in the nearest sewage tank but, on the contrary, they lapped up the punishment. Deutscher emerges from the 1967 Harpur College seminar as an old-style, bullying patriarchal preacher, wedded to his own early history, purblind to the fact that for the New Left traditional Marxist rhetoric was fatally associated with Stalinism. But he and his classical Marxism had seen everything, knew everything. His venerated vessel was not to be boarded, seized by young pirates, deflected into 'petit-bourgeois' cul-de-sacs. Yet he recognised that the stifling Cold War consensus was ruptured at last. He told Hamburg television: 'I have a great admiration for this other America, the unofficial one, which offers resistance to the official, conservative, neo-colonialist political character of the United States. . . . I hope this radicalism will finally seize the working class too.'[3]

The student-led upheavals in Europe and America inspired in Isaiah Berlin rampant distaste. Nineteen sixty-eight was already becoming the *annus mirabilis* of student revolution. The climate was threatening: major demonstrations in Europe had mutated into riots, causing a civic crisis in Berlin and then the fall of a French government. The disturbances reached Spain and Italy. Columbia and Berkeley had suffered dramatic upheavals, the London School of Economics came under siege, and everywhere professors were targets of protest, boycott – or worse. On 14 May, the General Assembly of the Sorbonne announced an Autonomous Popular University; the revolt now extended from students to some eight hundred junior faculty. Following upheavals and student occupations at the LSE, by 15 May all classes had been suspended at the Essex campus.

At one point during the Columbia student strike of 1968, Isaiah Berlin delivered a lecture so close to the police lines that his friends told him to wet a handkerchief to place over his mouth and eyes in case of tear gas. According to the *Oxford Mail* (22 May 1968) he spoke to the university's Humanists Group about the dangers of radical agitation: by using the university as a focus for disaffection, you risked destroying it. 'The University only reflects the evils of society,' he warned. 'You can only change the university by changing the outlook of society.'

'You can only change the university by changing the outlook of society' does, of course, carry a dimension of truth. The British government's resolve to expand higher education and render it available to wider sections of the young rather than the traditional 10 per cent, to build new universities, to fund the new sciences and technology – these vital decisions must be made at a political level. Yet the traditional structures, values and elitism of the universities equally influence the politicians and opinion-makers who have attended them. Effective protest may well begin within institutions: their hierarchies, their paternalist or authoritarian assumptions, serve as an *immediate* battleground. Berlin was not on record as expressing consternation about Oxford's record in admitting less than 10 per cent of its annual intake from state schools, although state schools accounted for more than 90 per cent of national secondary education. (In 2009, when Oxford's intake from state schools had risen to 53 per cent, this was still considered cause for concern by liberal opinion.)

When Berlin addressed the Oxford Humanists, the university was heading for more extensive trouble: by 3 June, the Clarendon Building, the administrative centre, was under siege, forcing the proctors to rescind their rule forbidding the distribution of leaflets. In October, a socialist faction sent an 'ultimatum' to Berlin's college, All Souls, whose warden, John Sparrow, had recently described radical students as long-haired 'sluts' whose sex could not readily be determined. The 'ultimatum' stipulated that All Souls must: (a) admit undergraduates for the first time in its five hundred-year history; (b) publish the College's real financial accounts; and (c) hold 'democratic elections' for fellowships. One anti-Sparrow slogan announced: 'Chairman Mao say, make sparrows into birds-nest soup.' By that time, 25 October, eight hundred students had occupied the LSE, with a further thousand converging outside.

'You can only change the university by changing the outlook of society' also brings us to the case of the many American universities about to conclude that social and educational privation in the black neighbourhoods required 'affirmative action', sometimes called 'positive discrimination', by rapidly admitting much higher proportions of young blacks to universities, despite their inferior high-school grades. 'You can only change the university by changing the outlook of society' – would Berlin have applied this nostrum to the contemporaneous Prague Spring? The Charles University had been a focus for reforming agitation since 1966, and it was the students who, in march after march, pressed for real national reforms, resulting in the election of Alexander Dubček as first secretary of the Party in January 1968. In April, a Student Parliament was established in Prague and the old Stalinist curriculum in the social sciences at the Charles University was no more.

Like Deutscher, Berlin discovered that the model of student behaviour he had grown up with was the best. As a faculty member at Columbia, the liberal literary critic Lionel Trilling observed events with bafflement. 'Like all my friends at college, I hadn't the slightest interest in the university as an institution. I thought of it, when I thought of it at all, as the inevitable philistine condition of one's being given leisure, a few interesting teachers and a library. I find it hard to believe that this isn't the natural attitude.' It was very much Isaiah Berlin's attitude. That autumn (1 October 1968) he wrote to Anna Kallin:

> The revolutionaries of my day had some respect for knowledge and intelligence and tried to learn from the enemy in order to use the weapons – whatever they may have been – philosophy or history or mathematics or technology for their own ends. This generation is complacently ignorant, uses mechanical formulae to dispose of anything that may be difficult or complicated, hates history on the whole. . . . The old Nihilists at least thought they respected science – these ones confuse crudity and sincerity and when culture is mentioned their hands really do automatically reach for a paving stone. But I must not go on with this lamentation, it sounds like some decayed liberal from Turgenev or some horrified old baronet in The Times.

Later in the same letter he mockingly extends his antipathy to the recently deceased Deutscher: 'What would the late Deutscher have said? Could he have brought himself to condemn Castro in this connection, for example?' (The context for this remark is not clear.) A month later he remarked in a letter to Franco Venturi (28 November 1969) that 'the rebellion of the repentant bourgeoisie against the complacent and oppressive proletariat is one of the queerer phenomena of our time'.[4]

The student movement did gain some faculty support but these voices were in a minority: Frederick Crews, Henry David Aitken, Kenneth Keniston, Martin Duberman, James A. Ackerman, and in Britain most eloquently E.P. Thompson. But the professorial consensus was overwhelmingly hostile to student radicalism. Among Berlin's close friends and colleagues, few if any embraced student causes, although most of them would have described themselves as liberals. The veteran diplomat and scholar George F. Kennan, a friend and correspondent of Berlin's for many years, came out with 'Democracy and the Student Left' in the New York Times, accusing the New Left of everywhere destroying the academy of pure learning. Admitting university involvement in defence contracts and commercial ventures, he argued that no one forced the student to talk with recruiters from the Marines or Dow Chemicals. Student demands that universities should divest themselves of securities in companies doing business in apartheid South Africa were 'absurd'; likewise student protests against Ian Smith's white regime in Rhodesia. Had not the Left always demanded African independence from Britain – so why complain when Ian

Smith did just that? (Oh dear!) As for Vietnam, America was given no credit for resisting a brutal communist dictatorship. Clearly Kennan was mixing two different lines of argument: the university should be no place for politics – and he did not like the politics it was getting. He concluded that if only the students had combined genuine intellectual curiosity with a proper detachment, they would have discovered that 'the decisive seat of evil in this world is not in social and political institutions . . . but simply in the weakness and imperfection of the human soul itself'.[5]

Berlin's longtime friend and now his colleague at City University Professor Arthur Schlesinger, Jr. drew congratulations from Berlin when he devoted part of his Commencement oration there to denouncing the radicals' vulgar existential politics – feel and act before you think – as 'fakery and fallacy . . . preposterous and depraved'. Another friend of Berlin, Hugh Trevor-Roper, Regius professor of history at Oxford, declared: 'They talk of "student democracy". In fact such demands are not only illogical; they are unattainable. The radicals who exploit them do not believe in them at all. They are generally foreigners . . . and they simply take advantage, as demagogues, of a captive mass of immature persons.' (But the majority of radical student leaders in Britain were as much natives at the professor.) The students also came under fire from the Old Left. Irving Howe concluded that 150 years of paternalism had been supplanted by 'a psychology of unobstructed need', which now merged unpleasantly with the 'authoritarianism' of the world-stage student leaders Tom Hayden, Daniel Cohn-Bendit, Rudi Dutschke. Even Professor Noam Chomsky of MIT, the most relentless scourge of American foreign policy, defended 'our legacy of classical liberalism . . . the commitment to a free marketplace of ideas'. Addressing a Columbia panel during the occupation of the university, Chomsky assured an increasingly hostile audience that MIT had never interfered with his freedom of speech, despite receiving funds from the federally funded Institute for Defense Analysis.[6]

In the course of his 1970 Romanes Lecture on Ivan Turgenev, Berlin presented dramatic parallels between Turgenev's time and his own: 'Fires broke out in the capital and university students were accused of starting them. Turgenev did not come to their defence. The booing and whistling of the radicals, their brutal mockery, seemed to him mere vandalism; their revolutionary aims, dangerous utopianism.' Turgenev wrote to a friend: 'Mud and filth were flung at me by the young. I was called fool, donkey, reptile, Judas, police agent.'[7]

Berlin turned to the contemporary scene (which may seem to be the central underlying purpose of the entire essay): 'The new insurgents of our time favour – so far as they can bring themselves to be at all coherent – something like a vague species of the old, Natural law.' The modern rebels believed, as Turgenev's fictional characters Bazarov and Pisarev believed, and Bakunin too, that the first requirement is the clean sweep, the total destruction of the present system; the rest is not their business. The future must look after itself. Confronted by such an eruption, 'this violent cry', modern liberals reacted like Turgenev's liberals, his Shubins, Kirsanovs and Potugins, 'the small, hesitant, self-critical, not always very brave, band of men who occupy a position somewhere to the left of centre, and are morally repelled both by the hard faces to their right and the hysteria and mindless violence and demagoguery on their left.'[8]

He expanded on the liberal predicament, the dilemma which he clearly saw as his own. The moderates find themselves assailed both by conservatives and radicals. (Berlin's conservative critics are hard to track down.) So moral courage is needed by those who cannot help seeing many sides of a case, as well as those who perceive that a humane cause promoted by means that are too ruthless is in danger of turning into its opposite. Here he invoked Erasmus and Montaigne, as well as the best representatives of the Girondins, the defeated Liberals in 1848, the 'stout-hearted' members of the European Left who refused to side with the Paris Commune in 1871. It was not weakness or cowardice that prevented the Mensheviks from joining Lenin in 1917, or the unhappy German socialists from turning communist in 1932. (One may wonder why the opponents of the Paris Commune needed to be so 'stout-hearted', given that all the Powers of Europe were on their side.)

The principled 'liberal' stance, it emerges, is part-heroic, part-tragic. 'The natural inclination of liberals has been, and still is, towards the left, the party of generosity and humanity, towards anything that destroys barriers between men. Even after the inevitable split they tend to be deeply reluctant to believe that there can be real enemies on the left.' And do not forget the temptations they have to transcend: 'To stretch themselves upon a comfortable bed of dogma would, after all, save them from being plagued by their own uncertainties, from the terrible suspicion that the simple solutions of the extreme left might, in the end, be as irrational and as repressive as the nationalism, or elitism, or mysticism of the right.'[9] One catches this note, these insidious 'temptations', more than once in Berlin's *plaidoires*; in his essay *Historical Inevitability* he remarks how 'tempting' and 'alluring' it would be to give up the struggle, to surrender to determinism, to abandon the notion of individual responsibility in history – how alluring to regard ourselves 'as soldiers in any army' no longer suffering 'the pains and penalties of solitude ... our goals are set for us, not chosen by us; doubts are stilled by authority'.[10] It seems as if Berlin, whenever confronting radicals, almost invariably imagined himself praying in the garden of Gethsemane, if not impaled on Golgotha.

He further explored the disastrously anti-rational discontents of the 1960s generation by way of a study of Georges Sorel (1847–1922), a figure of marginal influence in the European socialist movement after 1890, who managed to admire both Lenin and Mussolini (Lenin did not reciprocate). Sorel became a popular subject of study among academics opposed to the revolutionary outbursts of the 1960s and 1970s. Berlin's essay 'Georges Sorel' (1971) depicts an ultra-intellectual who despised intellectuals; a manic word-smith and ideologue who valued actions above words, passions above ideas, 'myths' above rationality, dreaming of largely undefined proletarian or syndicalist violence against the crapulent bourgeoisie. But what could logically connect Sorel to contemporary student radicalism? Berlin achieves this connection in three separate sentences: (1) 'Yet, if he were alive today, the wave of radical unrest could scarcely have failed to excite him'. (2) 'Like [Frantz] Fanon and the Black Panthers, and some dissenting Marxist groups, he [Sorel] believed that the insulted and the oppressed can find themselves and acquire self-identity and human dignity in acts of revolutionary violence.' (In fact, Sorel insisted that the proletariat alone was the pure, uncontaminated vector of necessary social violence.) (3) Although 'Che Guevara's or Fanon's concern about poverty, suffering and inequality was not at the centre of Sorel's moral vision ... they would have fulfilled his ideal of revolutionary pride, of a will moved by absolute moral values'.

But Berlin has to grant that Sorel 'hated disorder, bohemianism, the lack of self-imposed barriers, as symptoms of self-indulgence and decadence. . . . He would have been disturbed by their sexual permissiveness; chastity was for him the highest of virtues; their slovenly habits, their exhibitionism, their addiction to drugs, their formless lives would have enraged him; and he would have denounced their neo-primitivism, their Rousseauian belief that poverty and roughness are closer to nature than austerity and civilised habits, and therefore more authentic and morally pure.'[11]

Their 'formless lives'? Were the lives of Tom Hayden in America, Rudi Dutschke in Germany, Daniel Cohn-Bendit in France really 'formless'? Could the draft-resistance movement in the USA, resulting in many imprisonments, really be put down to 'exhibitionism'? What Berlin does is to take the hippie-yippie fringe, the Abbie Hoffmans and Jerry Rubins, the Fuck-You Motherfuckers, and cast them in all parts. Had he read the SDS's Port Huron Statement or Theodore Roszak's *The Making of a Counter-Culture* (1969)? No sign of it. Berlin's other self did, however, strive to understand why, as he put it, the students were alienated by faceless technocracy, by commercial manipulation, 'a society of consumers without authentic moral values of their own, sunk in vulgarity and boredom in the midst of mounting affluence, blind to sublimity and moral grandeur'. In 'The Bent Twig: On the Rise of National-ism', first published in *Foreign Affairs* (1972), he wrote: 'There is a growing number among the young of our day who see their future as a process of being fitted into some scientific well-constructed programme, after the data of their life-expectancy and capacities and utilisability have been classified, computer-ised. . . . Their protests sometimes take rational forms, at other times violently irrational ones, mostly exhibitionistic and often hysterical attempts to defy the ruling powers, to insult them into awareness of the totalitarian effect of such policies.'

Conspicuously lacking in any of Berlin's commentaries on the New Left are the specifics of contemporary politics. He does not mention the war in Vietnam, the Bay of Pigs, hegemonic practices sustaining dictatorial oligar-chies in Latin America or military conscription of the generation he derides. You would not guess that American ghettoes had been burning, or why. You catch no image of Lyndon Johnson and the Pentagon at work. The anger of the young, he thought, was 'about psychological malaise, hypocrisy, lack of love, lack of understanding, lack of acceptance, "alienation", class consciousness and class education, etc., and not oppression of the majority by a wicked or deluded minority'.[12]

The gurus popular among the New Left did not gain his esteem. In 1962, he had met Herbert Marcuse at Harvard and thought him an amiable café intellectual. He became increasingly disenchanted as Marcuse's influence rose. Returning from a spell at Columbia in May 1968, Berlin wrote to E.H. Carr about 'Marcuse's "Red Guards"', but himself admitted that the university authorities had acted with little sense. While reading *Encounter*, he came upon Marcuse's fatuous observation that 'the world of the concentration camps was not an exceptionally monstrous society. What we saw there was the image, in a sense the quintessence, of the infernal society into which we are plunged every day.' Berlin responded in a letter to Jean Floud: 'Wd you trust such a man with *anything*?' He went on to denounce Marcuse's 'terrible twisted Mitteleuropa in which nothing is straight, simple, truthful, all human relations and all political attitudes are twisted into ghastly shapes by these awful casual-ties who, because *they* are crippled, recognise nothing pure and firm in the world'.[13]

Deutscher shared Berlin's low regard for Marcuse but from a rather different vantage point. This became apparent during the second Socialist Scholars' Conference, held at the Hotel Commodore, New York, in September 1966, at which Deutscher delivered the lead address, 'On Socialist Man'. Writing in the *Nation* (10 October 1966), Harvey Swados described a standing ovation for Deutscher. Swados reckoned he was the star of the conference, 'almost the last of a breed effectively extinguished by Stalin and Hitler'. With his 'mid-European accent, bald Leninist dome and white Trotskyist goatee, [Deutscher] seemed like a character from a novel of the thirties, remarkably reincarnated.'[14]

Deutscher informed the conference that his reading of some nine classical Marxist writers indicated that their assumptions about human nature were neutral. They did not see man as wholly good or evil. He took issue with Freud's claim in *Civilisation and its Discontents* that *homo homini lupus* (man is a wolf to man) – the view that aggressive instincts are biologically predetermined and not significantly affected by changes in the structure of society. Freud viewed sexual drives as a lasting source of the aggression that would always continue to show itself in the nursery; but Deutscher did not believe this would be true in a communal nursery after the 'dissolution of the family unit'. He asked: 'Should one take it for granted that Socialist man will be subject to the Oedipus complex as we are?' (Presumably few in the audience were quite sure about that.) 'We suppose', Deutscher continued, 'that Socialist man will in childhood be far less subjected to paternal authority than his predecessors have been, or that he will not know it at all; and that as an adult he will be free in his sexual and erotic life, or, at any rate, that he will be incomparably freer than bourgeois man is to follow his emotional urges and need of love without coming into conflict with society.'[15]

(Proust reflected: 'We still light candles and visit doctors.' Adapted: 'We still light utopias and visit Marx.')

At one point in the discussion a letter from Marcuse was read out, proposing that traditional Marxism was outmoded since the working class could no longer be considered the agent of revolution. Deutscher riposted by lamenting infantile regression among American socialist scholars who, lacking live contact with the working masses of their own nation, had lapsed into self-centred revisionism. He insisted that the American working class remained the decisive agency of socialism. 'Do you really believe that they are so much more prone, and by nature conditioned, to be corrupted by the meretricious advantages of this war-flourishing capitalism than you are?' Socialist intellectuals must reach out to the young among the working class, shaking the sleeping giant out of his drugged myopia.

As for classical Marxism being obsolete: 'My argument is this. That on the contrary, Marx was so much ahead of his time, ahead of his society . . . that we are even now in so many respects still behind Marx and not ahead of him.'[16]

By the end of his life Deutscher's influence within the New Left was in the ascendant. His Trotsky anthology, *The Age of Permanent Revolution*, was said to be one of the three main sellers on bookstalls at the LSE during the student rebellions in the late 1960s. His Trotskyist adversary Tony Cliff recalled his concern over the dominance Deutscher exerted over audiences: 'I remember going to lectures by Deutscher at which there were 1,000 or more present. Twice I spoke up from the floor in the discussion criticising Deutscher's position, but I hardly cut any ice with the audience. . . . Our puny group, offering a tough approach to Stalinism, could not overcome Deutscher's soft soap.'[17] Among young admirers and militants in England, Deutscher in his self-proclaimed 'watchtower' maintained a somewhat magisterial and prickly reputation. Peter Sedgwick recalled 'that extraordinary semi-comic incident not long ago in which he summoned to his home the leadership of a certain British "Trotskyist" organisation which had connived at the brutal beating up of a rival militant: once he was satisfied of the evidence in the affair, "Deutscher's curse", magisterially invoking the dishonoured name of Trotskyism, rang through the house and he sent them packing.'[18]

He enjoyed a close-knit circle of disciples, who took some pride in their minority status and some satisfaction from their altercations with Cold Warriors (no chance of democracy under the CPSU), Stalinists (no criticism of the CPSU allowed) and orthodox Trotskyists (proletarian revolution in the West is the only solution). His key influence was on the editors of the *New Left Review* and, in France, Sartre's journal *Les Temps modernes*.[19] Marcel Liebman, professor of political science at the University of Brussels, produced a Deutscherite study of the Russian Revolution that rivalled the master's vocabulary for denigrating alternative schools of thought, including those who subscribed to 'order, obedience, resignation', or 'the lying and vulgar schematizations' of the Stalinists and orthodox Trotsykists. Deutscher himself wrote a combative preface, which displays him in full flow at the end of his life: 'That the enemies of the Revolution have been unable to produce a coherent account of the events that shook Russia and the world in 1917 is hardly surprising. . . . Most often class prejudice, resentment and ignorance colour their views . . . [they] see the upheaval of 1917 as the still active source of almost all the evils that have afflicted humanity ever since . . . an outrage against reason or human nature, an outrage committed by monstrous people and devils incarnate.' Deutscher evoked 'the heaven-storming defiance and courage and the warm humanity of the revolutionaries of 1917, their broad and open-minded intelligence, their world-embracing ideas and ideals, their fearless strategy, their supple tactics and their great inner-Party freedom.'[20]

Berlin's hostility to Deutscher (by then the late Deutscher) was to be exacerbated by the personal attacks he suffered from his young friends and disciples of the New Left, most notably Perry Anderson, an editor of the *New Left Review*, whose essay 'Components of the National Culture' first appeared in the July–August 1968 issue, reaching a wider audience the following year in a Penguin paperback collection, *Student Power*. Isaiah Berlin was affronted and, as his correspondence indicates, alarmed.

Anderson held Deutscher aloft for admiration: 'A larger figure than his compatriot Namier, Deutscher was reviled and ignored by the academic world throughout his life, and never secured the smallest university post. British culture accepted and promoted what confirmed its fundamental set: it put to the margin what departed from it.'[21] By contrast, Anderson located Berlin at the centre of the 'White emigration' that had 'rolled across the flat expanse of English intellectual life, capturing sector after sector'. He warned against the 'chloroforming effects of such [a] cultural configuration, its silent and constant underpinning of the social *status quo*'. 'In this intensely provincial society, foreigners suddenly became omnipresent. Again and again émigrés had provided the crucial, formative cultural influences.' Then came Anderson's list of these *maîtres d'école*, giving in each case the academic discipline and the émigré's country of origin:

Ludwig Wittgenstein, Philosophy, Austria
Branislaw Malinowski, Anthropology, Poland
Lewis Namier, History, Poland
Karl Popper, Social Theory, Austria
Isaiah Berlin, Political Theory, Russia
Ernst Gombrich, Aesthetics, Austria
Hans-Jurgen Eysenck, Psychology, Germany
Melanie Klein, Psychoanalysis, Austria
(Isaac Deutscher, Marxism, Poland)

The brackets granted to Deutscher signalled the shining ideological exception, though the attributed discipline, 'Marxism', might have been expressed as 'History'.

As Anderson saw it, those White émigrés from European unrest who admired British values chose to settle in England while other, more progressive émigrés like those from the Frankfurt School of Marxists – Marcuse, Adorno, Benjamin, Horkheimer and Fromm – initially sought refuge in France, then the USA. Anderson argued: 'The Intellectuals who settled in Britain were not just a chance agglomeration. They were essentially a "White" counter-revolutionary emigration.' (In fact, many of those listed by Anderson had been refugees from right-wing regimes: Namier from Polish Galicia under the

Habsburgs, Popper and Gombrich from the civil war and fascism of post-Habsburg Austria.) Even so, Anderson maintained that they had not only sought liberty in England but set out to flourish in a country where general ideas were disparaged and where Marxism could the more readily be disposed of by a process of intellectual travesty. 'Established English culture naturally welcomed these unexpected allies. Every insular reflex and prejudice was powerfully flattered and enlarged by the magnifying mirror they presented to it'. Anderson used the term 'philistines'. The British establishment duly rewarded the White émigrés with knighthoods.

From the Left, E.P. Thompson was later to castigate Anderson's *New Left Review* for its enthralment to Continental and particularly French thought (Louis Althusser) and its depiction of the mass of commonsensical Englishmen as passive, cowed, conformist, inert 'philistines'.[22] Anderson did not say how many of his list of White Guards were Jews but the answer – if we do not distinguish between Jewish and 'assimilated Jewish' parentage – is eight out of nine. Malinowski is the exception, the only non-Jew among them.

Anderson bracketed Berlin's perspective with Karl Popper's; both defined 'historicism' as an approach to the social sciences that assumes historical prediction to be their principal aim. The problematic and its negative answer were the same in Popper and Berlin, only the terminology differed. Anderson swept aside the charge of determinism: 'Hegel of course . . . explicitly refused all historical prediction.' Likewise, 'Marx and Lenin, of course, repeatedly emphasized that they analysed tendencies of social development, not absolute laws, and that therefore the predictions of natural science were impossible in history'. One can infer from this, as from E.H. Carr's writings, that the main thrust of Berlin's *Historical Inevitability* had lodged in the mind of Marxists anxious to disclaim determinism, although the defence raised by Anderson on behalf of Hegel, Marx and Lenin remained disputable.[23]

The impact of Anderson's essay was sharpened for Berlin when in February 1969 *Black Dwarf* accused him of calling Anderson 'anti-Semitic'. A month later Berlin explained his position to Jean Floud: he regarded Anderson's attack as more 'old-fashioned xenophobic' rather than anti-Semitic. That most of the co-called corrupters of British national tradition had been Jews was a matter of history, but Anderson's general indictment of 'wicked émigrés' reminded him of nationalist extremists 'from de Maistre to the anti-Dreyfusards and McCarthy' – the latter 'had his own pet Jews like Anderson' (meaning Deutscher). Berlin was infuriated to be included among those who set up a cry of anti-Semitism as soon as they were attacked. 'The vulgarity of it is intolerable.' Writing to Tamara Deutscher, he added: 'the New Left Review regards me as one of the terrible White termites, with Namier, Gombrich,

Popper, Wittgenstein and others, who have aborted the national radical tradition incorporated in D.H. Lawrence and Keynes.'[24]

We come to Vietnam, a crisis that can be said to have promoted Deutscher into a public figure, a platform tribune.

In June 1965, Isaiah Berlin hesitantly consented to be one of the academic sponsors of the Oxford Teach-In on Vietnam, held at the Oxford Union, his acceptance perhaps fortified by that of such esteemed colleagues as Sir William Hayter, A.J. Ayer and H.A.L. Hart.[25] When approached, he asked whether the *ad hoc* committee could vouch that the debate would be held on a fair and civilised basis – a good question given the rising temperature generated by the war. (Deutscher for some reason did not attend the Oxford Teach-In, though probably invited.) The organisers' aim was to invite a broad spectrum of speakers and to secure impartial chairmen, among them Christopher Hill, master elect of Balliol, who was an opponent of the war, and Professor Max Beloff, who broadly supported it. Berlin's endorsement, granted in the cause of free speech, may have encouraged leading politicians and academics to take part, but he himself had no wish to figure in the debate, which was eventually attended by thirty speakers and an audience of one thousand in the Union building.

To begin with – the first telephone calls – the wider establishment was having nothing to do with it. But this situation dramatically turned around after Lord Henry Walston, parliamentary under-secretary at the Foreign Office, persuaded Michael Stewart, foreign secretary in Harold Wilson's government, to undertake the main address.[26] Politicians of every stripe immediately scrambled for invitations. Having previously declined to cover the event, BBC Television experienced a change of heart. In addition, the Third Programme decided to scrap all its scheduled evening items in order to broadcast the debate continuously from 7.30 p.m. on the radio. US ambassador David Bruce indicated that Washington was looking to send a major figure who was not a member of the Lyndon Johnson administration – this turned out to be Henry Cabot Lodge,[27] a tall figure who arrived at the Union in an embassy car under police escort.

Cabot Lodge did not have an easy time. Misjudging his audience, he relied heavily on references to Churchill and the spirit of Dunkirk, and was astonished ('appalled', he later said) by the loudly derisive response from the hall. When he came to America's offer of 'unconditional negotiations' with the Hanoi government, a barrage of protest arose: was America's insistence on the enforced absence of the National Liberation Front, otherwise known as the Vietcong, from the conference table not a condition? (President Johnson and secretary of state Dean Rusk insisted that the National Liberation Front was simply the illegal, terrorist arm of the North Vietnam government.)

Foreign Secretary Stewart's sober speech was the highlight of the evening. He had been president of the Union in his student days and he understood his audience. Those who disagreed with his position had to respect his sincerity and his willingness to answer a barrage of difficult questions from the floor. BBC Television's *Gallery* programme accorded the lion's share of its coverage to the foreign secretary, its commentator Ian Trethowan announcing that the Teach-In had resulted in a triumph for Michael Stewart and a drubbing for the 'British Left' (of which the Labour government was evidently not part).

Isaiah Berlin stayed away. Much cultivated by the American establishment, he had been on various occasions invited to lecture before the cream of the Kennedy Democrats – JFK himself, Robert Kennedy, McGeorge Bundy, Robert McNamara, Arthur Schlesinger, Jr. and Walt Rostow. His contribution to *Authors Take Sides on Vietnam* (1967) was brief and equivocal. The questions posed by the editors to all contributors were the same, and only two:

'Are you for, or against, the intervention of the United States in Vietnam?'
'How, in your opinion, should the conflict be resolved?'

Berlin responded that Vietnam was a much more ambiguous issue than the Spanish Civil War: 'I was wholly pro-Spanish Republican.' America should not have intervened in Vietnam but, having done so, could not withdraw precipitately without a negotiated settlement and thus 'abandon people to massacre by their enemies'. He also accepted the domino theory, fearing 'a kind of terrorized joining of the bandwagon like that which took place in Central Europe in the last years of the 1930s'. He regretted having to cloud his answer with 'perplexities and qualifications'. By now it was Berlin's position on Vietnam, not Deutscher's, that was in the minority among intellectuals.[28]

Deutscher, meanwhile, came into his own as a tribune of the people at a series of Teach-Ins. His first was the National Teach-In, held somewhat incongruously at the Sheraton Park Hotel, Washington, on 15 May 1965. Invited by the Inter-University Committee, he reported to Professor Thomas F. Mayer at Ann Arbor: 'When I presented your invitation cables to the Consul here, he remarked: "But this is dynamite, Mr Deutscher, dynamite!"' The visa issue was referred to Washington.[29] A précis of his speech was issued as 'The Policy Context of the Cold War' but the published version carries the title 'Vietnam in Perspective'. The radio and televised relay went out to a hundred campuses. Andrew Kopkind described how Deutscher 'raced from the back of the huge hotel ballroom onto the stage, looking somehow like Lenin *and* Trotsky. He flailed his arms, shrugged exaggeratedly and berated the moderator with an accusing finger for no apparent reason except that he was closest to the rostrum.' The radical journalist I.F. Stone was overheard by Kopkind commenting to a disapproving TASS reporter from Moscow, 'Leave it to a Polish-Jewish Trotskyite to make the only significant contribution.' Hella Pick's report was less sardonic: 'Mr Isaac Deutscher's attack was in a class by itself. A Trotskyist with a Leninist beard, Mr Deutscher . . . went on to attack not just the US Government but the whole NATO alliance and especially the present British Government. He spoke not so much about Vietnam but about the cold war policy as a whole, arguing that it was the creation of the West and that Stalin had never had any expansionist ambitions. . . . Mr Deutscher agued that the Berlin and Cuban crises were the consequences of Western provocation, and that the same methods were being used to provoke China.'

McGeorge Bundy, President Johnson's special assistant on national security, cancelled his scheduled half-hour speech at two hours' notice, due to 'other duties'. He sent a message that the administration's objective in Vietnam was peace. Hella Pick reported the intervention of Arthur Schlesinger, Jr., no longer a member of the administration: 'He admitted that the US might have been wrong in supporting South Vietnam in 1954, but such mistakes, he said, were for historians, not policy-makers, to discuss. Once the US had committed itself, Vietnam had automatically become a vital US interest, and the Administration could not simply divest itself of past errors.' Schlesinger endorsed the domino theory, which displeased the audience. He wanted less bombing and more American forces on the ground: 'If we took the Marines we now have in the Dominican Republic and sent them to South Vietnam, we'd be a good deal better off in both countries.' Kopkind reported: 'The audience didn't know whether to clap or boo, so it did both.'[30]

Isaiah Berlin was a friend not only of Schlesinger but also of the absentee Bundy. In *The Color of Truth*, Kai Bird presents a study of McGeorge ('Mac') and William Bundy, describing the brothers as two of the dynastic technocrats who organised and justified the war in Vietnam. Formerly dean at Harvard, McGeorge Bundy had been appointed Kennedy's special assistant for national security affairs, with an office in the White House, work that involved him in the Bay of Pigs adventure. (When invited by the drama critic Kenneth Tynan to sign a condemnation of that operation, Berlin declined on the ground that Castro cared as little for civil liberties as Lenin or Trotsky. Berlin had earlier refused to sign a manifesto supporting the FLN in Algeria.)[31]

Working for Lyndon Johnson after Kennedy's assassination, Bundy became a firm supporter of escalating intervention in Vietnam, including bombing the North. With the conservative journalist Joseph Alsop, the Bundy brothers formed a reflective caucus in the tough-minded quarters of liberal Washington DC. Berlin's long-time friend Charles (Chip) Bohlen, made up an occasional fourth man. Berlin sent Alsop (20 April 1966) an account of a dinner with McGeorge Bundy: 'I have never admired anyone so much, so intensely, for so long as I did him during those four hours . . . his character emerged in such exquisite form that I am now his devoted and dedicated slave. I like him very much indeed, and I think he likes me, now, which was not always the case.' Mac Bundy returned the compliment, writing to Alsop in 1967 that he wished he possessed Berlin's stout resolution. But around them the tide of opinion was turning sharply. Alsop wrote to Berlin (March or April 1966): 'I cannot tell you how isolated and suddenly out of fashion I feel. The old way of looking at the world in this country, which was everyone's way from the defeat of Henry Wallace [in 1948] until about a year ago, is now increasingly outmoded among the intellectuals.' Berlin responded: 'I see the red line, formed by you and Mac [Bundy] and me, and Chip [Bohlen] – four old blimps, the last defenders of a dry, and disagreeably pessimistic tough and hopelessly outmoded position – one will perish at least with one's eyes open.'[32]

We return to Deutscher addressing the 1965 Washington Teach-In. 'All the misconceptions and illusions of the Cold War', he declared, were reproduced in Vietnam. 'Once again American policy is based on opposition to a genuine native revolutionary force.' Though the Vietcong was clearly backed by an overwhelming majority of the Vietnamese peasantry, the USA took refuge in blaming foreign communist powers, North Vietnam and the malignant Chinese colossus. 'The whole Western cold war strategy, having for nearly two decades moved in a maze of misconceptions and miscalculations . . . now stands helplessly before the blind Vietnamese wall.' Deutscher warned: 'The hostility between colonialism or neo-colonialism and the peoples of Asia, Africa and Latin America will not soon die down. . . . I still believe that class struggle is the motive force of history and that only a socialist world – one socialist world – can cope with the problems of modern society. But in our time class struggle has sunk into a bloody morass of power politics.'

('In our time'? When, one may ask, was it otherwise? Cromwell's England was almost permanently at war. The French Revolution was accompanied by continuous European wars, extending with Napoleon to the Middle East. The Paris Commune of 1871 was inseparable from defeat in a national war against Prussia, likewise the Bolshevik Revolution inevitably precipitated foreign military intervention. Twenty years later, foreign fascist intervention in the Spanish Civil War proved decisive. Where would one find the elegant model of pure class struggle free of foreign intervention dreamed up by Deutscher when he called for a situation whereby the 'divisions may once again run within nations, rather than between nations. We may give back to class struggle its old dignity'?)[33]

The Deutscher archive contains a typescript of his address that includes interjections like 'LAUGHTER', 'APPLAUSE', suggesting it was taken from an audio recording. Passages of not untypical demagogic rhetoric abound. He spoke of the need to awaken

> this sleeping giant, the American working class. . . . You must shake it and drag it with you to the struggle. (APPLAUSE) You must widen your move-ment. . . . I don't mean to say go out to the bureaucracy of your trade unions. (LAUGHTER, APPLAUSE). . . . I don't even say go and appeal to the middle-aged elderly American worker . . . who is, like the Russian peasant 100 years ago, bribed by his false semi or quarter-emancipation; by the television he has . . . by the crumbs that he has from the rich table of his own productivity that is being appropriated. . . . But go out to the young worker who couldn't have been bribed . . . and who surely feels that he is still an oppressed, alienated, exploited creature. Go out to the young worker. Go out to the young worker, appeal to him, carry to him the message of socialism . . . only socialism can allow us and can teach us to live. (APPLAUSE).

All rather patronising (bribes, crumbs, TV sets), one might think, and also misleading: the only Western workers who had taken action since 1945 against imperialist-colonial military ventures were dockers and some railwaymen belonging to the Stalinist French Communist Party and its trade-union wing, the CGTU. Even when Vietnam brought conscription to young America, the resistance was largely confined to students. Deutscher ignored the psycho-logical role of patriotism and racism in the prevailing populist outlook. For the white worker, staying above blacks and 'chinks' was a more pressing and feasible status-objective than expropriating General Motors.

On 11 June 1965, back in London, Deutscher spoke in the packed and sweltering Upper Refectory at University College, Bloomsbury, to five hundred students and faculty. This was the first British Teach-In. The *Guardian* described a warm response to 'Mr Deutscher's arm waving and his description of Mr Wilson as "the assistant gendarme of world counter-revolution"'. The US embassy had withdrawn both its promised speakers.[34] On 26 June, Deutscher was again on the platform at Church House, Westminster, along with left-wing Labour MPs like Michael Foot and Ian Mikardo. He was in America again for the second Vietnam Day rally in Berkeley on 21 April 1966, beginning his address: 'Ladies and gentlemen, my friends and comrades.' As a member of the Russell War Crimes Tribunal (alongside Bertrand Russell and Jean-Paul

Sartre), he described American intervention as 'the most barbarous act of warfare since the Second World War ... an act of the most intense class struggle waged by America's capitalist-monopolistic oligarchy (and its servants and puppets) against Vietnam's peasants and toilers'.[35] But by the spring of 1967 his view of the Tribunal, as privately expressed to his wife, Tamara (16 April), was bleak: 'My American experience made me regret that I got myself involved with the Tribunal. The Russell-Foundation here is dead ... the so-called American members treat it as a honorific marginal affair, as, I suspect, Sartre treats it: it is good publicity to be associated with Russell in this venture – that's all. I seem to have given more thought, time, and energy to it than all of them taken together. What a shame, and it's going to be a flop'.[36]

Should violence be used against 'America's capitalist-monopolist oligarchy'? Deutscher somewhat dodged the issue during his address at Berkeley. 'The October insurrection', he told his young American audience, 'was carried out in such a way that, according to all the hostile witnesses (such as the Western ambassadors who were then in Petrograd), the total number of victims on all sides was ten.' The leaders of the insurrection organised the upheaval 'with a very profound although unspoken concern for human lives'. (This claim may bring to mind Sergei Eisenstein's joke that more Russians were killed during the filming of his *October* than during the actual event.) But Deutscher justly pointed out that nearly ten million perished during the First World War. Then came the intervention of the Great Powers, the civil war. 'Violence had to be used on an increasing scale, just as the Viet Cong today have to use violence on an increasing scale.'

But what about armed insurrection here in America? According to Deutscher, Marxism still suited the industrialised West (where it was dormant) better than the undeveloped countries (where it kept taking over). He resorted to Marx's outdated prognosis of the pauperisation of the middle class into the ranks of the proletariat when he assured his audience that a revolution in the West would be carried out against 'a really small minority consisting of the exploiters. The need to use violence would be very limited.' How could he be so sure? In the next breath he insisted that Marxists must treat violence as a necessary evil. 'In the West we must foster a way of thinking which would not shirk realities.' Vietnam was not an accident, it was part and parcel of imperialism. 'If you accept this, you imply that the social order has to be changed. ... How is it going to be changed by non-violent methods. . . ?' But here he slipped in a caveat: he could imagine this being achieved non-violently in the USA on one condition: 'When you have the overwhelming number of Americans ready to use violence in order to bring about socialism, only then may socialism conquer the United States without the use of violence. The revolution's capital is its moral supremacy.'[37]

This was a scenario unknown to human history – anywhere. Deutscher as revolutionary tribune before a mass audience may remind us of Aesop's fable about the daddy frog who puffed himself up to impress his son until he burst.

PART SEVEN

TO BE A JEW

19

TWO JEWISH HERITAGES

WE COME TO the 'Jewish question', that is to say, the extent to which the Jewish heritage shared by Berlin and Deutscher exacerbated their antagonism, imparting a fratricidal intimacy to their wider ideological quarrel. When Berlin privately describes Deutscher as a *parshivy yevrey*, a 'mangy Jew', something is afloat.

For Berlin, a non-believer, it was a cause for some discomfort that his Latvian family had a direct kinship with the Schneerson clan who ran, and still run, the fundamentalist sect known as the Lubavitch or Chabad. Established in the 1780s by Rabbi Schneur Zalman Schneerson, the Lubavitcher were among the most mystical, messianic and devout of the Hasidic sects. Mendel Berlin used to attribute his son's memory and scholarly achievements to his rabbinical ancestors, a proposition dismissed as absurd by Isaiah. Menachem Mendal Schneerson, the charismatic Rebbe from Brooklyn's Crown Heights who opposed blood transfusions because they compromised unique Jewish DNA, was Berlin's cousin. The Rebbe elevated the Israeli soldier to the level of *tzadik*, a righteous person risking his life for the protection of another Jew. He sent his Chabad Shluchim apostles into battlefields and remote army posts to care for the physical and spiritual needs of these brave defenders of Israel. Isaiah Berlin regarded the modern Lubavitch Hasidim – with their three-quarter-length black frock coats, wide-brimmed hats, beards and ringlets – as alarming fanatics.[1]

Berlin found no god in the universe but he was exceptionally preoccupied by Jewishness. Bryan Magee, who came to know Berlin noticeably well, has recalled that in conversation Berlin would quiz him about MPs who were Jews. 'If he went to a concert he might start speculating about why so many musicians were Jews, or so many of the music critics, or so many of the concert agents. At the theatre he might start wondering why there were so few Jewish actors.... He was constantly telling Jewish jokes. His fascination with Jewishness, what it was and what difference it made, went right down to his foundations.'[2]

Doubts have been expressed about Isaac Deutscher's religious upbringing in Poland, as related by Isaac and Tamara. He depicted himself as a child steeped in religious faith: 'I wore my sidelocks and my long *kapota* until I was seventeen.'[3] In 1958, he claimed during an interview with the *Jewish Quarterly* that by the age of thirteen he knew the entire Talmud by heart. Professor Bernard Wasserstein has called this 'preposterous', in his *Isaiah Berlin, Isaac Deutscher and Arthur Koestler: Their Jewish Wars* (2009). Tamara described how at a young age Isaac relished a debate in Yiddish on an abstruse question about the saliva of the mythical bird the *kikiyon*, which appears over the world once every seventy years and spits on the earth only once. 'The saliva is extremely precious: it has miraculous qualities, for it can cure any illness or deformity.' The question presented to the young Isaac was: 'Is the bird's saliva *kosher* or *treyfe*?' So brilliant was his barmitzvah *droshe* (homily) on this question that Isaac's audience 'nodded their heads admiringly' and pronounced him fit to become a rabbi. Mother, aunts and uncles embraced him while his father tried to conceal his deep pride. Wasserstein is again unimpressed: 'The *kikiyon*, which appears in the Book of Jonah and is discussed in the Talmud, is not a bird but a plant. That the barmitzvah boy would be granted *semichah* (ordination as a rabbi) on the spot beggars belief and the notion has been disputed by at least one rabbinical authority.'[4]

One difficulty is that we are reliant on Deutscher alone for evidence of his early years. Given the intellectualism and linguistic intensity of his upbringing as he described it, it is perplexing to learn that, having apparently translated Hebrew poetry into Polish in his earlier days, he could by 1951 inform an acquaintance in Tel Aviv that he could no longer read the language. It is also said that he lost his Yiddish in later years. Wasserstein quotes one of Deutscher's acquaintances, the journalist S.J. Goldsmith: 'It must have been an act of will – Isaac was a very determined man – to forget Hebrew to the point of being unable to compose a single sentence, unless it was a quotation. . . . His Yiddish [too] was halting in his last years – as if he had learned it recently rather than given it up recently.'[5]

By his own admission, Isaiah Berlin never learned Hebrew properly. On receiving a brief, handwritten postcard message in Hebrew from Gershom Scholem in the 1960s, he expressed relief that he had understood the gist: when Scholem would arrive in London, where he would stay.

One can list, as Michael Ignatieff has most thoroughly done, the many aristocratic, or wealthy, or simply adoring Jews who befriended Berlin after he

was elected to All Souls, and whose company he sought. He showed no incli-
nation to distance himself from the high-born Rothschilds, d'Avigdor-
Goldsmids and Ginzbourgs, or the self-made millionaires like Isaac Wolfson.
Berlin's preferred Jews were proud to be British.

The conservative ethos of Anglo-Jewry might entail a degree of snobbery:
in Berlin's case an aversion to encounters with Jews in a crowd (as on board a
ship sailing between Italy and Israel), particularly if they hailed from Brooklyn
and displayed signs of mass distress or panic. Writing in April 1958 to Bernard
Berenson, a Jewish art historian whom he revered, from the S.S. *Theodore
Herzl* of the Zim line, he described the scene at the dockside in Naples when
the S.S. *Jerusalem* had arrived late from Israel: 'The passport room, designed
for about 50 persons, had 350 milling Jews in it, mostly American. The Italian
officials took their time. After an hour so, babies were crying, women threatening to faint, and all these affluent Yiddish speaking first class passengers
from Brooklyn or the suburbs of Chicago became a mob of desperate, helpless
refugees, human flotsam from some concentration camp, jostling, screaming,
with no vestige of self-control, shaming & horrible.' They did not calm down
until four hours later when they poured into the S.S. *Jerusalem* '& were given
cold meat and tea'. By contrast, the Israeli passengers did not speak Yiddish
and remained calm. 'Zionism really *has* turned them into decent, emancipated
human beings. It was the best advertisement for it I ever saw.' Jennifer Holmes,
coeditor of *Enlightening*, a volume of his correspondence, comments: 'A less
pleasant trait [of his letters] is the snobbery Berlin sometimes displays, particularly towards other Jews, such as the "Jews with colossal noses, who hate
Zionism, make jolly Jewish jokes, but ultimately *are* ashamed and aggressive."'
His descriptions of Jews in transit, she adds, are 'positively vicious and provoke
the same feeling of unease as his attempts in later life to rid his father's memoir
of any taint of Yiddish influence'.[6]

Deutscher was capable of a different form of anti-Semitism, that of Marxist
inverted snobbery. 'We all know how repellent are some of the Jewish milieus
of the West, the milieus in which there is nothing but a few taboos and a lot of
money. With us [in Poland], in the environment I knew, it was the reverse: no
money, no taboos, but an abundance of hope, ideas and ideals. We had a thor-
ough contempt for the *Yahudim* of the West.'[7] This obviously reflects Marx's
view.

Berlin's most profound unease, easily turning to aversion, was aroused by
the more radical Jewish scholars from European backgrounds not dissimilar to
his own. An impressive proportion of Berlin's *bêtes noires* were Jewish immigrant intellectuals from Central and Eastern Europe, who brought with them
foreign languages, Continental *savoir faire*, personal knowledge of the human

catastrophes of the Thirties and Forties, intense involvement with Zionism (one way or another). Without exception they had escaped the Holocaust by the skin of their teeth: Isaac Deutscher (from Poland), Hannah Arendt (from Germany) and Arthur Koestler (from Hungary and Germany). He did, however, maintain a personal relationship with Koestler after he provocatively proposed in print that Jews should either fulfil two thousand years of prayer by settling in Israel or abandon any separate identity in the disapora by way of deliberate assimilation, if only for the sake of their children's future. This touched a raw nerve. Berlin took him severely to task in 'Jewish Slavery and Emancipation' (1951), rejecting any obligatory choice between *aliya* (migration to Israel) and apostasy. However, this rather artificial debate, far removed from what divided Berlin and Deutscher, need not detain us further.[8]

Berlin's aversion to supercharged Jewish intellectual émigrés extended even to the following generation; for example, the young George Steiner, born in 1929 of Viennese parents and fluent in English, French and German, whose high-voltage cosmopolitanism and opinions on the Holocaust provoked Berlin to write to Anna Kallin: 'Steiner is what is meant by alienation – if ever there was "a rootless cosmopolitan" – unlike ourselves – it is he. He goes about the East Coast campuses preaching the virtues of the Jewish diaspora in embarrassing, tortured, madly conceited, ludicrously pretentious terms – I cannot believe there is anyone who has derived any benefit from his writing, but of course one can never tell.'

On the whole Berlin maintained cordial, not necessarily very close, relations with Jewish intellectuals who were reliably anti-Soviet and pro-Zionist: J.L. Talmon, Karl Popper and Raymond Aron, for example. But a high proportion of his favourite people, his lifelong friends, were Gentiles: Maurice Bowra, John Sparrow, A.J. Ayer, Stuart Hampshire, Stephen Spender, Arthur Schlesinger, Jr., Nicolas Nabokov, to name a few. He said he preferred Lord David Cecil to Harold Laski and the Jews he met at the University of Chicago – 'too smart and "prost" for me …'.[9]

All Cold War theology extends back to the holy ghost of Karl Marx or the Trinity of Marx–Engels–Lenin. Isaiah Berlin's first book-length project, as we have seen, was a biography of Marx, who was directly descended from two long generations of rabbis and suffered anti-Semitic jibes from fellow radicals during the greater part of his life. Visiting Marx's grave in Highgate's East Cemetery, Berlin was confronted by the main inscription beneath the bust, 'WORKERS OF ALL LANDS UNITE', an injunction unlikely to have won his full-hearted enthusiasm. More to the point, here was a Jew buried in a Christian cemetery; Berlin was to condemn Jews who evaded their inescapable identity, not least Marx, whose German father, Heinrich, had chosen to be received into the church in 1817, a year before Marx's birth. Having been baptised, Marx did not suffer from the legal disabilities afflicting German Jews, nor – Berlin was to complain – did he ever acknowledge his Jewish provenance: 'He rarely speaks about himself or of his life, and never about his origin. . . . His references to individual Jews, particularly in his letters to Engels, are virulent to a degree: his origin had become a personal stigma which he was unable to avoid pointing out in others.' In a letter to the editor of the *Jewish Observer and Middle East Review* (18 December 1959), Berlin renewed his castigation of Marx's anti-Semitism: 'He attacks Judaism as a parasitic growth upon society, neither race nor religion but an economic junction identical with money-lending and exploitation, which is the language of an anti-Semite.' In his late essay 'Benjamin Disraeli, Karl Marx and the Search for Identity' (1970), the perspective on Marx is unforgiving. In an 1843 letter to Ruge, Marx had called the Israelite faith 'repugnant', while in his essay *On the Jewish Question* (1844) he described 'the secular morality of Jews as egoism, their secular religion as huckstering, their secular god as money' – in Berlin's view, a diatribe that 'resembles many later anti-Semitic tracts . . . in the past and in growing measure in our own time'.[10]

And more: in his *Theses on Feuerbach* (1845), Marx called the Paris Bourse the 'stock exchange synagogue', losing no opportunity to highlight the Jewish origins of the leading financial families. In an article for the New York *Tribune* (1856), he remarked: 'every tyrant is backed by a Jew, and every Pope by a Jesuit'. Writing to Engels, he called the German labour leader Lassalle, who remained unbaptised and did not conceal his Jewish sentiments, 'the Jewish nigger'. Berlin accuses Marx of attempting 'to escape from intolerable reality' and 'self-hatred' (a term to be widely deployed by friends of Israel against its Jewish critics, including Hannah Arendt). Marx, he says, felt the need to eliminate every kind of nationalism, including Jewish nationalism, as a force in history. His refuge was to identify with the proletariat, as Benjamin Disraeli did with the inner core of the British upper class. Never able to become a member of the proletariat, Marx fashioned it into 'an abstract category' that embraces 'his own indignant self'. What is really speaking in him is 'the oppression of centuries of a people of pariahs, not of a recently risen class'. Berlin held that in reality Marx was addressing 'persons like himself, alienated members of the world-wide intelligentsia', rather than factory operatives. 'Marx's proletariat is to some extent a class constructed after Marx's own specifications, as a vessel to carry the vials of his justified wrath.'[11] We find here a clear link between Berlin's sense of an irrevocable Jewishness and his aversion to a long line of Marxists who attempted to escape from it.

Whereas Deutscher's commitment to Polish Jewry grew into contempt for West European Jewish capitalism, its self-enslavement (as he saw it) to the market economy, Berlin never departed from his family's subscription to the market economy. The young Isaiah's passage to England and his subsequent private education at St Paul's were on the back of Mendel Berlin's entrepreneurial profits from the timber trade in Russia, prudently stashed in a London bank. Isaiah Berlin himself was to embrace the welfare state but not socialism. For Deutscher, by contrast, the proper Jewish destiny was socialism in common cause with the non-Jewish working class. Rosa Luxemburg and Leon Trotsky were his Jewish figureheads, both ultimately martyrs to the cause of a regenerated future. Deutscher may have had Isaiah Berlin in his sights when he declared that all the members of his own, preferred Jewish pantheon were 'determinists, they all hold that the universe is ruled by laws inherent in it and governed by *Gesetzmässigkeiten* [regular principles of legitimacy]'. All of them believed 'that knowledge to be real must be active', that morality is inseparable from praxis. These 'non-Jewish Jews' were optimists, they believed in the ultimate solidarity of mankind.[12]

Clearly the intellectual who maintains his Jewish identity while assimilating into the wider secular society experiences that society both as insider and outsider. Berlin liked to regard himself as one of those clear-eyed Jewish observers who, as he remarked of Proust, 'turns his rootlessness into the kind of Archimedean point outside all worlds, the better to assess them from'. He likened such a Jew to an anthropologist studying a tribe; he could prosper only if he made himself more of an expert on the customs of the tribes than the natives – hence the poignant passion of the Jew for institutions that do not allow him truly to belong.[13] Yet Berlin could on occasion describe his own capacity for assimilation, his eagerness to fit in to English society, as almost a sin. Jews should not be so emollient or accommodating; ingratiation, the fatal eagerness to please, was a common Jewish failing, always hoping that one would 'pass'. He wished that he had been one of life's intransigents, those hard, difficult, 'impossible' characters who do not bend.[14]

Berlin never bent in the face of anti-Semitism. The fascinating story of his friendship, then falling out, with Adam von Trott zu Solz illustrates his unblinking stance in the face of Nazi anti-Semitism, but that complex episode is beyond our reach in these pages. Sufficient to say that while Maurice Bowra later regretted having turned against Trott, who was hanged after the 1944 bomb plot to kill Hitler, Berlin did not repent, and rightly so in the present writer's opinion. Indeed, he resented David Astor's passionate advocacy of Trott's integrity: 'David Astor was Trott's greatest friend and is a neurotic, muddled, complicated, politically irresponsible, unhappy adventurer, permanently resentful of somebody or something and a typical poor little rich American boy surrounded by a court of dubious toadies which gives his newspaper [the *Observer*] its queerly disoriented look.'[15] Much later, in 1986, Berlin wrote a polite tribute to Trott, professing ignorance of his career, not alluding to Trott's role in the Nazi bureaucracy, his acceptance of Germany's expansion in the east, or his ambiguity about anti-Semitism, and adding that David Astor was perhaps better informed. This whitewash carries little value.[16]

In 1951, Berlin took an outspoken stand against T.S. Eliot, who in 1934 had written that a society could not achieve cultural and spiritual unity as long as there were Jews in its midst. Berlin had contributed to Eliot's quarterly magazine *Criterion*, but took him to task as one of those 'fearful thinkers', 'those souls filled with terror', who sought to place Jews 'beyond the borders of the city' because their critical and discontented spirit jeopardised the unity of European Christian civilisation. In reply, the illustrious poet, more than twenty years Berlin's senior, politely complained that Berlin had misrepresented or misunderstood lines he had written in the Thirties describing Europe's Jews as aliens within a Christian civilisation; Eliot said that he had regarded the Jewish problem as a religious one, not a racial one. Berlin stuck to his guns, quoting chapter and verse; Eliot duly repented, although anti-Semitic images do surface in several of his poems. Sensitive to the status of Jews at his old school, Berlin was gratified when in July 1957 St Paul's elected its first Jewish president of the Old Pauline Club, the veteran Lord Nathan. But only four years later Berlin resigned from the Old Paulines when the school introduced a quota system. 'We try to keep the school 85 per cent Christian,' explained the headmaster.[17]

Berlin generally chose to observe the major Jewish festivals like the Passover Seder and Yom Kippur, reading from the scriptures in Hebrew, a language he barely knew. He did not believe. The religious creed was not for him. Bernard Wasserstein recalls: 'To judge from his demeanour during Kol Nidrei services in the Oxford synagogue, one might reasonably conclude that, like many others present, he regarded it more as a social than a spiritual occasion.' When Berlin was buried in the Jewish section of Oxford's Wolvercote Cemetery, the chief rabbi intoned in Hebrew and English: 'May his soul be bound in the bonds of everlasting life.'[18]

Deutscher's sentiments about an ineradicable Jewish identity were not so different. 'I am, however, a Jew by force of my unconditional solidarity with the persecuted and the exterminated. I am a Jew because I feel the Jewish tragedy as my own: because I feel the pulse of Jewish history.' In November 1963, when taking part in a London symposium on 'The Identity of the Jewish Intellectual', organised by the World Jewish Congress British Section, he criticised another speaker who said that he was 'opting for a Jewish identity'. Deutscher retorted: 'You don't opt for something that you *are*. You opt for something that you are *not* or for something you want to acquire.' But what manner of life did this 'you *are*' entail? For both Berlin and Deutscher, religion, belief in God, attendance at the synagogue were all optional – a man could choose to jettison the religious beliefs and rituals of his forefathers without loss of existential integrity.

That Deutscher had put behind him the religion of his upbringing was clear from his provocative address 'The Non-Jewish Jew in Modern Thought', given at Woburn House, Bloomsbury, an event tactfully described as 'controversial' by the *Jewish Chronicle* (14 February 1958). His remarks were frankly inflammatory: 'Yet I think that Marx went to the very heart of the matter when he said that Jewry had survived "not in spite of history but in history and through history", that it owed its survival to the distinctive role that the Jews had played as agents of a money economy in environments which lived in a natural economy; that Judaism was essentially a theoretical epitome of market relationships and the faith of the merchant; and that Christian Europe, as it developed from feudalism to capitalism, became Jewish in a sense.' That was why Marx used the Young Hegelian idiom to call for the 'emancipation of society from Jewry'. Deutscher went on to parade his pantheon of liberated 'non-Jewish Jews' who had sought a universal ethic, that of mankind, of the nationless society. 'Trotsky is still under anathema in Russia today. The names of Marx, Heine, Freud and Rosa Luxemburg were forbidden in Germany quite recently. But theirs is the ultimate victory. Spinoza had seized on the fundamental contradiction between a universal God and the God of one people only, the Jews. After a century during which his name was covered with oblivion, they put up monuments to him and acknowledged him as the greatest fructifier of the human mind.' It was tragic, Deutscher declared, that at a time when the nation-state had entered on its final stage of decay, the Jews should choose to embrace a concept that for centuries had been a factor for disunity and strife. (The decline of the nation-state was one of Deutscher's favourite mistakes.)

A not entirely coherent response came from the Ango-Jewish establishment in the shape of Israel M. Sieff. Sieff was certainly a Jewish merchant, soon to be chairman of the retail chain Marks & Spencer, and presently Baron Sieff. In answer to Deutscher, he claimed that the heritage of Abraham, Isaiah and Moses was indeed universal, likewise the teaching of Maimonides, Spinoza and Einstein. 'Their God, as evolved in Jewish history, as seen in Isaiah and Malachi, was the God of the man who loved justice and charity and was his neighbour's brother. He was the God of the Universe, which included all mankind.' On the difficult case of Spinoza, Sieff maintained: 'The expulsion of Spinoza from his community did not expel the philosopher from the Jewish spirit.... He was expelled only from the ritual of the community.' As for Deutscher's lauded radicals – Marx, Trotsky and Rosa Luxemburg – they were no longer Jews, said Sieff, having divorced themselves from the living body and spirit of Judaism, and in their guilt belittled what their fathers had deemed sacred. They had adopted the proletariat as the new Messiah. (This last phrase might or might not indicate Isaiah Berlin at his elbow – Michael Ignatieff mentions his invitations to the Sieffs' dinners in Park Lane.)[19]

We come to the fraught issue of Soviet anti-Semitism. For Berlin and others, a bone of contention was Deutscher's long silences or evasive utterances about the virulent anti-Semitic campaign of Stalin's last years. A Politburo resolution of 8 February 1949 disbanded associations of Jewish writers and banned miscellanies written in Yiddish. On 9 March, Jewish 'unpatriotic critics' were expelled from the Party and the Jewish theatre was shut down. The Jewish Anti-Fascist Committee, allowed prominence during the war, was accused of being a nest of spies working for American, British and Israeli intelligence. Aleksandr Fadeyev, secretary of the Writers' Union, wrote a letter (21 September 1949) denouncing two Jewish colleagues, several times introducing such emotive phrases as 'slither out of', 'his cosmopolitan friends' and 'close contact with bourgeois Jewish nationalists of the Jewish theatre'. Cartoons appeared of figures displaying Fagin-like profiles. Jews who had adopted Russian names were attacked – Yasny as Finkelstein, Gan as Kagan.[20] Konstantin Simonov hastened to publish an article, 'The Tasks before Soviet Drama and Dramatic Criticism' (Pravda, 28 February 1949), in the course of which he attacked 'the anti-patriots and the bourgeois cosmopolitans with their imitators who knowingly imitate them'. He listed a number of critics by name, mainly Jews, castigating their 'criminal activities' in important editorial posts. Simonov later admitted in Novyi mir (December 1956) that he and other writers had lacked the courage to resist the anti-cosmopolitan campaign.

The Prague trial began on 20 November 1952. Rudolf Slansky and thirteen others were accused of being 'Trotskyist Titoist-Zionist bourgeois-nationalist traitors, and enemies of the Czechoslovak people'. Most of them were Jews. Writing to Rowland Burdon-Muller (2 December), Berlin mocked the absurd list of defendants but shuddered at the assault on Jews while trembling for the fate of the ones he knew in Moscow. There was clearly no room for the Jewish appetite for debate and political liveliness in a 'State which is determined to crush all thought and all ideology and rule everybody in an absolutely wooden and iron way'.[21]

What did Deutscher have to say about Stalinist anti-Semitism or the Prague trial? On 7 December 1951, the London *Jewish Chronicle* reported a symposium on the question 'Can Jewish community life continue under communism?' held under the auspices of the World Jewish Congress: 'Mr Deutscher said he did not believe that one could accuse the Soviet Government of any special anti-Jewish attitude. It seemed to him that the Jew remained in Russia equal to every other citizen with regard to the law. He added that he dissociated himself from the assumption that seemed to be implied in the question.' Labedz here comments: '*Mein Liebchen was willst du noch mehr* [My darling, what more do you want?] – as Heine would have said.'

Elsewhere Deutscher reminded his readers: 'Despite all of Stalin's crimes we must remember that it was on his orders that 2½ million Jews from the invaded territories in Russia were helped to move towards the interior of the country and at least were saved from Nazi concentration camps and gas chambers. This is a fact which the Jewish nationalist Zionist press all too often tends to forget.' In 1948, Stalin joined hands with America in pressing for the recognition of Israel. Together they managed to dislodge the British from the Middle East. 'Whatever Stalin's calculations, it was to him that Israel, paradoxically, was indebted for its independent existence.' But then Golda Meir was greeted in Moscow by the Jews and Stalin turned towards anti-Semitism because, Deutscher explained, the Jews of Russia leant towards America and their relatives living there. If the American army had marched into Russia, it would have found sympathy and collaborators among the local Jews.[22] This makes unhappy reading. But Deutscher did (eventually) condemn the 1952–53 'Jewish doctors' plot', and Moscow's claim of an anti-Soviet conspiracy of world Jewry, as carrying 'the flavour of the Protocols of the Elders of Zion and of the concoctions of Goebbels's Ministry of Propaganda.' Even so, he managed to insist that it was fallacious to argue that Stalinism adopted racial hatred and anti-Semitism. 'Before embracing racialism and anti-Semitism any Soviet government would first have to ban the works of Marx, Engels and Lenin, that is to say destroy its own birth certificate and ideological title deeds.'[23] This was specious pleading: how could it explain the murder of Mikhoels, the disbandment of the Anti-Fascist Refugee Committee, the virulent anti-Cosmopolitan campaign, the proportion of Jewish defendants at the Slansky trial in Prague? That Deutscher did not entirely believe what he wrote publicly is reflected in his correspondence with a New York Jewish editor, William Zukerman, about the anti-Semitism on display in Pasternak's novel *Doctor Zhivago*. He wrote to Zukerman: 'It is curious to see that on this point Pasternak, allegedly the heroic non-conformist, lends, perhaps unwittingly, support to an official [Soviet] policy which found its expression in the liquidation of Jewish writers.'[24]

By 1958, Deutscher's public position remained unaltered. He told the *Jewish Chronicle* that he believed few Soviet Jews would wish to emigrate because evolution to a genuine socialist democracy 'must provide a source of hope to Jews of all political convictions.' (Another remarkable misjudgment.) When Evgeny Yevtushenko published his poem 'Babi Yar' (1961), then his *Precocious Autobiography* (1963, but banned in Russia), Deutscher apparently confined his warm appreciation to a desk drawer. His review of the French edition appears tacked on to the end of *Ironies of History* in 1966, no previous publication details being given. Deutscher did not here quote from 'Babi Yar' – 'The antisemites have proclaimed themselves/ The "Union of the Russian People"' – but he did cite Yevtushenko's description of an ardent young communist who insisted that all evil stemmed from the Jews and who exultantly celebrated the arrest of the Jewish doctors accused of plotting to murder Stalin.[25] But reading these pages, one is again struck by how much, across the preceding years, Deutscher knew yet had chosen not to say.

For Jewish Cold War intellectuals he expressed a hostility scarcely less intense than Berlin's for Deutscher and his cherished 'non-Jewish Jews' on the pro-Soviet Left. In his essay 'Who is a Jew?' (which emanated from a discussion sponsored by the World Jewish Congress in November 1963), Deutscher struck out fiercely:

> What is so striking about the Jewish intellectuals of the West is precisely their extraordinary conformism, political, ideological, and social. In the Cold War which has dominated our lives for more than 13 years, the Jews have been most prominent ... historians, politicians, sociologists, etc.... When one looks at the legions of Panglosses who proclaim that 'our American way of life' or 'our British way of life' is the best possible of all ways of life, one is sometimes tempted to pray that some *numerus clausus* should be imposed on the access of the Jewish intellectuals to the Pangloss profession in which they are so vocal and in such relative majority.[26]

This appears to have been written shortly after he had sought legal redress against the Congress for Cultural Freedom for publishing Leopold Labedz's polemic, 'Deutscher as Historian and Prophet, Part 1'. But Deutscher spoke in terms wide enough to ensure that Isaiah Berlin would identify himself as a Jewish Pangloss alongside Labedz.

Finally, on a note more positive and comforting, one would like to imagine that Deutscher might have won Berlin's sympathy for his sensitive 1965 portrait of Marc Chagall as a quintessentially Jewish painter. Deutscher points out Judaism's traditional hostility to the visual arts; the *shtetl* had its cantors and musicians, its bards and poets, but no painters or sculptors. Challenging the view that Chagall was indebted to Hasidism, the religious romanticism of East European Jewry and the medieval Cabbala, Deutscher sets out to demonstrate that Chagall's surrealist painting is authentically Jewish in a different sense: 'The Jewish imagination sought to escape reality or to make life fluid, bright, unpredictably miraculous; and Jewish humour and self-irony cried and laughed over the constant clash between hopes and realities.' Chagall caught the same mood as the Yiddish author Sholem Aleikhem who created in Menakhem Mendel a figure who was both Don Quixote and Sancho Panza. In his long series of Crucifixions, in red, white, blue and yellow, Chagall's Christ is the epitome of Jewish martyrdom, always wrapped in a Jewish prayer shawl and never able to overcome the suffering of the crowds of terror-stricken, fleeing Jews below him.

Deutscher took the opportunity to laud Bolshevik cultural policy under Lenin. Under the tsars, Moscow was almost out of bounds for Jews, but when after the Revolution the Yiddish State Theatre opened in Moscow, Chagall was able to produce his stage designs for the plays of Gogol, Chekhov and Aleikhem. Yet the good times were short-lived: by the early 1920s, Chagall found himself in Vitebsk, hemmed in between the Party line and the hostile doctrinaires of abstract art, Malevich and his suprematist school. He left Russia in 1922.[27] Deutscher did not chide Chagall for subsequently enlisting with the anti-communist renegades in the West, he simply did not mention it. (During an edgy luncheon with Picasso in the late Forties, Chagall took care to insult him: 'Since the Russians so much admire your politics, why won't they show any of your paintings?' It was their last meeting.)

20

ZIONISM

No issue more exacerbated the conflict between Berlin and Deutscher than Zionism and the birth of the State of Israel. In biographical terms, Berlin's involvement was the more intense. When the Balfour Declaration, granting a Jewish Homeland, was announced on 9 November 1917, immediately after the Bolshevik Revolution, Isaiah witnessed his family's excitement about this place called Palestine, and later remembered the blue, white and gold flags that he and other children were given to wave in a synagogue basement.[1]

In an essay on his mentor, the Zionist leader Chaim Weizmann, Berlin keeps returning to, and implicitly embracing, Weizmann's anglophilia. The England that Weizmann embraced was epitomised by those he regarded as the enlightened spirits of the ruling class: Joseph Chamberlain, Alfred Milner, Herbert Samuel, Edwin Montagu, Arthur Balfour, Winston Churchill – all friendly or not unfriendly to Zionist claims. As Berlin put it, Weizmann 'loved [England's] independence, freedom, dignity, style . . . the moderation, the civilised disdain of extremes, the whole tone of public life, the lack of cruelty, of excitement, of shoddiness . . . the love of the odd and idiosyncratic, the taste for eccentricity.'[2] Weizmann had discovered an England 'moved, in the last resort, by her moral imagination, and not by a short-view of her self-interest or passing emotion'.

This was also Berlin's view. Did it fit the Boer War, in which Churchill served, or its notorious concentration camps? As Berlin saw it, the English Jews who supported Herzl's Zionist vision espoused 'the most idealistic liberal conception of the White Man's Burden . . . essentially a civilizing mission . . . [bringing] the most humane culture of the West to the inchoate, rather wild, rather barbarous Eastern peoples'.[3] These obviously included the Arab population of Palestine. Much the same attitude had prevailed among the majority of Jewish immigrants to England since the late Victorian era, Zionists included, who readily associated themselves with the White Man's Burden or, in French terms, the *mission civilisatrice.*

Later, working for the British government in Washington during the war, Berlin was to find himself closely caught up in the conflict between David Ben-Gurion's uncompromising demand for a Jewish state to cover the whole of Palestine, on the one hand, and the British government's refusal to permit unlimited Jewish immigration. This tension turned to bloodshed after Berlin returned to Oxford and the Labour foreign secretary, Ernest Bevin, deployed British troops in an attempt to beat back the rising terrorism of the Zionist paramilitary group, the Irgun.

Isaac Deutscher, by contrast, had always belonged to the anti-Zionist wing of Polish socialism. He did not believe in a Jewish state – Jews and Gentiles should work together for the social and political liberation of their homelands. Then came the Holocaust and the desperate flight of the few survivors to Palestine, radically changing the moral contours of any debate. But from his own Marxist standpoint, Deutscher's reluctant, *faute de mieux* support for Israel's existence was flawed by his eagerness to meet its leaders, notably Ben-Gurion, and to extend his personal reputation in Israel through lectures, journalism and the translation of his books into Hebrew. When he travelled internally, it was often across land previously belonging to some 700,000 exiled Arabs. We shall see presently how, caught in this dilemma, he attempted to resolve it.

Berlin's Zionism was rooted in nationalism and ethnic-cultural allegiance, not religion, although in reality the claim on Palestine has to be rooted in the Hebrew Bible, the destruction of the Temple in Jerusalem, the tragic dispersion. Even the more secular Zionist leaders felt compelled to seek justification in God (theirs). As Weizmann puts it in *Trial and Error* (1949), 'I know that God promised Palestine to the children of Israel', adding: 'God had always chosen small countries through which to convey his messages to Humanity.'[4] Ben-Gurion told the Peel Commission: 'I say on behalf of the Jews that the Bible is our Mandate, the Bible which was written by us, in our language, in Hebrew in this very country.'[5] Yet Isaiah Berlin subscribed to no God or Bible.

In 'The Life and Opinions of Moses Hess' (1957), Berlin revives the reputation of this German socialist (born 1812) as a hero of good sense and modesty. In his *Rome and Jerusalem*, Hess discusses the Jews, what they are, what they should be. Religion apart, the Jews are a nationality, 'inseparable from the heritage of my fathers and from the Holy Land'. Nations are a natural growth, like families. Jews will never be respected so long as they act on the principle of '*Ubi bene, ibi patria*' – 'Where I do well, this is my country'. According to Hess, the modern Jew is despicable when he disowns his race because the heavy hand of fate oppresses it. Neither reformed religion nor baptism would save Jews from the racial prejudice of Germans. 'What the Germans hate is not so much the Jewish religion or Jewish names as the Jewish nose.' You can change your religion but not your nose. Yet German Jews adopt patriotic poses, change their names, take refuge in a reformed religion, only to witness Gentiles digging out their original names and pointing the finger. Jews would be despised as long as they were homeless. Without his own soil 'a man sinks to the status of a parasite, feeding on others'.[6] Isaiah Berlin embraced this vision, though eventually choosing not to live on his 'own soil'.

Although Hess was a socialist (he knew Marx), he recognised that a Jewish homeland could be achieved only through the support of one or other imperialist power – France, Turkey, England, Germany – currently occupying, governing, sometimes crushing, the Arabs. Hess looked to France for help in establishing *Eretz Israel*. The Turkish sultan might be won over by Jewish gold, but 'French democracy, Jewish genius, modern science, that was to be the new triple alliance that would at once save an ancient people and revive an ancient land. . . . The rich Jews must buy the land and train agricultural experts. . . . Jewish colonists must be led by men trained in modern methods of thought and action and not by obscurantist rabbis.'[7] Labour must be fully protected. Mosaic and socialist principles were the same. By way of workers' cooperatives the new state would peacefully pass to full socialism.

Fine – but the Arabs of Palestine remain out of sight. Hess regarded nationalism as a development of civilisation reserved for the European races. Later, at the turn of the century, Theodor Herzl sought to win over the sultan, the kaiser and the British despite Joseph Chamberlain's warning that Jewish colonisation of Palestine would encounter strong Arab opposition. Chamberlain offered Uganda instead. The English Jew Israel Zangwill was so impressed that he announced that if Britain could attract the world's Jews to its colonies she would double the white population, strengthening her hand against indigenous peoples. The Empire was viewed as a *tabula rasa*, a place for fresh starts. Jewish settlers would achieve *de facto* self-government, the Zionist dream.[8] Weizmann also played the imperial card: 'We had long pointed out to the British . . . that a Jewish Palestine would be a safeguard to England, in particular in respect to the Suez Canal.' (In 1956, when Britain and France joined forces with Israel in an attempt to seize back the canal, Isaiah Berlin wrote to Lady Eden that her husband had 'saved England'.) Reporting on a visit to South Africa, Weizmann remarked that the animals of the Kruger National Park 'have no Arab problem'.[9] The First World War finally brought the concession of Jewish immigration to a homeland from a victorious Britain. Yet the Zionism that the Berlin family brought from Russia was far from typical

among the Anglo-Jewish establishment at that time. The influence on Isaiah
Berlin of his parents, and later of Chaim Weizmann and Lewis Namier, was
essentially the Zionism of immigrants from Eastern Europe. Weizmann found
that the old Anglo-Jewish families whose support he assiduously sought were
in the main devoted to local philanthropy; as for Zionism and the call of 'If I
forget thee, O Jerusalem, let my right hand forget her cunning', they 'might just
as well have belonged to another world'.[10]

Palestine was not the 'empty space' of Zionist mythology. It was during the
second *aliya* (immigration) of 1908–14 that a new generation of Zionist
settlers brought a determination to replace local *fellahin* labour with Jewish in
properties purchased mainly from absentee merchant landlords living in the
coastal cities. This process was protected by the Ottoman Land Code of 1858.
Even so, only 12,000 Jews occupied some 44 agricultural colonies in 1914,
compared to some 600,000 Arab cultivators. Visiting Palestine in 1918,
Weizmann remarked to the British commander-in-chief, Allenby, how the
villages founded by Baron Edmond de Rothschild were 'oases of fertility . . . in
startling contrast to the Arab villages, with their mud hovels and dunghills'. In
the years following the Balfour Declaration, the Jewish National Fund was to
pursue the policy of replacing the *fellahin* with Jewish labour, although the
incoming Jews also continued to employ Arab labour.[11]

Writing as a Palestinian, but not entirely subjectively, Edward Said points
out how in Western eyes Jewish settlement corresponded to historical prejudices. The gallant Zionists were seen as pioneers, as 'us', struggling against 'a
mass of undifferentiated natives with whom it was impossible for "us" to identify . . . a definite image of the White settler hewing civilization out of the
wilderness'.[12] In 1936, Jews numbered 384,000 out of a total population of
1,366,692. By 1946, immigration had brought the figure to 608,225 out of
1,913,112. In 1948, the Arab majority still owned 90 per cent of the land. Isaiah
Berlin never explicitly addressed the Eurocentric prejudice described by Said
although he was by no means blind to the claims of the Arabs. As a young man
he visited Palestine in 1934, travelling to Amman to meet fiercely anti-Zionist
Palestinians. As he remarked to his parents, he would gladly have visited the
grand mufti himself if he had been in the habit of receiving Jews. The young
Berlin was not persuaded by the myth of a land without people given to a people
without land. He wrote to Marion Frankfurter (20 March 1935) that the Arabs
preferred to be governed badly by their own people than to be well governed by
the Jews; 'in fifteen years' time the Arab nationalists will be sincere, incorruptible, utterly brutal fascists. It is then that the real fun will begin.' On the way
home, on a ship bound for Italy, he encountered a real fascist, Abraham Stern.
When Berlin asked for his opinion of the recent British move to create a

legislative council for Palestine, Stern replied that the Jews would fight it by force because it gave Arabs representation in proportion to their demographic superiority. He went on to found the Lech'i, the most radical of the underground terrorist groups, known to the British as the Stern Gang.[13]

The Arabs resisted Jewish immigration, rioted, embarked on civil disobedience. Failing to square the circle, London attempted a succession of compromises, culminating in the White Paper of 1939, proposing to limit Jewish immigration to 750,000 over a five-year period. Weizmann was bitterly disappointed. The Zionist line hardened, terrorist groups took up arms. In 1942, under Ben-Gurion's leadership, the Biltmore Declaration demanded the whole of Palestine for a Jewish state. Ben-Gurion believed the Jewish state would have to be established unilaterally, if necessary by force.

Like Weizmann, Berlin regarded the British policy of limiting Jewish immigration as an abomination, but as a British official he was bound to defend it in America. Weizmann insisted on restraint, continuing to regard the British protectorate as vital for the future of a Jewish state. In Berlin's view, American Zionists overestimated their power to influence policy at a time when State Department officials in charge of Near Eastern affairs were as sensitive to Arab sentiment as their British counterparts. Hearing of a proposal to issue a joint US–UK statement condemning Zionist agitation, Berlin leaked the story to a Zionist newspaper publisher, who informed Henry Morgenthau, secretary of the US Treasury. Having thus tipped off the Jewish lobby, Berlin managed to disguise his own role from the irate British ambassador, Lord Halifax. Berlin experienced an acute sense of injustice: 'whenever the Arabs in Palestine made murderous attacks upon the Jews, the Mandatory administration always rewarded the Arab aggressors with concessions, and punished the victims because they were Jews.' He tended to refer to the Arabs cursorily, as 'the Arabs', not differentiating between the Palestinian population and the neighbouring Arab states. His prism was that of Western politics and personalities, and he did not publicly challenge the refusal of the USA and the UK to welcome Jewish refugees and Holocaust survivors in the required numbers.[14]

After the war the tough trade unionist Ernest Bevin was appointed foreign secretary in the Labour government. As Berlin put it: '[Weizmann] was treated with brutal rudeness by Bevin, who conceived for him, and for the entire Zionist movement, a notorious personal hostility which nothing staunched.' Berlin detested Bevin, whom he regarded as an anti-Semite, and there is little doubt that Bevin shared an outlook widespread in Britain and the British administration in Palestine, a view of Jews as pushy, arrogant, demanding. In later years Berlin invariably referred to Bevin with contempt and loathing. Well aware that the Zionist Biltmore Declaration of 1942 demanded Jewish governance of the whole of Palestine, Bevin wanted to see Britain hand the territory on as a unitary, undivided, democratic state, which would have reflected Arab superiority in numbers. Jewish terrorists of the Irgun responded to London's intransigence by blowing up the King David Hotel in Jerusalem, which housed the British administration, on 22 July 1946, with the loss of ninety-one lives. Weizmann consulted Berlin over a speech he was to deliver to the Zionist Congress in Basel in December 1946, and Berlin contributed a strong paragraph condemning terrorism as an insult to Jewish history and ideals, a contamination of appeals to the conscience of the world.[15]

Once British withdrawal was announced and the United Nations voted for partition, the main target for Jewish terrorism became the Arab population. In Haifa, the population was more or less evenly split; 65,000 Arabs, 70,000 Jews. Benny Morris reports: 'Late on the morning of 30 December [1947], IZL [Irgun] gunmen threw bombs into an Arab crowd milling about the gate of the Haifa Oil Refinery. Six died and some 50 were injured.' Local Arabs retaliated: 'Altogether, 39 Jews were murdered and 11 seriously injured in the hour-long pogrom.'[16] (One notices that even this comparatively objective Israeli scholar says that the Arabs 'died' while the Jews were 'murdered' in the course of a 'pogrom'. Anyway, the Jewish paramilitary organisation the Haganah then 'retaliated' the following night, raiding the villages in which many of the Arab refinery workers lived, killing men, women and children. Survivors fled to Nablus, Jenin and Acre. 'The essence of the plan was the clearing of hostile and potentially hostile forces out of the interior of the territory of the prospective Jewish State.' That meant all the Arab villagers.

In April 1948, the Irgun performed a calculated massacre in an unarmed and non-belligerent Arab village, Deir Yassin. Here some 100–120 old men, women and children were systematically murdered. The Irgun gave a press conference claiming responsibility and paraded captured Arabs through the Jewish quarters of Jerusalem, then released the prisoners to spread the message. Hannah Arendt was among Jewish intellectuals who publicly voiced horror – but nothing was heard from Berlin or, indeed, Deutscher.

This leads on to a wider Israeli claim that the Arab population fled in huge numbers under instructions from Arab radio broadcasts, without Jewish encouragement. About this claim Berlin appears to have remained silent. Erskine Childers (discounted by the Israelis as pro-Arab) concluded after investigation: 'There was not a single order, or appeal, or suggestion about evacuation from Palestine from any Arab radio station, inside or outside Palestine, in 1948.' Israeli commanders like Yigal Allon and Moshe Dayan executed attacks on Arab population centres that incited panic; Zionist forces attacked Jaffa's eighty thousand Arabs prior to the outbreak of war on 14 May.

Childers convincingly suggests the rationale: in the territory assigned by the UN to a Jewish state, fully 45 per cent of the population was Arab, as were considerable land holdings.[17] In his authoritative *The Birth of the Palestinian Refugee Problem Revisited*, Benny Morris confirms that the majority of Arabs did not leave voluntarily or under orders from the Arab capitals, but he also argues that the Arab exodus was not the result of a pre-planned Jewish policy of Transfer, of which he has found no trace in official Israeli documents.

However, the dream of Transfer was long-standing. Morris himself cites Theodor Herzl's diaries from 1895: 'We must expropriate gently. . . . We shall try to spirit the penniless population across the border by procuring employment for it in the transit countries, while denying it any employment in our country. . . . Both the process of expropriation and the removal of the poor must be carried out discreetly and circumspectly.' Morris also cites Israel Zangwill: 'And therefore we must gently persuade them to "trek". After all, they have all Arabia with its million square miles. . . . "To fold their tents and silently steal away" is their proverbial habit, let them exemplify it now.' Well, these were distant voices but in 1930 Weizmann suggested to the Labour colonial secretary, Lord Passfield (Sidney Webb), that the solution might be to transfer the Arabs to Transjordan and Iraq. David Ben-Gurion, chairman of the Jewish Agency and *de facto* leader of the Yishuv, the Jewish community in Palestine, confided in his diary: 'The compulsory transfer of the Arabs from the valleys of the proposed Jewish state could give us something we never had, even when we stood on our own during the days of the the First and Second Temples.' In 1938, the leading Russian Zionist, Menachem Ussishkin, reflected: 'We cannot start the Jewish state . . . with half the population being Arab.' He defended Transfer 'before the Almighty'. Throughout the Second World War Weizmann remained in favour of Transfer. In 1941, he told Ivan Maisky, Soviet ambassador to London, that half a million Arabs could be despatched to Iraq or Transjordan. According to Maisky's account, Weizmann said: 'The Arab is often called the son of the desert. It would be truer to call him the father of the desert. His laziness and primitivism turn a flourishing garden into a desert. Give me the land occupied by one million Arabs, and I will easily settle five times that number of Jews in it.' While Morris argues that all this did not amount to pre-planning expulsion, he does crucially concede that 'transfer was inevitable and built into Zionism'. Following the invasion of the Arab armies, Yitzhak Gruenbaum, minister of the interior, told an Israel cabinet meeting on 12 September 1948: 'In the past we had a plan, that we were able to transfer the Arab population to the Arab states . . . with assistance and financial help. Now, too, I see nothing wrong with this plan.'[18]

Morris confirms: 'From the first, the [Arab High Command] and the local [Arab] National Committees opposed the exodus, especially of army-aged males, and made efforts to block it.' However, women, children and the elderly were evacuated in many areas to clear the way for the battle to come. The confusion and disorganisation of the Arab leadership contributed to panic and the final outcome of over 700,000 refugees.

Morris describes in detail the military operations of 1948. By the middle of that year, the Haganah and the Israel Defense Forces were determined that none who had fled should be allowed to return.[19] This entire sequence of events appears to have met with tacit acceptance by both Berlin and Deutscher as the regrettable price of survival. Avishai Margalit has recalled Berlin's admiration for his uncle Isaac Landoberg (later Yitzhak Sadeh), whom the young Isaiah remembered from Petrograd days as a Socialist Revolutionary officer carrying a huge Mauser pistol. He later founded the Palmach, the strike units that played a decisive role during the 1947–48 war of independence. Berlin called this romantic figure, sportsman and art dealer the Jewish Garibaldi.[20]

The upshot was that more than 80 per cent of the entire territory of Israel consisted of land abandoned by Arabs in 1948. By 1954, one-third of the Jewish population was occupying 'absentee property', most of it sequestered by Israeli legislation.

Berlin and Deutscher were frequent visitors. For both, Nazi persecution and the Holocaust were unanswerable justifications for a Jewish state. Both also felt the pull of a distinctively East European or Russian tradition, described in Berlin's case by Shlomo Avinieri as 'a realisation of sorts of Russian ideals'. Following a visit in 1953, Deutscher wrote: 'Israel is more than a spiritual colony of the East European ghettoes. It is their great, tragic, posthumous offspring fighting for survival with breathtaking vitality.'

Chaim Weizmann, now president of Israel, a titular role without real power, urged Berlin to leave Oxford and settle in Israel as his chief of staff. Berlin wrote to Weizmann in September 1948, acknowledging that to choose Oxford 'in an hour of crisis for our people may seem unpardonable egoism and even a kind of levity', but if he did not settle down and do serious work, 'I should become worthless in my own eyes.' Weizmann was reportedly furious. Berlin did not want to give up his Oxford fellowship to enter a world of sharply polarised and bitter Jewish politics, but there was another factor: Zionists had always imagined that Israel would embody the best of Europe, but Berlin now found the emerging Israel to be Middle Eastern, Hebrew-speaking and anti-British. The Sephardim were coming. Ignatieff comments: 'There was an irony in all this: a life-long Zionist discovering that he had no place in Zion.'[21]

Isaac Deutscher was a frequent, if more sceptical, visitor to Israel. In 1950, he wrote to George Weidenfeld, then serving briefly as President Weizmann's chef de cabinet, accepting an invitation to lecture in Israel (where his stepsister was one of the founders of the Mishmar Ha-Emek kibbutz), 'I am not a Zionist, although I am not against Zionism now.'[22] Writing to Heinrich Brandler (16 September 1953), he did not mention Weidenfeld's invitation on behalf of Weizmann: 'I am about to undertake a long journey to Palestine with my family, staying about five weeks. I am invited by my Hebrew publisher, Am Oved, the publishing house of the Israeli trade unions.' He added: 'I have all my adult life been a strong opponent of Zionism. It is impossible to be an opponent of Zionism now; the millions of murdered Jews have given the State of Israel a tragic if only negative justification. However, I cannot be a Zionist either, even now.'[23]

Deutscher insisted that Israelis could not be blamed for the harm caused to Palestinian Arabs: 'People pursued by a monster and running to save their lives cannot help injuring those who are in their way and cannot help trampling over their property.' Israel was now 'a living reality ... animated by a fresh and strong sense of nationhood'. He added that the Israelis were justified in rejecting criticisms of 'any real or imaginary breaches of international commitments' from the so-called civilised world, which in one way or another had the fate of European Jewry on its conscience.[24] ('Strong sense of nationhood' was a remarkable volte-face by one who declared that 'the nation-state had entered on its final stage of decay ... a concept which for centuries had been a factor for disunity and strife'.)

Deutscher's sense of allegiance was no longer significantly different from Berlin's. He entered a few face-saving caveats. He hoped that Jews would find their way back to the moral and political heritage of universal human emancipation. 'I have nothing in common with the Jews of, say, Mea Shearim or with any kind of Israeli nationalists.' A temporary historical necessity need not be a long-term programme or ideal. (One may ask: how not?) It was when Deutscher turned to the Western diaspora that clear water opened up between himself and Berlin. He said he shared nothing in common with the congregations of the synagogues of New York, Paris, London; indeed, continued to believe that class divisions must eventually supersede ethnic solidarity. (But in reality Jewish communities, whether in Israel or New York, were no longer the poor of the shtetls, the bottom of the pile. Their political outlook was to become increasingly the one prevalent among the possessors.)

By this time (1953) Berlin was describing Israel as 'politically liberal, egalitarian ... with a mentality not unlike that of the Italian Risorgimento: on the whole, left of centre, of a kind rightly admired by English liberals and radicals in the nineteenth century. This is the kind of outlook which has its stamp upon the whole economic and social development of Palestine.' Little mention of the Arabs is found in this lecture, 'The Origins of Israel', apart from a warning to Jews that 'the Arabs are certainly consumed with hostile sentiment towards them; indeed with the desire to exterminate them'. He told Mrs Vera Weizmann (16 April 1956): 'I still think that it is morally the best society in existence,' although: 'To assimilate with it I cannot – I have often wished I could: I am like Catholisant who somehow cannot quite enter the Church but is willing to defend it all his life & even baptise his children into it.'[25]

During the course of 1956, Israel entered into a secret agreement with Anthony Eden and Guy Mollet, France's right-wing socialist premier, to attack Egypt following Nasser's nationalisation of the Suez Canal and its closure to ships bound to and from Israel. Writing (1 November 1956) to his long-standing friend Clarissa Eden, Berlin reported that undergraduates were demonstrating against the Suez operation in Oxford's High Street while dons were speechless with indignation against her husband. But not he: 'I should like to offer the Prime Minister all my admiration and sympathy. His action seems to me very brave very patriotic and – I shd have thought – absolutely just. I am prejudiced, I suppose, in favour of Israel, who have undoubtedly committed what is, at any rate technically, an act of aggression . . . & it seems to me that Anthony (if I may call him that) has behaved with great moral splendour. . . . I think his policy is in essentials absolutely right . . . he will, I believe, turn out to have saved England.' The letter ended with 'all my affection & devotion and good will and everything else that you may feel in need of . . . . With fondest love Isaiah.' The Labour leader, Hugh Gaitskell, had risen to denounce the military adventure as 'disastrous folly' and tabled a motion of censure in the House of Commons. Berlin added a P.S.: 'Gaitskell was awful. . . . I am glad I am not a socialist & torn with conflicting loyalty and contempt. Very wet he fundamentally is. If we must have Wykehamists I prefer Kenneth Younger. He may be mistaken but he follows principles and doesn't tergiversate (forgive this last word – remember I am a don after all.)'

Berlin changed his mind the following week after Eisenhower's interven-tion had brought the enterprise to ignominious failure. He now wrote to his wife's son Michel Strauss (8 November): 'That the British Government has committed a blunder cannot be seriously doubted. At the same time I am not prepared to sign letters, signed by 350 dons and 2000 undergraduates, complaining of this. I cannot feel morally indignant. I see that they were faced with a terrible dilemma.' He added: 'I have kept very silent and signed no letters or counter-letters, appeared on no platforms or counter-platforms, since I feel [I] might not be unbiased on the matter.' He did not mention his letter to Clarissa Eden, congratulating the prime minister on saving England. Addressing the Liberal icon Lady Violet Bonham Carter (10 January 1957), he veered dramatically from the plaudit sent to Clarissa Eden: 'Also about the mad Prime Minister. I certainly thought and think the "intervention" lunatic in the form it took, & being very pro-Israel, thought worse of their attack than anyone else I met ... we ought to have waited 4–5 days & then issued our ultimatum to U.N.'[26]

He was to become increasingly uneasy about the impact on the Arabs, writing to Johanna Lambert (20 May 1958): 'Arab rights have been trodden on – that a wrong to them has been committed – it seems to be morally shameful to deny. If you then ask me why I am pro-Zionist, it is because I think that where right clashes with right – or rather misery with misery – one must not think about rights, which always exist ... but of some calm utilitarian solution which produces on the whole the best or happiest solution in the end.'[27] He believed the reason for admitting the Jews to Palestine was that 'their misery had been too long and too great'.

Enter Deutscher. In a letter to David Astor (19 April 1958), Berlin thanked him for an invitation to write on Israel's tenth birthday in the Observer, but declined. 'The only thing that might have shaken me was your decision to invite Deutscher to do it, if I refused.' Deutscher, he went on, hated Israel, a living refutation of all that 'this still most fanatical of Marxists' believed in. Berlin reported that 'even the most left-wing socialists' he had met in Israel, those aligned to Aneurin Bevan and Barbara Castle, expressed 'deep personal aversion' to Deutscher as 'an embittered Leninist who had not deviated a millimetre from what he believed in 1930'. Deutscher told Israelis that they were merely 'a foolish temporary expedient to save the Jews from Hitler's wrath'. During the nineteenth century, Jews had sadly become identified with the merchant and capitalist class. History being cruel but just, their destruction as part of the condemned capitalist world was inevitable: such was Deutscher's view, according to Berlin. 'It was [a] pity that six millions perished as they did: but history will not be cheated, & they were on the wrong side, & deserved ("objectively") to be exterminated.' Berlin claimed that Deutscher advised the Jews of Israel to make their peace with the Soviet Union before it was too late. This delighted the few Israeli communists and fellow travellers but dismayed the Bevanites. 'You can imagine, then, with what curiosity I shall look at the Observer tomorrow: to see, if nothing else, how much of this bubbling hatred this incurable hater, who really does abominate the West, manages to conceal under those slow, cool & smooth sounding sentences that used to please The Economist so.'[28]

The most virulent sections of this letter are hard to credit. Would Deutscher ever have told anyone that the Jews 'deserved ("objectively") to be exterminated.' Would he ever have said that 'their destruction as part of the condemned capitalist world was inevitable and just'? Indeed, Deutscher wrote: 'It is an indisputable fact that the Nazi massacre of six million European Jews has not made any deep impression on the nations of Europe. It has not truly shocked their conscience. It has left them almost cold.'[29] And yet, if we move forward nine years to Deutscher's reaction to the Arab-Israeli war of 1967, we clearly encounter the long-standing patterns of thought that turned Berlin's stomach. As if again endorsing Marx's view in 'The Jewish Question', Deutscher now seemed, almost, to justify prewar anti-Semitism in Europe. 'European Jews paid a horrible price for the role they had played in past ages . . . as representatives of a market economy, of "money", among peoples living in a natural, money-less, agricultural economy. . . . The image of the Jewish merchant and usurer lived on in gentile folklore. . . . The Nazis seized this image, magnified it to colossal dimensions. . . . The impact of Nazi Jew-baiting was so powerful in part because the image of the Jew as the alien and vicious "blood-sucker" was to all too many people still an actuality.' Deutscher gives early Zionism (which he had not embraced) an opportunistic twist: Israel had promised to free the survivors from the 'fatal stigma' of Jewish usury: 'This was the message of the kibbutzim, the Histadrut, and even of Zionism at large. The Jews were to cease to be unproductive elements, shopkeepers, economic and cultural interlopers, carriers of capitalism.' But now, 'as agents of the late, over-ripe, imperialist capitalism of our days, their role is altogether lamentable.'[30]

That was written in 1967 but it expressed a long-standing motif in Deutscher's outlook, sometimes rising to the surface, sometimes subsumed by sympathy for Holocaust survivors. (Twenty years later, Berlin wrote that Deutscher 'regarded Jewish identification with capitalism as their most heinous persecution-inviting attribute'.)[31] Deutscher's article in the *Observer*, 'Israel's 10th Birthday', was in the event more accommodating in tone, despite its remark that 'The future of Israel may well depend on whether the Israelis are on guard against nationalist conceit and are able to find a common language with the peoples around.'[32] A further letter from Berlin to Astor followed (14 May 1958), expressing deep irritation. If Astor, who knew Deutscher better than he, extolled Deutscher's courage, integrity and independence, well, let his courage be granted – but as for integrity and independence, 'can one speak of such qualities in the case of real, convinced, incurable believers in a total creed?' Berlin complained that Deutscher instructed the Jews to make friends with the Arabs but did not say how: did he mean giving up the Negev or half of Galilee? He advised the Jews not to underestimate the technological progress of the mainly Soviet-aided

Arabs, warning that they could not survive in a hostile sea – but were the Israelis themselves not constantly aware of this, as if the 'tragic folly' of Suez in 1956 had not been an effort – 'mistaken perhaps' – to protect themselves against neighbours who made it plain that what they wanted was the elimination of the Jewish state? Berlin added: 'I was myself in a tiny minority in this country ... who thought the Israel attack of 1956 not necessarily a tactical error but morally wrong.'[33]

(As quoted above, he had written to Michel Strauss on 8 November 1956: 'I cannot feel morally indignant'.)

On 23 January 1959, Berlin wrote a 'Memorandum to the Prime Minister of Israel'. David Ben-Gurion had been consulting widely, among more than fifty eminent Jews, about how Israel should treat the offspring of certain types of mixed marriage, mainly the children of Jewish fathers and non-Jewish mothers, where the mother had not converted, but both parents desired to register the child as a Jew in Israel. Should persons who belonged to some other religion or none be registered as Jews by nationality in Israel?

Berlin advised Ben-Gurion that Israel should be a liberal state, not a theocracy. Any resident should be entitled to be married or divorced without resource to a religious ceremony of any kind, although at present Israel did not permit civil marriage. Expressing respect for the Orthodox (ruling) rabbinate's adherence to the rules of Halacha, he nevertheless recommended that those not qualified by Halacha be allowed to register as Jews. He favoured a broad category of persons entitled to identify themselves by nationality, but not by religion. Jews should be defined as those who regarded themselves as Jews or were so viewed by others in the Diaspora. Children of mixed marriages whose Jewish fathers desired them to be brought up as Jews should be entitled to register.

No doubt liberal as these recommendations were when measured against Israel's prevailing laws, one notices that they implicitly reserved citizenship for persons granted recognition as Jews by one criterion or another, placing Israel in a unique position among modern states – and excluding all Arab post-1948 refugees.

Deutscher hardly had time to absorb the implications of the Israeli-Arab war of June 1967 before death overtook him. His attitude hardened further. In an interview published in the *New Left Review* (23 June 1967), he now depicted Israel as a Western outpost in the Middle East involved in the conflict between neo-colonialism and the Arab peoples. Israel's economy had depended on foreign Zionist aid and American donations, 'a curse in disguise for the new state'. In recent years, up to $250 million annually had been received in grants and loans from the Western powers and in contributions from Jews abroad. This amounted to nearly $125 a year per head of the Israeli population. The typical wealthy American Jewish donor, at heart proud to be a member of the chosen people, exercised his influence in Israel in favour of religious obscurantism and reaction, viewing with a hostile eye even the mild socialism of the kibbutz, while helping the rabbis to maintain their stranglehold on legislation and education, thus keeping alive the spirit of racial-Talmudic exclusiveness and superiority.[34]

In this, his last interview on the subject, Deutscher recalls 'the seizure of their land, the fate of a million or more refugees'. He adds: 'From the outset Zionism worked towards the creation of a purely Jewish state and was glad to rid the country of its Arab inhabitants. No Israeli government has ever seriously looked for any opportunity to remove or assuage the grievance.' (Yet, as we have seen, in 1954 he had told readers of the *Reporter*: 'People pursued by a monster and running to save their lives cannot help injuring those who are in their way and cannot help trampling over their property.') Now, in 1967, he was torn between condemning the demagogic anti-Semitic propaganda issuing from Arab dictatorships (Egypt, Jordan) and the Israeli response: 'Conjuring up Biblical myths and all the ancient religious-national symbols of Jewish history, the propagandists whipped up that frenzy of belligerence, arrogance, and fanaticism of which the Israelis gave such startling displays as they rushed to Sinai and the Wailing Wall and to Jordan and to the walls of Jericho.' He prophesied that Israel's victory would 'be seen one day, in a not very remote future, to have been a disaster in the first instance for Israel herself. . . . Paradoxically and grotesquely, the Israelis appear now in the role of the Prussians of the Middle East.' He demanded withdrawal from the newly occupied territories.[35]

One cannot doubt what one commentator calls 'the burning, aching attachment most British Jews feel for Israel'. Jews may tear their hair out privately about this or that Israeli policy, but in public the majority's urge is to defend the country fiercely. Most still see Israel as the answer to a 2,000-year-old prayer; their loyalty to it is unbending. Israel is like a family relative; you might complain about her behind closed doors but no stranger is allowed to do so.[36] For many years Berlin abided by this logic and concealed his misgivings, but gradually, after Menachem Begin came to power and the Likud government invaded Lebanon while extending Jewish settlements in the West Bank, he began to voice his exasperation openly, aligning himself with the 'Peace Now' movement. On 16 October 1997, when the government of Binyamin Netanyahu was sidelining the Oslo agreements, he dictated a deathbed plea for compromise, urging Israel to accept a final partition of land with the Palestinians and warning that the alternative was a terrible cycle of terrorist chauvinism and savage war. The appeal was sent to his closest Israeli friends, Avishai and Edna Margalit, and published in Israeli newspapers.[37]

By the end of that year Berlin was dead, thirty years after Deutscher – whom he had perversely likened to Menachem Begin: 'they were brought up under very similar conditions and with very similar ideals.'[38]

21

THE BANALITY OF EVIL: BERLIN AND ARENDT

BERLIN'S ANTIPATHY TO Hannah Arendt merits examination here if only because it parallels closely – though far from exactly – his aversion to Deutscher. All three were Jews, born between 1906 and 1909, each forced into exile by either Soviet communism or German fascism, all three having established themselves in the English-speaking world as intellectual luminaries, as political theorists with strong views, and endowed with forms of erudition closely linked to their origins. All three felt obliged to take up public positions on their Jewish heritage, on Zionism and the State of Israel.

In later years Berlin was asked about Arendt by Ramin Jahanbegloo: 'Do you dislike her because she was not a Zionist?' He replied: 'No. She was a fervent Zionist when I first met her . . . in New York in 1941. . . . She was working at that time for an organization which tried to get Jewish children out of Germany to Palestine. . . . On the second occasion, when I met her, about ten years later, she attacked Israel. She was perfectly entitled to change her mind – I had nothing against that. It is her ideological writings which repelled me.' Berlin called Arendt 'egregious': 'I think she produces no arguments, no evidence of serious philosophical or historical thought. It is all a stream of metaphysical free association. She moves from one sentence to another, without logical connection, without either rational or imaginative links between them.'[1]

We may question whether Arendt's changing perspective on Zionism was not the root cause of Berlin's animosity – in so far as it conveyed a shift of allegiance towards what Deutscher called the 'non-Jewish Jew', although in Arendt's case devoid of Deutscher's Marxist scaffolding.

Like Deutscher, but unlike Berlin, Hannah Arendt became a refugee from the Nazi scourge. Born in 1906 in Hannover, she was the only child of progressive secular Jews (in 1918–19, her widowed mother was hosting social-democratic discussion groups). In 1924, she entered Marburg University, where she studied philosophy with Martin Heidegger and became his lover, but in 1926 she broke with him and moved to Heidelberg, where she studied with Karl Jaspers. She was initiated into Jewish politics by Kurt Blumenfeld, a Zionist; at his instigation she surreptitiously collected evidence in the Prussian State Library of businesses and other organisations discriminating against Jews. Arrested along with her mother, she was interrogated for nine days by the Gestapo. Mother and daughter escaped via Czechoslovakia and Switzerland to Paris, where she worked for Youth Aliyah, an organisation training young émigrés bound for Palestine in agricultural and artisan skills. Following the outbreak of war Arendt was imprisoned in Camp Gars but wangled release papers after the fall of France, escaped by boat from Lisbon and in 1941 reached the United States with her husband and mother.

From November 1941, when she got her first job in New York as a columnist for *Aufbau*, she began writing about the need to form a Jewish army to fight alongside the Allies, but her views began to diverge from those of American Zionists inspired by David Ben-Gurion and from the hardline 'Revisionists'. She condemned 'Jewish fascists' practising terrorism in Palestine.[2] Her arguments were practical as well as moral, believing as she did that those fighting for a Jewish state, as distinct from a 'Jewish Homeland' within a federal, collaborative Jewish-Arab Palestine, were hurtling to suicide. But her moral alienation from prevailing Jewish sentiment in the USA was abundantly clear when she referred in 1946 to 'that Jewish brand of chauvinism automatically produced by secularization, which somehow persuades the average de-Judaized Jew [that] ... although he no longer believes in a God who chooses or rejects, he is still a superior being simply because he happened to be born a Jew – the salt of the earth – or the motor of history'.[3]

Whereas Isaiah Berlin regarded Zionism as a legitimate form of an indispensable nationalism, Arendt's view of nationalism as an obsolete force was not dissimilar to Deutscher's – although there is no evidence of any interchange between them. While Theodor Herzl himself could not be blamed for having failed to foresee 'that the whole structure of sovereign national states, great and small, would crumble within another fifty years' (we may find the factual basis for this obscure), in Arendt's estimation Zionism had become a 'sectarian ideology' employing 'the categories and methods of the nineteenth century'. The new Jewish nationalism, she regretted, displayed no solidarity with other oppressed people, failing to build the essential trust with Arab neighbours advocated by Rabbi Judah L. Magnes. Convinced that the demand for a Jewish state could be established only at the expense of a Jewish homeland, she called for a federal structure based on joint Jewish-Arab councils.[4] By contrast, Berlin, like his mentor Weizmann, wanted a Jewish state.

In 1948 Arendt, together with Albert Einstein and other prominent Jews, wrote to the *New York Times* condemning the new State of Israel for containing extreme nationalists of a 'fascist' nature, who had recently carried out the notorious massacre at Deir Yassin. She lamented the Arab evacuation of Haifa and Tiberias following Deir Yassin and the bomb thrown by the Irgun into a line of Arab workers outside the Haifa refinery, one of the few enterprises where Jews and Arabs had worked side by side: 'It is unfortunate that the very men who could point to the tragedy of the Jewish DPs [displaced persons] as the chief argument for mass immigration into Palestine should now be ready, as far as the world knows, to help to create an additional category of DPs in the Holy Land.'[5]

Berlin met Arendt in America in 1941, and again in the early Fifties. Neither figures in the other's public writings. Moreover, as with Berlin and Deutscher, so with Berlin and Arendt there is no discovered correspondence, in itself evidence of estrangement in an age when intellectuals wrote to each other more frequently and copiously than today.

The first discovered example of a punitive strike by Berlin against Arendt occurs in 1959, when he was asked by Faber and Faber for his opinion of her latest venture into global political theory, *The Human Condition* (Chicago, 1958). Berlin's report was wholly negative, opening with the lines: 'I could recommend no publisher to buy the UK rights of this book. There are two objections to it: it will not sell, and it is no good.'[6] A separate UK edition never appeared, despite the book's success in America and praise from Mary McCarthy, Dwight Macdonald, Philip Toynbee and others. W.H. Auden said of *The Human Condition*: 'Every now and then I come across a book which gives the impression of having been especially written for me. ... It seems to answer precisely those questions I have been putting to myself. ... Miss Hannah Arendt's *The Human Condition* belongs to this small and select class.' Auden's admiration for the book was widely shared: for Sheldon Wolin, professor of politics at Princeton, it came 'as a deliverance in 1958 to those who were trying to restate a conception of political theory relevant to the contemporary world.'[7] Berlin wondered why Auden, McCarthy and Robert Lowell admired Arendt. 'When I asked Auden about this he remained silent and changed the subject.'

Berlin's second punitive strike(s) followed the publication of Arendt's highly contentious *Eichmann in Jerusalem: A Report on the Banality of Evil* (US, 1963; UK, 1964). This intervention, as we shall see, was likewise performed privately. On 11 May 1960, the Israeli Secret Service had kidnapped Adolph Eichmann and spirited him out of Argentina. His main responsibility during the war had been to organise transport across Europe to the extermination camps while bringing pressure on local Jewish leaders to collaborate, tasks he carried out with zeal and efficiency. Arendt proposed herself as the trial reporter to William Shawn, editor of the *New Yorker*. The trial took place from 11 April to 14 August 1961. Isaiah Berlin's animosity intensified with the appearance of Arendt's *Eichmann in Jerusalem*, first published as five articles in the *New Yorker* (February–March 1963). Her argument that European Jewry might have resisted the Holocaust more effectively incensed him. The thought that his own people, the gentle, unheroic Volschonoks and Schneersons of Riga, should be criticised from the safety of New York for having failed to stand up to the SS struck him as monstrous moral conceit. No moral judgment was possible from conditions of safety on the behaviour of those in danger. 'Praise and blame are out of place – normal moral categories do not apply.'[8] (This seems to run counter to the widely held view that 'moral categories' are most vividly evident in extreme, life-or-death situations.)

As for Arendt's expression 'the banality of evil', as applied to Eichmann and Nazi behaviour in general, Berlin would have none of it: 'I am not ready to swallow the idea about the banality of evil. I think it false. The Nazis were not "banal". Eichmann deeply believed in what he did, it was, he admitted, at the centre of his being.' Here Berlin seems to conflate 'banality' with 'insincerity', whereas it could more accurately be likened to 'conformity'. Arendt likened Eichmann to all those play-safe German 'family men' whom she accused of turning a blind eye to rampant evil for the sake of wife and children. Yet Berlin partly agreed with Arendt's analysis of Nazism: it was too glib, he said later, to call Nazis mad, pathological. The belief that Jews are *Untermenschen* brings you to 'a state of mind where, in a sense quite rationally, you believe it necessary to exterminate Jews – this does not spring from lunacy, nor is it mere irrational hatred. . . . No, these emotions are organized by means of belief in monstrous untruths, taught systematically by orators or writers.'[9] (That is to say, taught to normal, sensible people – would Arendt have dissented?)

The single sentence written by Arendt that most incensed her critics was quoted in one indictment after another: 'To a Jew this role of the Jewish leaders in the destruction of their own people is undoubtedly the darkest chapter of the whole dark story.' The 'darkest chapter'? Darker than Eichmann's role? Did she have no understanding, no compassion? No, of course she did not mean that, but her choice of words, as quite often with Arendt, was provocative; indeed, many accusatory passages in *Eichmann in Jerusalem* are woefully lacking in humility. The next two sentences proved to be almost equally inflammatory: 'Wherever Jews lived, there were recognized Jewish leaders, and this leadership, almost without exception, cooperated in one way or another, for one reason or another, with the Nazis. The whole truth was that if the Jewish people had been really unorganized and leaderless, there would have been chaos and plenty of misery but the total number of victims would hardly have been between four and half and six million people.'[10] Against the leaders of the Jewish Councils she pressed her indictment:

> it has now been exposed for the first time in all its pathetic and sordid detail by Raul Hilberg [in his] standard work *The Destruction of the Euro-pean Jews*. . . . In the matter of cooperation, there was no distinction between the highly assimilated Jewish communities of Central and Western Europe and the Yiddish-speaking masses of the East. In Amsterdam as in Warsaw, in Berlin as in Budapest, Jewish officials could be trusted to compile the lists of persons and their property, to secure money from the deportees to defray the expenses of their deportation and extermination, to keep track of vacated apartments, to supply police forces to help seize Jews and get them on trains, until, as a last gesture, they handed over the assets of the Jewish community in good order for final confiscation. They distributed the Yellow Star badges, and sometimes, as in Warsaw, 'the sale of armbands became a regular business; there were ordinary armbands of cloth and fancy plastic armbands which were washable.' In the Nazi-inspired, but not Nazi-dictated, manifestoes they issued, we can still sense how they enjoyed their new power – 'The Cen-tral Jewish Council has been granted the right of absolute disposal over all Jewish spiritual and material wealth and over all Jewish manpower,' as the first announcement of the Budapest Council phrased it. We know how the Jewish officials felt when they became instruments of murder – like captains 'whose ships were about to sink and who succeeded in bringing them safe to port by casting overboard a great part of their precious cargo'; like saviours who 'with a hundred victims save a thousand people, with a thousand ten thousand.' The truth was even more gruesome. Dr Kastner, in Hungary, for instance, saved exactly 1,684 people with approximately 476,000 victims.

The truth or accuracy of Arendt's accusations has been widely and repeat-edly contested, but such debates must lie beyond our scope. Reactions from her contemporaries were preponderantly negative. However, to take one example cited by Arendt, it is certainly the case that, between May and July 1944, Hungary's Jews were being deported to the gas chambers of Auschwitz at the rate of twelve thousand people a day – for 'resettlement', as the Nazis said. Dr Rudolf Kastner, vice-president of the Zionist organisation in Budapest, negotiated with Eichmann to allow 1,684 chosen Jews to leave instead for the transit camp at Bergen-Belsen, and thence for Switzerland, on what became known as the Kastner train, in exchange for money, gold and diamonds worth $1,000 per Jew.

The critical onslaught that descended on Arendt was punitive, perhaps unprecedented. The Jewish magazines that weighed in against her, often in the harshest terms, included the *Jewish Observer and Middle East Review; Facts* (journal of the Anti-Defamation League); *Commentary* (organ of the American Jewish Committee); *Jewish Chronicle; Chicago Jewish Forum; National Jewish Monthly; American Jewish History Quarterly; Jewish Currents; Judaism; Jewish Frontier.* Arendt herself voiced the suspicion that the 'Elders of Zion' were now as alive and powerful as they had once been in anti-Semitic myth under the tsars, taking the shape of pressure groups like the Anti-Defamation League, the American Jewish Committee, the World Jewish Congress, not forgetting the Israeli government, which sent Gideon Hausner, chief prosecutor in the Eichmann trial, to New York to refute Arendt's claims.[11]

Both Arendt and Isaiah Berlin attached cardinal importance to the innate human capacity for choice; both set themselves against those forces or regimes suppressing the individual's right to choose. On more than one occasion Berlin's outlook almost coincided with Arendt's, although he rejected the idea of any such convergence. Writing to George Kennan (13 February 1951), he had come up with a rather surprising example of infamy – how the Nazis had deceived Jews going to their deaths by reassuring them that the cattle cars were taking them to resettlement in the East: Why horrific? 'Surely because we cannot bear the thought of human beings denied their last rights – of knowing the truth, of acting with at least the freedom of the condemned, of being able to face their destruction with fear or courage, according to their temperaments, but at least as human beings, armed with the power of choice'. (Yet he later remarked, in discussion with Steven Lukes, that 'knowledge is sometimes incompatible with happiness ... If I know that I have cancer, I don't believe I am made happier by the knowledge.')[12] This complaint seems to run parallel to Arendt's indictment against the Jewish Councils for their failure to inform the mass of victims of their impending fate – the Councils, like the Nazis themselves, wished to avert the chaos of despair. But whereas Berlin wanted the victims of the Holocaust to be told the truth so that they could each choose to discover themselves in the face of certain death, Arendt valued the capacity for refusal, for defiance, for the *vita activa*, even if of necessity confined to passive non-compliance and non-obedience. Berlin always shrank from political or collective action, even from the contemplation of it – and what kind of 'choice' is contained in the capacity 'to face their destruction with fear or courage, according to their temperaments'. Did this apply to the children too? And Granny?

In short, Berlin could not agree with Arendt that the Jewish Councils and rabbinical leaders of occupied Europe had the choice of non-cooperation with the infernal machine, of refusing to oil the wagon wheels of the 'Final Solution'. Such a judgment by a single intellectual enjoying hindsight from the sanctuary of New York amounted to arrogance and worse. Many years later, when receiving the Hannah Arendt Prize in Bremen, Michael Ignatieff offered an explanation for Berlin's attitude: his uncle had been a member of the Judenrat of Riga under Nazi occupation, and Berlin believed that no one could judge how anyone else behaved in a situation of terror and fear. He felt that Arendt lacked pity, and that her assumed standards of responsibility were flawed by arrogance and cruelty. Ignatieff explained: 'He thought of himself as a shtetl Jew, a cosy Russian tea-drinking Jew, and he regarded Arendt as the quintessential Yekke, the punctilious, exacting and charmless German Jew'.[13]

Never mentioned in these discussions is Arendt's gender, her identity as a woman. No one could say so, but it was not a woman's place to raise her voice in this essentially masculine way – analytical and judgmental. It seems probable that some Jewish elders, including the secular rabbinate, found Arendt's strictures doubly unacceptable because expressed by a disturbingly challenging woman – the leaders of the Jewish Councils under the Nazis were obviously men. The major influences on her formation as a political philosopher, Heidegger and Jaspers, were existentialist men in quest of human self-realisation, and she herself developed what might be called a virile set of values – firm, assertive, proud to resist. (She described herself as a political theorist, not a philosopher, because, as she put it, 'men, not Man, live on the earth and inhabit the world'.) She had survived a nine-day interrogation by the Gestapo.

Following the death of her husband Heinrich Blücher in 1969, W.H. Auden proposed marriage to her (declined). Choosing to recall this, Berlin remarked that this was insulting to her, it was like trying to turn her into a German *Hausfrau* – she had urged Auden to buy himself a second suit of clothes that was not horribly stained.[14] Auden's admiration for her clearly rankled with Berlin.

When the debate about Arendt's offending book reached Britain, Berlin was involved in ways that were not publicly apparent. Initially the discussion took the form of a sharp exchange between Professor Gershom Scholem and Arendt in the January 1964 edition of *Encounter*. Himself a prominent contributor to the magazine and a member of its editorial committee, Berlin had by his own avowal talked to Scholem about Arendt's book and very probably encouraged him to voice his protest in *Encounter*, with whose editors, Melvin

Lasky and Stephen Spender, Berlin was on close terms. He later recalled: 'I asked Scholem why people admired Miss Arendt. He told me that no serious thinker did so, that people who admired her were only the "littérateurs", only men of letters, because they were unused to ideas. For Americans she represented continental thought. But anyone who was truly cultivated and a serious thinker could not abide her.' If the sentiments quoted were really Scholem's, they clearly met with Berlin's approval.[15]

But if, as Berlin attests, Scholem really told him that 'anyone who was truly cultivated and a serious thinker could not abide her', this may reflect the pique of an affronted patriarchy.

When subsequently Eichmann in Jerusalem was published in London, a majority of reviews, both Jewish and Gentile, were scarcely less hostile than those appearing earlier in the USA. But one assault on Arendt must, for reasons to be explained, command our special attention: this was 'Judges in Israel', the anonymous review in the TLS (30 April 1964). It was in fact the work of John Sparrow, warden of All Souls College and Berlin's close friend. Sparrow had been elected a prize fellow in 1929, three years before Berlin, and they had been on intimate – although far from uncritical – terms since. Berlin had supported Sparrow's election as warden, and such was the circle of friendship that Jenifer Hart wrote to Sparrow to let her hair down after Berlin broke off their affair in favour of his future wife.

The choice of Sparrow to review two books about the capture and trial of Eichmann (the other was a celebration of the deed by Moshe Pearlman) might seem curious. Neither the Holocaust nor Zionism had featured or would later figure among Sparrow's primary interests, though it should be granted that he, like Trevor-Roper, had a maverick streak, relishing contentious forensic forays into hot contemporary events. However, as reflected in his numerous anonymous reviews for the TLS during the six years preceding 'Judges in Israel', i.e. since 1958, his favoured subjects for both reviews and letters to the paper were poetry and the misadventures of sex.[16] The editor of the TLS, Arthur Crook, had been introduced to Berlin by Sparrow at a lunch in All Souls, and subsequently Berlin kept up a correspondence with Crook throughout his editorship, 'sometimes delicately suggesting reviewers whom he might like to consider ... sometimes congratulating him (as on Sparrow's review of Eichmann in Jerusalem – "the best piece on the whole tormented topic")'.[17]

Why did Crook not invite Berlin to review Arendt's book – a far more obvious choice than Sparrow? Probably he did; probably Berlin declined, not wishing to become publicly involved and having always avoided referring to Arendt in print. Anonymity could not have disguised his distinctive style, his unmistakable voice, and in any case literary London guarded few secrets – we shall see how Mary McCarthy was able from Paris to unearth the reviewer's identity even though Arthur Crook declined to reveal it. It is odds-on that Berlin suggested Sparrow, a proven regular in the review columns of the *TLS*.

The early, legalistic passages of Sparrow's review sound entirely his own – he had been a Chancery barrister – particularly when he quotes from the Christian Gospels or considers the legal aspects of the Eichmann trial and the status of the Israeli court; but later passages about the Jewish Councils fit Berlin's voice rather than Sparrow's. We can surmise that they talked long into the night about this very long, essay-length review, Berlin updating Sparrow on the controversy in American Jewish circles.

One notices – she certainly did – the review's mocking reference to 'the raptures of the self-consciously "Gentile" Miss Mary McCarthy', who had come out in vigorous defence of *Eichmann in Jerusalem*, explaining what her friend Arendt had really meant by the role of the Jewish leaders and Councils being 'the darkest chapter in the whole dark story'. Of course, said McCarthy in 'The Hue and Cry', Arendt could not possibly mean worse than the Nazi atrocities, she meant the hardest factor for Jews to contemplate.[18] McCarthy had written this in the left-liberal *Partisan Review*, a magazine that could not by any stretch of the imagination be counted among Sparrow's regular reading, whereas Berlin did regularly read it (reacting with indignation when it published Isaac Deutscher's review of *Doctor Zhivago*). More recently (7 May 1963), Berlin had written to its editor, William Phillips, disparaging Arendt, describing her as once a 'fanatical' Jewish nationalist but now an equally fanatical anti-Zionist. As for her ideological works, 'she indulges in a kind of metaphysical free association which I am unable to follow except that the premises seem to me inaccurate and unallowable'.[19] It seems likely that Berlin placed McCarthy's 'The Hue and Cry' on the arm of John Sparrow's chair.

Berlin's influence shimmers through Sparrow's review, as when Sparrow comes up with an anecdote that is most unlikely to have been a naturalised citizen of his own head: 'A party of Jews is being hidden in a house of a Gentile; discovery meant certain death not only for them but also for their protector; with the party was a baby, whose irrepressible wailing was sure – the searchers were drawing near – to give the hiding place away. What was to be done? To allow the whole party, the child included, to be consigned to extermination? Or ...? Either course meant committing murder, of a kind.' The anecdote strongly recalls to the present writer one of Berlin's favourite topics for light-hearted debate, 'When is the lesser evil worse than the greater?'

Mary McCarthy herself got it in one: as she was to point out in a letter of rejoinder to the *TLS* (25 June 1964), the extracts from her *Partisan Review* article singled out by the anonymous reviewer in the *TLS* echoed the extracts widely in currency: 'I am almost ready to believe that he [the reviewer] is not familiar with my article but knows it at second hand through paraphrase and a set of selected quotations.' McCarthy was struck by the reviewer's general portrait of *Eichmann in Jerusalem* as being 'with certain mild modifications ... [taken from] the same old book that [Arendt's] most violent detractors have been hawking around New York.' McCarthy listed some familiar phrases that 'seemed to come out of a mimeographing machine'. This struck her as suspicious, but where did suspicion point?

In his anonymous reply (same date), 'our reviewer' assured Miss McCarthy that he had read her *Partisan Review* article 'more than once'.

Did Mary McCarthy believe that Berlin had inspired the review? At around this time (late summer or early autumn 1964), Berlin, having congratulated Arthur Crook on the review, decided to write to McCarthy at her Paris address, expressing the hope that she did not think he had written it! Unfortunately, his letter is not found in the Bodleian archive, only her reply (which is odd, since his letters of that time were normally typed by a secretary, who kept a carbon copy). McCarthy's long delay of three months in replying (19 January 1965) must surely indicate distemper as well as suspicion – she had in fact been in correspondence with Arendt about it and had used the interval to investigate who did in fact write the review.[20] 'Of course,' she wrote to Berlin, 'I don't think you wrote the piece in the *TLS*. I wouldn't have thought so if you'd confessed it to me yourself. You *couldn't* have written that piece.' She had been in correspondence about it with the paper's editor: 'My analysis, as told to Mr. Crook, was that it was a Gentile, a lawyer or someone who'd had legal training, and a "layman" in that field. He [Crook] living up to his name, said I was way off the mark. But I gather that I wasn't. People say it was John Sparrow, and I presume this is true. . . . I did meet John Sparrow at a lunch you gave at All Souls.'[21] By this circumlocution McCarthy arguably registered her suspicion that Berlin, one way or another, was involved in the review. On the other hand, her correspondence with Arendt herself conveys no such suspicion.

At about this time Berlin wrote to William Shawn, editor of the *New Yorker*, which had commissioned Arendt's coverage of the Eichmann trial. Again Berlin's letter is not found but he was evidently in remonstrative mode if Shawn's reply of 4 January 1965 is to make sense: 'As for your own strong feelings against the magazine, I must tell you that they gravely distress me.' What could have occasioned such 'strong feelings', one asks, other than the publication of Arendt's reports on the Eichmann trial? But evidently Berlin was batting as well as bowling, for Shawn continues: 'Thank you for sending along J.H.A. Sparrow's article. Much as I admired it, I had to tell him, with reluctance, that it was outside the scope of the magazine.'[22]

PART EIGHT

A SEAT AT THE SAME TABLE

22

THE SUSSEX LETTERS

WE HAVE EXPLORED the wide range of issues, academic and political, ethnic and temperamental, that set Berlin and Deutscher at loggerheads. It is now time to describe what action Berlin took against Deutscher in March 1963, and its long-term ramifications. This action, it transpired, occurred at the time of Isaiah's conversation with me in All Souls, which suggested that Deutscher was then on the hunt for an academic past.

Material from the letters exchanged[1] is presented below in roman typeface, while the commentaries, paraphrasing and explanatory notes are in italics.

Deutscher is known to have enquired about a regular British academic post on at least one previous occasion, in October 1954, but he discovered that the advertised chair at St Andrew's was not in modern European history and would require teaching the history of Britain, for which he felt unqualified.[2] We begin here with Deutscher's application (9 November 1962) for an advertised senior lectureship in modern history and/or economics at Sussex University, recently founded. Candidates were advised that 'Most of the teaching will be tutorials of one or two students.'[3] He wrote: I can undertake to teach at the School of European Studies or any other School the following subjects: Modern European History, especially the history of Russia and the USSR in the XIX and XX centuries; the history of France from the French Revolution till our time; the history of Germany for the same periods; the history of Poland; the history of labour movements, especially of European socialism; the Economic History of Europe in modern times; the history of economic theory; the economic theory and practice of Marxism, with special reference to the economics of the Russian Revolution; and other subjects in philosophy and literature related to the subjects mentioned above.

He then reviewed his career, his journalistic posts, his publications. I am engaged at present on a major work on the history of European Socialism which I hope to complete in 1963. *(This project has not been traced.)*

I hold no academic degree and have not held any academic post, although I have repeatedly been offered such posts, especially by the great American universities, but have not been able to accept. I have a very large and, I think, rather successful experience in lecturing at Universities and academic institutions.

. . . I would probably give up most of my journalistic activities. My journalistic activity in recent years has consisted in writing syndicated articles for leading newspapers of many countries, and I would be willing to give up this activity altogether, but I could afford to do so only if my commencing salary as Senior Lecturer compensated me to some extent for the financial loss involved.

A senior lecturer earned £1,650 × £100 – £2,250 per annum. Deutscher gave as his two referees Professor E.H. Carr, Trinity College, Cambridge, and Donald Tyerman, Esq., editor of The Economist.

On 10 December, Martin Wight, professor of history, 1962–72 (his death), and founding dean of the School of European Studies, wrote to him on behalf of the Sussex faculty: All my colleagues would be delighted if you could be associated with us in some way. *Wight explained that Sussex worked on the tutorial principle,* as it used to be understood in its strict sense at Oxford. This means that every undergraduate does at least one piece of written work a week, and spends an hour discussing it with a tutor. Lectures are entirely ancillary. We are asking people we appoint to undertake 12 hours a week of tutoring, which is a very heavy load compared with Redbrick. *Lectures were optional but not regarded as* a medium of instruction. *In most cases students would come in pairs for tutorials. One essay was handed in beforehand and given back with comments, the other was read aloud.* So for our faculty, the tutorial system does mean ploughing through a good deal of written work out of the regular teaching hours . . . a good deal of this written work is mediocre in quality, and a good deal of it is illegible.

An appointment, whose principal duties were lecturing, such as your letter suggests that you had in mind, raises great difficulties here, which may indeed be insuperable. *In a handwritten note Wight added:* We have met occasionally at sherry parties since I was your slightly awed colleague at the Observer in 1946, but you probably won't remember the occasions. *The letter did not mention the subjects to be taught or the subjects that Deutscher had offered to teach in his letter of application.*

Deutscher replied to Wight on 17 December. Yes, he did remember Wight, and if I am not mistaken we met occasionally at Chatham House also. *He explained that he had heard good reports about Sussex, and hoped to be able to contribute* to creating something like a real centre for the study of Soviet history and Soviet affairs. But I must admit that I was thinking primarily in terms of lectures and seminars, especially seminars, which I have always found preferable to tutorials. Please forgive this most un-English bias. Unfortunately, you have guessed rightly that a twelve hours' tutoring minimum per week would be too heavy a load for me. If this is what you ask your teaching staff to undertake, then I shall have regretfully to withdraw.

The next found letter is from Wight to Deutscher, 8 February 1963. We have been having some interesting and hopeful discussions about what we might do here about Soviet Studies. Is it possible that you could come down and have lunch with us next Tuesday 12th February to talk things over?

Wight wrote again on 14 February after Deutscher came for lunch. We are most interested in the kind of approach to Soviet Studies which you were outlining to us. *It would have to be discussed at the university council in two weeks' time.* But the Vice-Chancellor asked me this morning to tell you how much he hopes that we shall be able to come to a satisfactory arrangement.

On 16 February, Deutscher wrote to Vice-Chancellor Fulton, thanking him for lunch. I have found this exchange of views highly stimulating and have since given further thought to the coordination of Soviet Studies with the teaching programmes of your Schools. May I wish you every success in your noble and exciting work of building up this new University.

In a letter to Wight of the same date, Deutscher mentioned that Patrick Corbett and Tibor Barna had been at the lunch, but he did not know their work. Could Wight suggest any titles? I would like to acquaint myself more closely with their way of thinking.

Here the discovered correspondence between Deutscher and the university terminates for a period of three months. We shall now discover why.

Isaiah Berlin served on the Sussex University academic advisory board as an external adviser. Vice-Chancellor Fulton wrote to him on 28 February 1963.

Dear Isaiah,

I am sending you, by agreement with James Duff, this note about Isaac Deutscher. When we advertised recently for a post in History we had an approach from Deutscher. This is, of course, a very interesting possibility. He came to see the Deans and lunched with a number of our senior colleagues. We would like to have him as our Professor of Soviet Studies. He would propose to live in London probably for the next three years (there is a problem about the health of a boy who is under medical treatment) but would probably thereafter move to Sussex. Asa Briggs, Martin Wight, Patrick Corbett and [Tibor] Barna would like to have him very much. *(Briggs was pro-vice-chancellor; Wight was dean of the School of European Studies; Corbett was senior tutor and professor of philosophy; Barna was professor of economics.)* The understanding would be that he would go on with his writing (as you will know the last volume of Trotsky has just gone to Press and he is to write for the O.U.P. a biography of Lenin). He has just been invited – but refused – to be head of a department of Soviet Studies at Wisconsin. He would do his full 12 hours a week, though it would have to be composed into only part of the week in order to give him time for his writing. We are perfectly agreeable to this. I think I ought to enclose a biographical appreciation prepared by Martin Wight. Of course you do not need to be told about this, nor that he is a Marxist. It is a proposal for a new Chair. We had in our Development Programme put down a Chair either in German or in Russian for next October. We would be abandoning the Chair in German (but as we have a Reader this is not a serious matter). What it means is that we are to make the Chair in Soviet Studies rather than in Russian Literature. But [Robin] Milner-Gulland seems to be holding the literary end up and can get more help below the professorial level.

Our Constitution requires that before an appointment to a Chair is made there should be a committee of academics. There must be a member of the Academic Advisory Committee and one from the Council to sit on this appointing committee. Both James Duff and I feel that you would be the right person to serve in this capacity on the appointing committee. I am, therefore, consulting you by correspondence in the hope that we can avoid the necessity for a meeting. The academics are unanimous and I think that the Council member (who will be Alderman Caffyn) will also be in favour of making an offer to Deutscher.

I hope that you will feel that you can back this. I think it is very important for our young people in Social Studies and in European Studies really to come to grips with what the other side of the Iron Curtain stands for and not just vaguely to react against it.

I look forward to seeing you here at the end of March.

Yours ever, John Fulton.[4]

Martin Wight's accompanying CV or appreciation of Deutscher stated that when his biography of Stalin was published in 1949, it immediately placed him in the front rank of contemporary historians. *The first two volumes of his biography of Trotsky were received with still higher praise than the Stalin. Deutscher was* a profound student of the politics of Western as well as Eastern Europe.[5]

Berlin replied to Vice-Chancellor Fulton within a few days (4 March 1963). The letter was marked 'Personal & Confidential'. Berlin avoids mentioning Deutscher by name.

Dear John,

Your letter puts me in a cruel dilemma. The candidate of whom you speak is the only man whose presence in the same academic community as myself I should find morally intolerable. How much of this is founded on objective judgement of his academic and intellectual activities and how much on personal feeling, I find it difficult to say. I feel it is very wrong to leave matters like this: and I certainly have no wish to oppose anything that Asa Briggs, Corbett and others want – nor would I dream of doing so, even if I had a right to do so, which I doubt. But I think there is a limit below which lack of scruple must not go in the case of academic teachers. If you would like to know my views in greater detail, I should be ready to communicate them in conversation – I would rather not put them down on paper. Alternatively, you may wish to ignore this attitude on my part altogether, which would greatly relieve me. The man in question is the only one about whom I have any such feeling – there is literally no-one [else], so far as I know, to whom I would wish to urge such objections – and of course I do not think that personal opinions, especially left-wing ones, should be any barrier to academic appointment by your or any university in England at the present moment. I should have supported the claim of [C.] Wright Mills, say, or [Eric] Hobsbawm, vigourously [*sic*: typist's error?].

Yours sincerely, [*No signature on the carbon copy*].[6]

Fulton replied by return (7 March):

Dear Isaiah,

I think we are in a troubled state of mind as a result of your letter – an entirely proper state of mind to be in, except for knowing what one ought to do. I wonder if you would be good enough to let Martin Wight come and talk to you fairly soon? He is the Dean of the School concerned and was the originator of the proposal and I am particularly anxious that one of the academics should talk to you before I do. There will be an opportunity for you and me to talk when you come to Brighton for the Academic Advisory Committee. The immediate result of your writing was to make us put the scheme into cold storage for the present. I do not think there is a great disadvantage in some delay.

I look forward very much to seeing you. If you can spend the night with us you know how much we would like it.

Yours ever, John Fulton[7]

The third meeting of the Academic Advisory Committee (AAC) took place within the month, on 27 March, at the university's Stanmer House. Berlin attended. We do not know whether he took up Fulton's invitation to discuss the matter privately with him during his visit to Sussex. Present at the AAC meeting were Sir James Duff, chairman, Vice-Chancellor Fulton, Berlin and five others. Among those called in for parts of the meeting were Wight, Corbett, Barna and Professor David Daiches. Apologies for absence were received from Asa Briggs.

The minutes of this meeting indicate that no chair in any subject was appointed in 1963–64. No mention is made either of Deutscher or a chair in Soviet studies – although Vice-Chancellor Fulton outlined the Senate's provisional programme for the creation of new chairs during the current quinquennium.

Circulated minutes normally avoid mentioning ad hominem *discussions, but the fact that Wight, Corbett and Barna were called in to the meeting, with Berlin himself present, suggests that the issue of Deutscher was discussed. All these gentlemen are now deceased, however, and there is no firm evidence.*

Evidently a dinner was held after the meeting, and it is to this that Corbett, senior tutor in philosophy, refers in a letter he wrote to Berlin a few days later (1 April 1963), regretting that he had not been able to talk to him at the dinner. Previously senior tutor at Balliol, teaching philosophy for Modern Greats, Corbett had known Berlin at Oxford. But his letter does not mention Deutscher. He sought Berlin's advice in his search for a scholar suitably qualified to edit a book of readings on Marxism and Culture.

Berlin replied (5 April 1963):

Dear Patrick,

I am sorry that I had to leave dinner so early – I looked forward to talking to you about anything about which you might want to talk, and also about Deutscher, etc. *Having run through a number of possible editors for Corbett's project on Marxism and Culture, Berlin brought Deutscher into the frame, although without reference to Deutscher's candidacy for a chair in Soviet studies. As cited earlier, he wrote:* Deutscher, as far as I know, has only ventured once into this field, namely with an attack on *Dr. Zhivago* considerably more violent than any delivered in the Soviet Union; it ended by costing him the favour of *Dissent*, the *New Left Review* and other non-Communist left-socialist publications, which decided to break off relations with him at the time, although the *New Left Review* have repented of this decision.[8]

The sole living survivor from those involved, Lord Asa Briggs, was, as already noted, not present at the AAC meeting. He writes: It was my idea to get Deutscher to Sussex and I was fully supported by the historians. I was not yet Vice-Chancellor and I was angry that Fulton had consulted Isaiah. I cannot recall Martin Wight being asked to see Isaiah: I don't think that he ever saw him. Isaiah never discussed the matter with me. I knew him better than Martin [did]. I was aware of his intense distrust of Deutscher who seemed to me a great 'acquisition.' As far as I can recall, Fulton did not tell me of Isaiah's veto, for that was how Fulton treated it. . . . In those early Sussex days I had considerable power to carry through appointments, but ultimately the Vice-Chancellor had his own veto powers, very seldom used. . . . I very much wanted Deutscher at Sussex.[9]

After three months' silence, Fulton wrote to Deutscher on 28 May.

I am sorry that I have been so long in writing to you since you came to lunch here and met some of my colleagues with me. As I am sure you know, we greatly enjoyed the occasion and found it most stimulating.

We have given a great deal of thought since then to the whole question of the place of Soviet Studies in the University; and greatly though we were attracted by the possibility we feel that we cannot in the light of our other commitments hope to develop it at this stage. So that I am afraid that we are not in a position to make an offer to you. I think we were all very sensible of the compliment you did us by taking an interest in our academic affairs, and if you feel disappointed at this decision I want to tell you that we share it also. You did say that you would continue to be interested in our fortunes and I hope that we may see you here before long to renew what was a very stimulating discussion.

It is interesting to note that at this time the university was planning a one-year MA in Russian studies, with a paper required on one of ten alternative subjects including many highly relevant to Deutscher's knowledge and teaching: Russian Government and Politics, Russia and the West, Russia and the East, the Russian Economy, Contemporary Russia, the Russian Mind. Miss Beryl Williams was named as director of studies.

Although the accepted code of practice obliged Fulton to conceal Berlin's role when writing to Deutscher, and it can be argued that Fulton was not morally obliged to inform any candidate why he had been turned down, one can only view his letter of refusal as a formulaic obfuscation of the truth. Deutscher was never informed by Sussex why he had been turned down despite enjoying virtually the entire faculty's support for his appointment.

Deutscher replied to Fulton briefly on 30 May: Naturally enough, I am disappointed at your being unable to make any offer, especially as I was given to understand that what was under discussion were only the particulars of an offer. However, I appreciate the very kind terms in which you have communicated to me the negative decision; and I must assume that the 'other commitments' to which you refer are of a very imperative nature. Whatever the disappointment, I do retain a very pleasant memory of our meeting in the University, and I also hope to renew the contact.

In the months to come, Berlin's flag was to fly ever higher at Sussex. The remarkable reach of his influence and prestige can be tracked in this reference note.[10]

The evidence of Deutscher's correspondence with friends and colleagues, or in fact the negative evidence, is that the refusal became an episode that he kept under wraps. His correspondence from this time, and indeed until his death four years later, carries no hint of his application to Sussex or the outcome. Although he had named Carr as one of his referees, his discovered letters to Carr contain no allusion to Sussex. How, or whether, he learned of Berlin's decisive role in the affair remains a subject for conjecture.

Five or six years passed before the episode reached the public domain, eighteen months after Deutscher's death. Black Dwarf, *published fortnightly in large format at 7 Carlisle Street, London W1, shared premises with the* New Left Review.[11] *The back page of its 14 February 1969 issue carried 'Dwarf Diary', written anonymously. An item, 'In Defence of Perry Anderson', referred to the latter's essay 'Components of the National Culture', published in the* New Left Review *(no. 50). The essay had come under attack:*

But by far the most serious rebuttal has come from Sir Isiah [*sic*] Berlin. ('Isaiah' *is misspelled throughout.*) A private rebuttal, needless to add. Berlin maintains that Perry Anderson is anti-semitic and cites as evidence the fact that all the émigrés he attacks are Jewish. This drivel is being repeated by Berlin's acolytes, notable among whom is Mrs Jean Floud of Nuffield College, Oxford. What Professor Berlin and his cohorts fail to mention is that Anderson was arguing that in 'liberal democratic' England the most distinguished and undoubtedly the most brilliant of the émigrés was one Isaac Deutscher (also a Jew, Professor Berlin!) and that he was ignored by the academic establishment because he was a Marxist. There are good reasons why Berlin prefers to ignore this. It was Berlin who was responsible for Deutscher being refused a university post at Sussex. He justified it by saying: 'You can't have a Marxist teaching history.' And of course Berlin was fully aware that Isaac Deutscher was not a person who could be integrated into the system. With a record such as his own Professor Berlin should think twice before he accuses Perry Anderson of being an [*the remaining words do not appear on the printed page but one can assume they include 'anti-Semite'*].[12]

On receiving a photostat of the Black Dwarf *article, Berlin wrote (18 March 1969) in some agitation to Jean Floud, named in the article as one of 'Berlin's acolytes'. Here he addresses the Deutscher affair:*

What he had said to Professor Wight, the only person I saw on the subject, was that he did not regard Deutscher as a suitable professor of Russian history (actually Soviet studies) unless there was a colleague in the same field, not quite so fanatical, *and able to give the other side of the case. Berlin told Floud that he would welcome Deutscher's presence in a university like Oxford or Cambridge, where more than one point of view could be heard. However, if Sussex University wanted him, Berlin would not oppose it or vote against him,* because I believe that universities should have the people they want. *He added that Fulton had consulted David Astor, an intimate friend of Deutscher, who said that he respected him but* he had become a furious propagandist, with no regard whatever for academic values. *After that the matter was dropped.* I knew there was some rumour among the students . . . that I had somehow vetoed Deutscher, but this is perfectly false.

Later in the letter he comes back to Deutscher:

I disliked him personally, read his books with some admiration, was not prepared to vote against him for any post, and would have voted for him for e.g. a Fellowship at All Souls or Nuffield or St Antony's.[13]

In view of what we know, this last claim beggars belief – Deutscher a fellow of All Souls! The claim that Martin Wight was the only person I saw on the subject runs into the difficulty of Berlin's initial letter to Fulton and the claim in the letter to Floud (found nowhere else) that Fulton subsequently consulted David Astor. This is interesting: it will be recalled that the previous year, 1962, Astor had severed Deutscher's retainer to write regularly for the Observer. *While we have no first-hand evidence of what Astor told Fulton, it seems unlikely that he would have said that Deutscher, whose Trotsky trilogy was now complete, had 'no regard whatever for academic values'.*

A further month passed. An undated letter from Berlin to his friend the BBC producer Anna Kallin encloses his first letter to Tamara Deutscher (22 April 1969). To Kallin he confided:

I did think Deutscher pretty awful, as you know, but I bent over backwards – perhaps unnecessarily – on the few occasions in which I was concerned in anything that concerned him. I have to admit that I did once suggest that he might not be an ideal person for writing the life of Dr. Weizmann, which had been suggested to me in Palestine. Apart from that I do not think that I offered any obstruction to his career. *He added:* Deutscher wanted me to write an introduction to 'The Non-Jewish Jew', but for obvious reasons I thought better not. *This claim is certainly surprising. If true, it could possibly indicate that until the end of his life Deutscher remained innocent of Berlin's fatal role in the Sussex debacle – indeed, innocent of Berlin's intense personal animosity. In another letter to Kallin, Berlin added sardonically:* I don't want Mrs Deutscher to think that I put a fatal obstacle in her husband's glorious career. *Would Anna Kallin please tell Mrs Deutscher that I am not a monster* – that I had no wish to do her husband harm, and indeed refrained from doing so, and of course I did not like his view of me, or his views in general, particularly about the Jews.[14]

Berlin added: I have now verified the text [his letter to Tamara Deutscher] with Mr Wight at Brighton, who consulted me about Deutscher, and he declares it to be accurate and true.

Berlin's letters to Tamara Deutscher are dated 22 April, then 2 and 12 June 1969. She replied on 13 May and 8 June. His first letter of 22 April to 'Dear Mrs Deutscher' was sent from the City University of New York.

He explained that he had received a cutting from a recent issue of Black Dwarf, *an anonymous article accusing him of attributing Perry Anderson's recent polemic in the* New Left Review *to anti-Semitism. Berlin was further accused of having blocked the appointment of the late Isaac Deutscher to* a Chair in Russian History *at Sussex University on the ground that Deutscher was a Marxist.* I need scarcely say that all these statements are false. And although the fact that they have been made seems to me scandalous, I do not, despite feeling great irritation, propose to controvert them in public, as 'The Black Dwarf' has been described to me by various left-wing Socialists to whom I have spoken here as the kind of publication that would take little notice of the fact that the statements ascribed to me were, in fact never made by me either in public or in private. *He had not accused Mr Anderson of anti-Semitism and did not care whether he was an anti-Semite or not. What concerned him far more was the libel about his behaviour with regard to the late Mr Deutscher.*

Berlin then apprised Tamara Deutscher of the facts, which were confidential and which therefore he did not intend to publish, *to the best of his recollection.*

At a time when he belonged to a committee responsible for reporting on academic standards of the then newly created Sussex University, and therefore liable to be made an elector to chairs in fields about which he had some knowledge, he had been asked whether he supported the idea of creating a chair in Soviet studies for Mr Deutscher. My view, which I communicated verbally to Professor Martin Wight, was that Mr. Deutscher's remarkable gifts would benefit the University most if he were not called on to create a field of studies but to reinvigorate an existing discipline. *Berlin would have been wholeheartedly in favour of the appointment if the department contained another expert to look after aspects of the field that Deutscher did not regard as central or relevant to what interested him most. Berlin would have supported his candidature in any institution that possessed a department, or at least one or two teachers, in this field, e.g. at Oxford or Cambridge; or for a research fellowship anywhere at all. But although he did not think Mr Deutscher ideally qualified for the Sussex job, if the university's own people nevertheless wished to appoint him, Berlin would not have resisted, since universities ought to be absolutely free to do what they thought it right to do.* I made it absolutely plain that I should not have lifted a finger to obstruct your late husband's appointment whatever my misgivings, nor ventilated my views on the subject to anyone, if the University in fact wished to give Mr. Deutscher the post in question.

He felt sure that Professor Wight and indeed the vice-chancellor at that time, Lord Fulton, would bear this out if Mrs Deutscher cared to ask them.

Berlin said he did not know what transpired. I gather that others closer to your husband than I (indeed I hardly knew him at all, for we met but twice) were consulted, and that, in the event, no post in this subject was created. But I know nothing of the circumstances; the only point I wish to make is that if the University had wished to appoint Mr. Deutscher to be Professor of Soviet Studies, they could have done so, in the knowledge that no opposition to this would come from me. Consequently the statement in 'The Black Dwarf' is wholly groundless.

(The statement others closer to your husband than I . . . were consulted *may echo what Berlin had more explicitly told Jean Floud: that David Astor had been consulted by Fulton and had replied that Deutscher had* no regard whatever for academic values.*)*

Berlin continued: the position attributed to him by Black Dwarf *that 'No Marxist should be professor of Russian history'* is a monstrosity of which no one who knows me could (I should hope) believe me to be guilty. (*Black Dwarf in fact alleged that Berlin had said, 'You can't have a Marxist teaching history.'*) Your husband disapproved of my views, if anything, more strongly than I did of his; nevertheless it would have been a betrayal of every intellectual value in which I believe if I had allowed this to sway my judgement consciously in judging his fitness for an academic post. *Indeed, when someone, sometime after the Sussex episode, had asked him whether he would be prepared to support Mr Deutscher for a research post at one of the Oxford colleges, he had said that he would be glad to do so – that Mr Deutscher would bring an element of passionate concern, however wrong-headed Berlin might think it to be, that Oxford could certainly do with. However, nothing came of this, and he had heard no more. He felt sure that Mrs Deutscher would agree that* no decent person could remain unmoved by a false charge of unjust behaviour towards another man, especially if he were brilliant, courageous, gifted, and had in all probability suffered a good deal for his political convictions.

Neither in this nor his two subsequent letters to Tamara Deutscher did Berlin mention his 'Personal & Confidential' letter to Vice-Chancellor Fulton of 4 March 1963, with its three crushing sentences: The candidate of whom you speak is the only man whose presence in the same academic community as myself I should find morally intolerable. *And:* But I think there is a limit below which lack of scruple must not go in the case of academic teachers. *And:* The man in question is the only one about whom I have any such feeling – there is literally no-one [else], so far as I know, to whom I would wish to urge such objections.

In an almost simultaneous letter to Anna Kallin (23 April), he made a plea: Do make it all right for me with Mrs Deutscher – I am told here that I really could bring a libel suit against Black Dwarf, and get quite a lot of money, but I shall not.[15]

No correspondence between Berlin and Wight has been found.

On 13 May 1969 Tamara Deutscher replied from 2a Kidderpore Gardens, London NW3.[16] *Her tone was polite but coolly sceptical, though not accusatory.*

Berlin wrote again on 2 June 1969, thanking her for her response. I ought to explain that I knew nothing (until your letter came) about the antecedents: the advertisement for the post of Senior Lecturer, the correspondence with Professor Wight, the luncheon on 12th February 1963 etc. (*Yet Fulton, it will be recalled, had originally advised him on 28 February 1963:* When we advertised recently for a post in History we had an approach from Deutscher. . . . He came to see the Deans and lunched with a number of our senior colleagues. . . . We would like to have him as our Professor of Soviet Studies. The academics are unanimous. *Fulton had enclosed Wight's recommendation of Deutscher for a chair.*)

After suggesting to her that Wight and Fulton would confirm his version, he added a further sentence, which is typed on to the carbon copy available: I have not communicated with him [Fulton] about all this. *Berlin repeated that he regarded the whole matter as confidential. He defended the practice of confidentiality in traditional 'neither fear nor favour' terms, adding that for his part:* I have absolutely nothing to conceal in this case, or even cause to look on it as particularly confidential. *He added that if a* serious publication *made such slanderous allegations as those in* Black Dwarf, *he would not hesitate* to take proceedings. *He concluded that he felt wounded that Tamara Deutscher* may still believe me to have behaved in some improper way in a matter that affected your late husband.[17]

Tamara Deutscher replied on 8 June. By this juncture nothing new was being disclosed.[18]

On 12 June, Berlin wrote again to Mrs Deutscher. Nothing new here, either: But the main purpose of this letter is to say that my original motive for writing to you was self-exoneration – I did not want you (in particular) to think that what the Black Dwarf said was true. It was painful to me to think that you could suppose me to have made the statement and behaved in a manner described in that publication.[19]

In summary: had Berlin forgotten what he had written to Fulton six years earlier? This is highly unlikely – that letter resided in his files. Or did he count on Fulton, if approached by Tamara, keeping the secret, which he surely would. Having entirely obfuscated, in his letter of 30 May 1963 to Deutscher, the university's reason for not granting him a chair, Fulton would hardly stamp himself a liar by coming clean to Tamara about Berlin's role. One notices that, when writing to Anna Kallin (23 April 1969), Berlin tells her that he has cleared his letter to Tamara with Martin Wight. If so, Wight himself may not have seen the original letter of veto from Berlin to Fulton. When attending the Sussex AAC on 27 March 1963 (the minutes record that Wight, Corbett and Barna were called in), Berlin may well have presented his case against Deutscher in the more objective terms later conveyed to Tamara Deutscher, omitting his lethal ad hominem *remarks found in the letter to Fulton. Such discussions may have continued since Fulton did not break the news to Deutscher for a further two months. But we can only conjecture, lacking conclusive evidence.*

On 1 July 1969, Tamara Deutscher wrote to E.H. Carr: I also got myself involved in a long correspondence with Isaiah Berlin, but this *entre nous* and I would like to show you the letters when I have a chance to see you. *Carr replied (8 July):* I am intrigued by your correspondence with Isaiah Berlin, and find it difficult to imagine the occasion or the subject. I saw him in Oxford a few weeks ago, and he bubbled as amiably as ever. *She wrote back (13 July):* To get the full flavour you must see the letters – if I produce the arguments in my own poor words, all piquancy will be lost. The correspondence deals with the old Sussex University appointment. Isaiah Berlin felt terribly unhappy at the mere thought that I might think he vetoed this appointment. (All this, of course, in confidence.)[20]

What seems apparent is that Isaac and Tamara Deutscher lacked conclusive evidence about Berlin's role in the Sussex affair. It was an episode they were reluctant to speak about openly. Peter Sedgwick's posthumous tribute to Deutscher deals with the matter cautiously, without naming Sussex: Towards the end of his days, when he sought an academic position in a British university in order to complete his *Life of Lenin,* free from journalistic chores, he was at first offered a full professorship, and then abruptly blacklisted, under pressure from certain senior dons.[21] *In 1971, the journalist Daniel Singer, a close friend of the Deutschers, published a version of events clearly derived from Tamara but offering only a single, noncommittal, allusion to Isaiah Berlin:* The new University of Sussex was looking for a senior lecturer. Deutscher expressed his interest. The response was enthusiastic: for such a distinguished candidate the offer was raised to a full professorship and the direction of a department of Soviet studies. Then came an awkward silence and an even more awkward withdrawal. The Board, which included such famous figures as Sir Isaiah Berlin, will one day have to answer publicly why the appointment was not confirmed. Quite naturally, they prefer to keep quiet.[22] *In 1978 Tariq Ali repeated the* Black Dwarf *allegation of 1969*: Isaiah Berlin blackballed Deutscher's appointment at Sussex University, and legend has it that this great believer in freedom and democracy was opposed to a Marxist teaching Soviet history. . . . As a result, Deutscher's research work had to be constantly interrupted by writing articles for the press in order to earn a living (*on this claim, see below*).[23]

E.H. Carr's biographer, Jonathan Haslam, reports that when he interviewed Berlin in 1983, he attempted to clear the air about the Sussex affair, emphasizing that he had not actually voted against Deutscher's appointment as Professor of History [*sic*], merely suggested that he was not qualified for the job.[24]

The late Christopher Hitchens recalled that, when reviewing Berlin's book Personal Impressions *for the* New Statesman, *he mentioned the old story of Berlin acting as an academic gatekeeper and barring the appointment of Deutscher to a chair at Sussex University. In the next post came a letter from Berlin, stating with some anguish that while he didn't much approve of Deutscher, his opinion had not been the deciding one. I telephoned Tamara Deutscher and others, asking if they had definite proof that Berlin had administered the bare bodkin, and was told, well, no, not definite proof. So I published a retraction. Later Hitchens, like Haslam, read Ignatieff's biography and saw the light.*[25]

Michael Ignatieff's account of the Deutscher episode is confined to half a page, but he does quote part of one deadly sentence from Berlin's letter to Fulton: the only man whose presence in the same academic community as myself I should find morally intolerable. *Rightly assuming that this letter 'put paid to Deutscher's chances', Ignatieff adds that Berlin remained troubled by his own part in the affair; he maintained that if Deutscher had been offered a chair in Marxist thought, he would have no objection. The difficulty lay in supposing that Deutscher could be counted upon to teach non-Marxist concepts with the fairness requisite in a university teacher.*[26]

Our final reflections on the affair appear below in roman type.

A common line of thought among Deutscher's admirers maintains that the denial of a chair at Sussex forced him to keep churning out paid journalism and away from his work on the biography of Lenin. This, it may be recalled, echoes Deutscher's statement of purpose when he first wrote to Sussex, yet he also told Martin Wight that he preferred seminars to tutorials and would find a minimum of twelve hours a week too much. After years in the British academic wilderness he was doubtless excited by Sussex's recognition that he was worthy of a chair, but one may doubt whether he would have found himself happy to shoulder the duties and obligations of such a post. Wight himself had rubbed in the problem by pointing out how many often 'mediocre' or 'illegible' essays had to be read outside the tutorial hours. One may add that a new chair in Soviet studies would inevitably involve a lot of non-teaching time establishing a curriculum, liaising with colleagues, drawing up reading lists, vetting candidates for admission, marking exam papers, supervising doctoral theses, sitting on committees, writing letters of recommendation. As a visiting professor in American universities, he came, he delivered, he departed. But a permanent chair at Sussex would entail time-consuming personal and even pastoral obligations to his students.

There was also the financial question. In his initial letter to Sussex, Deutscher explained that he currently wrote syndicated articles for a broad spread of newspapers, which he would be prepared to give up provided his starting salary compensated for the lost income. But in the case of a chair the starting salary – one can only speculate – would have been in the region of £3,000 p.a. (the peak for a senior lecturer being £2,500). We may therefore ask: what kind of income did Deutscher derive from his journalism? We have seen that he had recently lost his £2,000 p.a. retainer at the *Observer*, probably a factor motivating his application to Sussex. On the other hand, a statement of income for the year 1963 from his syndication agent, Robert Harben, puts the figure at £2,644 derived from about fifteen countries – but this did not include his British or American journalistic income, which Deutscher apparently negotiated on his own behalf. His desk swarmed with invoices, statements from his agent, handwritten lists of earnings.[27] That had long since become his *modus vivendi* and not easy to give up.

But the money was only one motive for his non-stop, prodigious journalistic output. He was born to write, to announce his views, to propagate his prophecies – to be himself. Could he happily surrender his political mission (and attendant publicity) to the undramatic, hidden-away routines of a very small, new university with only (at that time) about five hundred students? As Daniel Singer remarked, Deutscher relished the pressures of journalism and 'the smell of printer's ink', adding: 'So as to stimulate debate within the socialist movement, he was willing to write long essays for, say, *Les Temps modernes* or *La Sinistra*, without bothering about reward.' He also relished being interviewed by *L'Espresso, L'Express, New Left Review*, Hamburg television – *L'Espresso* allowed him to come up with the questions as well as the answers.

On top of that, as it turned out, Deutscher was soon to pitch himself into political agitation and mass teach-ins involving frequent and extended visits to America, time when he was clearly not bent over his biography of Lenin. In

May 1965, he flew to Washington for the first National Teach-In, then travelled on to Berkeley for another. In May 1966, he returned, speaking in Berkeley again and New York, where he addressed the Fifth Avenue Peace Parade on 23 May. He came to Harpur College (the State University of New York at Binghamton) for six weeks in March 1967, to conduct a seminar on 'Aspects of Soviet Society'. While at Harpur, he again took part in the Fifth Avenue Peace Parade in New York City, on 15 April 1967. The previous day he had spoken at the New School for Social Research to explain the Vietnam War Crimes Tribunal. He also lectured at New York University, Princeton, Harvard and Columbia in the spring of 1967. He joined the Russell Tribunal in Stockholm, addressing mass meetings in Copenhagen and Stockholm. These extended visits coincided with the spring and summer teaching terms at the University of Sussex. It is hard to imagine that his late-in-life emergence as a public celebrity, a tribune, would not have been more attractive to him than compiling reading lists, marking essays, setting exams, sitting on committees.

But this, of course, is speculation: I merely suggest that the time-free scenario to be provided by Sussex, as imagined by his sympathisers after his death, may be simplistic. To turn the question around, what would he have brought to the students at Sussex? Fame, a high profile, some excitement, yes. But can one easily imagine Deutscher handing out Soviet studies reading lists extending to the 'Cold War' scholars, to Wolfe, Schlesinger, Kennan, Fainsod, Laqueur, Schapiro, Ulam, Katkov, Seton-Watson, Keep, Zeman, Utchein, Hayward? To Berlin and Popper? One can doubt it. Indeed, if we leave aside Isaiah Berlin's motives, he may have done the University of Sussex, or its students, a small favour.

But the motives remain his legacy. His letter of 4 March 1963 to Vice-Chancellor Fulton fouls the nest of academic impartiality, transgressing the obligation to reveal personal grievances in full. Berlin's correspondence, when brought to light, reveals a succession of vehement attacks on Deutscher's views about Soviet history, Stalin, Trotsky, Marxism, historical inevitability, renegades from communism, the Cold War, the Soviet Union since Stalin, the New Left, Vietnam and, most passionately, Judaism and Israel. Every attack, sent in confidence and not for publication, came back to one or several of Deutscher's personal failings – a specious, dishonest, arrogant charlatan and an enemy of Israel – not forgetting how Berlin had detested and despised him since his review of *Historical Inevitability*. Surely Berlin should have come clean about a decade of personal and political animosity, and thus disqualified himself? Of course, such was Berlin's high standing that the effect of his frankness might have been no less fatal.

Notes

Preface

1. In recent times the ongoing publication of Berlin's letters has provoked mixed reactions. A somewhat brutal review of *Enlightening* by A.N. Wilson culminated in the faint praise of 'malicious, snobbish, boastful, cowardly, pompous'. Wilson's attack produced an ardent defence by Charles Rosen. See A.N. Wilson, 'The Dictaphone Don', *TLS*, 17 July 2009, 3–4; Charles Rosen, 'On Isaiah Berlin', *New York Review of Books*, 25 Feb. 2010, 26–28.
2. Peter Oppenheimer, 'Run Over by Isaiah', in Hardy, 84. The Deutscher case is briefly mentioned in Michael Ignatieff's biography.

1. Berlin – A Life

1. Ignatieff, 10, 12–13, 17.
2. *Ibid.*, 25, 309n2, citing Berlin to Roma Schapiro, 3 Nov. 1983, and unpublished interview with Harry Shukman, St Antony's College, 5 June 1986.
3. Jahanbegloo, 4.
4. Ignatieff, 24; Hitchens, 3–11 online.
5. Ignatieff, 26–27.
6. Jahanbegloo, 5; Ignatieff, 303–04.
7. Ignatieff, 29; Lukes, 76.
8. Ignatieff, 30, 31, 35–39, 310n3, 4, citing 'The Purpose Justifies the Ways', *New York Review of Books*, 14 May 1998, 53, and Mendel Berlin, 'Autobiographical Notes', 60.
9. Ignatieff, 38, 40–41, 44–45 n16, citing the *Debater*, 10, Nov. 1928, St Paul's School.
10. *Ibid.*, 49, 51.
11. *Ibid.*, 64, 66, 311n13, citing Virginia Woolf, *Letters*, V, 255, 410–11.
12. *Ibid.*, 156, 67, 58, 312n16, citing Berlin to Spender, Feb. 1935.
13. *Ibid.*, 72, 312n33, citing Berlin, *Personal Impressions*.
14. Berlin, *Flourishing*, 302–04.
15. For a witty description of being privately flown back to Oxford from a Rothschild weekend in Cambridge, see Berlin to Mary Fisher, c.17 Dec. 1937, in Berlin, *Flourishing*, 223.
16. Ignatieff, 172, 322n16, citing an interview with Clarissa Eden, June 1995, and interviews with Stuart Hampshire and Jenifer Hart.
17. An item in *Queen* (16 April 1969) indicates that Berlin was also a member of St James's Club at 106 Piccadilly.

18. Berlin, *Enlightening*, 208; Ignatieff, 222, 328n4, citing Berlin to Mary Fisher, 20 June 1957, Berlin to John Sparrow, 18 July 1957, Berlin to Morton White, 19 July 1957.
19. Lacey, 206; Berlin, *Enlightening*, 589.
20. Carpenter, 127.
21. Including Bernard Crick, Peter Laslett, H.G. Nicholas, S. Finer, Wilfred Harrison and John Plamenatz.
22. J. Hart, undated, MS Berlin 257, fol. 168–70.
23. Berlin, *Enlightening*, 522–23.
24. Ignatieff, 300. A photograph found in the Sparrow papers in All Souls and taken in 1976 shows The Club in black tie and stern expressions: Roy Jenkins, Robert Blake, Hugh Trevor-Roper, E.T. Williams, John Sparrow, William Hayter, Kenneth Wheare, Raymond Carr, Peter Strawson and Isaiah Berlin.

2. Deutscher: A Life

1. Deutscher, *Non-Jewish Jew*, 10.
2. Deutscher to Donald Tyerman, 25 Oct. 1954, Deutscher Papers, File 16.
3. Deutscher, 'La Tragédie du communisme polonais', 22–23.
4. Deutscher, *The Prophet Outcast*, 422.
5. *Times of Ceylon*, 6 Aug. 1970, Deutscher Papers, File 189.
6. Tamara Deutscher, letter to Friends [unidentified], 16 Nov. 1967, Deutscher Papers, Files 69–72.
7. Haslam, 138.
8. Labedz, 122.
9. Peregrine, *Observer*, 3 March 1946, Deutscher Papers, File 4.
10. Labedz, 120–22.
11. D. Cleverdon to Deutscher, 27 Nov. 1948, Deutscher Papers, File 1.
12. Trevor-Roper article reprinted from *Polemic*, 8, 1947, Deutscher Papers, Files 1, 194. Letter from J.H. Peck of the Foreign Office to Deutscher, 24 July 1951, Deutscher Papers, File 3.
13. Carew Hunt and Degras, Deutscher Papers, File 1.
14. Clive James, 'On Isaiah Berlin', *TLS*, 3 Sept. 2004.
15. Dan Davin to Deutscher, 7 July 1948; Deutscher to Davin, 8 July 1948, Deutscher Papers, File 92, Wasserstein, citing Berlin to Cater, 27 June 1949, Deutscher Papers, File 103.
16. Geoffrey Cumberlege to Deutscher, 2 July 1938, Deutscher Papers, File 92.
17. Donald Tyerman to Deutscher, 24 April 1947, Deutscher Papers, File 4.
18. John Brown of OUP to Deutscher, 21 March 1958, Deutscher Papers, File 95.
19. *Newsweek*, 3 Oct. 1949, 82.
20. Tamara Deutscher, 'Work in Progress', in Horowitz, 66–67.
21. *Ibid.*, 69.
22. *Ibid.*, 77.
23. Photo of Deutscher in 1962, Deutscher Papers, File 89.
24. No longer on the the staff of the *Economist*, Deutscher was offered a salary of £120 plus a retainer of £100 for freelance contributions. *The Times* commissioned an anonymous article on 'Soviet Diplomacy: Principles and Practice since the Revolution. From a Special Correspondent' (17 Dec. 1949). A second instalment appeared the following day, 'Spheres of Influence since the War: Communism in East and West'. Still a special correspondent for *The Times*, he contributed a further two-parter on 'The Russian Economy' (31 Jan. and 1 Feb. 1949). In Feb. 1949, the *New York Times* published an article by Deutscher about 'Stalin's Possible Successor', followed by 'The Possibilities of a Settlement between Germany and Russia', in the *New York Times Magazine* (June 1949), for which he was paid $200. In Jan. 1950, the Sunday edition of the *New York*

Times carried his article 'How Much Economic Communism Is There in Russia?' Melvin J. Lasky, a future editor of the CIA-subsidised magazine *Encounter*, and at that time editor of *Der Monat*, which operated out of the US Press Center in Berlin, offered Deutscher a two thousand-word reply to Franz Borkenau's review of *Stalin*, but Deutscher declined to answer 'direct falsifications, the like of which one usually finds only in Stalinist reviews'. Deutscher Papers, File 3.

25. Deutscher Papers, File 4.
26. Tamara Deutscher, 'Work in Progress', 82.
27. Deutscher to John Brown of OUP, 14 Dec. 1955, Deutscher Papers, File 95. Robert Harben to Deutscher, 22 Jan. 1964, Deutscher Papers, File 108. One discovered document indicates that he tried his hand in the textbook market as a contributor to *Comparative Labor Movements*, published in 1952 by Prentice-Hall.
28. Deutscher, *The Prophet Outcast*, 27–28.
29. Lecture of 2 April 1954, published in the *Journal of Royal Artillery*; letter to Imperial Defence College, 8 Nov. 1962, Deutscher Papers, File 46; letter to Conservative Political Centre, 9 Feb. 1963, Deutscher Papers, File 45.
30. Deutscher Papers, Files 16–17.
31. Tamara Deutscher to Isaac Deutscher, 30 March 1967, Deutscher Papers, File 90. Translations from the Polish by courtesy of Eva Sadowski. The Deutscher correspondence, both between themselves and with others, contains many sensitive references to their only child, Martin, born in 1950.
32. Berlin to Noel Annan, 11 Nov. 1966 (extract supplied by Henry Hardy).
33. On memorial meetings, Deutscher Papers, Files 69, 192. Tamara Deutscher, Letter to Friends, 16 Nov. 1967, Files 69–72.
34. Tamara Deutscher to A. Crook, 5 Dec. 1967, R. Maxwell to D. Tyerman, 13 Sept. 1967, both in Deutscher Papers, File 72. Letters were exchanged with the inner circle in England and with American admirers; Michael Foot, Fred Halliday, David Horowitz, E. H. Carr (a little), Daniel Singer (a close friend) and Christopher Hill (new on the scene). Her liaison with the *New Left Review*, she reported, was Quintin Hoare.
35. Tamara Deutscher, Memo, 17 July 1969, Deutscher Papers, Files 75–76.
36. Carr, *New Left Review*, 137, Jan.-Feb. 1983; Haslam, 273; Tamara Deutscher, an obituary by Daniel Singer, published in the *Independent*, 10 Aug. 1990; Ralph Miliband, 'An Historic Partnership', *Guardian*, 9 Aug. 1990; W.L. Webb, obituary note, *ibid.*

3. The Issues

1. Berlin, *Enlightening*, 495.
2. 'Zionist Politics in Wartime Washington', in Berlin, *Flourishing*, 690.
3. Wasserstein, 21, ref. 43, citing Deutscher to Henry Z. Walck, 30 June 1950, Deutscher Papers, File 99.
4. Hart, xiii–xiv.
5. See Herbert Butterfield, *The Whig Interpretation of History*, London, 1931, reprinted 1950.
6. Berlin, *Against the Current*, 286.
7. On Herzen, 'Herzen and his Memoirs', *ibid.*, 212; on Montesquieu, 'Montesquieu', *ibid.*, 161, 132; on Vico, 'The Sciences and the Humanities', *ibid.*, 110; on Belinsky, *Russian Thinkers*, London, 1978, 153.

4. Marx and Marxism

1. Berlin, *Karl Marx*, 282–84, 286.
2. *Ibid.*, 21.
3. *Ibid.*, 9.

4. Berlin to Alan Dudley, 17 March 48, in *Enlightening*, 46.
5. *Ibid.*, 8, 140, 10.
6. Berlin to Lindsay, 31 Oct. 1939, in *Flourishing*, 297.
7. Berlin, *Karl Marx*, 142, 140, 143, 42.
8. *Ibid.*, 39–42, 19.
9. *Ibid.*, 255, 271–72; Berlin, *Four Essays on Liberty*, 47.
10. Berlin, *Enlightening*, 623–25.
11. Jahanbegloo, 125.
12. Tamara Deutscher, Letter to Friends, 16 Nov. 1967, Deutscher Papers, Files 69–72.

5. What Is History?

1. Berlin cited by Haslam, 196.
2. Berlin's general outlook on Carr as a historian of Soviet Russia is replicated in a review of the first three volumes of Carr's *The Bolshevik Revolution* by the veteran American Sovietologist Bertram D. Wolfe, who alleged that only Lenin's persona carried weight in Carr's narrative. B. Wolfe, 'The Persuasiveness of Power', *Problems of Communism*, 4:2, March–April 1955, 43–48, cited by Haslam, 145.
3. Haslam, 139, citing Deutscher, 'Soviet Diplomacy: I. Principles and Practice since the Revolution', *The Times*, 17 Dec. 1947; 'II. Spheres of Influence since the War', 18 Dec. 1947.
4. Carr followed up with a strong review of *Stalin* in the *New Republic*. Carr again favourably reviewed Deutscher's *Soviet Trade Unions*. Cox, 130–31; Carr, *TLS*, 10 June 1949, 373; Carr, 'The Riddle of a Public Face', *New Republic*, 28 Nov. 1949; Carr, *TLS*, 17 Nov. 1950, 717.
5. *TLS*, 9 June 1950.
6. For a fuller account, see Haslam, 161–64.
7. Carr, 'Academic Questions', *TLS*, 16 April 1954, 249.
8. Berlin, letter to Denys Page, 17 March 1955, in *Enlightening*, 482, 484.
9. Haslam, 168, 140, the latter citing Deutscher to Brandler, 3 Jan. 1955.
10. Deutscher, 'Soviet Precept and Practice', *TLS*, 7 March 1952, 165; Deutscher, 'Lenin's Foreign Policy', *TLS*, 5 June 1953, 359.
11. Deutscher, 'Mr E.H. Carr as Historian of Soviet Russia', *Soviet Studies*, April 1955, 347; Carr, 'Recoil against Stalinism', *TLS*, 20 May 1955, 262; Deutscher, 'Mr E.H. Carr as Historian of the Bolshevik Regime', in *Heretics and Renegades*, 2nd edn, London, 1969, 91–110; Carr, preface to *ibid.*, 3–4.
12. Carr, 'Stalin's Foremost Foe', *TLS*, 7 Nov. 1963, 897.
13. Participants in the Geneva conference included Merle Fainsod, Bertram D. Wolfe, Leonard Schapiro, John Keep, S.V. Utechin, George Katkov, Marc Mancall, Boris I. Nicolaevsky, Alvin Z. Rubinstein, Jane Degras, Louis Halle, Richard Lowenthal, Jan Meijer, Walter Z. Laqueur, Adam B. Ulam, Matthew Gallagher, Vernon V. Aspaturian, George F. Kennan, Leopold Labedz, Stuart R. Schram, Boris Souvarine and Max Beloff.
14. Keep, 41, 89, 220.
15. Deutscher, 'The Road to Stalinism', *TLS*, 8 Oct. 1954, 633. See also Cox, 132–34.
16. Carr, 'De-Stalinization', *TLS*, 17 May 1957, 299.
17. Carr, 'Cold War in the Market', *TLS*, 21 April 1961.
18. Among those who did participate in Geneva were two colleagues of Berlin's, S.V. Utechin and George Katkov, whom Carr took the opportunity to savage when the opportunity arose. See Carr, '1917 and All That', *TLS*, 23 July 1964, 643; Carr, *TLS*, 19 May 1961, 306; Carr, 'The Unplanned Revolution', *TLS*, 6 April 1967, 288.
19. Carr, 'Watching the Kremlin', *TLS*, 1 Dec. 1966, 1117.
20. Carr, 'Fifty Years On', *TLS*, 3 Aug. 1967.

21. Carr, *The New Society*, 118; Carr; 'Reason and Progress', *TLS*, 28 Jan. 1955, 57, 106.
22. Carr, *The New Society*, 117–18; see also Carr, 'Progress in History', *TLS*, 18 July 1952; Carr, 'Character in History', *TLS*, 11 Jan. 1955. For an illuminating analysis of Carr's theoretical positions see Heath.
23. Quoted by Roger Hausheer, Introd. to Berlin, *Against the Current*, xxi. See Berlin, *Personal Impressions*, 2nd edn, 143.
24. Berlin, 'Historical Inevitability', in *Four Essays on Liberty*, 59.
25. *Ibid.*, 60–62.
26. *Ibid.*, 77, 73, 80–81.
27. 'Determinists All' appears not to have been reprinted in any of Deutscher's collections.
28. Berlin, *Enlightening*, 472, 474–75.
29. Carr, 'History and Morals', *TLS*, 17 Dec. 1954.
30. Berlin, *Enlightening*, 530–31.
31. Carr, 'History without Bias', *TLS*, 30 Dec. 1960; Carr, *What Is History?*, 44.
32. Ignatieff, 330n50. See also an earlier letter from Berlin to Carr, 3 Dec. 1954, in *Enlightening*, 460.
33. Berlin, 'Mr Carr's Big Battalions', *New Statesman*, 5 Jan. 1962, 16.
34. Carr, *What Is History?*, 40, 72; Mehta, 103.
35. Haslam, 188.
36. Deutscher, 'Between Past and Future', review of Carr's *What Is History?*, *TLS*, Nov. 1961.
37. In *Debates with Historians*, the Dutch historian Pieter Geyl had praised Berlin's *Historical Inevitability* for stressing that methods used in the sciences cannot be transferred to history.
38. Deutscher, 'Between Past and Future'.
39. Hill, 'The Theory of Revolution', in Horowitz, 128–29.
40. Deutscher, 'The Comintern Betrayed?', *TLS*, 18 June 1964, 521.

6. A Portrait of Stalin

1. Here Laqueur quoted a critique by the zealous ex-communist, Franz Borkenau, 'Stalin im Shafspelz', published in the American-subsidised magazine *Der Monat*, Nov. 1949.
2. Laqueur, *Fate*, 96–7, 102, 103.
3. Deutscher, *Stalin*, 295, 294; Deutscher, *Russia after Stalin*, 55.
4. Deutscher, *Stalin*, 318, 320–24, 325n1.
5. *Ibid.*, 325, 336–37, 342–44.
6. *Ibid.*, 294, 360–61.
7. *Ibid.*, 355.
8. Deutscher listed his sources: 'Official Soviet sources have given no specific account of the plot. Anti-Stalinist versions can be found in E. Wollenberg, *The Red Army*, pp. 232–64; M. Borbov, 'Zagovor ili Revolutsia [Conspiracy or Revolution]', in *Sotsialisticheskii Vestnik*, no. 10, 1947; and V.G. Krivitsky, *I was Stalin's Agent*.
9. Deutscher, *Stalin*, 1949 edn, 383, 380n1, 372, 486.
10. Laqueur accused Deutscher of refusing to alter his account in a later (1967) edition of *Stalin*, published after Khrushchev's secret speech to the 20th Congress in 1956 implied that the murder of Kirov was organised by Stalin himself. Khrushchev also publicly deplored Stalin's purges of military officers in the late 1930s. This occurred at the 22nd Party Congress in 1961, and was accompanied by a complete rehabilitation of Tukhachevsky which appeared in *Izvetsiia*. Heer, 248–49, citing Ia. Gorelov, 'Zolotoe oruzhie', *Izvestiia*, 29 Dec. 1961.
11. '[T]he real conspiracy was said to have been begun by the leaders of the army, Tukhachevsky and his associates. The exact circumstances are not known, *and some deny the existence of any plot, and maintain that Hitler's secret services planted the story*

of a conspiracy and forged evidence of it, on President Benes of Czechoslovakia who trans-mitted it to Stalin. According to this version the real forger was the GPU in Moscow and [sic] designed the whole plan with Stalin's connivance.' Deutscher, *Stalin*, 1967 edn, 379. The italicised words do not appear in the 1949 version. But Deutscher then leaves his caveats behind and presses ahead with the thesis that 'the generals did indeed plan a *coup d'état* from their own motives, not in contact with any foreign power' (1967 edn, 379): 'Tukhachevsky was the moving spirit of the conspiracy' (1949) becomes 'Tukhachevsky was regarded as the leader of the conspiracy' in 1967. In other words, there was indeed a military conspiracy to overthrow Stalin, whatever Deutscher's critics might argue.

12. *Ibid.*, 174–76; Deutscher, *The Prophet Armed*, 506, 515.
13. Crankshaw, 193.
14. Deutscher, *The Prophet Outcast*, 417, 419.
15. See Deutscher, *Stalin*, 380.
16. Solzhenitsyn, 7.
17. Deutscher, *Stalin*, 446.
18. *Ibid.*, 523–24.
19. *Ibid.*, 549–50, 569, 568.
20. Perry Anderson, Introd. to Deutscher, *Marxism, Wars and Revolutions*.
21. Deutscher, *Stalin*, 569.
22. Jahanbegloo, 130; Lukes, 90–91.

7. Images of Lenin

1. Jahanbegloo, 130.
2. Berlin to David Astor, 14 May 1958, in *Enlightening*, 624.
3. Berlin, 'Political Ideas in the Twentieth Century', *Foreign Affairs*, 29: 3, June 1950, in *Four Essays on Liberty*, 17–19.
4. Berlin, *The Soviet Mind*, 139.
5. Berlin, 'Russian Populism', in *Russian Thinkers*, 214, 217, 236–37, 222.
6. Deutscher, *The Prophet Armed*, 318–21.
7. Deutscher, *Ironies*, 169.
8. Berlin, *Fathers and Children*, 51.
9. Deutscher to A. Rosmer, 18 May 1955, Deutscher Papers, File 88.
10. Deutscher typescript, 'The Mensheviks', BBC Third Programme, 24 April 1964, Deutscher Papers, File 3.
11. *Listener* (4 Feb. and 1 April 1965); Deutscher, *Ironies*, 217, 207, 214.
12. Deutscher, *Ironies*, 219, 224–25.
13. MS Berlin 172, fols 163–65.
14. Deutscher, 'The February Regime', *TLS*, 30 June 1966, 565.
15. Deutscher, *Heretics*, 198–200.
16. Deutscher, *The Prophet Armed*, 311–12.
17. Deutscher, *The Prophet Outcast*, 241–42, 251.
18. Jahanbegloo, 148.
19. Deutscher, 'The February Regime', *TLS*, 30 June 1966, 565; Deutscher, letter, *TLS*, 14 July 1966, 615.
20. Z.A.B. Zeman was the author of *Germany and the Revolution in Russia* (1958) and *The Merchant of Revolution: The Life of Alexander Israel Helphand (Parvus) 1867-1924* (1965). Zeman listed several friends of Lenin including Radek, who maintained rela-tions with Germany's wealthy intermediary with Russian radicals, Alexander Helphand (Parvus), during the two years before the Revolution. The evidence is clear from Zeman's research that both Lenin and the German government were privy to an under-standing about payments. Zeman reckoned at 30 million marks the total funds allo-cated by Berlin for subversion in Russia. Zeman, 219, 35–52, 61, 230–31.

21. Deutscher, *Stalin*, 218-20.
22. Deutscher, *The Prophet Armed*, 492-93, 509.
23. Sedgwick, n.p., citing *The Prophet Armed*, 510, 513-14, and *The Prophet Outcast*, 437.
24. Deutscher, *The Prophet Armed*, 514, 335.
25. Deutscher, *Stalin*, 224, 225.
26. *Ibid.*, 175.
27. Deutscher, 'The Moral Dilemmas of Lenin', *Listener*, 5 Feb. 1959, in *Ironies*, 167-69.
28. *Ibid.*, 171-72.
29. MS Berlin 261, fol. 78.
30. *Ibid.*, fol. 80.
31. The *Oxford Concise Russian Dictionary*, 267, 711, translates *parshivy* or *parshivyi* as (1) mangy, (2) figurative 'black sheep', (3) colloquial 'nasty, rotten, lousy'. The spelling given for 'Jew' is *evrei*.
32. Jahanbegloo, 167.
33. Berlin, *The Soviet Mind*, 53.
34. Deutscher, Introd. to Lunacharsky, 20-21.
35. Deutscher, *The Prophet Armed*, 260.
36. Carr, 'Lenin and Gorky', *TLS*, 11 July 1968, 724.
37. Tamara Deutscher, *Not by Politics Alone*, 181.
38. *Novaya Zhizn*, 89: 304, 14 May 1918, in Gorky, 175-76, 184.
39. Deutscher, *Lenin's Childhood*, 45.
40. Lunacharsky, 68.

8. Trotsky the Prophet

1. Haslam, 170.
2. Trotsky had spent a year of internal exile in Alma-Ata, Kazakhstan in 1928, prior to his expulsion from the Soviet Union by Stalin.
3. Berlin, *Enlightening*, 455-56.
4. Fainsod, 'Was Leon Trotsky Responsible for his Own Downfall?', *New York Herald Tribune*, 21 March 1954.
5. He added: 'Neither Marx in the historical sections of *Das Kapital* and in his *Kleinere Schriften*, nor Mehring, nor Rosa Luxemburg (in the historical chapters of *Akkumulation*) confined themselves to "*trockene Tatsachendarstellung*" [dry description of facts] – and these are still the unsurpassed models of Marxist history writing, far superior to the "dry style" of the Kautsky or Pokrovsky schools.' Deutscher Papers, File 84.
6. Sedgwick, n.p.
7. Liebman, 101-04.
8. This perspective brought irate criticisms from the orthodox Trotskyites. See Cliff, *passim*. See also Hal Draper, 'The Two Souls of Socialism', *International Socialism*, 11, winter 1962.
9. *New Statesman*, 24 Aug. 1957, 217; Liebman, 108-10, 113, citing Deutscher, *Ironies*, 180.
10. Deutscher to Natalya Sedova, 7 Nov. 1959, Deutscher Papers, File 89. A former syndicalist, Rosmer had been expelled from the French Communist Party in 1924. The founding congress of Trotsky's Fourth International was held at his home outside Paris in 1938.
11. Deutscher to Alfred Rosmer, 27 Nov. 1959, Deutscher Papers, File 88.
12. Deutscher to Alfred Rosmer, 12 Feb. 1960, Deutscher Papers, File 88.
13. Deutscher, 'Notes on Talks with Natalia Ivanova in Paris', undated (1961?), Deutscher Papers, File 89. He wrote her obituary for *The Times*, 24 Jan. 1962, and contributed to 'Hommage à Natalia Sedova-Trotski', in *Les Lettres nouvelles*, Paris, 1962.
14. Deutscher, *The Prophet Outcast*, 384-86.

15. Deutscher, 'Notes on Talks with Natalia Ivanova in Paris', Deutscher Papers, File 89.
16. In *Against the Self-Images of the Age*, London, 1971, 53–59. Review of Deutscher, *The Prophet Outcast*, first published in *Encounter*, Dec. 1963.
17. Deutscher to Alfred Rosmer, 22 Nov. 1963, Deutscher Papers, File 88.
18. Deutscher, *The Prophet Outcast*, 246.
19. Deutscher Papers, File 81. Balabanoff was the author of *My Life as a Rebel*, London, 1938.
20. Anderson, *A Zone*, 73.

9. Berlin, Christopher Hill – and Deutscher

1. MS Berlin 104, fols 197–98.
2. As told to the author by Keith Thomas, 2011.
3. Lukes, 70–71; MS Berlin 105, fols 12, 13.
4. K.E. Holme, *Two Commonwealths*, London, 1945, *passim*.
5. MS Berlin 112, fols 112–14, 140.
6. Hill, *Lenin*, 1947, 221–24, 227.
7. Ignatieff, 174–75; May, *Critical Times*, 304, no date given.
8. Berlin, *Comrade Jacob*, London, 1961.
9. Berlin, *Enlightening*, 575.
10. MS Berlin 169, fols 9, 21; MS Berlin 172, fol. 98. Hill's second letter is handwritten and difficult to decipher.
11. *Listener*, 10 Aug. 1967, 172–73.
12. Hill, *Collected Essays*, vol. 3, 95; Hill in Horowitz, 120, 124, 129.
13. Deutscher Papers, File 70.

10. Two Concepts of Liberty

1. Berlin, 'Equality', *Concepts and Categories*, 81–102.
2. See Richard Wollheim, 'A Hundred Years After', *TLS*, 20 Feb. 1959, 89.
3. Jahanbegloo, 34–35.
4. Talmon, 2.
5. Berlin, 'Two Concepts of Liberty', in *Four Essays*, 124–25.
6. Berlin's former lover Jenifer Hart, fellow of St Anne's, was sent *Two Concepts of Liberty* in draft. She felt sad that she would probably not be there to hear the lecture delivered – 'I've never heard you lecture in fact.' But she was far from convinced by the text: 'I wish you had developed yr. point about there being no reason to think democracies safeguard liberty more than autocracies do – I don't feel convinced that this cd. be proved true if one looked at the empirical evidence. Anyway whose liberty? That of a few important people at the top or the many lower down? Certainly civil liberties were extended roughly with (and I shd. say partly as a result of) the extension of democracy in England in the 19th c.' J. Hart, undated 1958, MS Berlin 257, fols 157, 158
7. Berlin, 'Two Concepts of Liberty', in *Four Essays*, 133–34, 137.
8. *Ibid.*, 144, 152.
9. *Ibid.*, 156–57.
10. *Ibid.*, 126–27.
11. *Ibid.*, 123.
12. Crowder, 82.
13. Macpherson, 'Berlin's Division of Liberty', in *Democratic Theory*, 3–23, 95–113.
14. *Ibid.*, 101–02.
15. Macpherson, *Possessive Individualism*, 275.
16. Macpherson, 'Berlin's Division of Liberty', 115 and in general 95–119.
17. Cohen, 13n9.

18. Taylor in Ryan, *The Idea of Freedom*, 176–80. See also Richard Wollheim, 'A Hundred Years After', *TLS*, 20 Feb. 1959, 89.
19. Anderson, *A Zone* 71, quoting Berlin, 'Two Concepts of Liberty', 36.
20. Crowder, 83.
21. Berlin, 'Meetings with Russian Writers', in *Personal Impressions*, 169–70.
22. Gray, 89, 96.

11. The Hedgehog and the Fox

1. 'The Hedgehog and the Fox', in Berlin, *Russian Thinkers*, 22, 23. Originally published in book form in 1953 and as 'Leo Tolstoy's Historical Scepticism', *Oxford Slavonic Papers*, 2, 1951.
2. Deborah McVea and Jeremy Treglown, 'TLS Historical Acrhive, 1902–2005', www.timea.com/thetsis/researchTools.asp (cached); Carr, 'Fox and Hedgehog', *TLS*, 20 Nov. 1953, 743; Berlin to Annan, 13 Jan. 1954, in *Enlightening*, 423.
3. Berlin, 'Hedgehog', 36.
4. Berlin, 'Meetings with Russian Writers', in *Personal Impressions*, 169.
5. Turgenev, *Fathers and Children*, 9, 22.
6. Rowse, 101; Greenwood, *passim*.
7. Tolstoy, 151–52, 243, 173–74, 179.
8. Berlin, 'Tolstoy and Enlightenment', 39, 40.
9. Turgenev, *Fathers and Children*, 73–76.
10. Berlin, *Enlightening*, 7n1; Berlin, *Fathers and Children*, 14.
11. Schapiro, 201–02.
12. *Ibid.*, 260.
13. Berlin, Introd. to Aleksandr Herzen, *My Past and Thoughts*, vol. 1, xxi.
14. *Ibid.*, xxxiii, xxi.
15. Carr, *The Romantic Exiles*, 264–65.
16. Berlin, *Enlightening*, 528; Carr, 'Continuity in Russia', *TLS*, 20 April 1956, 229. Carr was reviewing a collection to which Berlin had contributed: Ernest J. Simmons, ed., *Continuity and Change in Russian and Soviet Thought*. Berlin had written about Herzen in a four-part series published in *Encounter*: 'A Marvellous Decade, 1838–1848: The Birth of the Russian Intelligentsia' (June, Nov., Dec. 1955, May 1956).
17. Turgenev, *Virgin Soil*, 234–37, 240.
18. Berlin, *Fathers and Children*, 17.
19. Jahanbegloo, 147.

12. Anna Akhmatova

1. Ignatieff, 123, 139–40.
2. Dalos, 18.
3. See Berlin, 'Meetings with Russian Writers', in *Personal Impressions*, 169, 187; Berlin, *The Soviet Mind*, 53.
4. Berlin, 'Meetings with Russian Writers', 177.
5. Berlin, *The Soviet Mind*, 91–93; Berlin, *Flourishing*, 625.
6. Ignatieff, 148, 319n2, citing Public Record Office/Foreign Office Papers, 371/56724, 21.
7. Akhmatova, 423.
8. Akhmatova's first husband, the poet Nikolai Gumilev, had been shot by the Cheka in 1921. Her common-law husband, the art historian Nikolai Punin, twice arrested, was to die in the Gulag in 1953 after four years of harsh incarceration. Her son, Lev Gumilev, suffered arrest three times and spent a total of eighteen years in camps. Dalos, 37, quoting Berlin's report to the Foreign Office on his trip.
9. Ignatieff, 157, 160, 320n31, citing Dalos, 162–63.

10. Berlin, *Enlightening*, 457, 457n2.
11. Dalos, 52, 50.
12. Berlin, *Enlightening*, 26.
13. Berlin, *The Soviet Mind*, 78.
14. Berlin, 'The Arts in Russia', 7, 56; Ignatieff, 161.
15. 1946 Central Committee Resolution on Leningrad journals, bilingual edn, Royal Oak Michigan, 1978.
16. Ignatieff, 165–67, 320n43, citing Heinrich Böll, *Stiftung, Stasi, KGB und Literatur*, Cologne, 1993, 115–26.
17. 'I eto bylo tak' – 'That's how It was: Anna Akhmatova and Isaiah Berlin.' For a lucid summary and analysis of the book's content, see Josephine Von Zitzewitz, 'That's How It Was. New theories about Anna Akhmatova and Isaiah Berlin, her "guest from the future"', *TLS*, 9 Sept. 2011, pp. 14–15.
18. Ignatieff, 168, 321n56, citing Berlin to Jean Floud, 31 July 1975; TV interview with Michael Ignatieff, BBC2, 14 Nov. 1997.
19. A wealthy heir to Whitney money, Straight was known to Berlin through the Rothschild connection and through Arthur Schlesinger, Jr. He was subsequently interviewed by MI5 and confessed to having been recruited into the Cambridge spy ring by Anthony Blunt.
20. Berlin, *Enlightening*, 388, 386.
21. Dalos, 127.
22. Berlin set these facts down in January 1996 while making notes on the Russian edition of Gennadi Kostyrchenko's *Out of the Red Shadows: Anti-Semitism in Stalin's Russia* (Amherst, New York, 1995); Ignatieff, 321.
23. Berlin, *Enlightening*, 540.
24. Berlin, *Personal Impressions*, 177.
25. Berlin, 'Thinkers or Philosophers', *TLS*, 21 March 1953, 197.
26. Letter to Rowland Burdon-Muller, 28 June 1958, in *Enlightening*, 637, 640.
27. Berlin, *Personal Impressions*, 186–87; Shostakovich, 65.

13. Boris Pasternak

1. Berlin, *The Soviet Mind*, 56; Jahanbegloo, 18.
2. Ignatieff, 143–47.
3. Berlin, *The Soviet Mind*, 60, 63.
4. *Ibid.*, 67.
5. Berlin, 'Boris Pasternak', in *The Soviet Mind*, 85–89.
6. Berlin, 'Conversations with Akhmatova and Pasternak', in *The Soviet Mind*, 68.
7. Quoted by Henry Hardy, Preface, *The Soviet Mind*, xxiv–xxv.
8. Berlin, *Enlightening*, 643–44, 652.
9. Deutscher to P. Rahv, 31 Dec. 1958, 16 March 1959; Rahv to Deutscher, 7 March 1959; Deutscher to William Philips, 18 March 1959, Deutscher Papers, File 31.
10. Deutscher, *Heretics*, 1969 edn, 261. A version of this critique was published in *Partisan Review*, 2:26, spring 1959, 248–65.
11. Pasternak, 366–67.
12. Deutscher, *The Prophet Armed*, 322.
13. Howe, 258.
14. Deutscher, *Ironies*, 264; Labedz, 134.
15. Deutscher, *Heretics*, 1969 edn, 253.
16. Jahanbegloo, 9.
17. Pasternak, 273.
18. Deutscher, *Heretics*, 264.
19. Irving Howe, 'The Life of Trotsky', *New Republic*, 21 March 1964.
20. Berlin, *Enlightening*, 223n1.

21. Deutscher, *Heretics*, 258-59.
22. These comments are reported in Hingley, 224-25, and Reeder, 365.
23. Berlin, *Enlightening*, 656n1.
24. Arguments against putting Pasternak on the cover of *Time* magazine, *Enlightening*, 761-62. See also Berlin, review of Pasternak's *Selected Writings*, reprinted in Victor Erlich (ed), *Pasternak: A Collection of Critical Essays*, New Jersey, 1978. Also Berlin, letter in reply to Gabriel Josipovici, *TLS*, 16-22 Feb. 1990, 171.
25. *Daily Telegraph*, 25 Oct. 1958; *Sunday Times*, 9 Nov. 1958.
26. MS Berlin 322, Sussex Academic Advisory Committee, fol. 79.
27. Deutscher Papers, File 30. See also 'The Jew in Modern Society', a conversation with Isaac Deutscher, *Jewish Quarterly*, winter 1966.

14. The Cold War and the People's Democracies

1. Deutscher, *Marxism, Wars and Revolutions*, 75, 76.
2. *Observer* cited by Labedz, 156; Deutscher to Donald McLachlan, 14 May 1951, Deutscher Papers, File 4.
3. Deutscher, *Marxism, Wars and Revolutions*, 77.
4. Robert Conquest citing Deutscher's essay, 'Vietnam in Perspective', published in *Ironies*; Conquest, *We and They*, 204.
5. Deutscher, *Ironies*, 154. On Yalta, Thomson, 788.
6. Deutscher, *Ironies*, 156, 158, 153.
7. Deutscher, *Marxism in our Time*, 86, 89; Deutscher, *The Prophet Outcast*, 518.
8. See Deutscher, *Stalin*, 535-36.
9. Deutscher, typed notes, 'First Talk with Brandler', 15 Feb. 1948, Deutscher Papers. File 1. In 1933, Brandler escaped to France, was interned in 1939-40, fled to Cuba in 1941 and left for Britain in 1948, where he first met Deutscher.
10. Deutscher to R. Hanke, 5 Sept. 1952, Deutscher Papers, File 4; Deutscher, 'Dialogue with Heinrich Brandler', *Marxism, Wars and Revolutions*, 144.
11. Deutscher Papers, File 84; Deutscher, *Marxism, Wars and Revolutions*, 149.
12. Deutscher, *Heretics*, 31-33.
13. Deutscher, *Ironies*, 44-45; Deutscher, 'La Tragédie du communisme polonais', 1675-77.
14. Labedz, 133, citing Deutscher in *Universities and Left Review*, 1: 1957, 10.
15. Deutscher, *Ironies*, 46; Sedgwick, n.p., Deutscher, *The Prophet Unarmed*, 462n1.
16. Berlin, *Enlightening*, 559, 559n1; Berlin, 'Moses Hess', in *Against the Current*, 248.
17. Deutscher Papers, File 181.
18. Born in 1920 in Simbirsk, Leopold Labedz had fled from the Nazis, then been arrested by the Soviets and deported to Siberia, where he spent the next three years. Released in 1942, he joined General Anders's army, serving in Palestine, Egypt and Italy. By the end of the war, he was the only surviving member of his family. He emigrated, enrolling at the LSE. Recruited by Walter Laqueur, founder of the periodical *Survey: A Journal of East and West Studies*, Labedz subsequently served as editor from 1962 to 1989. His books include *Revisionism* (1961), *The Sino-Soviet Rift* (1964), *International Communism after Khrushchev* (1965), *On Trial* (1967) and *The Use and Abuse of Sovietology* (1989).
19. Labedz, 125-30.
20. Deutscher Papers, File 83.
21. Labedz, 141-44. In a final note Labedz promised that a second instalment, devoted to Deutscher's historical writings, would appear in a forthcoming issue. In the event, the successor article did not appear until ten years after Deutscher's death, in *Survey*, 104, Summer 1977, 146-64.
22. Deutscher to Silverman, 10 April, 19 July 1962; Silverman to Deutscher, 26 April, 17, 26 July, Deutscher Papers, File 176.

23. Silverman to Oswald Hickson Collier, 31 July 1962, Deutscher Papers, File 176.
24. Deutscher Papers, File 176.

15. Orwell and the Renegades

1. For a fuller description of these cases see Caute, *The Great Fear*.
2. Deutscher to G. Cumberlege, 30 March 1948, Deutscher Papers, File 92; Deutscher to A. Ciliga, 21 Nov. 1948, Deutscher Papers, File 1.
3. Deutscher, 'The Ex-Communist's Conscience' (1950), reprinted in *Heretics*, and in Deutscher, *Marxism, Wars and Revolutions*.
4. Deutscher, *Heretics*, 50, 53.
5. Deutscher to H. Brandler, 10 Oct. 1950, Deutscher Papers, File 83.
6. Deutscher, *The Prophet Outcast*, 321.
7. Deutscher, *Heretics*, 54–55, 58–59.
8. Labedz, 123, 124.
9. Berlin, *Enlightening*, 624.
10. Deutscher, *Heretics*, 44.
11. *Ibid.*, 49–50.
12. See Labedz, 138, citing Deutscher, *Heretics*, 37.
13. Deutscher, *Heretics*, 66, 69.
14. Deutscher, *Stalin*, 361–62, no reference given for Dostoyevsky.
15. *Ibid.*, 37–75.
16. Deutscher, *Heretics*, 69–71.
17. This point is made by Labedz, 134n2.
18. Deutscher, *Heretics*, 48.
19. Deutscher, 'Dialogue with Heinrich Brandler', 144.
20. Carr, 'Recoil against Stalinism', *TLS*, 20 May 1955, 262.
21. Berlin, 'Political Ideas in the Twentieth Century', *Four Essays on Liberty*, 24–25 (see also *Liberty*, 77–78); Jahanbegloo, 41.
22. Orwell, *Collected Essays*, vol. 1, 576, 565; Thompson.
23. Orwell, 'The Lion and the Unicorn', 95.
24. Thompson, 225, 236.
25. Buber-Neuman, 323.
26. *Les Lettres françaises*, 19 Jan. 1950.
27. Deutscher to Brandler, 11 Oct. 1950, Deutscher Papers, File 83.

16. Post-Stalin Russia: The Prophecies

1. Deutscher Papers, File 5.
2. Mark Alexander, 'Counterfeit Freedom', *Encounter* 1:1, Oct. 1953, and Deutscher's reply, 1:3, Dec. 1953.
3. Deutscher, *Heretics*, 211–12.
4. Berlin, *Enlightening*, 474–75.
5. *Ibid.*, 488–89.
6. Deutscher, *Heretics*, 193–94, 197.
7. On the *Reporter*'s fees, Deutscher Papers, Files 104–05. On Deutscher's falling out with Ascoli, 1959–63, Deutscher Papers, File 107. He wrote intermittently for Freda Kirchwey at the *Nation*, see Deutscher Papers, File 3. See in general Deutscher Papers, File 14. For Deutscher's correspondence with J.J. Servan-Schreiber and J.M. Domenach, and his articles in *L'Express* 1954–55, see Memo, 12 April 1957, Deutscher Papers, File 95.
8. Ignatieff, 219.
9. Arendt, *The Origins*, 326, 367, 423–27. See also George F. Kennan, 'Totalitarianism in the Modern World', in Carl Friedrich (ed.), *Totalitarianism*, Cambridge, Mass., 1954.

See Merle Fainsod, *How Russia Is Ruled* 1953, 2nd edn 1963; Carl J. Friedrich and Zbigniew K. Brzezinski, *Totalitarian Dictatorship and Autocracy*, 1956.

10. Schlesinger, 49–52.
11. Hoffer, 16, 18, 84.
12. Deutscher, *The Prophet Outcast*, 456.
13. Deutscher, *The Unfinished Revolution*, 33; Deutscher, 'A Reply to Critics', *Heretics*, 201.
14. Deutscher, '22nd June 1941', in *Marxism, Wars and Revolution*, 21.
15. Deutscher, *Ironies*, 16–20, 43–44.
16. Berlin, *Soviet Mind*, 127, 164, 151.
17. Ignatieff, 232, citing Berlin to Violet Bonham Carter, 10 Jan. 1957.
18. Berlin, *Soviet Mind*, 158.
19. Berlin, 'The Arts in Russia', 59–63.
20. Deutscher, *Russia after Stalin*, 129–30; Deutscher, *Heretics*, 178; *New Statesman*, 29 June 1957; Deutscher, *The Great Contest*, 76–77.
21. Deutscher, 'Violence and Non-Violence', in *Marxism, Wars and Revolutions*, 260, a discussion organised by David Dellinger in Berkeley in 1966, in connection with a Vietnam Day of Protest.
22. Deutscher, *Marxism, Wars and Revolutions*, 236, 239; Deutscher, *Heretics*, 204–05.
23. See Memo on the Harvard Seminar, Deutscher Papers, File 4, and Christopher Hill, 'The Theory of Revolutions', 115–18.
24. Deutscher, *The Great Contest*, 17, 33.
25. Deutscher, *Ironies*, 159.
26. Deutscher, *Russia after Stalin*, 173.
27. We find him repeatedly in the *Manchester Guardian* in 1955: on 'Stalin's Heirs. First Beria, Now Malenkov'; on 'The Kremlin's Upheaval. How It Happened'; on 'Growth of Army Influence in Russia, the Power of the Three Marshals': *Manchester Guardian*, 9, 12 and 14 Feb. 1955.
28. For a hostile view see James Burnham, 'History à la Deutscher', *National Review*, 12 Aug. 1961, Deutscher Papers, File 184.
29. Victor Zorza, 'Mr Deutscher Answers Critics of his "Disclosures"', *Guardian*, 24 July 1961; Labedz, 140–41.
30. Deutscher Papers, File 102.
31. Berlin to F. Roberts, 15 Feb. 1962 (extract); letter to A. Walicki (extract), both supplied by Henry Hardy.
32. Labedz, 125, citing Deutscher, *The Great Contest*, 65.
33. *Ibid.*, 138, citing Deutscher in the *New Statesman*, 24 Jan. 1959, and Deutscher in the *Observer*, 28 Jan. 1962.
34. Deutscher, *Ironies*, 138.
35. Deutscher, 'Germany and Marxism'.
36. Anderson, *A Zone*, 73.
37. Jahanbegloo, 128, 143.

17. An Anglo-American

1. Berlin, 'L.B. Namier', 33–36.
2. Ignatieff, 101, 170.
3. Berlin, *Flourishing*, 584–85, 583.
4. *Ibid.*, 400–03.
5. Berlin, *The Soviet Mind*, 91–93.
6. Ignatieff, 170–71, 321nn5,6, citing Berlin to Churchill, 14 Feb. 1948.
7. Ignatieff, 195–97, 324–25, citing Berlin, 'Mr Churchill', *Atlantic Monthly*, Sept. 1949.
8. Bryan Magee, 'Isaiah As I Knew Him', in Hardy, *The Book of Isaiah*, 47.
9. Ignatieff, 170–71.

10. Berlin, BBC Third Programme, 21 Sept. 1949, *Listener*, 29 Sept.; Berlin, *Enlightening*, 743–48; Rodney Hilton, *Listener*, 27 Oct. 1949, 723,

11. Berlin, *Foreign Affairs*, 28, 1950, 198, and 30, 1952, 197–214; Berlin to Armstrong, 16 August 1951, *Enlightening*, 239.

12. Berlin, *Enlightening*, 100; Ignatieff, 324n14.

13. Ignatieff, 193; Berlin, *Enlightening*, 100.

14. On McCarthy, Berlin, *Enlightening*, 374; letter to Schlesinger, 30 May 1953, *ibid.*, 368.

15. Ignatieff, 240–42.

16. Tim Bayliss Smith, letter to *TLS*, 17 Sept. 2004.

17. Coleman, 1–13, for his general perspective.

18. The overall balance of the magazine may be indicated by Jeremy P. Howard's Oxford DPhil thesis (1994), which found 18 'exclusively political contributions', 37 pieces 'about general cultural issues', 24 short stories and 99 poems during *Encounter*'s first two years. Cited by Wilford, 271–72.

19. Ignatieff, 199.

20. Cited by Rees, 42.

21. *Ibid.*, 41–42.

22. MS Berlin 264. On CIA funding of *Encounter*, see fols 64–66, 87–97.

23. MS Berlin 283, fols 79–82.

24. MS Berlin 264. On Conor Cruise O'Brien's libel action see fols 52–56, 79–80.

25. Ignatieff, 199–200, 326n39, citing Berlin to J. Rees, 16 Nov. 1994.

18. The New Left and Vietnam

1. Deutscher, *Marxism in our Time*, 64–65, 67, 71.

2. *Ibid.*, 72–73, 76–77.

3. Deutscher, 'Germany and Marxism'.

4. MS Berlin 261, fol. 161. Ignatieff, 254, 256, 332n31, 333n36.

5. Kennan, 18, 107, 167–69.

6. For a more detailed account, see Caute, *Sixty-Eight*, 330–43.

7. Berlin, *Fathers and Children*, viii, 23, 31.

8. *Ibid.*, 56–57.

9. *Ibid.*, 50–53.

10. Berlin, 'Historical Inevitability', *Four Essays on Liberty*, 77.

11. Berlin, 'Georges Sorel', in *Against the Current*, 329.

12. Berlin, *The Crooked Timber of Humanity*, 257–58; Berlin to R.H.S. Crossman, 6 March 1963, information supplied by Henry Hardy.

13. Ignatieff, 252–53, 332n25, citing Berlin to J. Floud, 8 March 1969. By 'casualties' Berlin presumably meant the Frankfurt School, who had sought refuge, mainly in America, from the Nazis. This school of neo-Marxist interdisciplinary social theorists had been associated with the Institute for Social Research at the University of Frankfurt am Main. Marcuse, a Jew, had been a member before emigrating to the United States in 1934.

14. Deutscher Papers, File 178.

15. Deutscher, *Marxism in our Time*, 234–38.

16. *Ibid.*, 252–53; Tamara Deutscher, Letter to Friends, 26 Nov. 1967, Deutscher Papers, Files 69–72.

17. Tony Cliff, quoted by Davidson.

18. Sedgwick, n.p.

19. Among academics, his disciples or admirers included Marcel Liebman, Louis Menashe, V.G. Kiernan, Christopher Hill and Ralph Miliband.

20. Deutscher, Preface to Liebman, 11, 13.

21. Anderson, *English Questions*, 65.
22. See Thompson, *The Poverty of Theory*.
23. Anderson, 'Components', *Student Power*, 240–41.
24. Berlin to Jean Floud, 18 March 1969 (extract supplied by Henry Hardy); Berlin to Tamara Deutscher, 22 April 1969, MS Berlin 261, fol. 168.
25. Christopher Hill, Max Beloff and Wilfred Knapp were among the co-sponsors. The present writer was among the organisers of the event.
26. Telephone conversation between Lord Walston and the present writer, June 1965.
27. New England patrician, Republican senator for Massachusetts, 1947–53, US ambassador to the UN, 1953–60, Nixon's running mate in bid for the presidency in 1960 and a former US ambassador to Saigon.
28. Cecil Woolf and John Bagguley, *Authors Takes Sides on Vietnam*, New York, 1967, 20–21.
29. Deutscher to Thomas F. Mayer, 1 May 1965, Deutscher Papers, File 177.
30. Kopkind, *New Republic*, 29 May 1965; Hella Pick, probably *Guardian*, 17 May 1965 (unattributed press cutting in Deutscher Papers, File 177).
31. Ignatieff, 234, citing Berlin to Tynan, 1 May 1961. On Berlin refusing to sign a pro-FLN manifesto, see Ignatieff, 330n43, citing Berlin to Stephen Spender, 11 Nov. 1960.
32. See Bird, 192, 359–60, 459n52, citing McGeorge Bundy, interview, 3 Nov. 1994; *Ford Foundation Annual Report, 1966*, 94; Joseph Alsop letter to Sir Isaiah Berlin, 25 April 1966.
33. Deutscher, *Ironies*, 161–63.
34. *Guardian*, 12 June 1965; *Tribune*, 18 June 1965.
35. Deutscher's 'Vietnam and the Russell Tribunal' was delivered at the New School for Social Research, New York, on 14 April 1967, and published in the *London Bulletin* of the Bertrand Russell Peace Foundation, Sept. 1967.
36. Isaac Deutscher to Tamara Deutscher, 16 April 1967, Deutscher Papers, File 90.
37. Deutscher, 'Violence and Non-Violence', in *Marxism, Wars and Revolutions*, 257–58, 260, 262.

19. Two Jewish Heritages

1. See Ignatieff, 15.
2. Bryan Magee, 'Isaiah as I Knew Him', in Hardy, *The Book of Isaiah*, 45.
3. Deutscher, *Non-Jewish Jew*, 44.
4. *Ibid.*, 6–7; Wasserstein, 9, ref. 15. On the *kikiyon* Wasserstein cites Tamara Deutscher's 'The Education of a Jewish Child', in Deutscher, *The Non-Jewish Jew*, 5. Wasserstein cites a review of *The Non-Jewish Jew* by Rabbi Jeremy Rosen, *Jewish Echo* (Glasgow), 13 Dec. 1968, in Wasserstein, 10, ref. 18.
5. Wasserstein, 22, ref. 45, citing Deutscher to J. Glouberman, 4 June 1951, Deutscher Papers, File 6; Wasserstein, 22, ref. 46, cites J. Goldsmith, 'Deutscher in Marxland' (review of *The Non-Jewish Jew*), *Jewish Observer and Middle East Review*, 22 Nov. 1968.
6. Berlin to Berenson, 11 April 1958, in *Enlightening*, 617–20. Holmes here quotes from a letter to his mother, Marie Berlin (20 Nov. 1955); Hardy, *Book of Isaiah*, 241.
7. Deutscher, *Non-Jewish Jew*, 45.
8. See A. Koestler, 'Judah at the Crossroads', in *The Trail of the Dinosaur* (New York, 1955), 106–41; Berlin, 'Jewish Slavery and Emancipation', *Jewish Chronicle*, reprinted in *The Power of Ideas*. For a discussion of this exchange see Wasserstein, 11–15.
9. Berlin to Anna Kallin, 23 April 1969, MS Berlin 261, fol. 171; letter to Marie Berlin, 20 Nov. 1955, *Enlightening*, 508.
10. Berlin, *Karl Marx*, 253; Berlin, 'Isaiah Berlin and Moses Hess', *Jewish Observer and Middle East Review*, 18 Dec. 1959, 17, reprinted in *Enlightening*, 710–11; Berlin, *Against the Current*, 277.

11. Berlin, *Karl Marx*, 282–84, 286.
12. Deutscher, *Non-Jewish Jew*, 32, 34–35.
13. Ignatieff, 184, 323n57, citing Berlin to Goronwy Rees, 23 Dec. 1952, and Avishai Margalit, 'Address', Sheldonian Theatre, 21 March 1998.
14. *Ibid.*, 35.
15. Berlin to Rowland Burdon-Miller, 18 Jan. 1951, in *Enlightening*, 208.
16. 'A Personal Tribute to Adam von Trott (Balliol 1931)', *Balliol College Annual Record* (1986), reprinted in Berlin, *Flourishing*, 717–19. See also his letter to Trott, July 1934, in *Flourishing*, 89–91.
17. Berlin's remarks are found in 'Jewish Slavery and Emancipation', Oct. 1951, in *The Power of Ideas*, 181, 184. Ignatieff, 186, 323n65, citing Berlin to Eliot, 30 Jan. 1952. On St Paul's, Michael Frayn, 'Miscellany', *Guardian*, 23 Jan. 1961, in MS Berlin, fol. 790.
18. Ignatieff, 42, 293–94, 300; Wasserstein, 16.
19. *Jewish Observer and Middle East Review*, 21 Feb. 1958, Deutscher Papers, File 184; Ignatieff, 63.
20. *Christian Science Monitor*, 10 Jan. 1950.
21. Berlin, *Enlightening*, 339.
22. Deutscher, 'The Russian Revolution and the Jewish Problem', *Non-Jewish Jew*, 78–82.
23. Deutscher, *Russia after Stalin*, 112–13.
24. *Jewish Chronicle*, 14 Nov. 1958; Deutscher to Zukerman, 15 Nov. 1958, Deutscher Papers, File 30.
25. Deutscher, *Ironies*, 275–77.
26. Deutscher, *Non-Jewish Jew*, 59. In Voltaire's *Candide* (1759), Dr Pangloss views situations with unwarranted optimism.
27. Deutscher, 'Marc Chagall and the Jewish Imagination', a Third Programme talk (14 Aug. 1965), in *Non-Jewish Jew*, 153–62.

20. Zionism

1. Ignatieff, 27.
2. Weizmann, who became a British subject in 1910, was another Jewish son of the Russian Empire – indeed, both his father and Berlin's were timber merchants.
3. Berlin, 'Chaim Weizmann', in *Personal Impressions*, 52–54; Berlin, 'The Origins of Israel', (1953), in Laqueur, *The Middle East in Transition*, 207.
4. Weizmann 280, 474.
5. Cited by Cruise O'Brien, 225.
6. Berlin, *Against the Current*, 213–31, 233.
7. *Ibid.*, 237–41.
8. Rochelson, 141.
9. Weizmann, 243, 430.
10. *Ibid.*, 150.
11. See Khalidi.
12. Said, Introd. to Said and Hitchens, 5–6.
13. Ignatieff, 79, 313n8, citing Bernard Wasserstein, 'Staying to Get Out', *TLS*, 24 April 1998; Ignatieff, 80, citing interview with Berlin, 13 Dec. 1988.
14. Ignatieff, 118, 316n29; Berlin, 'Zionist Politics in Wartime Washington', in Berlin, *Flourishing*, 663–93. Bills introduced in both Houses of Congress allowing 100,000 survivors to emigrate failed to pass, the result being that during the Holocaust fewer than thirty thousand Jews a year reached the United States and some were turned away.
15. See Berlin, 'Chaim Weizmann'; Ignatieff, 177, 322n27, citing speech to Zionist Congress, Basel, 12 Dec. 1946.
16. Morris, 101.
17. Childers, 145–50; Laqueur, *The Israel-Arab Reader*, 282.

18. Morris, 41, 47, 50, 53, 60, 61.
19. *Ibid.*, 163–64, 603, 589.
20. Avishai Margalit, 'Tribute', in Hardy, *Book of Isaiah*.
21. Ignatieff, 179, 322n45, citing Berlin to Weizmann, 16 Sept. 1948; Ignatieff, 179, nn37,38,39, citing Berlin to Frankfurter, 12 Sept. 1949; and Berlin interview, 5 April 1989.
22. Wasserstein, 18, ref. 40, citing Deutscher to Weidenfeld, 2 April 1950.
23. Deutscher to Brandler, 16 Sept. 1953, Deutscher Papers, File 4.
24. Deutscher, 'Israel's Spiritual Climate', *Non-Jewish Jew*, 94.
25. Laqueur, *The Middle East in Transition*, 219–20; Berlin, *Enlightening*, 525.
26. Berlin, *Enlightening*, 547–48, 549, 551, 565.
27. *Ibid.*, 630.
28. *Ibid.*, 621–22
29. Deutscher, *Non-Jewish Jew*, 38.
30. Deutscher, 'The Israeli-Arab War', in *Non-Jewish Jew*, 150–51.
31. Berlin to Chimen Abramsky, 11 Dec. 1978 (extract supplied by Henry Hardy).
32. Deutscher, *Non-Jewish Jew*, 122, 125.
33. Berlin, *Enlightening*, 624–25.
34. Deutscher, 'The Israeli-Arab War', 130.
35. Deutscher, *Non-Jewish Jew*, 128, 133–40; Wasserstein, 19 ref. 42.
36. Jonathan Freedland, programme note for the National Theatre's production of Ryan Craig's play *The Holy Rosenbergs* (2011).
37. Ignatieff, 297–98, 337n18, citing interview with the Margalits in 1997.
38. Berlin to Robert Silvers, 2 Feb. 1970 (extract supplied by Henry Hardy).

21. The Banality of Evil: Berlin and Arendt

1. Jahanbegloo, 81–85.
2. From 1944, she wrote for the *Partisan Review*. By 1946, she was also contributing to the *Nation* and *Commentary* while becoming an editor at Schocken Books.
3. See Arendt, 'The Jewish State: Fifty Years After. Where Have Herzl's Politics Led?', *Commentary*, May 1946, 1:7, reprinted in Arendt, *The Jew as Pariah*, 170.
4. Magnes, 1877–1948, a native of Oakland and co-founder of the Hebrew University of Jerusalem, spoke out for a binational Palestinian state. See Ronald Beiner, 'Arendt and Nationalism', 45, citing Arendt, *The Jew as Pariah*, 173, in Villa.
5. Arendt, *The Jew as Pariah*, 188, 216, 192.
6. Berlin, *Enlightening*, 676n4.
7. May, *Hannah Arendt*, 80–81.
8. Ignatieff, 253, 332n26,27, citing 'Between Philosophy and the History of Ideas', a conversation between Berlin and Steven Lukes, Berlin Archive, Wolfson College. This is published in Lukes, 52–134.
9. Jahanbegloo, 81–85, 38.
10. Arendt, *The Jew as Pariah*, 111.
11. A comprehensive survey of the critical literature is Michael Ezra, 'The Eichmann Polemics: Hanna Arendt and her Critics', *Democratiya*, 9, summer 2007, online at dissentmagazine.org/democratiya/article _pdfs/d9Ezra.pdf.
12. Berlin, *Enlightening*, 216; Lukes, 101.
13. www.hks.harvard.edu/cchrp/pdf/arendt.24.11.03.
14. May, *Arendt*, 124.
15. Jahanbegloo, 84, 85. For 'An Exchange of Letters' between Scholem and Arendt, see *Encounter*, 22:1, Jan. 1964.
16. His subjects included Roger Casement, medieval Latin poetry, the Lady Chatterley trial, Oscar Wilde, 'Hymns and Poetry', 'Feliciano and Mantegna', Mark Pattison,

John Donne (frequently), A.E. Housman (on several occasions), Milton, Shakespeare's Sonnets.

17. May, *Critical Times*, 372.
18. McCarthy, 'The Hue and Cry', 82–94.
19. Berlin to William Phillips, 7 May 1963, in *Enlightening*, 430n2.
20. In an early letter to Arendt (10 April 1953), McCarthy had described Berlin as a 'serpentine dove, moralistic, familial, perhaps not very brave'. She wrote to Arendt on 9 June 1964: 'I suppose you saw the piece about you in the *TLS* [30 April 1964]. Sonia Orwell has promised me to find out who wrote it, but so far she hasn't delivered. It seemed to me a particularly nasty job and done by someone who is authentically stupid.' The *TLS* had solicited a reply from her, but not from Arendt. Later, a letter from McCarthy to Arendt from Paris (22 Dec. 1964) does not mention Berlin's letter to her but she does say that John Sparrow 'seems clearly to have been the author of the *TLS* attack on you'. A further letter of 18 Jan. 1965 likewise does not mention Berlin. See Brightman, 14, 166, 167, 170.
21. MS Berlin 172, f. 88.
22. This was most likely Sparrow's essay on the Profumo scandal, rejected by the *TLS* under veto from Sir William Haley, the editor of *The Times*. See Sparrow, 'The Press, Politics and Private Life', in *Controversial Essays*.

22. The Sussex Letters

1. Based on the Bodleian Berlin Archive, the Isaac Deutscher Papers at the International Institute for Social Research, Amsterdam, and other sources.
2. Deutscher to Donald Tyerman, 18 Oct. 1954, Deutscher Papers, File 16.
3. The correspondence following in the text is found in File 48 of the Deutscher Papers.
4. MS Berlin 322, fols 41, 42.
5. Wight, MS Berlin 322, fol. 43.
6. MS Berlin 322, fol. 44.
7. MS Berlin 322, fol. 45.
8. MS Berlin, Sussex Academic Advisory Committee, 322, fol. 79.
9. Lord Briggs to the author, 21 June and 19 Sept. 2011.
10. On behalf of the AAC, the registrar, A.E. Shields, invited him (1 Oct. 1963) to sit on the Joint Committee to select a professor of psychology. MS Berlin 322, AA/3/5, fols 76, 77. In Oct. 1965, he was appointed the AAC's representative on the Joint Committees to appoint (a) a chair of comparative literature, (b) a chair of German, (c) a chair of sociology, (d) a second chair of economics. The chairman of the AAC, Sir James Duff, appointed Berlin as the AAC's representative on the Joint Committee set up to appoint a chair in Russian. Duff also moved the resolution 'Sir Isaiah Berlin to be appointed to the Joint Committee on the Chair of Politics'. MS Berlin 322, fol. 146.
11. *Black Dwarf* claimed direct heritage from the radical sheet first launched in 1817 by Thomas Wooler. Published between May 1968 and 1972, it was edited by Tariq Ali until the editorial board split in 1970 between Leninists and non-Leninists. The former, including Ali and other member of the International Marxist Group, went on to found *Red Mole*.
12. *Black Dwarf*, British Library, shelf mark TAB.583.A.
13. Berlin letter to Jean Floud (extract supplied by Henry Hardy).
14. MS Berlin 261, fol. 175.
15. MS Berlin 261, fols 170–71.
16. The correspondence between Berlin and Tamara Deutscher is found in Deutscher Papers, File 73. Copies in Berlin MS 261, fols 115–16, 120–21, 125–26. Her letter of 13 May reviewed the steps by which Sussex moved beyond a senior lectureship to a proposed chair in Soviet studies, including the lunch on 12 Feb. 1963, 'at which a very

detailed plan of the coordination of Soviet Studies in the context of the School's programmes was discussed'. Two days later Martin Wight informed Deutscher that 'the Vice-Chancellor asked me this morning to tell you how much he hopes that we shall be able to come to a satisfactory arrangement'. There followed three-and-a-half months' silence. Tamara Deutscher ended her letter on a note of asperity: 'Incidentally, on the first page of your letter you refer to "the facts which are confidential." I do not quite see what should be treated as "confidential" in the whole letter.' Deutscher Papers, File 73.

17. MS Berlin 261, fols 180–81.
18. Tamara Deutscher's subsequent letter to Berlin, 8 June 1969, is found in MS Berlin 183, fols 180–81, Deutscher Papers, File 73.
19. MS Berlin 183, fol. 91.
20. Deutscher Papers, File 73.
21. Sedgwick, n.p.
22. Daniel Singer, 'Armed with a Pen', in Horowitz, 48–49.
23. Ali, xxiv.
24. Haslam, 242, 242n14.
25. Hitchens.
26. Ignatieff, 235, 330n48, dates Berlin's letter to Fulton as 4 April rather than 4 March 1963. Ignatieff's claim that *Black Dwarf* 'published the confidential correspondence' is not correct.
27. Deutscher Papers, File 108.

Bibliography

Archival Sources

Isaiah Berlin Papers, Bodleian Library, Oxford (MS Berlin) *mainly open, some sections closed. References to this collection are given as MS Berlin (number), fol. (number). This archive holds what was in Sir Isaiah's possession at the time of his death in 1997, including carbons. On the history of this collection, by its curator, see Michael Hughes, 'The Berlin Papers in the Bodleian Library', in Henry Hardy (ed.), *The Book of Isaiah*, Woodbridge, Suffolk, 2009. According to the website, 'Most correspondence later than 1980 is closed. Correspondence and papers relating to confidential university business are closed for 80 years; certain other administrative files are closed for 30 years.' The researcher may find an obstacle in the category 'Confidential University Business'.
www.bodley.ox.ac.uk/dept/scwmss/wmss/online/modern/berlin/berlin.html

The Isaiah Berlin Virtual Library. Since Berlin was Wolfson College's founding president (1966–74), some of this material tends to be celebratory as well as interesting. Dr Henry Hardy (Wolfson College), who maintains this website on behalf of the Isaiah Berlin Literary Trust, holds some letters by Berlin retrieved from their recipients and not yet deposited in the Bodleian.
http://berlin.wolf.ox.ac.uk

All Souls College, Oxford (Codrington Library) *application required.
www.all-souls.ox.ac.uk/content/The_Codrington_Library
Isaac Deutscher Papers, International Institute for Social History, Amsterdam (Deutscher Papers) *not restricted. References to this collection are given as Deutscher Papers, File (number).
www.iisg.nl/archives/en/files/d/10748983full.php

The British Library
www.bl.uk/catalogues/listings.html

Works by Isaiah Berlin Cited in the Text

— *Karl Marx: His Life and Environment*, London, 1939, 1947
— *Against the Current: Essays in the History of Ideas*, ed. Henry Hardy, Introd. Roger Hausner, London, 1979. (Includes 'Herzen and his Memoirs' (1968); 'Montesquieu' (1955); 'The Sciences and the Humanities' (1974); 'Moses Hess' (1959); 'Georges Sorel' (1971); 'Benjamin Disraeli, Karl Marx and the Search for Identity' (1970))

— *Russian Thinkers*, ed. Henry Hardy and Aileen Kelly, London, 1978. (Includes his essay on Belinsky in 'Russian Populism' (1960); 'The Hedgehog and the Fox' (1953))
— *Four Essays on Liberty*, Oxford & New York, paperback edn, 1969. (Includes 'Two Concepts of Liberty' (1958); 'Historical Inevitability' (1954); 'Political Ideas in the Twentieth Century' (1949))
— *Liberty: Incorporating Four Essays on Liberty*, ed. Henry Hardy, Oxford, 2002
— *Flourishing: Letters 1928–1946*, ed. Henry Hardy, London, 2004
— *Enlightening: Letters 1946–1960*, ed. Henry Hardy and Jennifer Holmes, London, 2009
— *Concepts & Categories: Philosophical Essays*, ed. Henry Hardy, Oxford, 1980. (Includes 'Equality' (1956) 'The Concept of Scientific History' (1960))
— *The Soviet Mind: Russian Culture under Communism*, ed. Henry Hardy, Washington, 2004. (Includes 'Boris Pasternak' (1958); 'Conversations with Akhmatova and Pasternak' (1980); 'Four Weeks in the Soviet Union' (*c.* 1956, published 1980))
— *The Power of Ideas*, ed. Henry Hardy, Princeton, NJ, 2000, (Includes 'Jewish Slavery and Emancipation' (1951))
— *Personal Impressions*, ed. Henry Hardy, London, 1980, 1998. (Includes 'Chaim Weizmann' (1958); 'Meetings with Russian Writers' (1980))
— *The Crooked Timber of Humanity: Chapters in the History of Ideas*, ed. Henry Hardy, London, 1990. (Includes 'The Bent Twig: On the Rise of Nationalism' (1972))
— Introd. to Aleksandr Herzen, *My Past and Thoughts*, vol. 1, trans. Constance Garnett, London, 1974
— 'Tolstoy and Enlightenment', *Encounter*, 20:2, Feb. 1961
— 'The Arts in Russia under Lenin and Stalin', *New York Review of Books*, 47:16, 19 Oct. 2000
— 'The Question of Machiavelli', *New York Review of Books*, 4 Nov. 1971. www.nybooks.com/50/Machiavelli
— 'Thinkers or Philosophers', *TLS*, 21 March 1953
— 'Jewish Slavery and Emancipation', *Jewish Chronicle*, Oct. 1951
— review of Pasternak's *Selected Writings*, *Partisan Review*, 17, 1950, 748–51, reprinted in Victor Erlich (ed.), *Pasternak: A Collection of Critical Essays*, New Jersey, 1978
— 'L.B. Namier: A Personal Impression', *Encounter*, 27 Nov. 1966
— *Fathers and Children* (The Romanes Lecture 1970), Oxford, 1972
— 'The Origins of Israel' (1953), in Walter Laqueur (ed.), *The Middle East in Transition: Studies in Contemporary History*, London, 1958
— *Zionist Politics in Wartime Washington: A Fragment of Personal Reminiscences* (Yaachov Herzog Memorial Lecture, Jerusalem 1972), in Berlin, *Flourishing*, 663–92
— Interviews and conversations. See below Jahanbegloo, Ramin, and Lukes, Steven

Works by Isaac Deutscher cited in the text

— *Stalin: A Political Biography*, London & New York, 1949 (rev. edn 1967 with postscript: 'Stalin's Last Years')
— *The Prophet Armed, Trotsky: 1879–1921*, vol. 1, London & New York, 1954
— *Russia after Stalin*, London, 1953
— *Heretics and Renegades*, London, 1955. (Includes 'The Ex-Communist's Conscience' (1950); 'The Tragic Life of a Polugarian Minister' (1950); 'A Reply to Critics' (1954); 'Mr E.H. Carr as Historian of the Bolshevik Regime' (1954); ' "1984" – The Mysticism of Cruelty' (1955).) 2nd edn, London, 1969, includes Introd. by E.H. Carr
— *The Prophet Unarmed. Trotsky: 1921–1929*, London & New York, 1959
— *The Great Contest: Russia and the West*, London & New York, 1960
— *The Prophet Outcast. Trotsky: 1929–1940*, London & New York, 1963
— *Ironies of History: Essays on Contemporary Communism*, London & New York, 1966. (Includes 'Pasternak and the Calendar of the Revolution' (1959))
— *The Unfinished Revolution: Russia 1917–1967*, London & New York, 1967

— *The Non-Jewish Jew and Other Essays*, ed. Tamara Deutscher, London & New York, 1968. (Includes 'Israel's Spiritual Climate' (1954); 'The Russian Revolution and the Jewish Problem' (1964); 'The Israeli-Arab War' (1967))

— *Lenin's Childhood*, London & New York, 1970

— *Marxism in our Time*, ed. Tamara Deutscher, London, 1972

— *Marxism, Wars and Revolutions: Essays from Four Decades*, ed. Tamara Deutscher, London, 1984. (Includes 'Violence and Non-Violence' (1966, edited 1984))

— 'La Tragédie du communisme polonais', *Les Temps modernes*, 145, March 1958

— 'The Jew in Modern Society', a conversation with Isaac Deutscher, *Jewish Quarterly*, winter 1966

— 'Germany and Marxism', an interview for Hamburg television, 23 July 1967, transcript in *New Left Review*, 1:47, Jan.–Feb. 1968 (online)

— Preface to Marcel Liebman, *The Russian Revolution*, trans. Arnold J. Pomerans, London, 1970 (Paris, 1967)

Works by Tamara Deutscher cited in the text

— 'Work in Progress', in David Horowitz (ed.), *Isaac Deutscher: The Man and his Work*, London, 1971

— *Not by Politics Alone . . . – the Other Lenin*, London, 1973

— 'The Education of a Jewish Child', in Deutscher, *The Non-Jewish Jew*

Other Works

The most quoted work in the present study is Michael Ignatieff's excellent *Isaiah Berlin: A Life*, London, 1988. (All references are to the Vintage edition, 2000.) There is no comparable study of Isaac Deutscher's life.

Akhmatova, Anna, *Complete Poems of Anna Akhmatova*, trans. Judith Hemschemeyer, Boston, 1989

Ali, Tariq, *1968 and After: Inside the Revolution*, London, 1978

Anderson, Perry, 'Components of the National Culture', in *Student Power*, ed. Alexander Cockburn and Robin Blackburn, London, 1969. Revised in Perry Anderson, *English Questions*, London, 1992

—, Introd. to Isaac Deutscher, *Marxism, Wars and Revolutions*, London, 1984

—, *A Zone of Engagement*, London & New York, 1992

—, *English Questions*, London, 1992

Arendt, Hannah, *The Origins of Totalitarianism*, New York, 1951

—, *The Jew as Pariah: Identity and Politics in the Modern Age*, New York, 1978

Bar-Yosef, Eitan, and Nadia Valman (eds), *'The Jew' in Late-Victorian and Edwardian Culture: Between the East End and Africa*, Basingstoke & New York, 2009

Berkowitz, Michael, *Zionist Culture and West European Jewry before the First World War*, Cambridge, 1993

Bird, Kai, *The Color of Truth: McGeorge Bundy and William Bundy; Brothers in Arms*, New York, 1998

Bowra, C.M., *Memories 1898–1939*, London, 1966

Brightman, Carol (ed.), *Between Friends: The Correspondence of Hannah Arendt and Mary McCarthy 1949–1975*, London 1995

Buber-Neumann, Margarete, *Under Two Dictators: Prisoner of Stalin and Hitler*, trans. Edward Fitzgerald, London, 1949

Carpenter, Humphrey, *The Envy of the World: Fifty Years of the Third Programme and Radio 3*, London, 1996

Carr, E.H. *The Romantic Exiles: A Nineteenth-Century Portrait Gallery*, London, 1933

—, *The Soviet Impact on the Western World*, London, 1946

—, *The Bolshevik Revolution 1917–1923*, vol. 1, London, 1950

—, *The New Society*, London, 1951

—, *Socialism in One Country 1924–26*, vol. 1, London, 1958

—, *What Is History?*, London, 1961

Caute, David, *The Great Fear: The Anti-Communist Purge under Truman and Eisenhower*, London & New York, 1978

—, *Sixty-Eight: The Year of the Barricades*, London & New York, 1988

Childers, Erskine, 'The Other Exodus', *Spectator*, 12 May 1961, reprinted in Laqueur (ed.), *The Israeli-Arab Reader*

Cliff, Tony, 'The End of the Road: Deutscher's Capitulation to Stalinism', *International Socialism*, 1st series, 15, winter 1963

Cockburn, Alexander, and Robin Blackburn (eds), *Student Power*, London, 1969

Cohen, G.A., 'Capitalism, Freedom and the Proletariat', in Ryan

Coleman, Peter, *The Liberal Conspiracy: The Congress for Cultural Freedom and the Struggle for the Mind of Postwar Europe*, London, 1989

Conquest, Robert, *Common Sense about Russia*, London, 1960

—, *We and They: Civil and Despotic Cultures*, London, 1980

—, *Russia after Khrushchev*, London, 1965

Cox, Michael (ed.), *E.H. Carr: A Critical Appraisal*, London, 2000

Crankshaw, Edward, *Russia by Daylight*, London, 1951

Crowder, George, *Isaiah Berlin: Liberty and Pluralism*, Cambridge, 2004

Cruise O'Brien, Conor, *The Siege: The Saga of Israel and Zionism*, London, 1986

Dalos, György, with the collaboration of Andrea Dunai, *The Guest from the Future: Anna Akhmatova and Isaiah Berlin*, trans. Anton Wood, London, 1998

Daly, Lawrence, 'A Working-Class Tribute', in Horowitz

Davidson, Neil, 'Isaac Deutscher: The Prophet, his Biographer and the Watchtower', *International Socialism*, 104:2, 2004

Fainsod, Merle, *How Russia Is Ruled*, Cambridge, Mass., 1953, 1963

Friedrich, Carl J., and Zbigniew K. Brzezinski, *Totalitarian Dictatorship and Autocracy*, Cambridge, Mass., 1965

Galipeau, Claude J., *Isaiah Berlin's Liberalism*, Oxford, 1994

Gidley, Ben, 'The Ghosts of Kishniev in the East End: Responses to a Pogrom in the Jewish London of 1903', in Bar-Yosef and Valman

Glover, David, 'Imperial Zion: Israel Zangwill and the English Origins of Territorialism', in Bar-Yosef and Valman

Gorky, Maksim, *Untimely Thoughts: Essays on Revolution, Culture and the Bolsheviks 1917–1918*, trans. and with an Introd. by Herman Ermolaev, London, 1968

Gorny, Yosef, *Zionism and the Arabs 1882–1948: A Study of Ideology*, Oxford, 1987

Gray, John, *Isaiah Berlin*, London, 1996

Green, S.J.D., 'The "Freemantle Affair" and the Destruction of the *Ancien Régime* in All Souls, 1857–1864', 343–71, in S.J.D. Green and Peregrine Hodren (eds), *All Souls under the Ancien Régime: Politics, Learning and the Arts, c.1600–1850*, Oxford, 2007

— and Peregrine Hordern, *All Souls and the Wider World: Statesmen, Scholars and Adventurers, c.1850–1950*, Oxford, 2011

Greenwood, Walter, *Love on the Dole: A Tale of the Two Cities*, London, 1933

Hardy, Henry (ed.), *The Book of Isaiah: Personal Impressions of Isaiah Berlin*, Woodbridge, Suffolk, 2009

Hardy, Henry, Kei Hiruta and Jennifer Holmes (eds), *Isaiah Berlin and Wolfson College*, Wolfson College, Oxford, 2009

Hart, Jenifer, *Ask Me No More: An Autobiography*, London, 1998

Haslam, Jonathan, *The Vices of Integrity: E.H. Carr, 1892–1982*, London & New York, 1999

Heath, Amelia, 'E.H. Carr: Approaches to Understanding Experience and Knowledge', PDF version, 2010

Heer, Nancy Whittier, *Politics and History in the Soviet Union*, Cambridge, Mass., 1971

Hill, Christopher, *Lenin and the Russian Revolution*, London, 1947
—, 'The Theory of Revolutions', in Horowitz
—, *Collected Essays*, vol. 3, *People and Ideas in 17th-Century England*, Brighton, Sussex, 1986
Hingley, Ronald, *Pasternak: A Biography*, London, 1985
Hitchens, Christopher, 'Moderation or Death', *LRB*, 20:23, 26 Nov. 1998
Hoffer, Eric, *The True Believer: Thoughts on the Nature of Mass Movements*, New York, 1951
Horowitz, David (ed.), *Isaac Deutscher: The Man and his Work*, London, 1971
Howe, Irving, 'The Politics of Boris Pasternak: An Exchange', *Partisan Review*, 2:26, spring 1959
Ignatieff, Michael, *Isaiah Berlin. A Life*, London, 1999 (Vintage edition, 2000)
Jahanbegloo, Ramin, *Conversations with Berlin*, London, 1992
James, Clive, 'On Isaiah Berlin', *TLS*, 3 Sept. 2004
Keep, J.H. (ed.), *Contemporary History in the Soviet Mirror*, London, 1964
Kennan, George F., *Democracy and the Student Left*, Boston & London, 1968
Khalidi, Rashid, 'Palestinian Resistance to Zionism before World War I', in Said and Hitchens
Labedz, Leopold, 'Deutscher as Historian and Prophet', *Survey: A Journal of Soviet and East European Studies* (London), 41, April 1962
Lacey, Nicola, *A Life of H.L.A. Hart: The Nightmare and the Noble Dream*, Oxford, 2004
Laqueur, Walter Z., *The Fate of the Revolution: Interpretations of Soviet History*. London, 1967
— (ed.), *The Middle East in Transition: Studies in Contemporary History*, London, 1958
— (ed.), *The Israel-Arab Reader: A Documentary History of the Middle East Conflict*, London, 1969
Liebman, Marcel, *The Russian Revolution*, trans. Arnold J. Pomerans, London, 1970 (Paris, 1967)
Lowe, John, *The Warden: A Portrait of John Sparrow*, London, 1998
Lukács, Georg, *The Historical Novel*, trans. Hannah and Stanley Mitchell, London, 1963
Lukes, Steven, 'Isaiah Berlin in Conversation with Steven Lukes', *Salmagundi*, 120, Fall 1998
Lunacharsky, Anatoly, *Revolutionary Silhouettes*, trans. and ed. Michael Glenny, London, 1967, reproduced in Tamara Deutscher, *Not by Politics Alone*
Luxemburg, Rosa, *'The Russian Revolution' and 'Leninism or Marxism'*, Introd. by Bertram D. Wolfe, Ann Arbor, Mich., 1961
Macintyre, Alasdair, *Against the Self-Images of the Age*, London, 1971
Macpherson, C.B., *The Political Theory of Possessive Individualism: Hobbes to Locke*, Oxford, 1962
—, *Democratic Theory: Essays in Retrieval*, Oxford, 1973
McCarthy, Mary, 'The Hue and Cry', *Partisan Review*, 1, winter 1964
May, Derwent, *Critical Times: The History of the Times Literary Supplement*, London, 2001
—, *Hannah Arendt*, London, 1986
Mehta, Ved, *Fly and the Fly-Bottle*, London, 1963
Menashe, Louis, 'The Dilemma of de-Stalinization', in Horowitz
Morris, Benny, *The Birth of the Palestine Refugee Problem Revisited*, Cambridge, 2004
Orwell, George, *Animal Farm*, London, 1945
—, *Nineteen Eighty-Four*, London, 1949
—, 'Inside the Whale', in *Collected Essays*, vol. 1, *An Age Like This 1920–1940*, London, 1968
—, 'The Lion and the Unicorn: Socialism and the English Genius', in *Collected Essays*, vol. 2, *My Country Right or Left 1940–1943*
Oxford University, *The Report of Commission of Inquiry. I. Report, Recommendations, and Statutory Appendix*, Oxford, 1966
Pasternak, Boris, *Doctor Zhivago*, London, 1958
Popper, Karl, *The Open Society and its Enemies*, London, 1945

Reeder, Roberta, *Anna Akhmatova: Poet and Prophet*, London, 1955

Rees, Goronwy, 'Column', *Encounter*, Sept. 1966

Rochelson, Meri Jane, 'Zionism, Territorialism, Race and Nation in the Thought of Israel Zangwill', in Bar-Yosef and Valman

Rowse, A.L., *All Souls in my Time*, London, 1993

Ryan, Alan, ed., *The Idea of Freedom: Essays in Honour of Isaiah Berlin*, Oxford, 1979

—, 'Sir Isaiah Berlin (1909–1997)', *Oxford Dictionary of National Biography*, Oxford, 2004

Said, Edward, and Christopher Hitchens, *Blaming the Victims: Spurious Scholarship and the Palestine Question*, London, 1988

Schapiro, Leonard, *Turgenev: His Life and Times*, London, 1977

Schlesinger, Arthur, *The Vital Center: The Politics of Freedom*, Boston, 1949

Sedgwick, Peter, 'Tragedy of the Tragedian', *International Socialism*, 31, winter 1967–68

Shostakovich, Dmitry, *Testimony: Memoirs as Related to Solomon Volkov*, London, 1979

Solzhenitsyn, Aleksandr, *The Gulag Archipelago, 1918–1956*, vol. 1, trans. Thomas P. Whitney, London, 1974

Sykes, Christopher, *Troubled Loyalty: A Biography of Adam von Trott zu Solz*, London, 1969

Talmon, J.L., *The Origins of Totalitarian Democracy*, London, 1952

Taylor, Charles, 'What's Wrong with Negative Liberty?', in Ryan

Thompson, E.P., 'Outside the Whale' (1960), in *The Poverty of Theory and Other Essays*, London, 1978

Thomson, David, *Europe since Napoleon*, London, 1957

Tolstoy, Leo, *What Is Art? And Essays on Art*, trans. Aylmer Maude, London, 1930

Trevor-Roper, H.R., 'Mr Carr's Success Story', *Encounter*, 84:102, 1962

Turgenev, I.S., *Fathers and Children*, trans. Constance Garnett, London, 1913

—, *Virgin Soil*, part 1, trans. Constance Garnett, London, 1896

Villa, Dana (ed.), *The Cambridge Companion to Hannah Arendt*, Cambridge, 2000

Wasserstein, Bernard, *Isaiah Berlin, Isaac Deutscher and Arthur Koestler: Their Jewish Wars*, Amsterdam, 2009

Weizmann, Chaim, *Trial and Error*, London, 1949

Wilford, Hugh, *The CIA, the British Left and the Cold War*, London, 2003

Zeman, Z.A.B., *Germany and the Russian Revolution, 1915–1918*, London, 1958

Index